PRAISE FOR

STARTUP PROGRAM DESIGN

"This book sheds a whole new light on the world of startup programs and how they can be designed. Drawing on their own experiences and systematic research with other experts in the field, the authors have written a must-read book that is filled with valuable insights, examples, and practical advice for anyone interested in understanding, starting, or working with startup programs in the business, public, and social sectors."

—**PIERA MORLACCHI,** Associate Professor of Entrepreneurship and Organization Studies at the University of Sussex Business School

"Never more than today it's evident how technology and innovation are crucial to every business, to adapt to rapidly changing conditions. At my company we source ideas both internally and externally, test them and transform them into new ventures and business lines. Working with startups is like having hundreds of test labs outside of our own. *Startup Program Design* by Adam and Paolo accumulates many ideas in one place, and ties together great examples of both what to do and not to do with startup collaboration programs. It's comprehensive in nature, a very valuable read for anyone in corporate innovation around the globe."

—**KRISTIN WELCH,** Mobility Industry Investor, Mentor and OEM Innovation Leader

"Scaling startups in the social impact space provides the opportunity to solve some of the world's most pressing challenges. This is a great read to learn how to set up a program that accelerates startups—and what is needed from partnerships and VCs to support that."

—**BERNHARD KOWATSCH,** Head of Innovation Accelerator, UN World Food Programme

"The key to a great startup program is a focus on access with a process. Critical outcomes for businesses and entrepreneurs in these programs depend on meeting the right person, with the right resources and the right opportunity, at the right time. Paolo Lombardi and Adam Berk's new book, *Startup Program Design*, is THE handbook for how to do just that. If you have been tasked with the big job of partnering with startups to solve big problems, you should keep this book on your desk and refer to it often."

—**JOHN LYNN,** Cofounder of Cela

"The innovation potential doesn't stop at the boundaries of established corporations. Among the options of open innovation, partnering with startups has developed to be one of the core options. To be crystal clear about the goals you aim to achieve helps to navigate the many obstacles ahead. Paolo Lombardi and Adam Berk dissect these concepts in a new light and give expert advice that only veteran insiders of our industry possess."

—**STEFAN PERKMANN BERGER,** Managing Director and Cofounder of WhatAVenture

"Corporate startups are the vehicles that drive business-building from innovation. But how should companies build their programs to come up with these startups and engage with startups from external ecosystems? Adam Berk and Paolo Lombardi tell you how. Their book breaks new ground. It fleshes out what to do to get the set-up for success right—hence increasing the odds for success significantly."

—**FRANK MATTES,** advisor to corporate innovators and author of *Scaling-Up Corporate Startups* and *Lean Scaleup*

"As someone who has worked at the interface of Industry and Government for decades, I can speak to the importance and value of good design."

—**RICK MYLLENBECK**

STARTUP PROGRAM DESIGN

A PRACTICAL GUIDE FOR CREATING ACCELERATORS AND INCUBATORS AT ANY ORGANIZATION

PAOLO LOMBARDI & ADAM BERK

New York Chicago San Francisco Athens London Madrid
Mexico City Milan New Delhi Singapore Sydney Toronto

1 2 3 4 5 6 7 8 9 LCR 27 26 25 24 23 22

ISBN 978-1-260-46325-5
MHID 1-260-46325-7

e-ISBN 978-1-260-46326-2
e-MHID 1-260-46326-5

Library of Congress Cataloging-in-Publication Data

Names: Lombardi, Paolo, author. | Berk, Adam, author.
Title: Startup program design : a practical guide for creating corporate accelerators and incubators at any organization / Paolo Lombardi and Adam Berk.
Description: New York : McGraw Hill, [2022] | Includes bibliographical references and index.
Identifiers: LCCN 2021042671 (print) | LCCN 2021042672 (ebook) | ISBN 9781260463255 (hardback) | ISBN 9781260463262 (ebook)
Subjects: LCSH: New business enterprises. | New products. | Entrepreneurship.
Classification: LCC HD62.5 .L653 2022 (print) | LCC HD62.5 (ebook) | DDC 658.1/1—dc23
LC record available at https://lccn.loc.gov/2021042671
LC ebook record available at https://lccn.loc.gov/2021042672

Icon illustrations by Sara Gioria (https://www.instagram.com/saragioria/)

McGraw Hill books are available at special quantity discounts to use as premiums and sales promotions or for use in corporate training programs. To contact a representative, please visit the Contact Us pages at www.mhprofessional.com.

McGraw Hill is committed to making our products accessible to all learners. To learn more about the available support and accommodations we offer, please contact us at accessibility@mheducation.com. We also participate in the Access Text Network (www.accesstext.org), and ATN members may submit requests through ATN.

To Mariella and Renzo who taught me to never stop learning, and to Elizabeth who taught me to never stop loving.

PAOLO

To Karen, you are to me what words are to a book. ILYSM

Goldie, Oliver, Julian, Mom, Dad, and Jenn, olive you. PS, Oliver, this is just the beginning of the story . . . not DN.

Paolo, thank you for including me on this journey and for being the convergence to my divergence! We did it:)

ADAM

Contents

Introduction

What do Google, the Nobel Prize laureate World Food Programme, Ford, Microsoft, the Chilean government, the city of Tulsa, the Vatican, the Canadian city of Calgary, BMW, the National Geospatial-Intelligence Agency, and a 100-year-old cement corporation all have in common?

They all work with startups.

Moore's Law seems to apply to startups as well as semiconductors: the number of new startups continues to increase while the cost to launch a startup has plummeted. Startups are growing, and startup ecosystems are thriving.

Meanwhile, the average length of time for a corporation to remain on the S&P 500 Index has steadily declined. Entire regions and countries are trying to reinvent themselves in the face of global economic changes. Calgary is trying to move on from its reliance on fossil fuels and develop new ways to drive its economy. The World Food Programme is relentlessly tackling hunger as climate change poses new threats to traditional cultivations. BMW is delivering the next generation of mobility services, diving into artificial intelligence and electric power. Many other organizations are turning to innovation to address social justice, health crises, or inequality.

All of these things point to one positive trend: an increase in cooperative programs between the biggest, oldest, most inside-the-box organizations in the world and the smallest, newest, and most outside-the-box thinkers—the startups. Startups have been engaged to help tackle some of the world's most pressing problems—world hunger, malaria, inequitable funding for female and underrepresented founders, plastic in the oceans, among other as well as mitigate the internal cultures that contribute to and exacerbate some of these problems. Startups are also helping corporations solve day-to-day product innovation challenges like higher-capacity batteries, simpler tax software, or a better razor blade.

Partnering Can't Be Ignored

Organizations have always had the same three cliché options for innovation, growth, and reinvention: build, buy, or partner. This classic phrase only tells part of the story, however. In truth, these solutions are not mutually exclusive.

Each of these strategies has significant limitations and risks if pursued in isolation. "Build" (the exclusively internal route) is often ineffective and can feel like pushing water uphill. Organizations are literally conceived to execute known ideas and reject distractions. Employees join these companies for precisely that reason—they recognize themselves in the mission. It should be no surprise that many internal change and transformation efforts come up short.

"Buy" (the exclusively external route) is not bulletproof either. Integrating talent and technology is often complex, and corporations and industry groups can grow like chimeras, generating odd conglomerates without a cohesive strategy or even a reason to coexist.

"Partner" at first sight appears the perfect bridge between those two worlds: it allows a similar customization as provided by a "build" strategy, without absorbing the external partner completely like in a "buy" strategy. But partnering without intent risks simply becoming the trivial hybrid of two vague ideas. What are you partnering for, exactly? Revenue? Growth? Talent? Technology? Each will require a different contribution by your partner. Partnering works when the other side is as engaged as you are, and it's like love between two hedgehogs: it must happen at the right distance. In contrast to build or buy, in partnering two players expect a gain. All these aspects make partnering far from trivial.

From classic M&A to skunkworks-style labs to corporate venture capital—there has been a clear trend of companies to solve the "ambidexterity" problem of conducting both search and execution by separating those functions and developing parallel internal and external routes to innovation. Build, buy, and partner coexist in most organizations as pieces of the general game of adaptation, transformation, and invention.

This game is as complicated as four-dimensional chess, however, without a clear winning move. Innovation is not a precise science; it cannot be planned. It is uncharted territory, and it requires trial and error, iteration, and continuous learning. Putting all your eggs in one basket—be it build, buy, or partner—is almost certainly a recipe for disaster, so a thorough innovation strategy must comprise all three.

That is why partnering can't be ignored. But to be successful, it must be done with intent. Partners can be of various nature: suppliers, customers, distributors, players in other industries, universities, startups, and so on.

Working with startups is one of the external strategies that can help you win the innovation game. Partnering with startups doesn't need to be exclusive, but if done with intent it works. Like any good strategy, it needs to be designed and executed based on objectives and resources. As any systems thinker knows, corporate growth and regional innovation are today inextricably linked to startup ecosystems. Since this is a foregone conclusion, you may as well do things earlier and with intent.

Open Innovation and Entrepreneurial Ecosystems

This book pulls together the collective wisdom of hundreds of real-world startup engagement programs. It stems from 3 years of research and cumulatively draws on over 20 years of interactions with program managers and industry experts across the globe, not to mention helping to design and mentor some of the very programs that are leading the way.

When mature firms collaborate with external startups or when public institutions foster new entrepreneurship, they use similar tools of startup engagement, just in different contexts. For businesses, startup engagement is a particular case of open innovation. Sometimes an established company engages with external startups to grow its own business or enter new markets. Other times, startup engagement is about investments in disruptive technology and business models, positioning the company as innovative, or improving internal culture. For public institutions, startup engagement is aimed at economic and social development or tackling global challenges such as climate change or hunger. In some cases, public institutions use startup relationships to source innovative solutions, similar to businesses.

Notwithstanding their different organizational structures, missions, and goals, both private businesses and public institutions employ the same tool when they engage with startups: the *startup program*. Accelerators run by mature businesses resemble those run by public institutions. And the same holds true for incubators, hackathons, challenges, competitions, matching events, cocreation workshops, and so on. The startup program as a common tool seeks to define a new category—or, perhaps better, an entirely new industry, of *startup engagement*.

Why a Book on Startup Programs

We initially embarked on writing a book about startup incubators and accelerators run by mature businesses or public institutions that engage with external startups. However, we soon realized during our research that the process was far more nuanced and complicated than just planning a curriculum, bringing in the right mentors, and creating an appealing offer for the startups.

This book is about startup programs, and not just accelerators or incubators. Over the years, we have reviewed countless definitions that attempt to draw a line between these two categories, but they all sounded too theoretical.[1] Truth be told, at some point we got lost in a forest of contradicting terminology, and even we—supposedly the experts—were in doubt when asked to classify specific real-world programs as either incubators or accelerators. The task became even more difficult when we encountered more hybrid programs that dramatically altered their form, mixing and matching their structure and content to meet their own particular goals. For instance, what would you call a two-week entrepreneurial curriculum ending with a demo day and targeted at post-seed startups? Would that be a "very short accelerator"? Or maybe a "pre-accelerator for seed startups"? Or is it a "bootcamp with an investor demo day"?

That's when we realized that, perhaps, the whole problem of classification was ill-posed. We wondered if classification mattered at all, at least to practitioners. Scholars need categories to study a phenomenon, but were the best operators sticking to the definitions? The (perhaps not so) shocking answer was "not frequently." When we answered no to that question, we discovered an opportunity to build a new framework that would question the boundaries between accelerators, incubators, challenges, hackathons, venture builders, venture clients, or venture funds more than ever before.

What Is a Startup?

In this book, a "startup" is an independent entity that innovates a product, business model, process, or market employing an explorative approach and transformational or disruptive technology.

Note that this is not the most common definition. According to lean startup expert and Silicon Valley authority Steve Blank, a startup is "a temporary organization formed to search for a repeatable and scalable business model."[2] In the Valley, a startup is synonymous with rapid growth, venture capital investments, disruption, and multibillion-dollar exits.

But outside of Silicon Valley, "startups" are often perceived as best-in-breed teams developing novel technologies, products, or services, without any additional expectations. Some term researchers, students, or professionals who team up for an innovative project, with or without any future as a company, "startups." Others use the term for small to medium-size enterprises that innovate outside their core business with an experimental unit to differentiate or eventually spin off. These initiatives might seek venture funding, but they are just as likely to prefer nondilutive grants. Maybe they will scale their business, maybe not. And yet they are among the sources of innovation with which corporations and public institutions might want to engage. Explorative methodologies and transformational or disruptive power are the two key elements that, we believe, make the collaboration with these diverse entities attractive.

What Is a Startup Program?

Referencing our definition of a startup, a *startup program* is a process to engage with external startups and create new temporary innovation partnerships in a way that can be managed, repeated, and improved. While the collaboration in itself may last from a day (in a hackathon) to several years (in the case of equity investment), its effects might have a more prolonged impact.

This definition is intentionally inclusive and purposely neglects more defined delineators such as the absence of equity investments or having specific goals.[3] Equity becomes a configuration parameter that the designer can use or not, depending on the context. Goals are a part of that context. They may be as diverse as financial return, innovation search, economic and social development (for governments), encouraging self-employment in specific social groups (for NGOs), fostering technology transfer (for universities), or rejuvenating an out-of-date or "stuck" organizational culture.

When used with external entrepreneurs to pursue some objective, formats such as accelerators, incubators, challenges, hackathons, venture builders, and even venture funds are all startup programs.

The keyword *organization* also deserves some clarification. In this book, it is meant as an umbrella term to capture the mirror image of the startups. It may refer to a corporation, a medium-to-large business, a government agency, an international institution, a university, or a nongovernmental organization (NGO). In short, an organization is any entity engaging with startups, and it's often sponsoring or cosponsoring the startup program. "Internal" refers to the organization, and "external" indicates something outside the organization.

What Veterans Do That Novices Don't

During our research, we have realized that veteran experts in the field don't follow any specific model by the book (even if most of them call it by the same name): they take inspiration from others but constantly adapt a model to their context. Initially, we were surprised. If accelerators such as Y Combinator or Techstars are the gold standard, why do new models keep emerging—especially from the best programs and most brilliant people? After all, those formats have been tested and refined through more than a decade and hundreds of startups.

Indeed, copying and pasting are what most novices do. They experiment in (what is to them) an unknown space with known processes (made by others). They also create Frankenstein programs out of more than one format, taking what seems like any good idea and adding it into the mix. That's not bad in principle, but most of the time it does not work. The effectiveness of Y Combinator or Techstars does not reside only in the model but also in the assets they possess, such as exceptional mentors, a global brand, and an unparalleled network of follow-on investors (plus, initially, also the first-mover advantage). When an organization lacks the assets and the drive that enabled the original version, any copycat model will underdeliver—guaranteed.

Intentional design and behavioral economics are the keys to hone success in multistakeholder actions such as startup programs, and veterans know that. First, to the question, "How can we build an accelerator?" (or any other program type), they answer with another question: "What are you trying to accomplish?" Starting with *why* is fundamental in startup programs, as in many other design problems, but startups are not the only client here—the sponsoring organization is another. Collaborative programs are platforms for exchanging value, and each model is best at a certain type of exchange. Consequently, veterans interview dozens of internal stakeholders or run cocreation workshops to map the needs and available means for startup engagement before deciding what model to implement. Last, when they build crossovers of models, they select the features that maximize the value and useful metrics for that particular context.

The idea for this book stems from the realization that many inexperienced operators make the same mistakes we had made early on with our first program and our clients: Novices don't mix program features with intention. They don't understand the behavioral consequences of design choices for either the external startups or the internal stakeholders. They sometimes invest time and budget in a complex program such as a corporate accelerator when they just need a hackathon. Or, vice versa, they may expect from a hackathon what nothing short of an accelerator can deliver.

Veterans Still Lack a Framework

The open innovation category is still young, and startup engagement from both corporations and governments has a long way to go. New open innovation models are still emerging as we write, but the problem behind innovation is as old as time, going from R&D to M&A to internal transformations and corporate startups. After several decades of experimentation and data in adjacent areas of innovation and startup collaboration, we believe it is time to look for patterns and systemize a theoretical framework.

We aimed for a new theoretical framework while providing practical anchors to apply it straight away. Theory must be simple enough to be general, yet it must explain what happens in the phenomenological world. In line with the prevalent trend in design, we resorted to a Canvas to visualize our framework for context analysis. We then created a list of challenges and checkpoints that a startup program designer must address when choosing the features.

As with talking to customers or testing a beta version, selecting the right startups and program is not as trivial as it may seem. Our goal is to help you pick the startups you need to work with, based on your objectives and the organization that supports the program. Then, we help you choose the program and its features, but with a certain freedom, not limiting you to a silo such as "the best practices for accelerators" or any other mainstream program template. In some rare cases, we intend to empower you to create a new template.

Startup program design, in our view, falls in the sweet spot between complexity and diversity. Large organizations are complex but not diverse. Entrepreneurial ecosystems and startup communities, on the other hand, are both varied and complex—but complex to a point where no one can manage the chaos. Startup programs are the liaisons that simplify the relationship between these multiple complex systems.

Now It's Your Turn

If you are reading this book, you might be about to start working with startups but have no plan. Or you might already be working with startups but are unsatisfied with your program or have no program at all. You might be looking for a new model of startup engagement, or you have one and need to refine it. You might have been hired by a corporation, government, NGO, international institution, or university to design an accelerator, an incubator, or a hackathon series.

Now, you are ready to step up and take responsibility for the design, but you want to avoid mistakes and create value for both the startups and the organization sponsoring the program.

Part One introduces a new framework for context analysis and shows how different contexts call for different startup program templates. Part Two discusses one by one the main challenges of startup program design and offers tips for overcoming them. Part Three looks at combining programs into a coherent system and discusses what external providers you may need to hire and when.

This book is not for venture capital investors. We discuss the mathematics of exits only briefly. We don't refer only to the next Google, Baidu, or Moderna when we speak of startups. This book is for large organizations prioritizing strategic goals over financial goals when they engage with startups. We believe that strategic goals change everything.

This book will not attempt to convince you to engage with startups. It postulates that you are already convinced. We believe in the old saying, "If you want to go fast, go alone; if you want to go far, go together." Working with startups can help solve some problems within an organization. Startups tend to attract talent that is difficult to hire in large organizations,* and typically have the ability to implement new technological solutions faster. In the end, the thesis is simple. To work effectively with startups, you need first to know who you are, what you are trying to accomplish, and what your organization is capable of.

---

* Startup CEOs make excellent managers, but they might be a tough hire through "normal means" (who, for instance, would hire Elon Musk?!).

A Word of Gratitude

Our experience alone wouldn't have brought us here. We owe gratitude to more than 120 operators and program designers from corporate, government, university, and independent consultancy companies that agreed to share their knowledge with us. These are amazing people who strive every day to facilitate entrepreneurs; to meaningful impact their communities—and beyond; and to solve global problems such as poverty, climate change, or famine with entrepreneurship.

Their work is often less celebrated than the entrepreneurs' success, but it is no less valuable. Startups are infant organizations, and as such, they need to be nurtured, encouraged, and supported. These professionals have the insight, experience, passion, and guts to fight for a better world of higher inclusion, social mobility, constructive change, and relentless improvement.

In addition to the interviews we conducted, we reviewed almost 500 programs, from top tier to almost unknown. We watched dozens of hours of videos on innovation, participated in workshops and fireside chats, and interacted with the speakers' lives and social media. We read hundreds of blog posts and surveyed heaps of scientific papers.

Without the richness of experience coming from these innovators who shared their knowledge and passion to the public or privately to us, this book would not exist.

Among all those who participated, directly or indirectly, in this work, we would like to express our special gratitude to our interviewees, whom we list in the Acknowledgments at the end of the book. Descriptions and references of programs mentioned in the text, and descriptions of program templates and models can be found on the companion website to this book: http://startupprogramdesign.com.

PART ONE

A UNIFIED FRAMEWORK

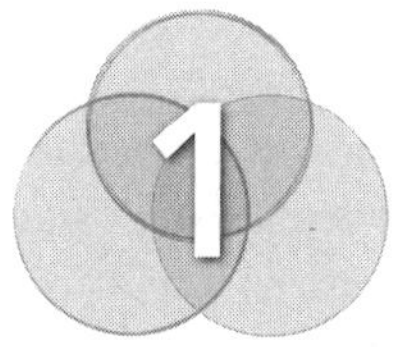

STARTUP ENGAGEMENT

If humans like predictability, large organizations even more so. The status quo is a feature, not a bug, and change is hard. In the savannah, adopting a different behavior from the pack literally got you eaten by a lion. In the boardroom, proverbially so. Yet change and innovation are necessary to cope with the ever-dynamic business landscape. Engaging with external startups is increasingly becoming not just an alternative way for organizations to pursue innovation but a must-have. On the other hand, working with startups is relatively new, and organizations are continuously exploring new collaboration models. Startup programs are the perfect vehicle for organizations to initiate and encourage change in a managed and directed way. While large organizations have internal means to innovate, startup programs provide organizations with options that often don't exist in-house, such as a patented technology or early customer data in a new and emerging market. Internal-external partnerships are quickly becoming the norm, and the startup programs that enable this new model of innovation are continuously evolving and hybridizing.

External Innovators

Partnering with external startups can solve problems that organizations cannot address internally or simply buy their way out of. Startup engagement can be initiated by established corporations, businesses, or public institutions—what we collectively call "organizations" in this book.

For businesses, startup engagement is one possible implementation of the open innovation approach. Startup collaborations have become a powerful tool for experimenting with new technologies and business models. Cooperation with external startups can help organizations create new offerings, gain a competitive advantage, stay relevant for existing customers, and open new markets. Internal research and development or internal innovation labs can, of course, address the same problems, but innovation is complex. Organizations simply cannot do everything alone because the pace of change is accelerating—a trend that is partially due to startups. Partnering with external innovators is one approach[1] to solving organizational ambidexterity.[2] It can contribute to existing innovation projects, provide superior technology or a missing element faster, or enable an organization to experiment with a long-term perspective. It might also prepare a gateway for future mergers and acquisitions (M&A) or contribute to reviving internal culture or external market positioning.

For example, Procter & Gamble launched an award-winning teeth-whitening product under its Crest brand thanks to an innovative technology produced by Corium International Inc., a venture-backed biopharmaceutical company.[3] In another example, from a serendipitous collaboration with a pharmaceutical startup incubated in AstraZeneca's BioVentureHub in Sweden, a hosting facility for external companies, the corporation simplified its clinical test methods, leading to considerable gains.[4] Ex-startups such as Salesforce, Google, or recently IPOed Snowflake engage with younger startups through accelerators, venture arms, and challenges. Salesforce was a startup launched by former Oracle executives, so all the startups in Salesforce's programs are the third generation—metaphorically, they could be Oracle's startup grandchildren.

Several public institutions or nonprofit organizations nurture an interest in startups as well. Along with being suppliers of innovative solutions or helping transform internal culture, external startups can also contribute to such entities' core mission, tackling hunger, climate change, social and economic development, and so on. The Nobel Peace Prize 2020 laureate, the World Food Programme (WFP), created an Innovation Accelerator that helped Tanzanian startup Imara Tech to produce portable threshing machines that can provide $10 per hour of earnings to small farmers—and allowed Imara Tech to expand its operations and reach 10,000 farmers.[5] The city of St. Louis, Missouri, developed the local entrepreneurial scene with Arch Grants, a startup competition started in 2011 that has helped participants collectively create over 2,300 jobs in Missouri and attract more than $355 million in follow-on capital to the region.[6]

The Big Bang of Startup Programs

But this was not always the case. Until the late 1990s, corporate venture capital was the only game in town for organizations wanting access to startups. Corporations used venture arms even if they were not interested in M&A—for market exploration, revenues, self-disruption, solving a specific innovation need, corporate social responsibility, or pushing a more entrepreneurial internal culture. This concentration of tasks in one (limited) box created the ground—a critical mass, so to speak—for an explosion of models, each better than CVC at a given task and in a given context: a kind of Big Bang of startup programs.

This interest of established private and public organizations in startups has spawned thousands of startup programs worldwide over the past few decades. During our research, we mapped and analyzed almost 500, but that's just the tip of the iceberg. Many more exist. Some have opened and closed, often because of a perceived lack of value, prevailing short-termism, or leadership and strategy changes. Many had sufficient internal support but failed because they lacked a strategic and tactical design. Others are still alive but with a different name and goal following an internal reorganization.

Before the Big Bang: Corporate Venture Capital

M&A was once the only way to engage with startups, and it is essentially a way to buy revenue, talent, or technology. As this strategy became more competitive and as startups grew in number, some sophisticated companies looked upstream to invest in growth rather than just buy it at a premium—and thus, the early corporate venture capital (CVC) funds were born.

Corporate investments in new, external companies have been documented since the early 1900s, but corporate venture arms became more formalized in the 1960s as companies such as DuPont, Boeing, and Monsanto strove to diversify.[7]

CVC funds soared in the late 1990s and have further exploded in the last few years. Before the 2008 financial crisis, about 600 corporations were involved in US venture capital transactions. In 2018, that number had more than doubled, with 1,400 CVCs. In 2018 alone, a record 264 new CVCs entered the scene, coming both from traditional industries, such as Porsche Ventures, and from ex-startups turned corporations, such as Coinbase Ventures, the arm of a blockchain startup founded in 2012.[8] Perhaps counterintuitively, CVC investments did not decline during the 2020 pandemic; they represented over 25 percent of US deals and more than 51 percent of deal value.[9]

For many decades, corporate investments and successive mergers and acquisitions were the only managed, measurable, and repeatable processes for partnering with startups. Other collaborations existed, of course, but there was no other "program" behind them; they were developed on a case-by-case basis. If a corporation wanted to engage with a startup, it had to pony up cash and buy it (partially or entirely).

The recent intensification of CVC activity signaled a major shift in corporate innovation: in the classic dilemma of "build, buy, or partner," we are seeing a general shift of build and buy strategies toward partnering. While for many organizations CVC is viewed as simply a cheaper and earlier stage of M&A, for many others, it is employed to simply open the door to diversified technologies, talent, and markets.

The Unbundling of CVC

Until the early 2000s, CVC was overloaded with tasks, and it still is in many organizations. Scouting for startups was one: CVC was the corporate front line searching for external novel technologies and business models. Financial return was another: CVC, like every other business unit, had to prove its economic viability, and it was often compared with private venture capital (VC). CVCs have always struggled to walk the tightrope between strategic goals and financial returns.[10] Ecosystem building was a third: CVC startup portfolios were built with the strategic plan of creating an external innovation network.

With the emergence of accelerators, CVC got unbundled for the first time. The reasons to differentiate became evident—CVC had too many jobs and, in that form, could not compete with private VC on the same ground. As the types of startup program models increased, specialization quickly followed, creating a long tail of dozens of hybrid models. Challenges, for instance, are highly specialized scouting tools without any educational or equity aspect. Venture accelerators are investment vehicles, the complement to CVC for early-stage startups. Hackathons, or a series of them, are ideal for idea creation and testing. Coworking spaces and content-intensive programs such as non-venture accelerators can also perform ecosystem building. Consequent to this unbundling, in very recent times, CVCs such as Microsoft's M12, now free of other tasks, are refocusing on financial goals.[11]

Equity ownership is a powerful tool because it provides legal rights to open the hood, look inside a startup, and decide when and how to steer its course. However, it's very invasive for the entrepreneur and costly for the investor. In some respects, it is like having a hammer as the only tool in your toolbox when what you really need is a screwdriver (it may—or may not—get the job done, but in either case odds are the results won't be pretty). The new models emerging from the Big Bang are more precise and targeted, and and large organizations are pivoting from CVC to using the right tool for their needs.

The Big Bang: Accelerators

After the first startup accelerator, Y Combinator, opened its doors in summer 2005 in Boston, Massachusetts, corporations and other large organizations saw a new model that could de-risk startup engagement compared to CVC (and cost less to boot). Between 2008 and 2012, several major corporations such as Microsoft, Google, Sprint, and T-Mobile opened corporate accelerators for external startups. Digital and telecommunication companies were first movers because this model, with its three-month duration and small-ticket investments of about $50,000, works best with fast and low-cost digital startups. Many other corporations followed suit in diverse industries, such as pharmaceuticals

(Bayer, Sanofi), banks (Wells Fargo, Barclays, BBVA), and transport (Boeing, British Airways, Mini). Governments did the same, setting up accelerators to attract entrepreneurs to their regions, such as Start-Up Chile or TechPeaks in Italy.

Even as the accelerator detached from CVC, the story repeated itself, like a Russian doll nested in another. During the period 2008–2012, as the accelerator was exported from its origins in the investment community to the corporate and government settings, it became clear that the accelerator model too was doing multiple jobs, such as sorting, resourcing, educating, connecting, staffing, and expanding new businesses, as well as piloting new applications. Consequently, accelerators also adopted slightly diversified models, giving birth to their own mini Big Bang with at least three categories: (1) the venture accelerator, led by investors and focused on financial return; (2) the ecosystem accelerator, led by public institutions to develop local entrepreneurial communities, or by corporations to create innovation networks; (3) the matchmaking accelerator, led by businesses to solve specific innovation problems.[12]

Accelerators can manage early-stage startups or even prestartups or informal teams—engaging with 10 to 20 such ventures with the same effort and cost as one CVC investment. Under these aspects, an accelerator complements CVC and can prefilter startups to be later considered for CVC and M&A.

More Big Bang: Incubators, Coworking Spaces, and Other Programs

For many observers, accelerators are a specialized form of startup incubation.[13] Incubators, named after neonatal intensive care units, were introduced in 1959 in the United States at the Batavia Industrial Center, New York—a shared building for multiple businesses,[14] establishing a model that would be replicated in Europe from 1984.[15] With the internet economy boom, corporations and private investors began to employ the same model, but for digital startups and focusing on networking services. In the early 2000s, incubators also experienced their own mini Big Bang, with at least four types and two meta-models.[16] The main differences were in the business model (e.g., sponsorship, rent), the backers (e.g., corporate, university, government), and the offering (e.g., office only or also networking).

In 2005, the first official coworking space in the United States opened in San Francisco, California, taking inspiration from European hackerspaces of the early 1990s. Beyond sharing a physical workspace, this new concept included intentional cooperation between independent workers.[17] WeWork, a private company and itself a startup, climbed to fame during its wild expansion and blurred the idea of coworking space with a serviced office. Often crossing that same grey line, governments and corporations have also been using coworking spaces as tools of startup engagement for at least a decade, sometimes offering them in overlap with incubation or acceleration.

Hackathons followed a similar path, from independent events to tools of startup engagement. First conceived as a hacker event in 1999,[18] they have been used at least since 2007 to aggregate local entrepreneurial communities (e.g., Startup Weekend)[19] or for idea crowdsourcing, especially by government agencies or corporations such as PepsiCo and Capital One. When large organizations adopt the hackathon format, they often create a program consisting of a series of events, like the Space Apps Challenge by NASA.[20]

Challenges gained traction in established businesses and governments in the last decade, but they likely have roots in XPRIZE, founded in 1994. Today, players such as Comcast, Pfizer and E.ON run challenges to source innovations from startups.

Case Study: Corporation—Wayra

Before continuing with our thesis, let's look at two examples from the private and public sectors to appreciate the startup program phenomenon better.

Telefónica, a Spanish telecommunication operator with vast operations in Europe and Latin America, started Wayra as its corporate startup accelerator in 2011.[21] Wayra "Academies" spread across 14 countries in 2014, with a mission to aggregate and create entrepreneurial ecosystems around them. In the beginning, Wayra invested a fixed 50,000-euro (about $60,000) ticket for a 5- to 10-percent equity share in seed-stage startups, later moving to similar amounts but utilizing a convertible bond.

In 2018, the program was relaunched to accelerate more mature companies with a sharp fit with Telefónica's strategic projects. Academies became "Open Innovation Hubs"—they focused more on being a partnership enabler while reducing the ecosystem activities. Today, Wayra's average investment has grown to $250,000, and promotional services have replaced the demo day. The program team identifies itself as a micro-CVC instead of an accelerator.

Business development is now one of Wayra's leading key performance indicators. Wayra UK and Germany together generated over $25 million in contracts for their startups in 2019. Wayra still assists its startups in the go-to-market actions, but the process is now highly customized and involves at least one more business unit. Out of over 500 active startups in the Wayra portfolio, more than 170 are working with Telefónica or its customers (with revenue-sharing agreements).

As of 2020, Wayra had invested €54 million ($64 million), almost a third of the total startup investments made by Telefónica in its history, and attracted another €600 million ($715 million) in coinvestments from third parties. It successfully exited 70 of its investments with a positive financial return.

Wayra changed throughout its lifetime, staying aware of a mutating context and adapting its model to the strategic goals of the parent company. Its identification changed as well, going from corporate accelerator to open innovation hub and micro-CVC.

Case Study: Government—Start-Up Chile

The Chilean Economic Development Agency (CORFO) initiated a program named Start-Up Chile (SUP Chile) in November 2010 to encourage Chilean entrepreneurship through examples of foreign startup founders visiting the country for six months.[22] Participants received nondilutive grants in the range of $20,000 to $100,000. But to unlock the disbursement, they were required to elevate the entrepreneurial culture and skills in Chilean universities and local small businesses via so-called return value or give back activities consisting of event participation, talks, lectures, and free consultancy.

Following a change in the government in 2016, the new leadership prioritized transforming the economy and reducing the country's dependence on the mining industry. Consequently, the program refocused on promoting domestic startups. It also increased the effort to create collaborations with the 200 international companies headquartered in the country.

In addition to funding, the program offers perks (such as free office space and free cloud service credits), a mentorship program, access to the SUP Chile partner network, a one-year visa, soft-landing services, and access to the SUP Chile community of alumni.

Since launching, SUP Chile has served 1,960 startups, 54 percent of which were active at the end of 2020. Their revenues amounted to $1.27 billion with an estimated aggregate valuation of $2.1 billion. No less than 300,000 Chileans were involved in innovation events and entrepreneurial mentoring.[23] As an indication of the program's achievements, more than 10 emerging countries have initiated programs modeled after Start-Up Chile, including, among others, Parallel18 in Puerto Rico.

Why Startups?

> *Startups are solving the world's important challenges with agility, innovative technology, and determination. Google is proud to help.*
>
> —Google for Startups official website

Rather than partnering with startups, mature organizations can address the same problems with internal research and development (R&D), skunkworks,[24] established suppliers and value networks, consultants, or traditional promotion and public relations. So why engage with startups specifically?

First and foremost, startups come at the end of an ideal line that moves from inside to outside sources and internal to open innovation. Startups are the most external sources after R&D (internal), skunkworks (just "outside the building" but still inside the organization), and traditional suppliers (outside the organization but more tightly controlled than startups because they don't have ambitions of market disruption).

There are also other strategic reasons, and they are different for each organization. One of the general problems that innovation tries to solve is that complacency leads to obsolescence.

While this is often understood, many people still default to "justifying their paycheck" when faced with a perceived change or threat. And all the time they spend doing this puts even more distance between where they are and where they need to go. External innovators can help break the internal inertia.

Sometimes you can't see the forest for the trees—when you are too close to a problem, you need to take a step back and gain a new perspective. Startups tackle issues with their technology and an independent drive. Hence, they are unlike any R&D department, skunkworks, or consultancy. Startups have proven that today's innovation paths can be entirely external to any established organization and still be as effective if not better (or even much better)—long gone are the days when innovation was the sole or even primary purview of established corporate giants (IBM, Lockheed Martin, Monsanto), as the thousands of successful startups over the last decades have proven; so partnering with them has become a must, as anything less risks being cut out of innovation.

In some cases, there's only one startup in the world that solves a particular problem, and it will be thanks to superior technology that no one else possesses. This might be the case when a research-based startup possesses a substantial and unique intellectual property, or when a startup had a dramatic head start in adopting and developing a new business model.

Other times, there may be several competing possible solutions but you don't have one specific solution in mind, and you want to explore many different routes before committing to one. In this case, the diversity and number of startups present hundreds of innovation labs "in a box," each already staffed with talent and able to deliver on a technology, from which an organization can pick and choose. This virtually unlimited expanse of options represents a long tail of innovation sources that is customizable depending on your engagement process. You change the terms of the offer, and you can attract precisely the right startup to address your needs.

Startups can be a good option also when you need to quickly set up an equivalent of a skunkworks to experiment beyond the reach of internal politics or bureaucracy, or to avoid risking your brand with an unproven cutting-edge project or in an unfamiliar market.

Finally, startups are compelling partners to help shift your business (or your regional economy, for public institutions) toward digital transformation, green energy, modern biotechnology, or another frontier specialization. They can provide a cultural example to your staff (or regional established businesses), pollinating managers and employees with explorative innovation skills and a failure-as-learning mindset.

Why Startup Programs?

> *Innovation can only be fostered, not planned, because it's an inherently stochastic process that follows a Pareto distribution. It means that running an experiment with a startup now and then is completely useless. To achieve returns, one must run many experiments—and startup programs are an efficient way of doing precisely that.*
>
> —Augusto Coppola, CEO Cloud Accelerator

Suppose you have decided to engage with external startups: Why use a "program" instead of case-by-case engagements?

Many organizations begin their journey in startup collaborations with one-off partnerships, with terms and exceptions created ad hoc around one single case. While one-offs are not bad per se, the lack of structure in this approach may cause several unintended problems. For instance, different organizational units could act disorderly and without coordination, unknowing of each other's startup initiatives. You want to avoid a situation in which startups chaotically reach out to one or another department in a desperate attempt to engage. Sometimes a startup might end up speaking with different units at the same time, landing discordant deals without the units even being aware of it.

Another problem originates from the higher uncertainty and unpredictability of the one-off approach. Innovation projects are inherently risky because they contain many unknown unknowns. On top of that, a startup is usually still proving its technology or business model, and the collaboration with your organization is just a stepping stone in that ongoing process. The outcome of one specific collaboration is hard to predict. In this

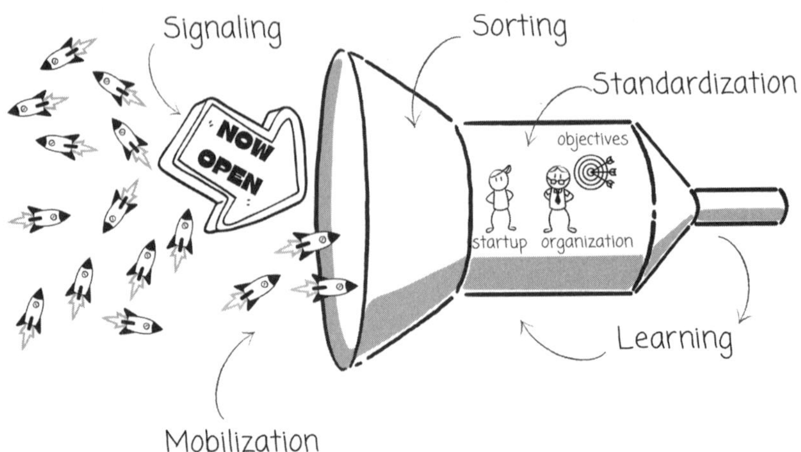

FIGURE 1.1 Startup programs provide multiple functions to an organization, including signaling, mobilization, sorting, and partnering process standardization.

situation, the rational approach dictates to spread the risk over a range of startup collaborations.

Startup programs provide a more efficient way of controlling risk and generating results. They create an organizational avenue to engage with startups.[25] As Tobias Gutmann, formerly with Siemens Next47, put it, "Programs are necessary to translate chaos into a linear process because corporates like linear but startups are chaos." Figure 1.1 illustrates some of the most prominent benefits of programs:

- **Signaling and Mobilization.** Programs have a signaling function, communicating the organization's intention to engage—both outside and inside the organization. Outside, they mobilize dozens of startups simultaneously, catalyzing attention when the organization wants and needs it. They lay out the goals and terms of future collaborations, empowering the startups to decide if there is a strategic fit before they apply. Inside, startup programs can generate momentum, triggering the attention of top management and critical parts of the organization and fostering coordinated action from diverse departments. A program might even be able to lock in resources that a one-off collaboration cannot obtain, creating a barrier against short-termism.

- **Standardization.** One-off collaborations are often seen as exceptions and rarely produce a new permanent process. Vice versa, a startup program can become an organizational process, with some (or total) standardization, thus providing a common language and smoother interactions across diverse departments such as legal, administration, engineering, research, operations, or sales. A standardized startup program can also be used as a neutral zone or a "sandbox,"[26] allowing specific procedures to be simplified, temporarily suppressed, or run as exceptions, thus assuming risks typically avoided in large organizations.
- **Sorting.** Because innovation inherently contains unknowns, an organization needs a portfolio of options[27] to distribute its bets. A program provides the framework to grow such a portfolio because it engages with multiple startups simultaneously. This parallelism enables two forms of sorting. One is embedded in the admission process, when you select startups that enter the program. The second comes at the end, after using the program as a due diligence tool before committing to deeper stages of the collaboration.
- **Faster Learning.** Higher parallelism also provides an opportunity to analyze cause/effect relationships across the entire program to learn more quickly what works and what doesn't, and help improve your processes in the next iteration. You can develop a playbook for the program to be repeated and improved over time.

There are two more advantages to programs when seen through the lens of this book: flexibility and systems thinking.

Flexibility originates from the multitude of design dimensions that characterize startup programs. By tweaking parameters such as duration, location, educational curriculum, interactive activities, and so on, a program can pursue a wide range of goals—as diverse as tackling lack of new products, improving brand awareness, expanding in new markets, reviving a stagnant company culture, developing an entrepreneurial ecosystem, or fostering employment. Whatever your objective for startup collaborations, you can create a program that maximizes it. Furthermore, organizations can proceed at their own pace, initially focusing on cheaper and leaner startup programs, such as hackathon series or competitions, to test the water before plunging into more demanding models, such as accelerators or CVC.

Systems thinking is an essential and unavoidable component of successful startup programs. Indeed, we will argue in this book that the lack of systems thinking is at the origin of many failed programs. Startup programs are connectors of different systems, and as such they create larger systems. They are "team players" by definition. Whereas one-off partnership address a single, isolated need, startup programs pull together loose strings inside and outside your organization creating the platform to potentially solve many issues. Since it's so interconnected and interdependent on the systems around it, a single program usually affects multiple actors and objectives simultaneously. For example, an accelerator can pursue revenue and cultural goals at the same time.

Putting together flexibility and systems thinking, an organization can even build a family or "system" of programs (Google for Startups and its six subprograms are an example), each addressing a different problem or working with startups at different maturity levels. Programs in a system can work in synergy or create artificial internal competition to help overcome complacency. They can also cooperate or compete with alternatives, such as internal R&D, skunkworks, or consultants (discussed in detail in Chapter 16).

The Startups' Perspective

For startups, approaching a large organization is often a riddle. The points of contact might be unclear or contradictory, and navigating the various procedures and red tape can be staggering. Startup programs act as an interface to the complexity of internal hierarchies and guarantee friendly terms and conditions, removing roadblocks that would potentially kill the initiative.

Startups are eager for resources, funds, talent, distribution channels, and customers—all things that large organisations possess. Finding the right launching customer, financial partner, or strategic alliance can give the startup an unprecedented push. Winning a long-term collaboration can provide even more—vetting, revenues, more opportunities.

Startup programs can provide a startup with a mix of these benefits in an approachable and accessible way. Compared to one-off partnerships, programs generally offer clearer terms, faster processing time, and useful perks. For example, a founder of a Series D, very mature startup told us he preferred going through a startup program rather than standard procurement when approaching a potential corporate client, because of less red tape and lower requirements—otherwise impractical for a startup.

Table 1.1 compares a startup program with a one-off partnership, putting together the organization's and startup's perspectives.

TABLE 1.1 Comparison between one-off, case-by-case engagements and a startup program

Function	One-off partnership	Startup program
Signaling	Typically self-referential and might not signal the organization's interest outside in a continuous and clear way.	Creates a clear gateway and indicates the intention to engage.
Mobilization	Opportunistic contact with one startup based on a specific need. The startup must typically be known already.	The program's promotion solicits startups to signal their reciprocal interest to engage. Such bottom-up mechanism may reveal unknown startups.
Sorting	The single-case partnership decision is made in isolation, making it hard to compare different cases distant in time, or made by different units.	The program provides a benchmark and a wider choice of partners all at once, and processed under one coordinated action.
Standardization	Hard to standardize because the internal actors involved may change, and they may not follow the same process.	The program can potentially become a unified process across different units inside the organization. It can be standardized (up to a level or completely) across different startups.
Repetition	Can be repeated independently, but often requires restarting the internal coordination process from scratch every time.	The program can develop a playbook which can be distributed to other units or locations.
Learning	Harder to transfer the experience across different, unconnected partnerships.	Success metrics and issues can be tracked over subsequent editions and can foster continuous improvements.
Interface	The interface might be set up and changed on a case-by-case basis.	The program provides a clear point-of-contact and a process to initiate a new partnership.

Why Startup Program Design?

> *Acceleration looks easy, right? You run a call, you do some mentorship, and it's done. Nope.*
>
> —Gianluca Dettori, General Partner Barcamper Ventures and a Kauffman Foundation Fellow

If you accept the idea of adopting a startup program, why not just copy and paste what others do or hire an external provider? Why go through the trouble of designing your own program? When does "design" matter?

Design matters when the problem is general but the context is specific, or in other words, when you must adapt an idea or model to different constraints from those of its original setting. And when a large organization is involved, the context is often overwhelmingly specific for at least three reasons.

First, goals for startup engagement tend to be strategic rather than financial. Models can be exported with relative ease when goals are purely measured by dollars returned on investment. But strategic objectives change everything. And because strategic needs are different for each organization, the details of that role are specific too. Therefore, a startup program model created for financial return, such as an archetypal accelerator, venture fund, or venture builder, doesn't work "as is" when applied to strategic goals—they are out of context. Consequently, these models need to be adapted or entirely redesigned when used by large organizations instead of investors. The same applies to hackathons, which hackers created to hack, or for incubators created by building owners to maximize rent. When you change the goals, you must adapt the model, too.

Second, because the strategy determines the role of a startup in the partnership, the "right" startup also changes. All (or almost all) investor-driven accelerators and VCs look for the same characteristics in a startup: rapid growth, disruption, and a potentially lucrative exit. But these characteristics might not be a priority for an organization's strategy. They could be substituted with entirely different ones—such as customizing a product or relocating to a different region. Consequently, the program's offer should be designed to appeal to these other startups, which imposes more changes to the model.

Third, every organization is unique in what it can or can't provide in a partnership. Some can contribute funds in the form of grants, while others can open a channel to unique kinds of customers or users. While investors almost always compete only on investment terms and access to networks, large organizations can (and should) compete in very different dimensions. Such dimensions define the opportunities and constraints on the "how" a program can (or should) be implemented.

As you can see, the level of complexity surrounding a startup program is nontrivial. If an organization doesn't intentionally plan to cope with all these factors *simultaneously*, its startup program is prone to failure. In truth, one of the main reasons why many corporate or government programs have failed is that they ignored context-aware and goal-driven design.

A Must, Not Just an Option

While the Big Bang of startup programs was positive in that it added more options, it can plunge novices into the paradox of choice,[28] which increases the chance of getting the model wrong. In the current cornucopia of startup program models, where what exactly is meant by terms like "accelerator" or "incubator" becomes ambiguous, copying and pasting blindly and without intentional design is a recipe for letting luck decide instead of management—failure becomes commonplace. In the assortment of options, picking the right program is more important than running it perfectly. And for those opting for hiring external providers of startup programs, choosing the right provider requires an understanding of the internal dimensions of this industry—or you may end up throwing millions to a fund without any clear upside.

Design is a problem-solving tool to make any given thing more approachable and valuable. Internal stakeholders (e.g., senior leaders or other units) should be enabled to "use the startups" and extract value from them. Likewise, the program's customers—the startups—should be able to profitably "use the organization" simultaneously. Each side has their needs and objectives, and these needs change each time the players are different; it is through design that a proper interface is built to make these needs compatible.

One Design Space, One Industry

> *We are trying to use the label "accelerator" for a wide variety of business types, from university programs to one that wants to create a deal flow for later funds, to a government program that creates jobs.*
>
> —Marius Ursache, CEO and Cofounder at Metabeta

Following the fragmentation and specialization of formats from the Big Bang, startup program models now overlap in scope and mechanics. Each form has its characteristics, but they are becoming fuzzier every day. Hybrids are on the rise. Witness the recent proliferation of chimeric names such as "inculator"[29] (a crossbreed of incubator and accelerator), "excubator"[30] (a sort of post-incubator), "ideathon"[31] (a student event to generate new ideas), and so on.

Hybridization is so common that it has become the norm rather than the exception. And, we argue, it could not be otherwise: customization of startup program models is a must, not an option. Startup program design is the new normal. There is no such thing as a holy grail or a one-size-fits-all startup program model—not anymore, at least. An accelerator, an incubator, a hackathon series, or any individual program in that respect is just one permutation of an infinite number of startup programs based on different objectives, different startup types, different contents, and different structures.

It's time to move one step past the Big Bang and recognize "startup engagement" as one single industry. What we need today is a paradigm shift from thinking in silos to embracing a unified framework. The venture fund, accelerator, incubator, challenge, hackathon, and so on, are the silos. The unified framework is the "startup program," and it applies to both the private and public sectors alike.

Instead of the question "How do I build my corporate accelerator?" we hope that after reading this book the question shifts to "How do I solve startup engagement?" The answer might not be "with an accelerator," or, for that matter, with any other known model. You might have to tailor one or more models to your needs or, in some rare cases, even invent an entirely new category.

Design Dimensions

We argue that startup program design should collect the design dimensions common to all startup programs—duration, location, educational curriculum, funding scheme, terms and conditions, mentorship framework, intake scheme, and so on—inside one single design space. Table 1.2 shows some of the most prominent dimensions—the dimensions used in this book. But there could be many more. Tobias Gutmann of EBS Business School, for example, has built a configurator with 47 "modes of innovation."[32]

Design dimensions are adjustable, like the controls on a music mixer used to obtain a unique combination and sound quality, or chromosomes in the human genome that can generate various phenotypes.

A specific model is a configuration of features in those dimensions. For example, duration is short in hackathons, longer in accelerators, and even longer in incubators—but it's still a design feature connected with what you want to accomplish, with whom, and in what time frame (as a constraint or opportunity).

In our framework, besides managerial aspects such as governance, design dimensions and program features fall in three categories: offer, ask, and structure.

Offer and Ask

The startup program acts as a platform on which value flows from the organization to the startup (*offer*) and vice versa (*ask*)—eventually creating additional mutual value in the process (Figure 1.2). The offer consists of content, such as the educational curriculum, mentors, or networking events; and benefits such as funding, office space, and perks. The ask is the ensemble of terms and conditions imposed on startups that help the organization achieve its objectives, such as equity, temporary relocation, exclusivity, and information disclosure.

TABLE 1.2 A list of design dimensions used in this book. Some may contain other features (content features contain funding, educational curriculum, mentors, etc.).

Design Dimension	Description
Admission process	A selection process that is done at graduation, before the beginning of the empowerment stage.
Content	Content features comprise the support for startups (e.g., funds, seminars, mentors, or introductions) and activities made for externalities—part of the offer.
Duration	The duration may vary from a few hours (hackathons) to a few weeks (accelerators) to several years (incubators).
Funnel structure	A program's stage-gate structure describes a funnel through which input startups can be progressively filtered. Each substage has its content.
Governance	Programs can be independent units or projects inside a corporate team (e.g., innovation) or an execution unit (e.g., a division).
Graduation process	A selection process that is done at graduation, at the end of the empowerment stage.
Input startups	Startups enter the program's funnel in a particular input state. Different programs target different startup segments, each segment having an archetypal input state.
Intake process	Startups can be admitted on a rolling basis, first-in, first-out, or in cohorts (or batches or classes) with a given deadline for applications.
Location	Where the startup program takes place. It can be an office building, a coworking space, or a virtual location (remote programs).
Metrics	How the program measures itself: input metrics, process metrics, output metrics, outcome metrics, or any variation that works in your organization.
Outcomes	The outcomes a program is attempting to produce. Outcomes may not occur before graduation.
Outputs	The outputs a program will produce in order to advance the outcomes. Outputs are always produced at graduation or before.
Program team	The program's management team is usually in charge of operations and input, process, and output metrics. It is not always accountable for outcomes.
Schedule	The distribution of activities, resources, and assets available to startups inside the program (in its substages). The schedule is part of both offer and ask.
Terms and conditions	A part of the ask, what the startups have to abide by so that the organization can capture value from the partnership.
Payback period	The time frame at which the organization expects to receive its returns.

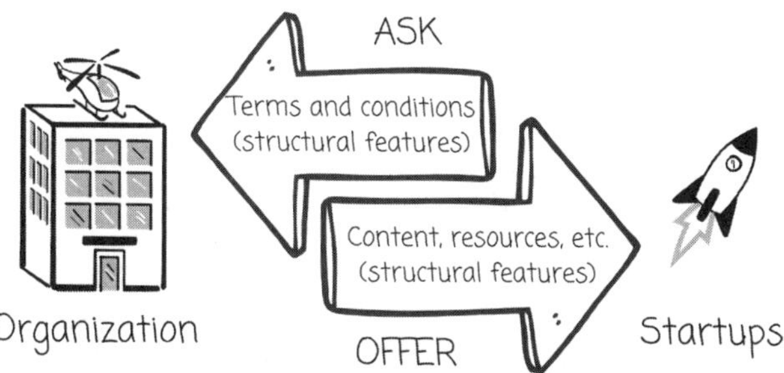

FIGURE 1.2 The offer and ask represent the flows of value in the program.

For example, LH Startup MAQER, the venture client unit of cement producer LafargeHolcim, targets startups in industry automation, logistics, and the retail customer experience. The ask is to be prototype-ready with a specific solution and customize it for the corporation. The offer is a commercial deal and follow-up support to solution implementation. The commercial agreement is a tool for creating mutual value: LH sees its problem solved, and the startup tests its product and processes while building its reputation with a global brand (Figure 1.3).

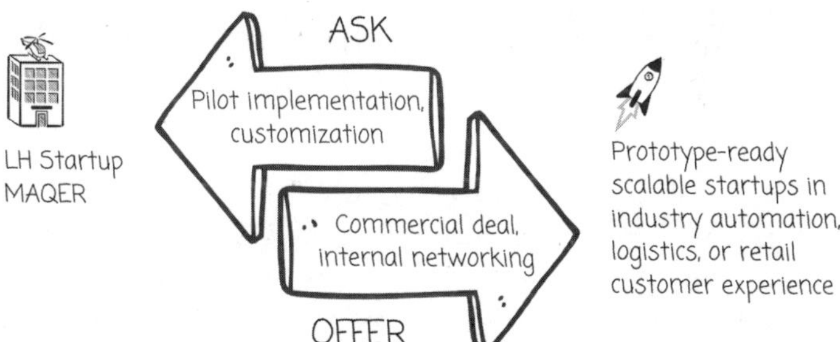

FIGURE 1.3 LH Startup MAQER: LafargeHolcim agrees to commercial deals only with prototype-ready startups.

Structure

Structural features are schedule, duration, location, intake mode (e.g., rolling or by cohorts), and the program funnel with selection processes, criteria, and gates.

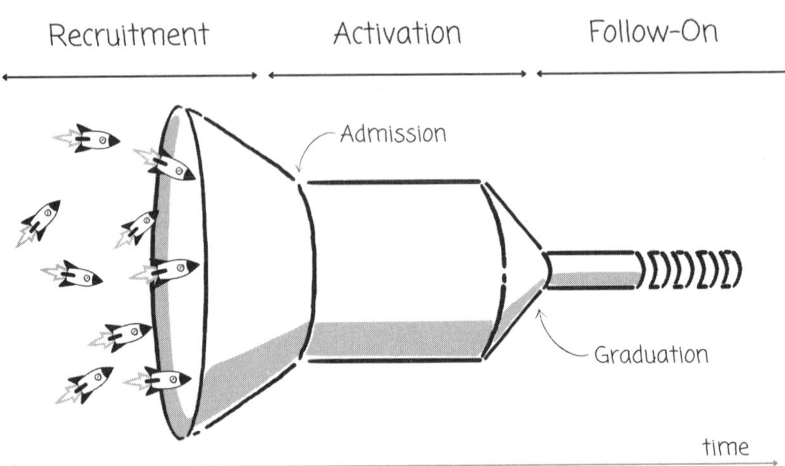

FIGURE 1.4 This book uses a unified framework to describe the program funnel, with three stages (recruitment, activation, and follow-on) and two gates (admission and graduation). Some program models may have more stages and gates, or some might have fewer.

The accelerator model has a structured funnel that spans a few months, from launching a new call for applications up to demo day, which is the typical graduation event involving the investor community. In a typical accelerator funnel, we can distinguish a series of stages and gates (Figure 1.4):

- **Recruitment stage.** The program signals the intention to engage, mobilizes startups to apply through inbound (e.g., call, promotion) or outbound channels (e.g., scouting), and screens the applicants.
- **Admission gate.** Recruitment ends with a decision gate that designates the admitted startups.
- **Activation stage.** The program continues with the bulk of activities, including an educational curriculum, mentors, networking events, and so on. Even though the terms "program" or "programming" are commonly used to describe this stage, we use "activation stage" to avoid confusion between this particular stage and the program as a whole.
- **Graduation gate.** Accelerators normally end with a demo day, a graduation event celebrating the startups'

improvements and presenting them to the investors. Graduation can sometimes be a gate where startups are ranked, and some are given prizes or extras.

- **Follow-on stage.** After demo day, accelerators maintain contacts with alumni through networking activities or online platforms. This part is commonly called "post-program," but the term "follow-on stage" communicates how some operators consider this still a part of the program—just another stage.

We describe this model as a funnel because the number of startups in the alumni network (follow-on stage) is typically less than the initial applicants at the program launch. Most startups are stopped at the admission gate (admission rate in accelerators is about 3 percent), others drop out during the programming activities, and more—in some formats—are filtered at the graduation gate. Furthermore, the activation stage might be divided into substages and contain one or more intermediary gates.

We generalize this structural pattern to other models as well. Some models don't incorporate one or more of these structural elements, but the general funnel still applies. In this generic funnel pattern, each stage has its duration, location, and schedule. Consider the following examples:

- **Hackathons.** Recruitment is the event promotion. Most hackathons don't have an admission gate (all those who pay the ticket enter), and the graduation gate is not a demo day but a pitch night (it's a gate because a winner is declared). The activation stage lasts two or three days instead of months. Hackathons don't usually have a follow-on, although some offer extra services to the winners.
- **Incubators.** Most incubators don't have a recruitment stage; their intakes are on a rolling basis and follow a logic of first come, first served. The activation stage lasts for the whole period of residence inside the incubator, typically one to three years, and might contain occasional networking activities, but mainly it provides office space. The follow-on stage is generally absent.
- **Venture funds.** For closed funds, recruitment goes on for two to five years as the fund looks for startups. The

activation consists of terms negotiation and funding. The follow-on stage contains board of directors' meetings and harvesting.

- **Challenges.** The recruitment stage is similar to accelerators, but there's no admission gate: everyone willing to compete can do so. Activation is usually left to participants, who individually develop their solutions, which are then judged to assign the prize at graduation. Follow-ons might include only the winners and might entail further implementation of the idea or solution.

In this book, we reference diverse stages, but always with the general funnel pattern in mind. Even when future models eventually appear, they will deploy one version or another of this generic scheme. Chapters 13 and 14 will analyze the structure and selection in more detail.

Ecosystem Effects and the Feedback Loop

The funnel structure introduced in Figure 1.4 might be misleading in one aspect. It looks as if startups were entering and exiting an impermeable tube. The figure doesn't portray any interaction with the outer world, save for the input and output.

In reality, a startup program almost always has repercussions on the world beyond the program, willingly or not. The reason is that a startup program, to function and produce results, involves many players and partners: startups, internal units, mentors, top management, investors, universities, and so on. This involvement produces reactions, cultural changes, social connections, information flow, knowledge exchange, and so forth. In this book, we collectively call these by-products *ecosystem effects.*

Such by-products occur even as a new program is announced. For instance, the program's offering will grant a new lens to measure the organization's intention and commitment to partnering with the startup community. It may inspire new entrepreneurs to break the ice and give their idea a chance. Other ecosystem players might react to the new program too: some will look for partnerships while others will create competitive offering. Later, after the program has run for one or more editions, the startup and investor communities will be influenced by the program's reputation and track record when interacting with the organization.

Repercussions are likely to also occur internally. Other organizational units may become supporters or detractors of the program, mutating their plans on how they interact with startups. Some colleagues might change, for good or bad, their approach to working with startups or, in general, to their job. Some will be inspired to become more entrepreneurial, and a few might even leave the organization and found a company of their own.

We could continue with the list of examples, but the takeaway is the following: you can't avoid ecosystem effects. They come with the package. In our model, these effects are represented as a *feedback loop* onto the world beyond the program. Our claim is that such feedback is inevitable. It can be weak or strong, positive or negative, but it's there. Edition after edition, a startup program modifies the people, culture, society, and institutions around it.

Note that ecosystem effects are distinct from startup benefits. The program affects the participants and, in parallel, also the surrounding ecosystems. Once you accept this truth, it becomes a designer's duty to take ecosystem effects into consideration when designing a program.

Evidence of Ecosystem Effects

Every experienced startup program manager will confirm that ecosystem effects are a fact, although seldom measured and thus hard to quantify. Recent research provides evidence for the effects of some specific types of programs such as accelerators, hackathons, and incubators.

Two independent studies indicate that accelerators positively affect the availability of venture capital in the region where they operate, not just for the accelerated startups, but in general for all the startups participating in the local ecosystem.[33] The same research highlights how accelerators can help increase entrepreneurial activity in a region when they involve locals who are not program participants—through mechanisms such as weekly happy hours, inspirational talks from outstanding entrepreneurs, internships of university students with accelerated startups, and so on.

Hackathons were also found to be effective to communities. They play a role in activating an entrepreneurial spirit in the participants or raising awareness to other participants that entrepreneurship is an option.[34]

Finally, studies on incubators suggest they might have positive outcomes in terms of enterprise survival and higher employment growth.[35]

Entrepreneurial Ecosystem and Organizational Ecosystem

For clarity and simplicity, we posit that two ecosystems exist around every startup program: one external and one internal to the organization. As we will argue in Chapter 2, a startup program sits at the junction between these complex ecosystems, connecting them to each other. Because it's at the junction, it feeds ecosystem effects on both sides.

On the external side stands the *entrepreneurial ecosystem*, identifiable as the ensemble of people, organizations, institutions and networks that collaborate in informal and formal ways to the creation and growth of innovative startups.[36] It includes universities, research institutions, support institutions (e.g., business incubators), investors, service providers (e.g., legal, financial), and corporations, on top of startups at diverse stages of maturity, from entrepreneurs with just an idea and little else to companies with several hundreds of employees challenging and disrupting an entire industry. Brad Feld and Ian Hathaway deeply discuss the ins and outs of entrepreneurial ecosystems in their book *The Startup Community Way*.[37] Startup programs always have effects on the entrepreneurial ecosystem they operate in. Since they later often source startups from the same ecosystem, this creates a feedback loop (Figure 1.5).

On the internal side, the *organizational ecosystem* comprises the people, units, governance structures, and procedures operating the organization, whether private or public. It encompasses everyone somehow involved in innovation activities and also beyond innovation, in the day-to-day operations—often including departments such as R&D, product, marketing, procurement, communication, human resources, and executives. Startup programs always have repercussions on the development of the innovation ability of this ecosystem too, although the program's by-products often require more planning and effort to

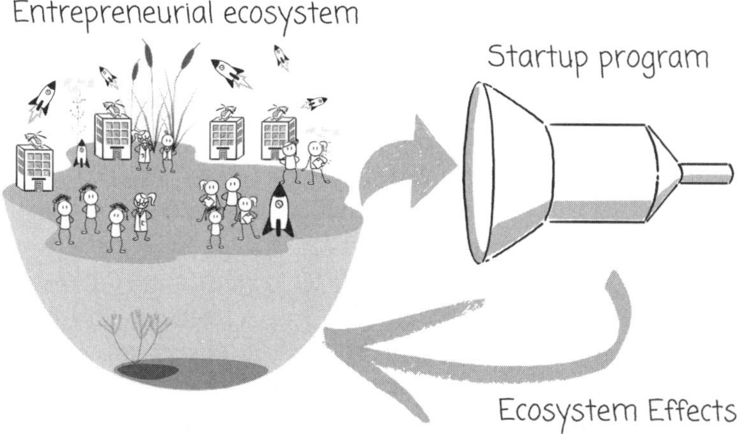

FIGURE 1.5 An external feedback loop forms because of side effects on the same entrepreneurial ecosystem (pictured as a pond throughout the book) from where startups are sourced and where they strive after they graduate.

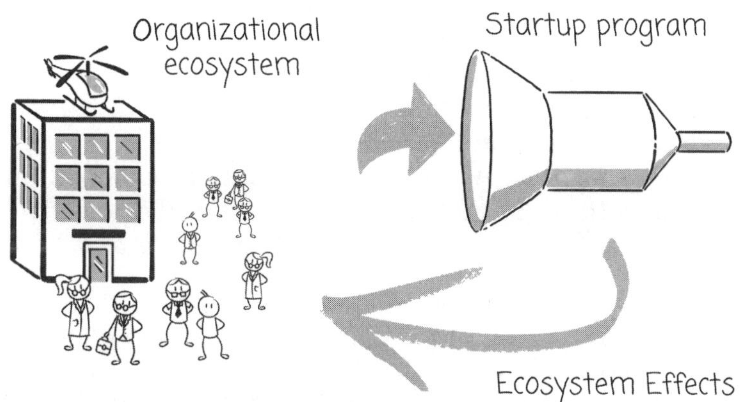

FIGURE 1.6 Another feedback loop forms internally, because the program's by-products affect the organizational ecosystem that sustains the program.

take root internally because of proverbial corporate inertia, time conflict with the execution business, and less self-motivation for entrepreneurial behavior. Because startup programs involve internal allies to operate in the current and future editions, the internal spillovers also create a feedback loop (Figure 1.6).

When a startup program is co-run by multiple organizations, the ecosystems are more than two: one entrepreneurial ecosystem and as many internal ones as the organizations involved in the program. Sometimes the multiplicity of ecosystems is on the external side, as it happens in programs embracing startup communities across different geographies or industries.

A Different Output to Design For

In our model, ecosystem effects are separate from funnel outputs. Funnel outputs are related to the direct effects on the startups participating in the program. Ecosystem effects are related to nonparticipating actors, such as internal or external partners, mentors, investors, other nonparticipating entrepreneurs, or the organization's employees. They may concern:

- The density, connectivity, diversity, and fluidity of an ecosystem.[38] Examples are connecting different social tribes important for innovation (such as researchers with investors), or helping diversify the local entrepreneurs.
- The reputation of the organization as an innovator. A burnished reputation will make it easier to attract partners and startups in the future.
- The cultural improvement about innovation and entrepreneurship. A fervent innovation culture that reframes failure as learning and knows how to judge the potential of a business idea will help procure new quality inputs.

The difference resides on whether participants are affected directly or not: if yes, that's a program funnel's output; if not, that's an ecosystem effect. Ecosystem effects and the activities generating them should be accounted with separate metrics from those that measure the participants' performance. Reasonable metrics are cultural improvement, positive press and media coverage, partners engagement, or long-term transformational effects on society or the organization.

In truth, the startups graduating from the program are, themselves, a potential source of ecosystem effects. They could create new jobs in their industry, contribute to attracting fresh capital to the region, or be a role model for the next generation of entrepreneurs. These secondary effects coming from good startup performance are also worth accounting for, although they are intermediated by the startups themselves and thus less in control of the program designer or management team.

Sometimes ecosystem effects are an explicit program objective, as it was in the case of developing the entrepreneurial skills of the Chilean ecosystem for Start-Up Chile. Until 2016 at least, SUP Chile was essentially hiring foreign entrepreneurs to educate Chileans and position the country internationally. The program intentionally contained specific features to hone ecosystem effects, such as startup road shows in universities, inspirational talks open to the general public, panels between mentors and local stakeholders, and public updates on alumni progress. These are examples of activities that can be explicitly designed and carried out by the program team to enhance the program's spillovers. Their outputs can be measured in terms of engagement and increased entrepreneurial activity.

The concept of feedback is what commands design and control of these side-effects. Feedback provides a powerful reinforcement with long-term impact. If it's positive, over time it nurtures the health of the complex ecosystems that the program bridges and uses to function. It can make more venture capital available, create more new startups, or promote a more entrepreneurial culture. In turn, these elements will improve the deal flow and quality of future applicants, and the opportunities of future graduates. If it's negative (e.g., a compromised reputation), it can harm the program outcomes by making the surrounding ecosystems less supportive toward the program.

KEY TAKEAWAYS

- **Successful external innovators.** Startups have proven that today's innovation paths can be entirely external to any established business or public institution and still be successful or even more successful. Engaging with them is a must rather than an option, as an alternative or a synergic completion of internal R&D, skunkworks, established suppliers, or consultants. Startups are a virtually unlimited expanse of options, a long tail of innovation sources that is customizable depending on the settings of your engagement process, like with an equalizer.
- **Startup programs are elective means.** Startup programs create new (temporary) innovation partnerships, potentially with long-term effects and resulting in a portfolio of options. Programs create an internal framework for interdepartmental coordination. They facilitate and develop several functions: signaling, mobilization, sorting, standardization, monitoring, repetition, improvement, and sandboxing, among others.
- **Startup engagement is one industry.** Fifty years ago, the only methodology to engage with a startup was to buy it, and CVCs and M&As were the how. Then, like a Big Bang from that one point, several other programs appeared, each more specialized: accelerators, incubators, venture builders, venture clients, hackathon series, and others. Since hybridization became the norm rather than the exception, a new industry has emerged—startup engagement.
- **A unified design framework.** Different startup program models are just configurations of design dimensions that are common to all startup programs. Offer, ask, and structural features can be combined to create the current and future models. A structure of recruitment, activation, and follow-on stages can be traced in any of today's models.
- **Ecosystem effects are inevitable.** Research shows that startup programs are effective tools for changing the surrounding ecosystems, including the external entrepreneurial ecosystem and internal organizational ecosystem. Ecosystem effects form an inescapable feedback loop and can be designed for, like any other output.

CONTEXT-AWARE DESIGN

Designing the right startup program and its features is more important than flawless execution. And if you don't pick a known template, it's even more critical to design with intent. A startup program connects at least two complex systems—the innovation ecosystem internal to the organization, and the external entrepreneurial ecosystem—in order to pursue chosen objectives. This chapter discusses that complexity and introduces a simple framework to help focus the strategic design on the operative context of the program, aligning (1) the opportunities you can offer, (2) your objectives, and (3) the specific startups that can benefit from the former and contribute to the latter.

The Only Way a Startup Program Can Succeed

Professionals are divided on how to measure the success or failure of a startup program. One rationale is to measure success in terms of benefits for the startups. "[Corporate] accelerators should be all about the startups, not the corporates," declared Lennaert Jonkers of DevelopMinded.[1] The mirror image is to measure success in terms of benefits for the sponsoring organization. According to this perspective, the corporate or public sector managers who approve the program are the final customers, and meeting or exceeding their expectations should be the main preoccupation. Without their support, there would be no program and there will be no next edition.

Both points of view have their obvious downsides. If you optimize only for yourself, exploiting startups, not communicating well, not listening, not writing checks (or writing too many checks as a way to compensate for not listening), your ability to engage with the most meaningful startups for your organization will diminish in the medium term. Likewise, if all you do is cater to startups' every whim and show no discipline, your ability to work with startups will diminish even quicker as the program will lose the needed internal support.

In the last decade there has been an explosion of new models. Startup programs are hybridizing and evolving to solve specific problems. Success metrics are following a similar arc, diversifying and growing in specificity. Nonetheless, all startup programs deliver one fundamental function: to connect. Startup programs operate at the meeting point of at least two complex systems:[2] the organization or organizations willing to engage with startups, and the startup community with its companies, talents, investors, influencers, activists, and future program participants. Any startup program is always a part of a more extensive system—actually, it connects different systems to each other, creating a new, larger system. Its function is to make those different systems work together with the lowest possible friction.

A Startup Program Is a Systems Connector

From systems theory, a system is a whole that consists of parts, each of which can affect its behavior or its properties. The behavior of a system is not given by the sum of its parts, but by their interactions.[3]

Once you accept that startup programs are systems connectors, and that, by connecting systems, they create a new, broader system consisting of the organization and the startup (at least), you must also accept the consequences. Startup programs can't create value alone, but only through the interactions with all of the other parts of the new system, namely, the organization (or organizations) and the startup community. You can't design a successful startup program without studying and predicting how it will interact with the other parts—all of them, no one excluded.

Create Mutual Value or a Fair Reciprocal Exchange

The only way a startup program can succeed is through creating value for all of its stakeholders, both the organizational (internal) and the startup (external) sides. Our research has uncovered two ways to achieve this situation (Figure 2.1). The first is when organization and startup are in perfect alignment about what creates value for both of them simultaneously, and a program supporting that "thing" will create *mutual value*. The second is when each side wants something the other has, and the program facilitates a *fair exchange of value*.

An example of the first category is when a startup aims for rapid growth and a financial exit with a high multiplier, and the organization looks for high-risk/high-return investment opportunities. In this case a successful exit is a win for both parties simultaneously. In other words, *both* the startup and its investor want the same thing: growth and exit. Consequently, a startup program can create mutual value by supporting the startup to achieve just that. Another example is when a company wants to buy new technology and the startup wants a new customer. Both startup and organization want a commercial deal, and if the program helps them close one it will have created mutual value. In these cases, the interaction the program fosters will create more value than just the sum of its parts.

However, not all startup programs walk this route. Some programs evolve deliberately toward establishing a form of trade or quid pro quo. For an example of this second category, consider an idea challenge in which a prize is promised to startups who suggest the best use case for a corporate technology. The organization wants new ideas, the startups want the prize. As long as the competition is fair and the award provides a relevant compensation for the startups' participation, that's fine: everyone will get what they want. Here, the program reallocates value like a marketplace would do, each party receiving a different "thing" than the other and for different goals.

In conclusion, the performance of a startup program always depends on how its stakeholders mesh and cooperate, not on how they act or benefit separately. You want to identify what the organization can do for startups, and, mirroring that, which startups can contribute to the organization's success. That's invariant across all good startup programs. However, whether a program achieves this through mutual value creation or a fair exchange of value has consequences on what features you need to add to the mix. The quid pro quo mechanism is not forcedly worse than mutual value creation, it's just different. But, as we will see in the rest of the book, it's important to recognize such distinction to design with intention and improve the chance of success.

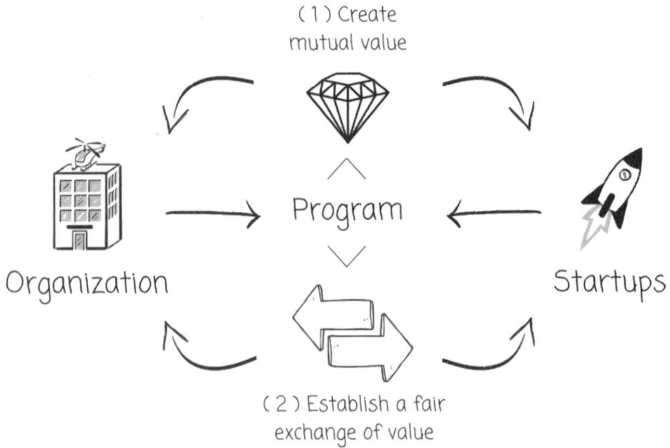

FIGURE 2.1 A good startup program must create value for at least two complex systems, the organization (internal stakeholders) and the startup community and participants (external stakeholders). If it does not create new mutual value, it should at least establish a fair exchange.

Explore the Context Before Designing the Solution

> *The list of top reasons for corporate accelerator failure, in rough order of commonality: (1) the organization did not provide the program enough time to succeed; (2) overpromising; (3) located where talent won't stay; (4) lack of internal support (and not knowing what that support entails); (5) investments viewed as competitors to internal projects (or giving that impression).*
>
> —Paul Orlando, accelerator founder in Hong Kong, Los Angeles, and Rome

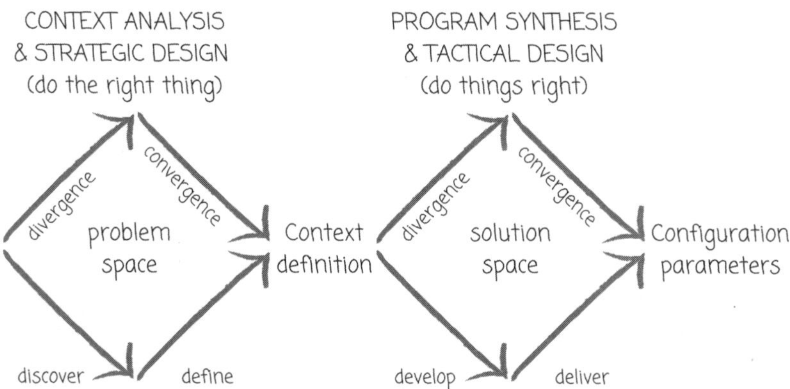

FIGURE 2.2 In the double diamond model of a design process, divergence and convergence are first applied to defining the problem, and only later to defining the solution. In startup program design, the first diamond is about defining the context, and the second about defining the feature configuration.

We believe that when startup programs fail, it's because they have not been considered within the context of systems thinking. You can succeed only when you properly position the startup program within the context in which the program operates that is, as a systems connector. Startup program design is first and foremost about strategic analysis. Only then can you drill down to the particulars. Peter Drucker underlined the difference between "doing things right" and "doing the right things."[4] Both are important, but "doing the right thing wrong" is far better than "doing the wrong thing right." In the earlier case you can learn, adjust, and iterate. In the latter case, instead, you are just executing on the wrong program, and even if you push hard, it will consistently deliver below expectations.

In design theory, this concept is captured by the double-diamond design process, in which the problem's strategic analysis precedes solution development (Figure 2.2). In startup program design, the first diamond assesses the context and determines what combination of organizational offer and participating startups will generate mutual or reciprocal benefits (effectiveness). It is about *context analysis* and *strategic design.* The second diamond defines the configuration of parameters and program features (such as duration, educational curriculum, funds staging, or mentors, for example) that best deliver those mutual benefits (efficiency). We call this second phase *tactical design* and *program configuration.*

If these two stages are inverted the program cannot be intentionally embedded within the adjacent systems, and the embedding is left to good luck. That's what happens when an organization sets off to design a corporate accelerator, a hackathon series, or any other template before even understanding their own objectives or the startups it wishes to partner with. Choosing the template before analyzing the context (or problem) is likely to set you on a course of optimizing the "wrong thing."

> *Accelerators don't exist as a category. Each is a project, starting with unique assumptions, local people, local ecosystem, individual goals and its own idea of what success resembles.*
>
> —Marius Ursache, Metabeta

The Startup Program Strategy Canvas

We have devised a canvas to help you capture all the factors that represent a startup program's operating context—the results of the problem space analysis (first diamond). We call it the Startup Program Strategy Canvas, and our research shows that three contextual elements matter:

1. The organization engaging with startups (its potential and drawbacks)
2. The specific objectives set for the program (by its initiator or manager)
3. The prospective participants and their startup community (needs and state)

A Canvas diagram captures a finite number of elements and lays them out in a simple, constrained visual representation. Even if those elements are self-evident, the Canvas helps as a checklist and a tool for reasoning. Especially in design, canvases have proven successful in conceptualizing, conceiving, and communicating ideas and models.

A Startup Program's Ikigai, *or Reason to Live*

To introduce the canvas, let's first look at a concept rooted in Japan's cultural fabric for centuries: that of *ikigai*, or a person's "reason to live."[5] A person's ikigai lies at the intersection of what one loves, is good at, can be paid for, and what the world needs (Figure 2.3).

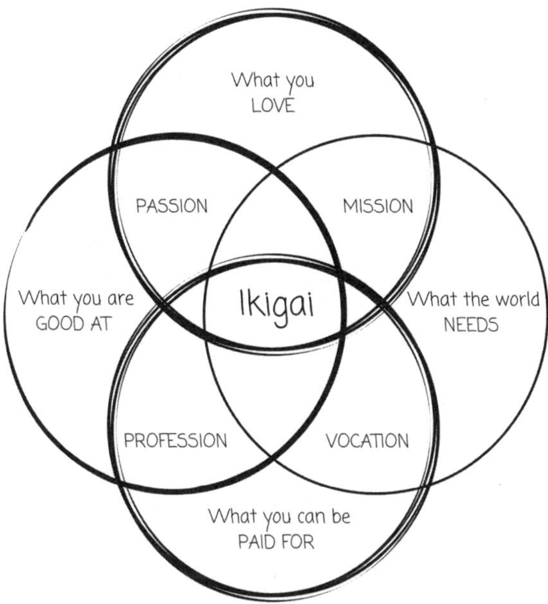

FIGURE 2.3 In the Japanese tradition, the ikigai expresses your reason to live.

Similar to the ikigai, a startup program should occupy the point of balance at the Intersection of three elements, represented by three circles:

- **Circle 1:** What the organization is "good at."
- **Circle 2:** The program's current objectives—a compromise between what it "loves" and what it can be "paid for": its vision and mission.
- **Circle 3:** What the startups themselves and the startup community "need."

That balance point, and that point only, gives the program a reason to exist (Figure 2.4). We call that central position the Intersection of the Startup Program Strategy.

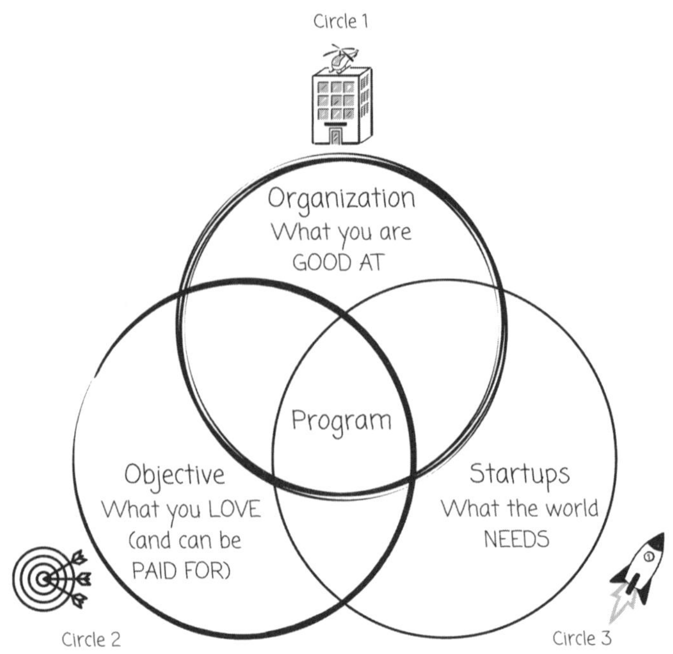

FIGURE 2.4 A startup program's context is described by three factors: the organization, the program's objectives, and the startups.

The Startup Program Strategy Canvas describes the results of problem definition (end of first diamond, Figure 2.2), enabling intentional and context-aware tactical design (second diamond). Circles 1 and 3 derive directly from the considerations of the previous section: they represent the two complex systems that the program should connect. Circle 2 stems from the need to make objectives explicit—starting with why. Goal-driven design is the glue between Circles 1 and 3. The following sections will introduce each Circle, and Chapters 8, 9, and 10, respectively, will review each in detail.

Circle 1: Organization's Uniqueness and Readiness

The best startup programs leverage the unique assets, networks, resources, and knowledge of the sponsoring organization (or partnership of organizations). Especially when competing with investor-driven programs for similar startups (e.g., Silicon Valley–style aspirant unicorns),[6] corporations and public institutions should adopt differentiation strategies based on what they alone can bring to the table. For instance, Wayra gives access to Telefónica's mobile users for product and market tests, and it devolves an internal business development team to help startups close new deals with its business client network. Investor-driven accelerators such as Y Combinator or 500 Startups cannot offer these features.

On the other hand, each organization also has intrinsic limitations regarding what offering it can deliver effectively and efficiently. The complex system of a mature organization requires careful analysis to uncover any bottleneck, strategic or operational, that might not be evident at first sight. As mentioned, corporations and government agencies frequently offer additional features beyond funding that private investors cannot offer. However, such extras don't originate simply from more budget but depend on business units outside of the program team. In the example above, Wayra involves the business unit controlling the relationship with relevant clients before greenlighting a startup needing access to that market. If the colleagues don't have the resources to assist the startup, Wayra doesn't offer it.

Circle 1 is essentially the embodiment of the ancient Greek maxim "know thyself"[7] applied to the organization, for both its strengths and weaknesses. It encompasses the following aspects, each affecting what program is feasible or viable.

- **Potential assets, networks, resources, and knowledge.** The potential unique offer of the organization to startups. Google can potentially contribute technology platforms, whereas Disney can potentially give access to studios. The governments of Chile or Tulsa, Oklahoma, can potentially activate local partners in a way that private players cannot.
- **Delivery readiness.** Some features of the potential offer are ready for delivery and others not. Unavailability might be due to resource overload, too much overhead, procedural problems, policies, internal politics, or other reasons. In the example above, a Telefónica unit might be currently on overload and unable to assist.

- **Cultural readiness.** Appreciating the uncertainty, sense of urgency, and disregard for rules and bureaucracy typical of startups is far from automatic in a culture of order, silos, and performance indicators.
- **Level of internal support.** Because complex politics inevitably entangle large organizations, the level of internal buy-in—from senior leadership down to the operational colleague—also delimits the boundaries of what is doable.
- **Program team.** Many things change if the leader is a startup community veteran or a corporate manager. The program team affects program culture, the ability to hire capable team members, the management of startups and mentors, the program's ability to expand its network, and ultimately its credibility and appeal.
- **Startup community foothold.** The existing partner network and brand recognition inside the startup community can largely affect the trust in the organization and, therefore, the outreach and attractiveness of a program.

Circle 2: Program Objectives

Defining a program's specific objectives in a large organization can be much harder than it sounds. Sometimes the objectives are too vague, such as "let's innovate with startups." Other times, they are self-contradictory or self-restrictive, to the point of making the action almost impossible, such as "let's do a ten-multiplier financial return in two years." They can be aligned or unaligned with the general strategy, and intentionally or unintentionally so. Or the senior leadership team can disagree or be misaligned about them. There are many possible reasons for this variety of situations, including internal politics, level of coordination with the leadership, type and quality of internal innovation governance, ambition and personal agenda of the program's initiator and management team.

An additional complication comes from the size and extent of large organizations, which inevitably allows or forces the creation of silos or backyards. A new startup program's objective often interferes with internal politics to the extent of mobilizing corporate antibodies and generating opposition. For instance, sometimes a startup program is assigned such a broad scope that it inevitably conflicts with the power backyard of another unit. Other times, if the objective is too unambitious or self-siloed, the program ends up being too peripheral to be of any use to either the organization or the startups. In some other cases, a program starts without a clear objective, or it starts in stealth to endure as long as possible out of the spotlight until it has results to show, or it may have just a political purpose to contrast with another internal initiative.

Notwithstanding all these possible difficulties about a program's objective, Circle 2 is here to remind you that a good startup program should always have a goal—at least in the mind of its creators, managers, and internal sponsors—even if it is the wrong goal and will be changed down the road, in future editions. Methodologies such as OKR[8] or V2MOM[9] can be helpful to express that goal, including measures of success. The managerial literature available on those and similar methodologies abounds, so we deliberately do not describe them in this book.

Note that Circle 2 is about the program objectives in the present (or imminent) edition, not to be confused with the general strategy of the program as a multiyear or multi-edition initiative. It's critical to understand this distinction to use our Canvas properly: single-edition objectives and multi-edition objectives can differ, and usually they do. For instance, Start-Up Chile as a multi-year program aimed at reviving the entrepreneurial economy of Chile, but the initial editions had prevalently cultural objectives and the objectives became more financial only after 2016.

It's important to understand that each design exercise for each edition is separate, and Circle 2 should reflect this fact. In effect, the content of Circle 2 may change and evolve from an edition to the next, following a multiyear strategy. So, continuing with the example, if you were designing Start-Up Chile in 2010 you would put "cultural growth in universities and SMEs and more Chilean first-time entrepreneurs" in Circle 2, whereas in 2016 you would put something more along the line of "economic growth in terms of higher value of innovation projects dealt by Chilean companies."

Twelve Reasons Large Organizations Work with Startups

While program objectives can be very diverse, the following are recurrent examples in corporate and government startup programs:

1. **Trend discovery and market intelligence.** Because the startups' business is, in essence, to find and exploit the next big thing, startups are like canaries in coal mines for new technology and emerging markets.
2. **Ideation or validation.** Startups are adept at problem solving and new idea generation by trade. They are trained in explorative methodologies (such as lean startup or design thinking) and validated learning. They are also tinkerers and ideal early adopters of a new technology the organization has produced and wants to be tested.
3. **Mindset shift and organizational culture.** Founders can be role models for internal teams regarding experimentation, collaborative practices, coachability, change orientation, intrapreneurship, and reframing failure as learning.
4. **Talent.** Startup talents can cross over and temporarily help internal teams, or, eventually, some founders might find a new career within the organization if the startup folds. "One of the main goals of corporate accelerators in China is to attract any founder who does anything technical," said Jelte Ansgar Wingender of Innoway, for example.
5. **Press and media coverage.** Surely the wrong reason if it's the only one, the hype generated by a call for startups or a visible prize can be useful—several programs have historically been funded exclusively on a corporate marketing and communication budget.
6. **Reputation and networks.** The organization may seek to strengthen or reposition its brand in the innovation landscape[10] and build a network in the entrepreneurial ecosystem with private investors, other startup programs, or research institutions.
7. **Strategic hedging.** A partnership or even an informal relationship with a startup can provide strategic hedging options,[11] such as access to alternative technology, defensive self-disruption, or a foot in a strategic whitespace.[12] Having

the option is generally enough; the organization will exercise it only if and when the need arises (e.g., convert a minority investment into M&A).

8. **Financial return.** Rare for a large organization with high revenues or budgets, but not unheard of, the financial return can be related to exits from equity investments or, when equity is not involved, to rent of underperforming real estate or program participation fees, for example.
9. **Innovative solution sourcing.** The organization seeks superior technology and solutions for an innovation problem, from the generic (e.g., customer care automation) to the very specific (e.g., predictive models for geomagnetic storms[13]).
10. **Innovation ecosystem building.** Innovation ecosystems[14] consist of a network of allies contributing to innovation for the ecosystem's focal firm. They have been a competitive frontier since Nokia lost its dominance in mobile handsets to Apple and its ecosystem of App Store developers in 2009.
11. **Entrepreneurial ecosystem building.** Entrepreneurial ecosystems[15] are networks collaborating in the creation and growth of startups. Governments, public institutions, universities, or grassroots communities develop entrepreneurial ecosystems in pursuit of economic and social improvement.
12. **Transformational impact.** Some organizations use entrepreneurship to advance a cause, like fighting inequality, hunger, poverty, or climate change. The organization fosters a transformation (such as from unemployed to entrepreneur, or from local company to international scale-up) potentially producing a direct or indirect impact on that cause.

A bank may do a startup program simply for positioning—towards not only the public but also their corporate clients. If startups become suppliers or wealthy customers later on, that's a bonus.

—Andrea Landini, Head of Community at Gellify.

Pre-graduation and Post-graduation Objectives

Not all objectives are made equal. One very important concept that came out of our research for this book is the significant distinction between objectives that organizations can achieve before graduation and those they can achieve only after. As you may recall from Chapter 1, graduation is the moment that marks the end of the activation stage. We borrowed the term from curriculum-intensive programs such as accelerators and extended it to all program types. It turns out that graduation is a pivotal point when it comes to control and accountability of a program's chance of success.

Pre-graduation objectives are those that can be achieved through intelligence gathering and interactions as a principle of value creation. Both intelligence gathering and interactions prevalently occur during the recruitment or activation stages. Objectives 1 to 7 of the previous section provide some examples of pre-graduation objectives. You can perform trend discovery (objective 1), for instance, by looking at startup profiles when they reply to a call for applications or at how a startup performs, what issues it encounters, and so on, during the incubation period (such as in an accelerator) or event duration (such as in a hackathon).

Post-graduation objectives, instead, are dependent on long-term partnerships that typically extend well after the activation stage. For example, financial gains from an accelerator or a venture fund appear only several years after the investment. Therefore the partnership must last that long and is usually formalized through legal and financial (e.g., equity ownership, convertible debt) or governance (e.g., a board member or observer seat) means. Ecosystem building is another example. Ecosystems grow through participation, so startups that break the partnership and leave the ecosystem are lost bets. Items 8 to 12 of the previous section are all examples of post-graduation objectives.

Post-graduation objectives introduce a disparity between organization and startup. Startups always pocket some value just through participation—from mentors, funding, or networking with peers and investors, for instance. Of course, more extended partnerships can potentially produce higher value for the startup, too, but the initial payoff on the startup side usually begins with the program admission. The organization can milk value for pre-graduation objectives around the same time as the startup starts gaining value (Figure 2.5). In contrast, in the case of post-graduation objectives, the organization must wait (Figure 2.6). If the organization has only post-graduation objectives, its gains are delayed compared to the startup.

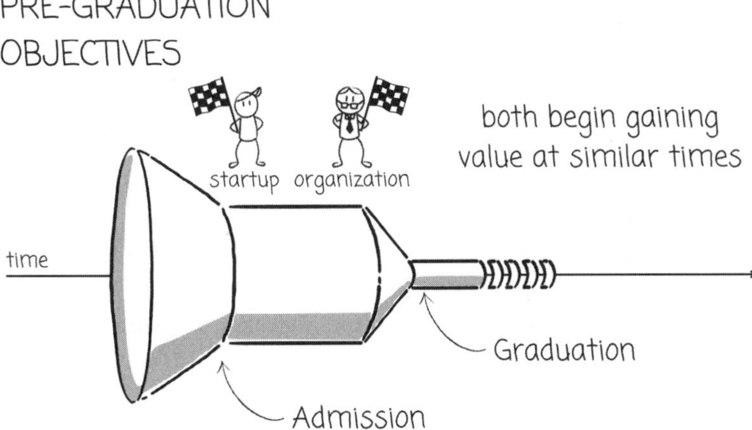

FIGURE 2.5 When the organization has pre-graduation objectives for the program, both parties start gaining during the programming activities.

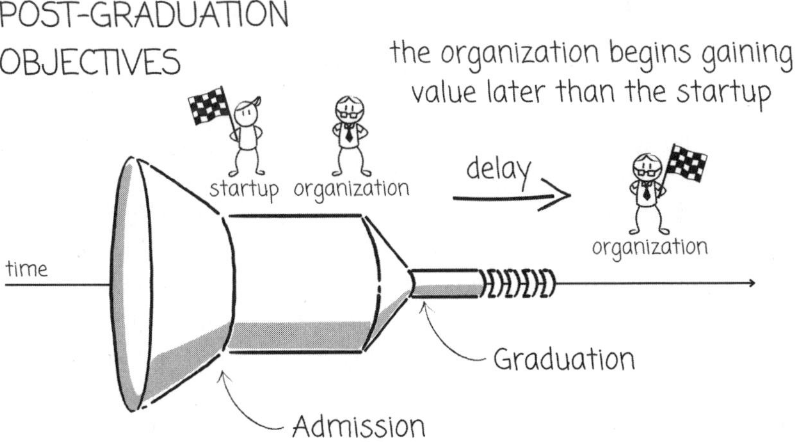

FIGURE 2.6 When the organization only has post-graduation objectives, its gains are delayed compared to the startup.

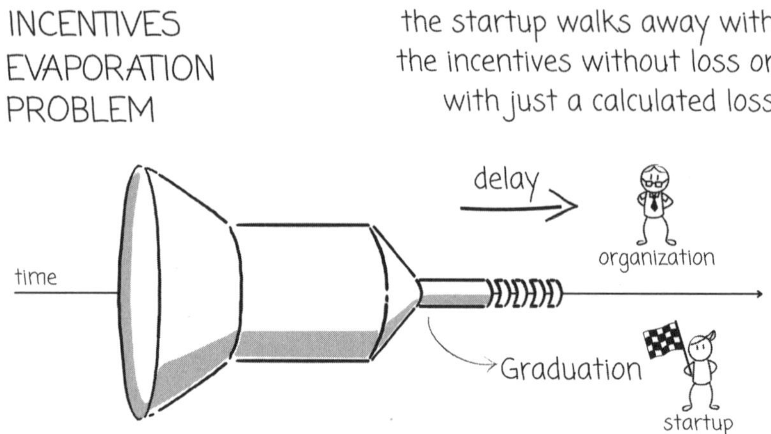

FIGURE 2.7 When the incentives provided by the startup program dry up, startups can break the partnership at little or no cost, walking away and taking the value generated by those incentives with them. If the organization has not yet realized any value, it incurs a complete loss.

The Incentives Evaporation Problem

Whether you are pursuing only pre-graduation objectives or also post-graduation objectives has major consequences on startup program design. The most evident is how far in time you must plan. Pre-graduation objectives require design only until graduation and can be achieved via a fair quid pro quo offering. Post-graduation objectives, instead, impose planning and management of the follow-on, too, and must focus on mutual value creation.

Furthermore, post-graduation objectives often suffer from what we call the "incentives evaporation problem": startups can break the partnership at little or no loss after the incentives brought by the startup program cease to flow to them. For the organization, however, that would account for a total loss if it has not yet pocketed its share of value—that is, if it has only post-graduation objectives, which are not yet achieved (Figure 2.7).

For instance, pre-accelerators investing for financial gain in very early-stage teams of students depend on their continuous commitment. If the students find a job in a corporation after spending the funds provided by the pre-accelerator, the pre-accelerator loses almost everything. The students, on the other

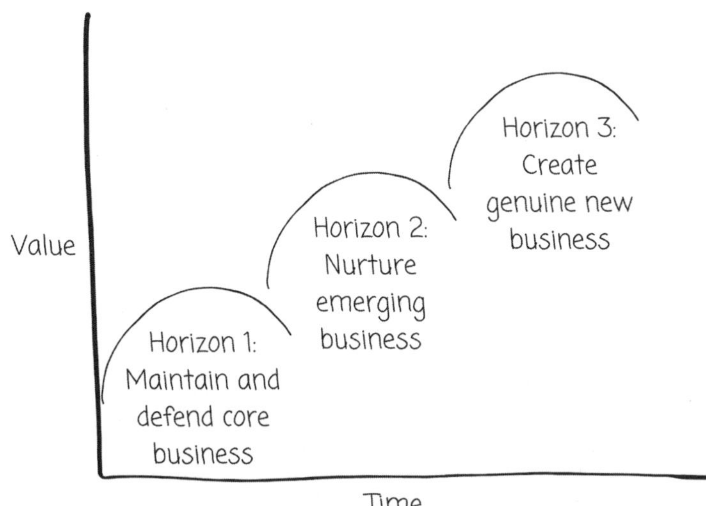

FIGURE 2.8 McKinsey's Three Horizons model.

Source: Adapted from Baghai, M., S. Coley, D. White, 1999, "The Alchemy of Growth—Practical Insights for Building the Enduring Enterprise." 1999 © McKinsey, Orion Business.

hand, have already cashed in—benefiting from valuable experience and gaining a sought-after entry for their curriculum vitae.

Horizons and Proximity to the Core

So far we have used a descriptive terminology for the objectives, without leveraging the vast innovation literature on this topic. In this book, we will mostly stick to descriptions such as the 12 objectives listed in a previous section. Nonetheless, we wish to acknowledge here two widely used frameworks for categorizing innovation objectives. The first is McKinsey's Three Horizons framework[16] (Figure 2.8), where each horizon H1, H2, and H3 indicates the expected onset of the innovation into the organization's core business. McKinsey's horizons can inform the timeline for measuring the outcomes of a startup program, or, vice versa, it can help identify realistic expectations starting from a preset timeframe.

Note how these horizons are independent of the pre- or post-graduation distinction made in the previous sections. Some objectives, such as cultural crossover, are related to pre-graduation activities, but the targeted innovation could be in H2 or even H3.

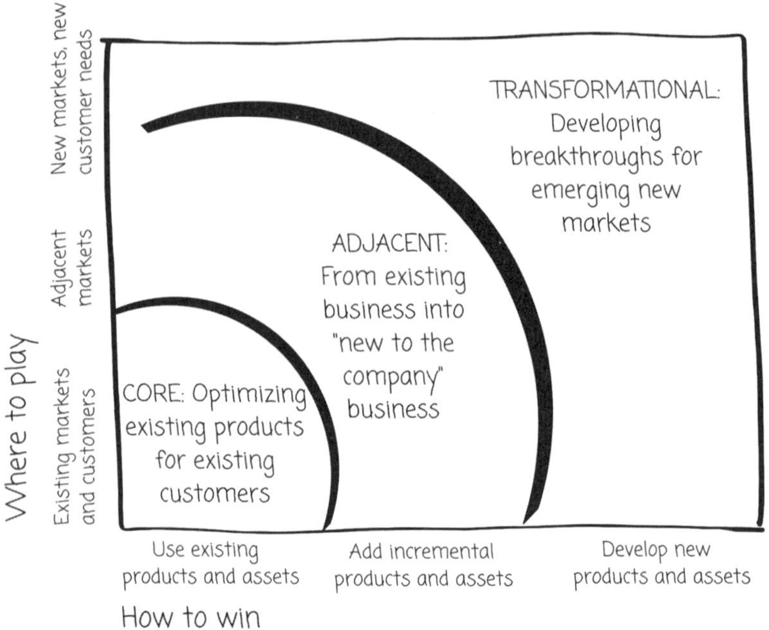

FIGURE 2.9 The Innovation Ambition Matrix.

Source: Adapted from: Nagji, B., and G. Tuff, 2012, "Managing Your Innovation Portfolio," *Harvard Business Review* 90(5), 66–74.

Vice versa, some post-graduation objectives, such as solution sourcing, can target H2 or even H1 and yet require a handover of the startup to a client business unit after the activation stage.

The second framework is the Innovation Ambition Matrix introduced by Nagji and Tuff (Figure 2.9) and building off of Ansoff's matrix.[17] This matrix can inform the governance of a startup program. Startup programs targeting core or adjacent innovations benefit from a close connection with the day-to-day business. Vice versa, transformational innovations are better pursued from a distance, allowing the startups to escape the gravitational pull of the organization's norms and expectations.

Nagji and Tuff also discovered a golden ratio of resource allocation in companies with higher share-price performance: 70 percent to core innovation, 20 percent to adjacent experiments, and 10 percent to transformational endeavors. The golden ratio can be used in at least two ways. First, startup programs might aim at a golden ratio when selecting startups for admission. Second, an organization might organize a golden-ratio portfolio (or system) of programs (see Chapter 16), such as, for example, launching several startup challenges per year with objectives distributed in a golden ratio.

Circle 3: Target Startups

Circle 3 describes the segment within the startup community targeted by the startup program, specifying its availability, quantity, quality, readiness, ambition, geography, industry, technology, business model, stage of maturity, and so on. It is the circle of "what the world needs" in the ikigai representation, describing the "world" in terms of the target segment and what it "needs" in terms of why it would join the program.

Startups Are Not Just Tools

Sometimes we refer to startup programs or startups as tools. And, in a sense, that's accurate. You could think of startups as innovation tools the program makes available to the organization. However, calling startup programs or even startups tools unfairly represents the balance of power. Startups "use" organizations and startup programs just as well as corporations and governments use startups and startup programs. The difference is that the organization (Circle 1) is often the one doing the design. When it's not, the initiator, program team, or a consultant designer is likely setting the vision (Circle 2). Because of this, the startups may be seen as customers when, in fact, they should always be considered partners.

Six Reasons Why Startups Join Startup Programs

Most startups think of joining a program for at least one of the following reasons (in rough order of influence on triggering the decision, in our experience):

1. **Funds.** Startups are generally cash-burning initiatives, so more funds will fuel more experimentation and runway.
2. **Customers.** Customers are not just a synonym of revenues but also testing, feedback, and experience (and recognition, next item).

3. **Recognition.** Associating the startup with the program's or the sponsoring organization's brand can procure the vetting necessary to open more opportunities.
4. **Networks.** A broad category including access to contacts with hard-to-get partners, such as mentors, investors, peers, talents, cofounders, suppliers, distributors, and institutions.
5. **Knowledge.** Entrepreneurial education, market intelligence, or technology training might not be otherwise accessible, so some startups join for that reason alone (e.g., a hackathon on a pre-launch, brand-new device).
6. **Perks.** Office space, labs, free credits, accessible technology, free counseling, a cool location, or other support to lower costs, enhance product and market development, or improve the quality of life.

Deep Motives

> *The most challenging problem is often managing the expectations of people who participate, because they may be in it for the wrong reasons.*
>
> —Paul Sturrock, Cofounder at FastForward London

Crafting an enticing offer that responds to needs is just one part of the equation for attracting the right startup. Aligning with the founders' deep motives about their enterprise and why they want to partner is also fundamental—especially in case of post-graduation objectives. In this book we use a classification of startups' motives based on two dimensions (Figure 2.10):

- **Ambition and drive.** Since our definition of a startup (see Introduction) includes individuals and informal teams, participants might join purely for personal reasons (P), such as their personal growth and career. When they have a business in mind (at present or planned for future incorporation), it might be a rapid-growth (R) startup hurrying toward an exit, in Silicon Valley unicorn style, or a company with the steady and solid advancement of a camel[18] (B). P-type startups can usually contribute just to pre-graduation objectives (except for transformational impact directed to individuals). R-type startups are a

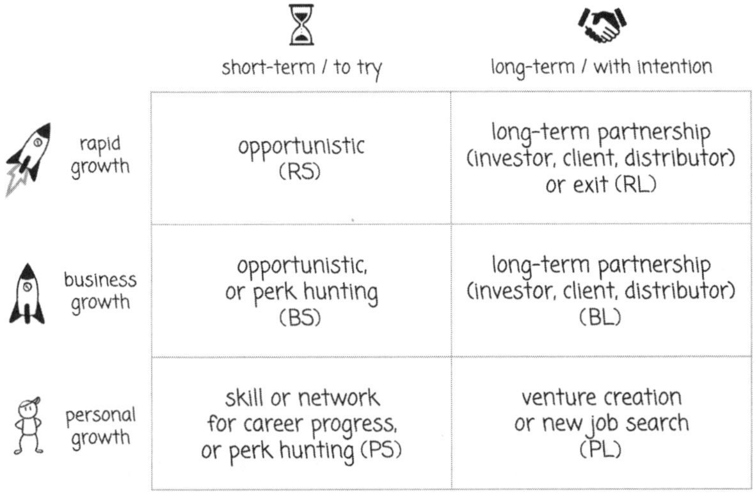

	short-term / to try	long-term / with intention
rapid growth	opportunistic (RS)	long-term partnership (investor, client, distributor) or exit (RL)
business growth	opportunistic, or perk hunting (BS)	long-term partnership (investor, client, distributor) (BL)
personal growth	skill or network for career progress, or perk hunting (PS)	venture creation or new job search (PL)

FIGURE 2.10 Startups' motives for the program depend on their general ambition (P, B, R) and their interest in building (L) or not (S) a long-term partnership with the organization.

requirement for financial investments, while B-type could serve an ample range of the other objectives.

- **Vision for the partnership.** The level of commitment and importance a startup attributes to a collaboration with the organization can be crucial and long-term (L) or secondary and short-term (S). S-type startups are more sensitive to perks and quick rewards, but they don't often contribute to post-graduation objectives. L-type startups are often the most desirable but hard to sort from the others.

In this book we use the acronyms PS, BS, RS, PL, BL, and RL to indicate the six categories resulting from this classification.

The Startup Journey and Maturity Stages

A startup seldom follows a linear journey of growth. The Lean Startup movement[19] celebrates hypothesis-driven exploration, experiments, and iteration as the elective processes to discover a new business model and market a new technology. What may look like progress one day may turn out to be a mistake the next day, or vice versa (Figure 2.11).

FIGURE 2.11 A startup's journey toward growth and success is anything but linear.

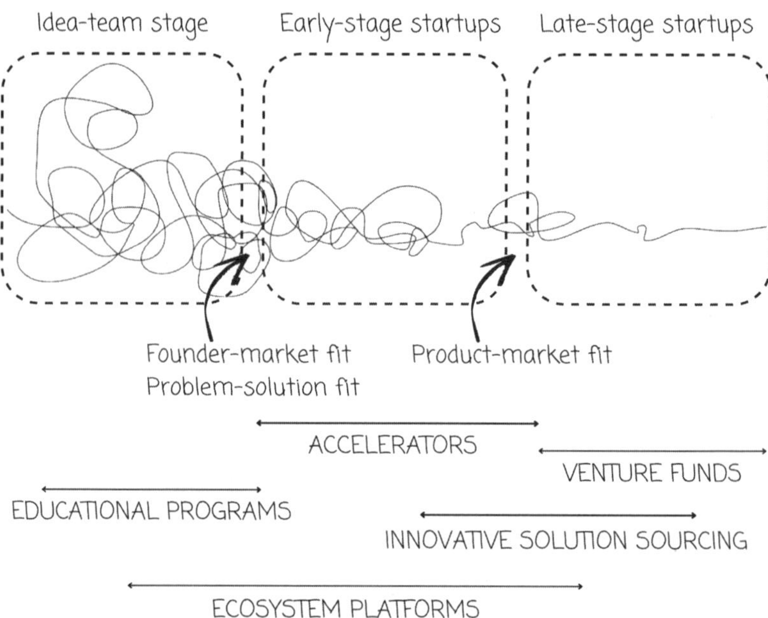

FIGURE 2.12 The conventions adopted in this book: the "idea-team" stage is until the problem-solution and founder-market fits; the "early" stage is until the product-market fit. Startup program templates typically address a given maturity range.

It is conventional to divide the startup journey into maturity stages, although universally accepted definitions do not exist. As a working definition, we distinguish three stages: idea-team stage, early stage, and late stage (Figure 2.12). Needs tend to change with the stage: earlier-stage startups generally still lack a strategy, while later-stage startups prioritize customer acquisition.

In an initial "idea-team stage," founders team up and start pivoting around a business idea. In this stage, a solo founder or incomplete team pursues a rough, undefined idea until they fill in missing cofounders and reach a fit between founders and market (a "founder-market fit")[20] and customer problem and solution (the "problem-solution fit").[21]

The "early stage" proceeds through product and market validation until the startup reaches a product-market fit,[22] while still generating low or zero revenues. VC-backed startups raise their seed or Series A rounds, up to a few million dollars.

The "late stage" is a growth trajectory after the product-market fit when a startup generally generates revenues, although it might not be yet at breakeven. As operations and employees scale up, some companies begin international expansion. They may have raised Series B or C rounds—in the range of tens of millions of dollars.

The Startup Program Is the Wedge

> *When we start with a new program, customer discovery is key. Building based on their ever-changing needs is critical to success. Once a program is built, don't be afraid to pivot. Keep doing the best of what worked and discard what did not work. Iterate as you go.*
>
> —Lisa Cashmore, Vice President at Communitech

Our thesis is that a good startup program is a solution to the context problem set forth by the Startup Program Strategy Canvas, a wedge that fits those three factors together. You can't integrate only two Circles and ignore the third—the puzzle must be complete on all three fronts (Figure 2.13).

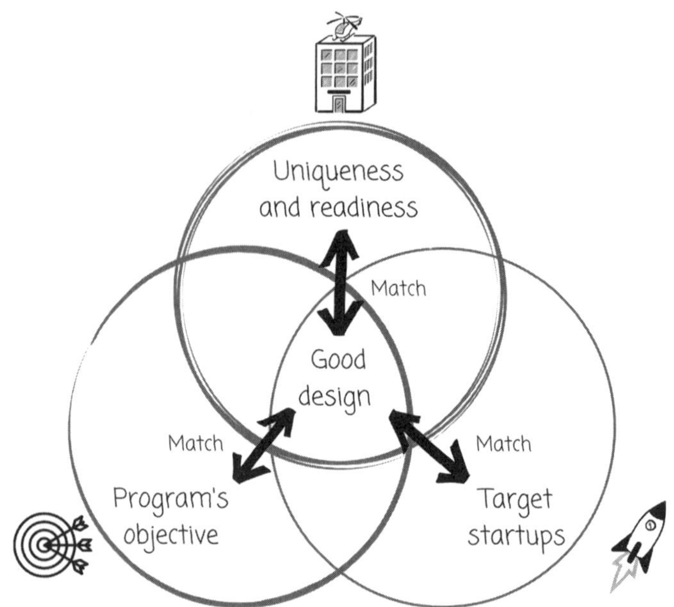

FIGURE 2.13 **A well-designed program matches all the contextual assumptions at once.**

Designing a Startup Program Starting from Templates

Using other programs as templates and tinkering with their features is a common practice. A template is a specific configuration of parameters that was proven to produce results in a given context.

For instance, if you create a new accelerator, you could take inspiration from a leader in the industry such as Y Combinator (YC), Techstars, or AngelPad and copy some features while altering or discarding those that don't apply. You could keep Techstars' curriculum but assign mentors differently, or run a program like AngelPad from within a corporation with corporate managers on the investment committee.

Copying good ideas from other programs and recomposing them is not the problem—everyone, even the most expert designers, copy. However, you must be intentional about the consequences of each feature, and the way to do that is to ground your choices on the context of the Startup Program Strategy Canvas:

- **Spot implicit assumptions.** Be particularly wary of the implicit assumptions coming from the original template (Figure 2.14). For example, equity investments imply that your business model is based on exits. This strategy might not fit a university pre-accelerator targeting teams of fresh graduates (although Velocity at the University of Waterloo, Canada, experimented with equity instead[23]).
- **Stay flexible on the template.** Use the template for inspiration, not as a rigid playbook for success. Don't replicate all features blindly. Try to understand if your context supports each of them. For instance, generally corporate accelerators can't compete with YC or Techstars directly because their brand and reputation are not comparable. Differentiating is a smarter strategy than a copycat.
- **Fit all three Circles.** Remember the ikigai and prioritize your Circles over the template's features. All of the Circles should be considered simultaneously.

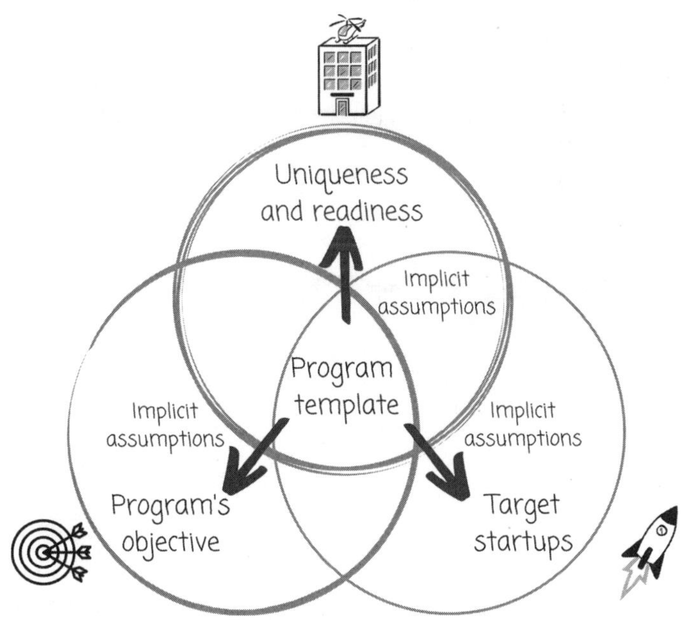

FIGURE 2.14 When you apply a program template, it imposes implicit assumptions to the Circles.

Copycats in Large Organizations Are Dangerous

A startup program model is neither good nor bad in general; its effectiveness and efficiency always depend on the context. Therefore, copying another model will work only if the original context is similar to the new context (Figure 2.15); otherwise, it will either break itself (i.e., it will underdeliver or not deliver at all on the expected objectives), or break the context (i.e., it will cause conflicts in one of the circles, such as attracting the wrong startups from Circle 3 or failing to involve the needed organizational allies from Circle 1).

In truth, copycats aren't always problematic. For instance, some investor-driven or community-driven programs tend to converge to proven models, such as Y Combinator for an investor-driven accelerator or Techstars Startup Weekend for a community-driven hackathon.

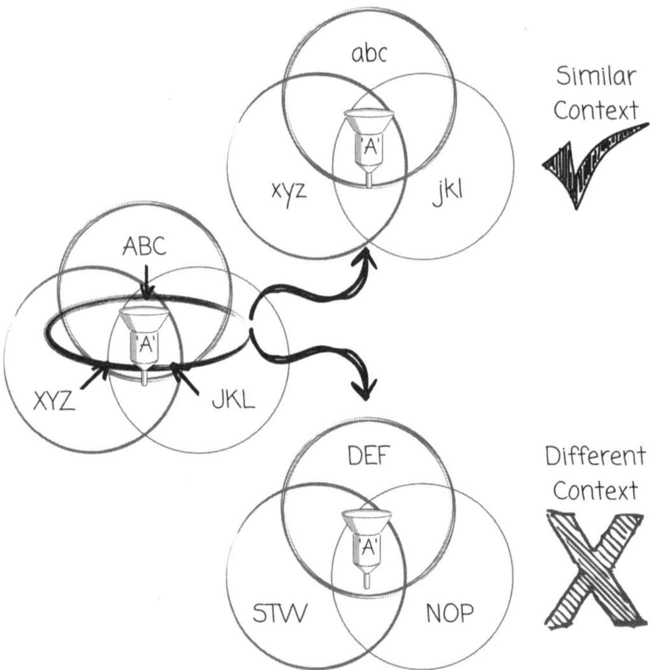

FIGURE 2.15 When you apply a template "A" created in a given context (left) to a similar context (top), it may work. In very different contexts, it will either break itself or break the context (bottom).

However, the complex system of a large organization is highly likely to differ from the systems of other organizations because of its internal processes and readiness (Circle 1) or the industry and external ecosystem it operates in (Circles 1 and 3). Consequently, using another organization's template almost always requires redesign and adaptation.

A Difference in Any Circle Also Alters the Model

Because a well-designed program serves all three Circles simultaneously, a difference in any Circle might require a leap to a completely different model.

Consider, for example, what happened to the venture fund model when the internet economy produced startups in much higher numbers than ever before, shifting the competition for successful startups toward the earlier stages. The classic investor-driven venture fund, such as Sequoia Capital or Kleiner Perkins, is based on the following assumptions (Figure 2.16):

- Circle 1: Professional investors with at least $50 million under administration
- Circle 2: Financial return on investment (ROI)
- Circle 3: Hockey-stick startups with a potential for high growth and exit, typically due to unique intellectual property (IP) or proven traction metrics and momentum

In a venture fund, the selection is rigorous—less than 2 percent of proposals get invested; startups exchange ownership for funds; and support comes with networks but without any educational programming or mentors.

When Circle 2 stays the same, but Circle 3 addresses earlier-stage startups, the model has to shift from venture fund to venture accelerator (Figure 2.17). But this change implies a completely different program, although the strict selection and equity investments stay as a common denominator. For one, the program must now include an educational curriculum because of the business inexperience of first-time technical founders. Second, mentorship must intervene to help founders refine the strategy. Without mentors, pre-seed startups could pivot indefinitely or fall in love with the wrong details of the business idea.

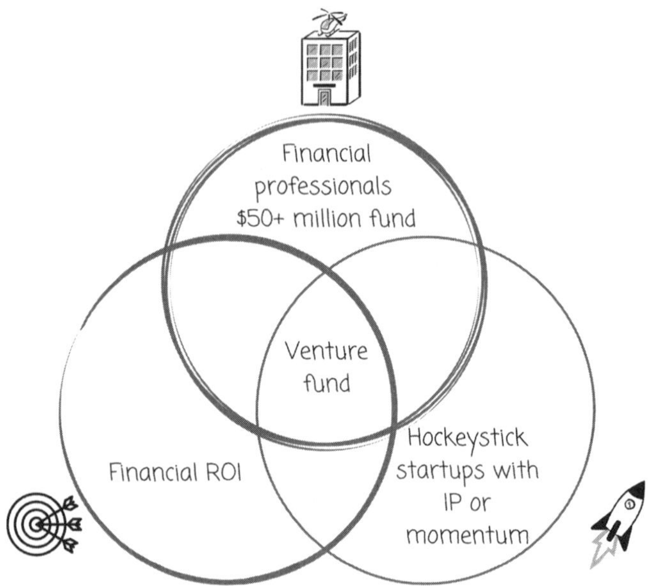

FIGURE 2.16 The Startup Program Strategy Canvas in the case of a venture fund.

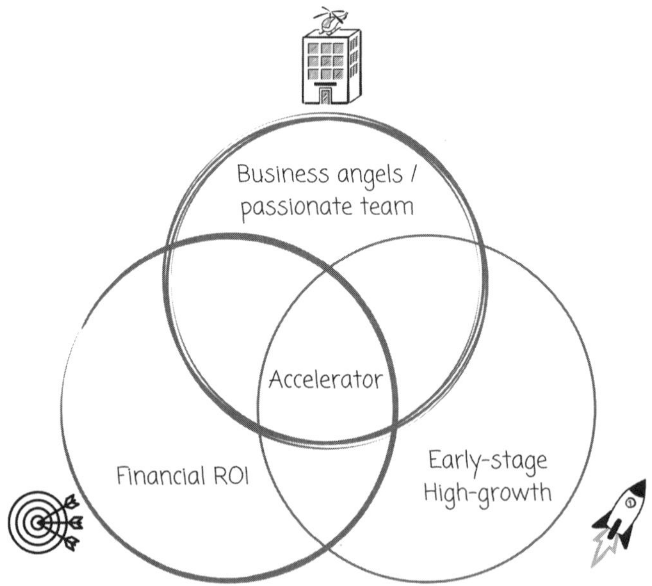

FIGURE 2.17 The Startup Program Strategy Canvas in the case of Y Combinator in its first instantiation.

Finally, Circle 1 has to change—at least in regard to the program team, which should be more similar to the passionate Y Combinator founding team who launched that program in summer 2005. Accelerator managers often pay themselves much less than VCs and are committed to a longer term. Venture funds, with their expensive staff, management fees, carried interests, and closed funds, can't afford the long waits and high risks involved with the pre-seed startup investing model.

Introducing the Next Chapters

Objectives that require a partnership to continue in the follow-on stage are tougher to articulate into effective programs. The startup program must create the conditions for the collaboration to continue after the incentives dry up. A straightforward solution is to keep the incentives for longer, hoping to trigger a deeper motivation to stick together.

Another solution is to use the program's offer, ask, and structure to set the right conditions for a longer-term partnership, a commitment to stick with it beyond the pre-graduation stage. The models reviewed in Chapters 3, 4, 5, and 6 utilize this latter strategy in a way that positions them to be champions of a a type of post-graduation objective (objectives 8–12 from our list in a previous section).

Case Study: Designing TechPeaks

In June 2013, the Italian prime minister welcomed 70 entrepreneurs from all over the world in a theater hall crammed with journalists in Trento, a town in the Alps that's about the size of Boulder, Colorado. TechPeaks – The People Accelerator was opening its first round. The program had received ample funding of $16.7 million dollars. It was embarked on a mission to launch the digital startup ecosystem in partnership with the University of Trento, a top school in Italy, and the international artificial intelligence research center FBK (Bruno Kessler Foundation).

TechPeaks accepted applications from founders without a team or a business idea alongside already incorporated pre-seed startups. It offered a stipend for six months, lodging and board, central office space, world-class mentors flown in from

New York City and Silicon Valley, a non-dilutive grant, and a live cast demo day. Founders were offered access to original artificial intelligence technology from the two research partners, totaling 500 researchers in AI and a vast international network. In exchange, they were asked to relocate to the Italian Alps for six months, train local students and entrepreneurs in the Lean Startup methodology, and possibly create partnerships, bonds, or new startups with the locals.

On paper, this was an ideal setting. Yet the program design was far from trivial and the program team had to iterate before finding a good program-context fit.

Initial Context Analysis

When the program team collected specifications from the local government on the intended objectives, the situation stood as follows (Figure 2.18):

- **Circle 1: Government agency with little experience.** The local government wanted to deploy funds via grants (not equity investments) and through a government agency, not a professional intermediary such as a venture fund. The program team had previously made only one investment.
- **Circle 2: Attraction of capital to the region.** The measure's stated objective was to incentivize private venture capital funds to invest in the area.
- **Circle 3: No requirement.** The profile of target startups was left open, provided they had an operative office in the region. At that time, there were less than a dozen active startups in the region, and all in the pre-seed stage (with no VC funding).

Solution

The solution was modeled like a Frankenstein creature after successful programs like Y Combinator, Start-Up Chile, and Startup Weekend. Given the lack of startups in the local community, TechPeaks set forth to create them. The design started by imagining a six-month-long Startup Weekend in which strangers were put together in a high-pressure environment to develop new teams and ideas, like atoms in a molecular reaction. Because the startups were early stage and digital, the educational curriculum

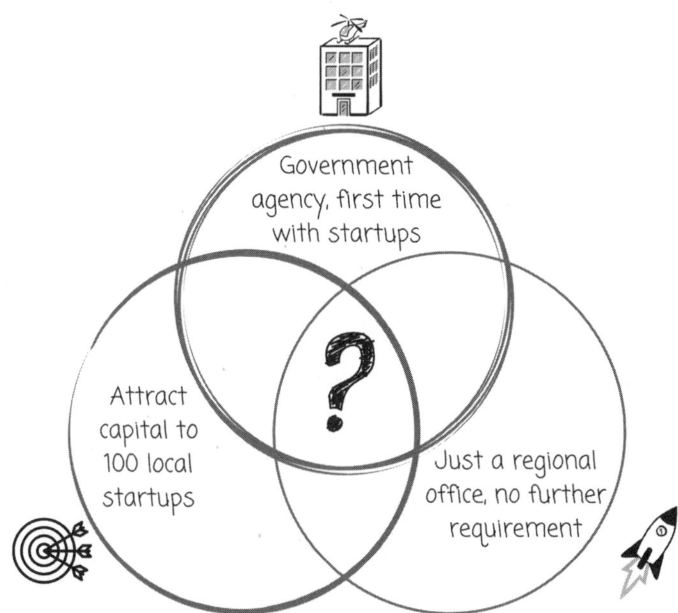

FIGURE 2.18 The context at the beginning of the design task for TechPeaks.

of YC seemed a perfect fit. Finally, from Start-Up Chile, the program team took the duration and the mix of activities, including the cultural "return value" activities intended to elevate the local entrepreneurial ecosystem.

Contextual Mismatch

The result of this fusion exercise was a hybrid without a distinct category. Nowadays, programs such as Entrepreneur First and Antler use a similar model, but back in 2012, the TechPeaks team was in uncharted territory.[24] On paper, the idea seemed to work: top-notch mentors would infuse solo entrepreneurs with Silicon Valley magic; in turn, the newly formed teams would create new startups with the help of local technology. However, the designers didn't consider the clashes with their context:

- **Circle 1:** The organization was not ready for a YC model. The program team was inexperienced, and the internal stakeholders disagreed on a learn-by-doing path. Local mentors numbered less than half a dozen and had no previous mentoring experience, leaving the new startups alone in the task of setting roots into the local business ecosystem.

- **Circle 2:** The program team incorrectly aimed the first edition to build a reputation without the explicit agreement of the internal stakeholders, who instead expected retention of new startups locally. None of the inspirational models was designed for retention—not even Start-Up Chile, which at that time was an educational program for locals.
- **Circle 3:** The targets of YC and Start-Up Chile were international entrepreneurs without any roots or interest locally, and with Silicon Valley dreams. These same people made up most of TechPeaks' applicants, reducing the levers for retention even further.

In its second edition, the program pivoted to explicitly incentivize retention while abandoning some features of the three inspirational models. Opposite to YC and Start-Up Chile, the funds were distributed at the end of the program. And opposite to Startup Weekend, TechPeaks selected individuals with a good mix that could facilitate retention rather than optimal unicorn-style teams.

KEY TAKEAWAYS

- **Systems connectors.** Startup programs are systems connectors, and by connecting systems they create a new, broader system made of the organization and the startup. The design of a successful startup program is based on predicting how it will interact with the other parts—all of them, not one excluded.
- **Context-aware design is a synonym of effectiveness.** Modeling the operating context comes before choosing a template or a feature configuration (the double-diamond design model). The ingredients defining the context of a startup program are the organization (what you are good at), the objectives (what you love / can be paid for), and

the target startups (what the world needs). The Startup Program Strategy Canvas provides a way to visually represent the results of context analysis (the problem space).

- **Good startup program design is a threefold wedge.** Like the Japanese ikigai, the startup program must wedge all three factors at once. Taking inspiration from well-known templates is the norm, but blind copycats are dangerous—especially for large organizations. You should stay flexible on how you implement a template until you are reasonably sure a feature is a good fit for your context.
- **Post-graduation objectives are the hardest.** Pre-graduation goals require only that you offer a fair quid pro quo. Post-graduation objectives need to go one step further and create a solid ground for the post-graduation partnership (connecting with other units, or with fair equity deals that allow follow-on investors in, etc.). The next four chapters will delve into these issues.
- **Mind the incentives evaporation problem.** If the organization only has post-graduation objectives, the startup could break the partnership without loss or with just a calculated loss. The startup still gains from the incentives bestowed by the program, whereas the organization incurs a total loss.

OBJECTIVE: GROWTH

The previous chapters discussed how startup program models depend on the context of objectives, organization and target startups, and how post-graduation objectives require the creation of a long-term partnership between organization and startup that continues after the program. Next, we will analyze four cases in which post-graduation objectives are at play (Chapters 3–6). These are frequent objectives that a large organization—private or public—determines to pursue through startup engagement in any specific edition of a startup program.

This chapter will present startup programs that capitalize on startups that are ready, willing, and able to grow (Figure 3.1).

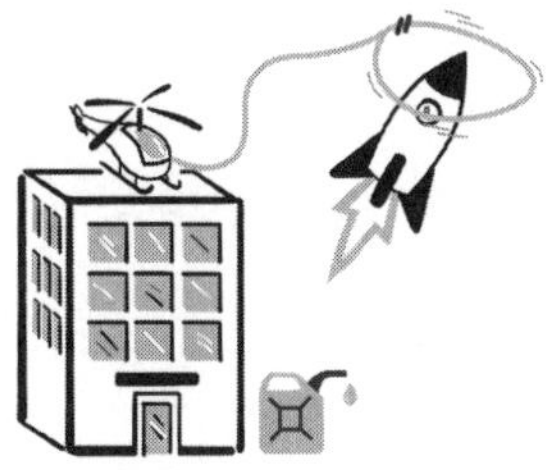

FIGURE 3.1 The startup receives resources to grow and, through a formal partnership, the organization shares in the startup's success.

The assumption is that the startup's *growth* will lead to eventual success for both parties involved, where "success" equals creating value for another company (acquisition) or the stock market (IPO, direct listing, SPAC, etc.). In this chapter, the parties' objectives and acceptable costs are (Figure 3.2):

- **Circle 2.** The organization wants a share of the startup's *growth* and *success* in exchange for resources to foster the startup's growth. The organization's interest stems from financial goals, financial hedging, or strategic hedging.
- **Circle 3.** The startups want resources to propel growth, and they are ready to pay what is needed, to the point that they are willing to trade in control and ownership (equity).

These programs require a mechanism directly connected to growth to transfer the startup's success to the organization. In most cases, this transmission belt is an equity position in the startup.

FIGURE 3.2 In this chapter, the value exchange creates alignment around the startup's growth and success.

Why Use a Program to Invest in Startups?

Asset classes for financial investments abound, so why with startups? And why through a temporary organization (a program) and not just a series of well-aimed, stand-alone investments?

Why Startups

Investing in startups can be both lucrative and impactful. Institutional venture capital firms (VC) drive innovation through exposed bets on new technology and the entrepreneurs who can scale it. Venture funds, financial accelerators, and business angels are hunters of the best ideas and products that revolutionize how we do things. Without risk capital, game-changing companies such as Google or Moderna Inc. might not be impacting our everyday lives as they do.

Corporate investors enter the game for a mix of financial and strategic reasons. Corporations have long invested in startups, and especially now that unlikely teams can disrupt entire industries from a garage. But these partnerships have often been about more than just financial gain. Even though the $240 million Microsoft investment in Facebook in 2007 resulted in a spectacular 50x rate of return, it accounted for a minimal amount of Microsoft's net profit, and the implications vis à vis its competition with Google[1] and the lessons Microsoft learned in the dawn of the advertising boom should not be overlooked.

Governments, for their part, see the strategic role of startups in the economy. High-growth startups account for as many as 50 percent of gross jobs created in the United States and an average of 2.9 million net jobs created annually between 1980 and 2010.[2] Government can stimulate the attention of private venture capital on specific niches of strategic interest.[3]

Why Programs

Beyond impact, individual bets can return financial gains in the range of 10x or even 100x in 10 to 12 years. Venture-backed companies accounted for 43 percent of all US IPOs (initial public offerings) in 2019,[4] showing how VCs and stock markets are tightly connected.

The portfolio's return depends on the industry, geography, and fund vintage. Still, the average US venture capital fund has an IRR[5] (internal rate of return) in the range of 15 to 20 percent in the years after 2010, with the upper quartile scoring 22 to 27 percent IRR.[6]

However, the average dispersion from the median to the top percentile is up to nine times higher than for other asset classes, such as small-cap stocks, which means that selection is fundamental.[7]

Additionally, the industry displays consistent returns from the same firm over different funds, meaning that good investors are consistently overperforming and inefficient investors are, vice versa, often underperforming.[8] Accessing the best deal flow[9] appears to be a discriminating factor for success. Notoriety wins because the best startups seek successful firms' backing, creating a positive loop for a winner-take-all situation.

In such an industry, pseudorandom one-off investments are too risky, and diversifying risk over a startup portfolio is crucial. Opening a venture fund or an accelerator provides the signaling and mobilization needed to access valuable deal flow and the pipeline to enact the required selection.

Rapid Growth as a Precondition to Winning

In startup investments, investors acquire securities when they are undervalued by the market, because no one else sees their potential, or because the investors know they can add value that no one else can. They then sell them for multiple returns (ROI) in an exit, that is, a divestment event.

The most common security is a minority equity position in the company. Equity, acting like a transmission gear put inside the startup growth value engine, transfers return on investment from the startup to the financial investor (Figure 3.3).

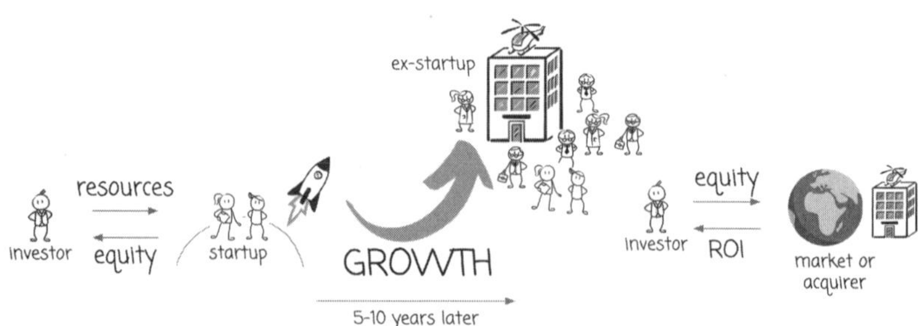

FIGURE 3.3 The startup's growth is a precondition for the investor's capital gain.

Venture capital works because, through the equity position, success is truly shared among the entrepreneur, investors, and other stakeholders. Investors cash in a capital gain only when the company issues an IPO or is acquired. If financial goals drive the investors, supporting the startup and founders is in their interest. Unless other strategic factors enter the room, any organization with pure financial goals (anyone in Circle 1) has a total alignment of intents with the startup's growth.

Venture capital investments are, by definition, illiquid. To be a viable alternative to other asset classes, the time to exit must stay within a reasonable horizon, typically six to eight years for early-stage startups and five to seven years for late-stage.

Consequently, startups are investable if they are scalable and can potentially achieve rapid growth. The entrepreneurs behind them must be long-term players with a vision and ambition to bring their companies to an exit (i.e., they have RL motives according to our classification—Figure 3.4).

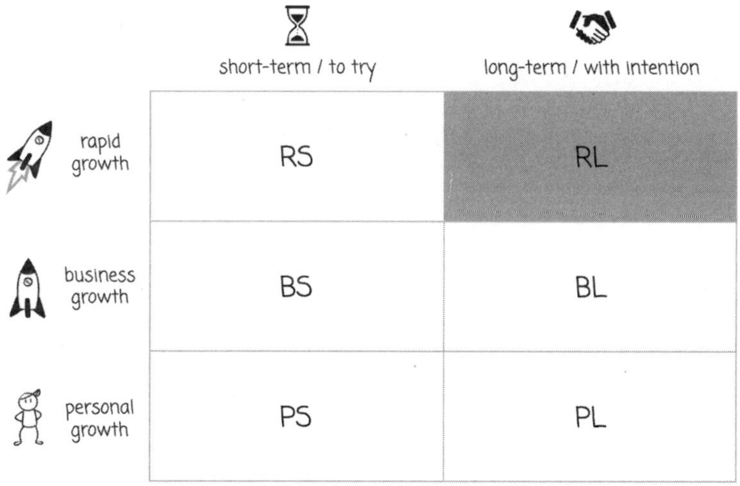

	short-term / to try	long-term / with intention
rapid growth	RS	RL
business growth	BS	BL
personal growth	PS	PL

FIGURE 3.4 Rapidly growing, long-term, committed founders are the only possible target for venture capital investors.

Even though investing in startups is a hazardous and illiquid way of seeking financial gain, it can find its place in a diversified investment portfolio thanks to its strong relationship with the real economy.

Key Functions of Growth-Based Programs

Startup programs aiming to share in the success of rapidly growing companies must implement most of the tasks that Chapter 1 illustrated:

- **External signaling.** The most significant asset that VC funds and CVC&A (corporate venture capital and accelerators) can have is access to the best-performing and most impactful startups. Signaling the investing activity to the startup community can discover new deals and unsolicited applications from startups the organization didn't even know they exist.
- **Mobilization.** The richer the pipeline, the more selective a program can be. Any investor in the venture capital industry, independently of the format used (venture fund, accelerator, or incubator, for instance), sees about 100 proposals for each investment made. Deal selection is, according to venture capitalists themselves, the most impactful factor for success.[10]
- **Partnership.** Given the long wait before capital returns, building a solid and aligned collaboration is critical. Deal negotiation can be case by case for VCs or more standardized for accelerators, but finding a win-win deal is crucial. Professional investors want the company ripe for further investments to fuel even more growth. Thus, terms and conditions should always strike a long-term balance.

Different Program Forms

Many growth-based programs have financial gain as the primary objective (Circle 2) and target rapidly growing, long-termist startups (RL, Circle 3—Figure 3.5). However, the program form changes between closed venture funds, accelerators, evergreen funds, and more. This section will give a tour of the diverse formats, keeping Circle 2 anchored on financial gain and sticking to these models' original inventors: noncorporate private investors.

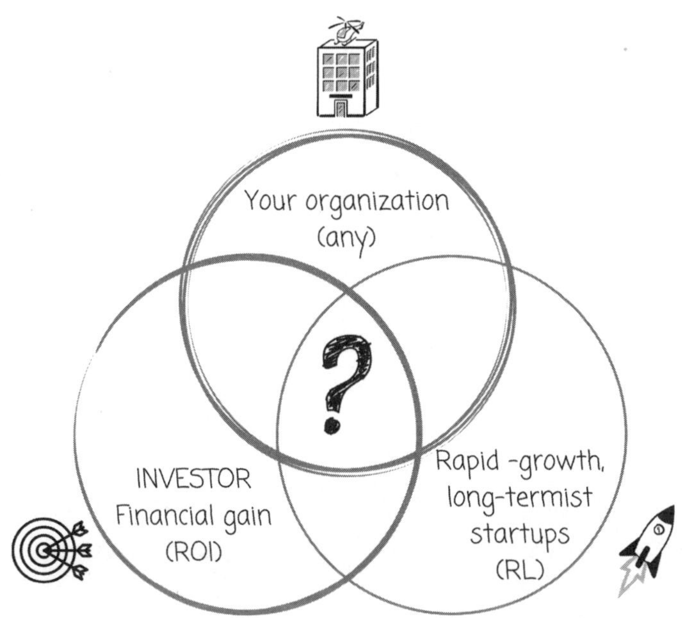

FIGURE 3.5 This chapter's anchors are financial goals (Circle 2) and RL startups (Circle 3).

Startup Maturity

> *We use acceleration as due diligence. We would have invested with our venture fund in one case if we didn't have acceleration as an option, but acceleration revealed it would have been a mistake.*
>
> —Gianluca Dettori, Barcamper Ventures

The different target startups' maturity stages dictate the differences between venture funds and accelerators (Figure 3.6).

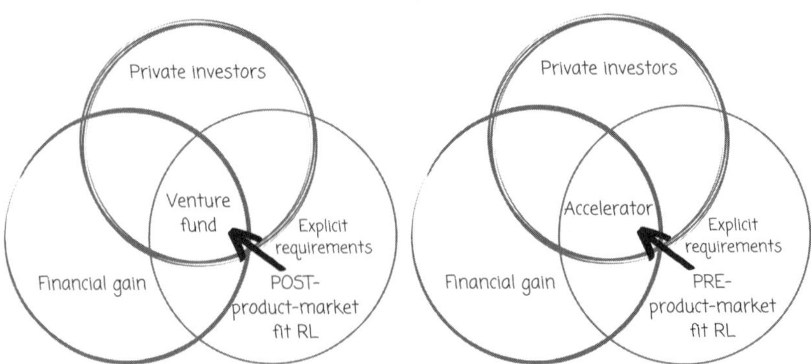

FIGURE 3.6 The differences between a venture fund and accelerator models stem from target startups being post- or pre-product-market fit.

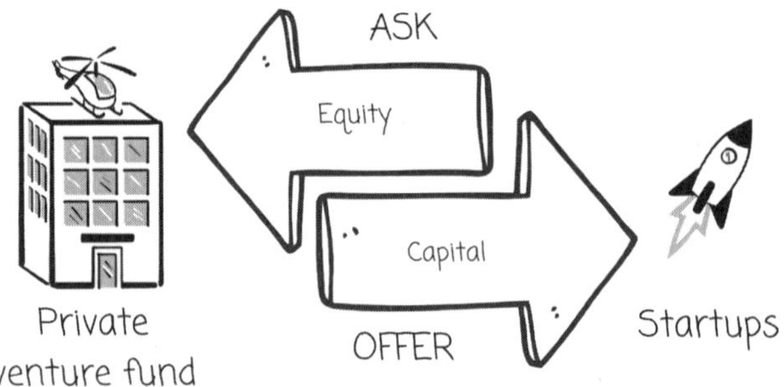

FIGURE 3.7 The value exchange for venture funds is capital for equity.

Circle 3: Post-product-market fit dictates a venture fund. Examples: Sequoia Capital, Kleiner Perkins, Andreessen Horowitz, Accel Partners. Venture capital funds engage with startups with early evidence of a product-market fit and finance the Series A, B, or C investment rounds to scale the experiments to confirm the fit and start growth. Valuations fall in the range of $5 million to $50 million, meaning venture funds may invest $2 million to $20 million on average per startup (including follow-on rounds). Here, equity for funds determines the central exchange of value (Figure 3.7).

Circle 3: Startups not yet at product-market fit dictate an accelerator. Examples: Y Combinator, Techstars, 500 Startups, Startupbootcamp. Accelerators engage with very early-stage startups before product-market fit—sometimes even still searching for the problem-solution fit. Valuations are lower, in the range of $300,000 to $2 million. Everyone knows that the offer in accelerators comprises educational aspects as well as assistance in incorporation, legal, and go-to-market strategy. This difference with venture funds is not random, and it's clearly explained by our Canvas. When Circle 3 switches from post- to pre-product-market fit startups, program managers must inject new features to cope with the different targets. First, the extra support addresses the lack of business experience of startups in this segment, especially those with technical founding teams. Second, the accelerators' full-dedication requirement tackles the higher risk intrinsic with the earlier stage by providing a more extended due diligence before any follow-on investment decision is taken (Figure 3.8).

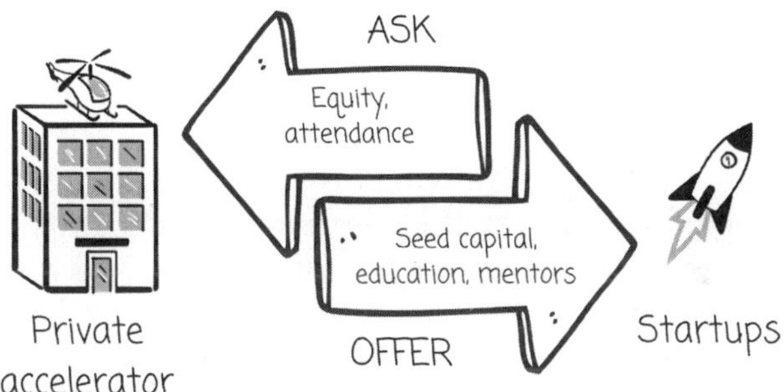

FIGURE 3.8 The value exchange for accelerators adds mentorship and education, which startups must attend, because of the early stage.

Dropping the Rapid-Growth Requirement

If Circle 3 changes into slow-growth startups (BL), the closed-fund model typical of venture capital and several accelerators breaks (Figure 3.9).

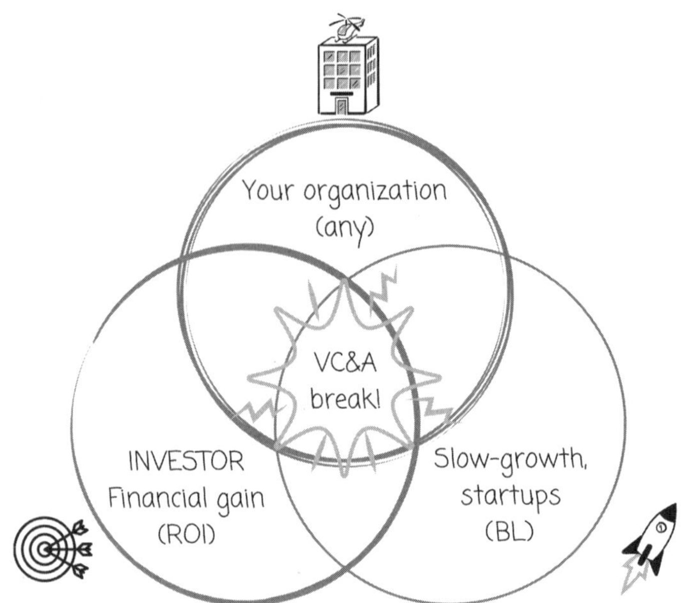

FIGURE 3.9 If input startups are slow growing (BL), Circle 3 breaks the venture fund and accelerator models.

In a closed fund, the investing firm must distribute the capital gain to limited partners within a pre-agreed deadline, typically 10 to 12 years after launch. If startups are BL and not RL, the increased illiquidity due to the slower growth will lower the internal rate of return (IRR). The financial mathematics of the closed-fund model simply stop working. This is why Sequoia Capital or Y Combinator are continuosly on the hunt for companies that will reach over $1 billion dollar valuation, the so-called unicorns.

Peter Thiel, the cofounder of PayPal and first investor in Facebook,[11] publicized the concept that the value of startup investments follows a power-law statistical distribution: the potential for financial returns is all concentrated in the top 3 percent of startups. His advice to venture capital investors is stark: "First, only invest in companies that have the potential to return the value of the entire fund. This is a scary rule because it eliminates the vast majority of possible investments. (Even quite successful companies usually succeed on a more humble scale).

This leads to rule number two: Because rule number one is so restrictive, there can't be any other rules."

To make it work with slow-growing but eventually successful companies in Circle 3, organizations have a couple of options, both involving more relaxed expectations for financial gain in Circle 2:

- **Patient capital.**[12] In this scenario, the financial investors are willing to forgo a competitive IRR in favor of impact, often sustained by a philanthropic spirit, such as impact investing in environmentally and socially responsible enterprises. Patient capital also often forgoes the closed-fund model for evergreen funds, where the profit is reinjected (in part) into the fund itself for future investments. Sting, a Swedish incubator cofunded by the City of Stockholm and KTH (Royal Institute of Technology), takes 2 percent of equity from accelerated startups and reinvests it for the incubator's self-sustainability.
- **Different primary goals.** This scenario breaks the anchor of Circle 2 and switches from prioritizing financial goals to prioritizing other purposes while still keeping financial return to sustain the initiative. For instance, a government fund investing in startups for a country's economic development could also tolerate slow growth. Several programs that go down this path start with a venture fund or accelerator as an inspirational model. Still, they take very different forms, including dropping any transmission belt with the startup's success. Instead of equity, they turn to debt or even non-dilutive grants.

Shared Features

Models capitalizing on startup growth share the following features.

Equity or Another Growth-Related Cog

All of these models must tie the organization to the upside of the startup's success. Equity, convertible debt, venture debt, venture leasing, investment rights, discounts in later rounds, or revenue sharing can all be viable alternatives. Equity brings the benefits of observer rights to gain insights into the technology or market, and sometimes director rights to steer strategy.

Long-Term Horizon and Funds Lock-In

Horizons 2 or 3 are the inevitable time horizons for these programs. ROI appears with considerable delay from the deployment of funds, and rarely before five years. Investors looking for a quick positive return should look elsewhere.

Potentially, CVC&A can be much more patient capital than private investors because corporations (and governments, when applicable) can take a much longer perspective than the 10- or 12-year closed funds typical of the venture capital industry. However, changes in leadership or corporate politics can suddenly impose a less patient strategic course and make CVC&A accountable on similar metrics as its noncorporate colleagues. Consequently, to function correctly, these programs should lock in their financiers' funding (e.g., limited partners, corporate sponsors, or partner business angels) like venture capital funds do.

Metrics of Growth

While ROI is the ultimate lagging indicator because of Circle 2 choice (financial gain), the leading indicators are related to startup growth: valuation, traction, revenues, employment, and funds raised.

Brand and Track Record

As noted in a previous section, financial returns in the venture capital industry are highly skewed in the top tier. Brand power in this market is overwhelming and poses a severe obstacle against new entrants. Building visibility and a track record is a top priority for any kind of growth-based program. Quality deal sourcing depends on that.

Internal Push

CVC&A often present startups to internal business units (in a demo day or with dedicated introductions) in an attempt to find synergies and create mutual value.

This is what we call "internal push." It's a push operation because startups were selected based on ROI or growth-related criteria that are independent of the internal market's needs. In other words, they were not selected for the business units, but they are later proposed to them as elective partners.

When done wrongly, this approach aliments the general thesis of innovation theatre—some business units find themselves involved with startups without really knowing why.

To make this push mode work, you must create a tight and intentional collaboration between the program team and the execution units. For example, Robert Bosch Venture Capital has staff dedicated to creating liaisons and procuring commercial deals between startups and the parent organization.

Another example is In-Q-Tel, a non-profit venture capital firm connected to the CIA (the United States Central Intelligence Agency). In-Q-Tel is independent of the CIA and yet the CIA has an office fully dedicated to coordinating with the venture firm, to foster the alignment of investments with both the startup's growth and the innovation needs of CIA.

When It Breaks: Strategic Investing

As you may recall, this chapter assumed financial goals in Circle 2. Enter now corporate venture capital (CVC) and the corporate accelerator (CA). Depending on the maturity stage of startups it targets, an organization may lean toward one or the other model. Many corporations have both CVC and CA: GV and Google for Startups Accelerator (Alphabet), M12 and Microsoft for Startups (Microsoft), or Novartis Venture Fund and Health Hub Accelerator in partnership with Wayra UK (Novartis).

Corporations and governments have applied the venture fund or accelerator templates created for financial gain to strategic investing. In practice, they adopted the central template as is, in a context in which Circle 1 (not a professional investment firm) and Circle 2 (strategic goals) were different. As Chapter 2 noted (see Figure 2.15), such an adoption transfers implicit assumptions on the context, for instance, the maturity level of target startups (Figure 3.10).

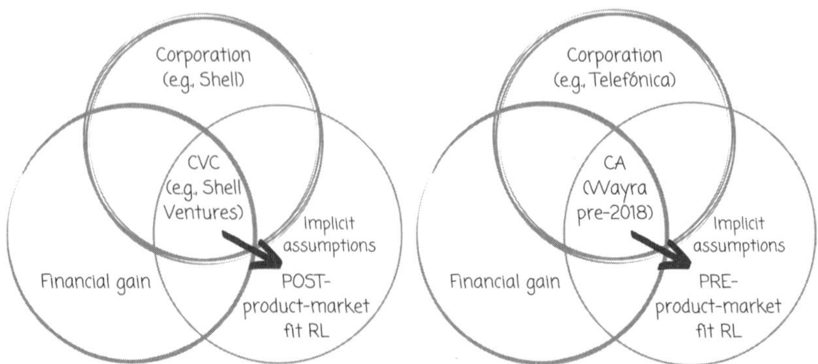

FIGURE 3.10 A private investor's template transfers its implicit assumptions onto the new context where it is applied.

Even when Circle 3 correctly matches the template in use, there could be issues. If our theory of context-program match holds, the equilibrium we observed in the financial case should break because of a different Circle 2, if not also of Circle 1. And that's the case—at least in the most traditional expressions of CVC and CA.[13]

CVC has presented contradictions from the start:[14] the tension between financial and strategic aims, the contradictory evidence over whether startup investing works as a form of "outsourced R&D," and the difficulty in competing for the best deals.[15] And CA experienced similar conflicts, struggling to convince budding startup stars to relinquish 5 to 10 percent of their shares to an industrial incumbent before approaching private investors. Why have these programs historically struggled more than their financial cousins?

Problem #1: Direct Competition Without Artillery Support

First, copying a template drags its contextual assumptions with it. Figure 3.10 shows each template's consequences on Circle 3: the venture fund template implies later-stage startups, while the accelerator template imposes earlier-stage startups. These are the private counterparts' exact target segments, putting corporate programs in direct competition and forcing the corporate versions to search their competitive differentiators in Circle 1.

However, the organization (Circle 1) has norms and culture, assets, processes, and resources all devoted to the core business, not to speeding the growth of alien startups. If that was not enough to create conflict, the startups might disrupt the corporate core business, namely, the very source of differentiation for CVC&A. Not surprisingly, across all industries and types of organizations, CVC&A reportedly has a hard time winning internal support.[16] It is as if CVC&A was infantry going into battle without the execution business's heavy artillery support.

Problem #2: Financial Metrics Stick Around

The template in the Intersection also has consequences on Circle 2 (objectives). CVC teams instructed to pursue strategic gains are compensated and assessed based on financial returns,[17] as implied by the template. In an interview with *Harvard Business Review* in 2016, GE Ventures' David Mayhew declared, "You can't focus only on strategic fit. Anyone in corporate venture capital who says they don't also focus on financial goals won't be around very long"[18] (Figure 3.11).

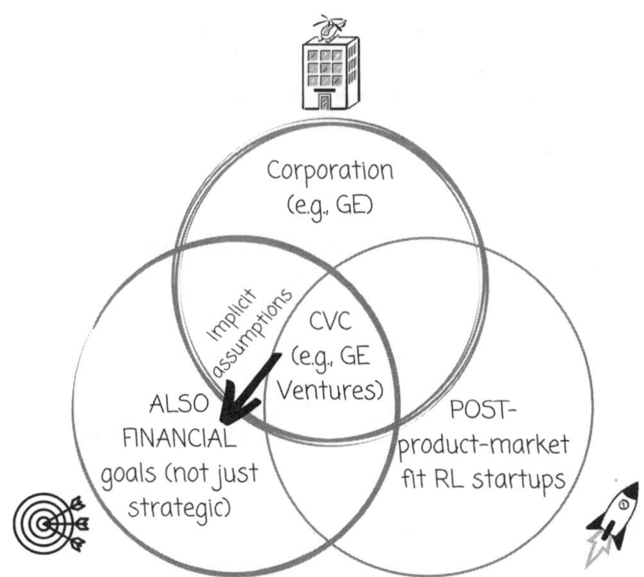

FIGURE 3.11 All contextual Circles are affected when an organization adopts a template. To Circle 2, a template passes assumptions on metrics and benchmarks.

The absence of commonly accepted measures of strategic impact accentuates this problem. While financial investing benefits from the numerical clarity of profit, "strategic investing" has a vague meaning. Instead, it is defined as any form of investment with a different primary goal than pure financial gain.[19] Strategic metrics are highly dependent on the context, making it impossible to build a reference benchmark for comparison and management purposes.[20]

Problem #3: Growth Is No Longer an Engine of Alignment

> *The corporations' capability of absorbing innovation is much smaller than the consumers', and even the best program will take months, not weeks, to make a proof of concept happen. For a corporation, it may not make sense to invest in disruptive innovations that it can't absorb.*
>
> —Michele Giordani, cofounder of Gellify

While we showed how financial gain is tightly dependent on the startup's success and growth, the spectrum of strategic goals does not exhibit this dependence in its entirety. Conversely, many scenarios of a strategic win for the organization do not require that a startup grows, for example:[21]

- **Strategic option creation.** An organization may acquire an equity position to monitor a startup, access its market data, and open a doorway to a future acquisition (lengthy diligence). In this case, what matters is to create the option, not to exercise or sell it. The organization already wins when the deal is closed; any financial gain is just icing on the cake.
- **Exploring strategic whitespace.** Gathering information on new markets and emerging needs not currently addressed by the organization occurs even if the startup does not draw a hockey stick on a chart via exponential growth "up and to the right."
- **Developing a backup technology.** The hedge provided by an alternative startup technology is per se an advantage, even if the new technology never becomes a plan A. The

organization wins if the technology is solid and valuable; it does not matter if it is a commercial success or stays on a lab shelf.

- **Experimenting with new capabilities.** When the invested startup develops interesting new processes unrelated to the current ones, the experimentation can be successful in and of itself, even if the startup does not grow.

This weak or absent tie to growth in CVC&A cancels the rationale for long-term alignment that characterizes its financial cousins. Equity alone, no longer an engine of alignment, does not guarantee the organization's long-term commitment in the startup. It should not surprise, then, that CVC&A has been sometimes accused of being a conflicted investor that does not care about the startup's rapid growth, to the point of being frowned upon by private venture capital and startups alike.[22]

Historical Motives Do Not Hold Anymore

The adoption of CVC&A was historically more connected to opening a channel with the startup community than for financial gains. CVC&A can't move the needle of a large organization's P&L.

CVC&A has been, in truth, a gateway to establish a direct relationship with the growing numbers of digital golden geeks. But copying the VC or accelerator model just to "get close to startups" is like starting a restaurant just to hang out with celebrities. Maybe it will work, but it misses the point, and it's not an efficient use of capital. In the dawn of startup programs, there was only one choice, and those ill-informed just took it off the shelf even when they had no idea how to use it. Now, there are more tools, and this book will help you understand what tools to use with what job.

Repairing the Broken Models

Organizations worldwide repair the problems of corporate venture funds and accelerators illustrated in the previous section in at least four ways, each acting on one of the Circles or the Intersection of our Canvas (Figure 3.12).

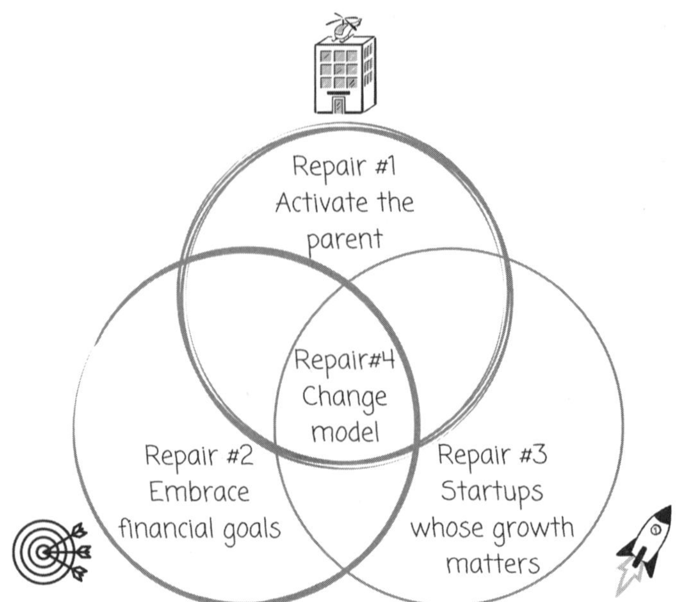

FIGURE 3.12 Organizations repair the broken models with at least four strategies, one per Circle plus the Intersection (the program model itself).

Repair #1. Smarter push mode (Circle 1). CVC&A has often fallen short on its promise to create a bridge with the internal business units. As the open innovation industry matures, more corporate programs have understood the importance of creating a link to the core business and task a part of the program team to market the parent organization's portfolio startups. Shell Ventures, among others, doubled down on this effort when it hired several full-time "implementation managers" dedicated to internal business development.

Repair #2. Embrace financial goals (Circle 2). Adopting a bolder financial investment strategy and putting the entrepreneurs' success over everything else realigns CVC&A with the original mission of the venture fund and accelerator models.

Some rare CVC examples have always emulated institutional VC firms and maximized their financial returns, with Intel Capital, Qualcomm Ventures, and GV on the lead. But since 2010, that trend has grown: CVC arms have spun out of the parent company and rebranded themselves to signal a stronger financial orientation. Names such as Sapphire Ventures (previously SAP Ventures, separated from SAP in 2011) or Mouro Capital (formerly Santander InnoVentures, separated from the Spanish bank and rebranded in 2020) hide their corporate LPs behind a veil.

"Among many CVCs, the strategic goals are slowly giving way to a growing emphasis on financial returns. As part of that shift, more CVCs have learned to approach investing in the same way that a traditional VC firm would," said M12, Microsoft's venture fund's Nagraj Kashyap at the Mind the Bridge Open Innovation Bootcamp in 2020.[23]

Repair #3. Partner with startups whose growth matters (Circle 3). Strategic investing aligns with startup growth in some specific occasions:[24]

- **Promoting a standard.** When startups directly or indirectly promote a technology standard favorable to the organization's growth.
- **Stimulating demand.** When the startups produce complementary products increasing demand for the organization's core business.

The Salesforce Platform Fund, for instance, is a fully committed $100 million fund dedicated to startups building apps and components on the Salesforce Platform.[25] After its relaunch in 2018, Wayra has focused on more mature companies that had a precise fit with Telefónica's strategic projects.[26]

Repair #4. Change the model (Intersection). With the emergence of new startup engagement models, organizations have a new toolbox that complements and sometimes substitutes CVC&A. New modes of open innovation directly address some strategic goals (i.e., a different anchor in Circle 2), such as solving innovation problems or creating innovation and entrepreneurial ecosystems. Because sharing in the startup's success and growth is not essential for those goals, most new models abandon equity investments as the elective intermediary to building a startup collaboration. The following chapters will dig into the details of these alternative models.

KEY TAKEAWAYS

- **Financial goals require a long partnership.** The first group of startup programs leveraging long-term collaborations focuses on aligning the organization with the startup's growth. Equity investments are a tool to secure such alignment while also providing a formal way to monetize the collaboration through an exit. Financial return is the most common objective. Archetypes of this group are venture funds (for later stages) and accelerators (for earlier stages).
- **Alignment with the startup's growth.** Access to a rapid-growing, disruptive deal flow is a precondition to be profitable. Participants must be committed to such rapid growth too; otherwise, there is no fit. Although some programs may drop the rapid-growth requirement while keeping the focus on the startup's success (e.g., patient capital), most programs that drop that requirement also break the alignment.
- **Strategic goals can be achieved without growth.** Corporate venture capital and accelerators (CVC&A) historically have displayed tension between financial and strategic aims. Unlike venture capital firms, CVC&A can achieve strategic wins that do not require that a startup grows, such as strategic option creation, exploring strategic white space, developing a backup technology, and experimenting with new capabilities. Consequently, keeping the alignment long term is much harder: the organization can score a win even when the startup doesn't. The model breaks, and the startup bears the cost of the divorce.
- **Fixes to the misalignment generate other models.** Organizations worldwide have endeavored to repair the problems of CVC&A in at least four ways: (a) activate the parent company to provide more than just capital (Circle 1); (b) embrace financial goals exclusively, so play like a VC (Circle 2); (c) partner with startups whose growth matters to the organization, such as those promoting a standard or stimulating demand for the core business (Circle 3); (d) change model (following chapters).

OBJECTIVE: SOLUTION SOURCING

Chapter 2 introduced a triumvirate of categories that inform the choice and design of a startup program. Chapter 3 discussed models of startup programs in which the organization has similar goals to a financial investor (Circle 2 was "investor"). Change the startup stage (Circle 3 going from "late stage" to "early stage") even when every other detail is the same, and you have a vastly different program—from venture fund to accelerator.

This chapter will continue to show how changes in the Startup Program Strategy Canvas affect the final design of a program. Where in the last chapter you were an investor, this time in Circle 2 you have similar goals to a *client* wishing to acquire, integrate, and capture innovation from external vendors (Figure 4.1). Circle 1, as the reader, does not change: you are still a corporation or a government agency, with its peculiarities. But your role changes, and that's reflected in different goals in Circle 2.

This change in goals in Circle 2 has a very specific effect on Circle 3, the one of target startups. Whereas in the previous chapter you could choose their maturity stage and consequently select an associated model (venture capital or accelerator), we will see how this time your client role will impose a nontrivial search

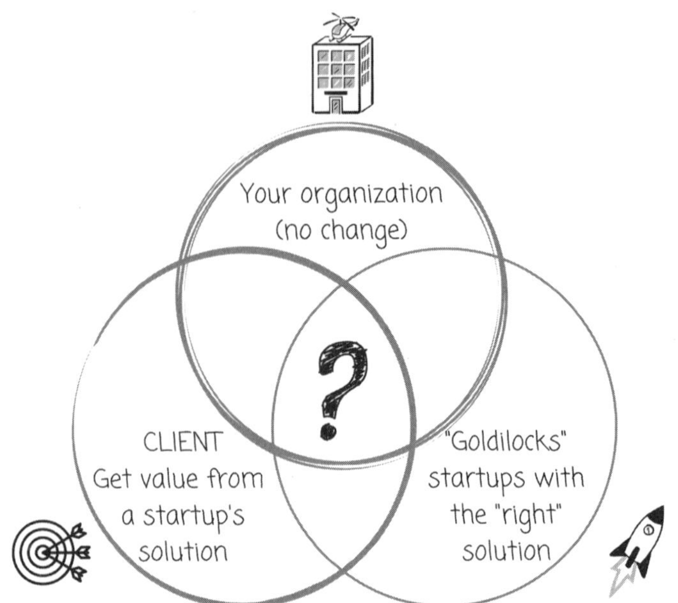

FIGURE 4.1 This chapter's anchors are solution sourcing (Circle 2) and "Goldilocks" startups (Circle 3).

for the "right" stage, not too early and not too late, in a sort of Goldilocks dilemma.[1] Startups should not be too late-stage, or otherwise they will not customize the solution for you. And they should not be too early-stage to customize just anything because they will have no traction and no vision. In other words, nobody wants a discount heart surgeon—not just because the cheapest solution is rarely the best, but because it might not be a solution. Furthermore, there is a scarcity issue in finding solutions for complex innovation problems. Sometimes it is hard to find even one heart surgeon—forget about three or five.

The exchange of value in this chapter is based on (Figure 4.2):

- **Circle 2.** The organization often wants a customized solution to a challenging business problem (for itself or its customers or partners), or the startup's superior technology to improve its offering, its internal processes, or those of its customers.

- **Circle 3.** The startup wants a commercial deal with a valuable launching customer (for validation, learning, or brand building).

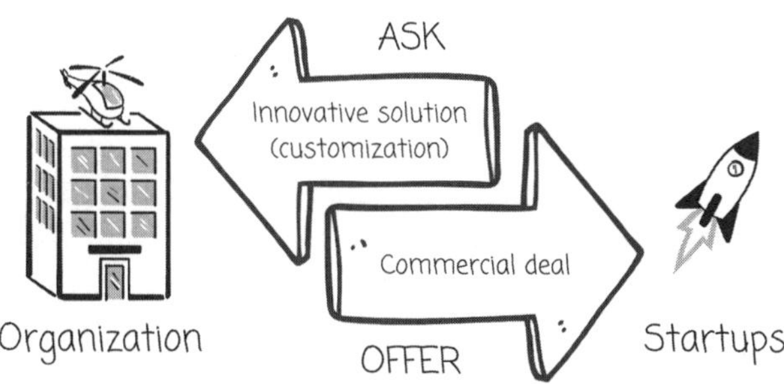

FIGURE 4.2 The value exchange is a customized solution for a commercial partnership (launching customer).

Why Use a Startup Program to Source Innovation?

> *With CVC, the corporation risks millions of dollars to acquire a non-controlling equity stake to get access to a low number of startups. Instead, corporate problem-owners can just buy and immediately use a few units of the product of many top startups that welcome smart new clients.*
>
> —Gregor Gimmy, founder of BMW Startup Garage

Why Startups

All organizations solve business problems with a combination of internal and external resources. That mix is what, in part, defines the business model of any organization. A startup becomes relevant if it has a superior solution than the organization can create internally or source from established partners. This superiority may be in the form of outstanding technical performance, cheaper implementation, quicker deployment, or defensive response to an emergency or an aggressive competitive attack.

In producing superior technology, startups have an unfair ally: venture capital. Corporations must compete with billions of dollars in venture capital funds, dwarfing the capital investments in corporate R&D. "We will remember February 4th, 2017, for the Black Sabbath moment," said Johannes Grabowski of Open Bosch[2] and a fan of the heavy metal band. "Not only was it Black Sabbath's last concert, but it's also when venture capital investments statistically surpassed the total corporate R&D expenditure in transformational innovation in OECD countries. I see this trend taking off across all the industries in which Bosch is active."

Why Programs

Without a dedicated approach, corporations are way less likely to understand what's out there and to manage the deal flow of innovations from startups. Even when they are able to manage the startup database, they are still likely to suffer from the problem of integrating innovative solutions and scaling them. A startup program is needed to manage the entire process from end to end, or at least until the validation of the startup's solution, otherwise, it breaks. Only when an organization duly prepares itself to accept the solution does a startup's solution truly become valuable for the organization. A startup program can:

- Discover known and unknown problems that startups solve best
- Signal readiness to the startup community
- Make startups aware of the real needs of the organization
- Make the organization aware of the need for startups
- Screen many diverse alternatives
- Open a procedural harbor for startups to land safely in the execution business
- Create a sandbox to test before buying, codeveloping, or customizing the solution

All the models in this chapter need to address these issues, as we will see.

Example: quick test deployment. LafargeHolcim, a giant Swiss conglomerate in cement and construction, uses a startup program based on the venture client model to quickly test new solutions before scaling them to the entire organization. In one instance, it helped a regional business unit adopt a chatbot for HR during the Covid-19 pandemic when many employees worked from home.[3] Its venture client unit, called LH Startup MAQER, supported Holcim México partnering with Leena AI, a startup. Within a matter of days, the startup deployed a test chatbot, which the corporation subsequently decided to roll out across three continents.

Example: signaling a need. The German car manufacturer Mercedes-Benz has traditionally counted on retail car dealers for sales and largely abstained from online channels. So when it started experimenting with online sales direct to customers, new challenges suddenly arose. Can you guess, what hour customers buy cars? It turns out it's late at night, when customer support is sleeping—with all the related consequences. After spotting this problem, Mercedes-Benz decided to call for startups to help. It teamed up with The Builders to run a commercialization program for enterprise-ready ecommerce and automated customer care solutions, communicating this specific scenario of late-night buys to the startup community. Startup entrepreneurs cannot imagine this kind of situations alone, so they would never think of approaching a car manufacturer to sell a solution to this problem unless solicited. In this example, the startup program was used to signal an organizational need and elicit proactive proposals.[4]

Integration and Scaling-up as Preconditions to Winning

Any new solution, internal or external, must be integrated and scaled to be truly valuable for the organization. Integration and scale-up are often the preconditions for a return on investment. Integration also creates long-term alignment through the economic value for both sides of the a supplier-customer or supplier-distributor partnership (Figure 4.3).

FIGURE 4.3 The preconditions to capture value are integration and scale-up.

These preconditions have implications on the maturity stage of the input startups:

- **Not too early stage.** Because the organization must test the product adequately, generally for 6 to 24 months from the initial engagement, the product must be the earliest usable prototype, maybe not industrialized and shippable at a large scale yet, but with all the characteristics needed to scale up once the partnership gets solidified.
- **Not too late stage.** If the startup already has a mature sales process and sales organization, it may be inclined to refuse the terms and conditions offered by a program and sell directly. However, there are exceptions to this rule. Sometimes even mature startups find it easier to open a conversation with a large organization through a startup program, rather than just sending salesmen to knock at the corporate door. A Series D startup[5] complained about the absence of a prospective customer organization's startup program. The entrepreneur would have gladly traded the hassle of going through the program instead of the standard procurement procedure.

In short, startups cannot be too early or they would not be helpful, nor too late or they would refuse to partner and customize their solution—but would prefer to sell instead (without or with too little customization). Finding this middle range is a mandatory condition to succeed in startup engagement for solution sourcing. The hard thing is that defining such a middle range is application-specific, and there is no general rule. Only the final user of the innovation, who can leverage firsthand knowledge of the problem, can tell what is "right," in the sense of Goldilocks.

The good news, however, is that unlike the models in Chapter 3, solution sourcing can afford to engage also with short-termist startups (RS, BS). While long-termist startups (RL, BL) may evolve into an acquisition, BS and RS startups can still provide resolutive products for the need at hand (Figure 4.4). It is understood that if the startup grows, the organization will grow as well. However, it's the superior product and the capability to scale it that counts here, not any kind of exit or acquisition.

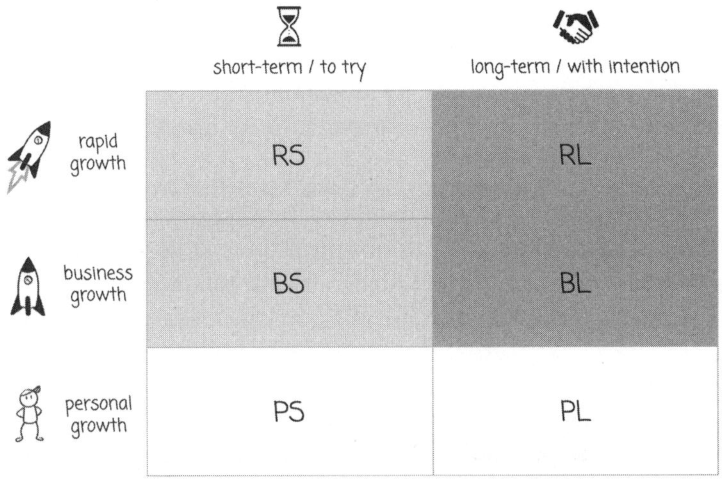

	short-term / to try	long-term / with intention
rapid growth	RS	RL
business growth	BS	BL
personal growth	PS	PL

FIGURE 4.4 While RL and BL startups are the ideal partners for solution sourcing, RS and BS are options too.

Buying from a Startup Is Worth It—but Challenging

Sometimes startups can solve problems no one else can solve, thanks to patents or a head start in frontier technology. Solution sourcing from startups can be very strategic and rewarding for an organization for one of two purposes:

- **Innovate internally.** Solution sourcing may directly impact the internal processes or the offering—for example, digital transformation technology, new material, new manufacturing technology, or new patented component.

Success metrics may include cost efficiency, performance, time to market, security, reliability, or yield.
- **Distribute to customers or partners.** Alternatively, the organization can redistribute the solution to its customers or partners. The goal is to improve their satisfaction, convenience, the spectrum of options, or loyalty to the organization's brand. For example, a Generali Bank in Italy complements its main retail offering with a bitcoin wallet managed by a startup. Success metrics may include customer satisfaction or a new revenue stream (agency fee, revenue sharing, co-sales, upselling).

On the other side, there are obstacles that come with solution sourcing which standard procurement does not experience to the same extent, or at all:

- **Unique, not just rare.** There may be many startups in the world capable of a solution within the specs, but sometimes there is only one. Forget about asking for three or five bids as in traditional procurement. Even finding one source can be tricky, and then you still need to convince that source to collaborate—but maybe that's easier if you can be its ideal client or partner.
- **Unfinished product.** Early-stage startups, especially deep-tech or research-based, might only have a working prototype, not a product—nothing you can test off-the-shelf without a degree of interaction and customization. Here is where the Goldilocks principle comes into play: startups cannot be too advanced and rigid, and yet they cannot be so early that the organization cannot test the product.
- **Uncomparable.** Startups compete more often on differentiation than on performance. It is hard to prefer one startup over another or an off-the-shelf product without testing the solution.
- **We don't speak the same language.** Startups don't know how to sell to large organizations, and large organizations don't know how to talk to startups. This goes beyond moving too slow or being too aggressive—no one knows who to talk to, how to ask for changes, how to run a negotiation, and so on.

- **What about IP (on both sides)?** Furthermore, startups are often very protective of their intellectual property because it is the single factor that will enable the business to scale and exit. At the same time, they might not have access to appropriate legal counseling. Organizations, on the flip side, tend to display a very defensive and conservative legal attitude.
- **The quick and the dead.** Finally, startups—still in a fragile phase of their business growth—suffer particularly from slow or aggressive payment terms.

For all of these reasons, large organizations often have to partner with a startup first before they can buy from it. That's where a startup program can help.

Key Functions of Programs for Solution Sourcing

The tasks of startup program models are to solve the goal-specific problems related to innovation sourcing (Circle 2).

External Signaling

Startups need to know that an organization is willing to collaborate. A program identifies a permanent channel (such as a website) where innovation needs are announced in the form of challenges, briefs, or calls for applications. Having a permanent channel gives out a strong signal and allows interested and qualified startups to engage despite the fact that innovation needs often arise at irregular intervals. This helps keep promotion costs under control.

Internal Signaling

The importance of internal signaling is often underestimated. A startup program catalyzes the attention of internal units, scopes their involvement, sets the rules of engagement, and encourages them to open up to external ideas and think more innovative. It tells the entire organization that it's now on a mission to search for external innovation, integrate it, and scale it.

Internal Pull

As a best practice, a solution sourcing program first creates an inventory of needs from internal units, and later searches for startups that can solve those problems. We call this a "pull" mode because effectively it's the business units that proactively pull innovative solutions from the startups, with the program basically acting as a matching facilitator. If you think about it, it's quite logical: because the objective is to eventually adopt the startup's solution through a partnership or simply as an early customer, the program must first make sure the internal buyer is interested. Therefore, it's critical to tightly collaborate with internal units in all phases, from selection to post-graduation, and not just have them one-off in a jury. Creating the inventory of needs and fostering such heavy involvement of other units requires strong internal advocacy before and during the program. Unlike with CVC&A, having dedicated liaison staff in this case is a must, it's not an option.

In some more mature startup programs, you can start to see a natural blend of objectives, in a way that the two modes of pull and push operate simultaneously. Some mature CVC&A select startups for ROI and growth while also keeping in mind the effect (direct or indirect) the startups' technology can have on revenues or other key business indicators—sometimes including business units in those decisions upfront (pull) while other times relying on the push mechanism we described in Chapter 3. The result is a strategic mix that sees a diversification of equity investments (with ROI in mind) in startups whose growth advances the business or mission of the organization.

Mobilization

These programs do preventive scouting to keep the pond stocked even if the innovation need is still not fully defined. Having an entire pipeline of startups serves at least two purposes:

- **Optionality.** More startups in the pipeline or network can offset the lack of uniformity and comparability of offers, effectively substituting the three bids of standard procurement.
- **Emergency response.** Like in the example of LH Startup MAQER above, finding the proper startup at the right time can be crucial.

Be careful in this instance; many programs use this feature without adding value back to startups. It's fine to have an "insurance policy" or save for a rainy day, but remember to keep the startups in mind.

Cultural Translation

As noted above, the parties speak two very different languages. These programs' educational activities are about cultural translation, process education, how to partner, and processes for selling to or buying from each other.

Lowering Transaction Risk and Cost

A significant function of these programs is to reduce risk in one or more diverse aspects of the transaction:

- **Test and customization.** Testing the product in a real scenario grows confidence in the value of a longer-term partnership and increases the likelihood of closing a commercial deal.
- **Transaction time.** A straightforward interface, a repeatable process, and pre-negotiated or partially pre-negotiated terms can speed up the transaction—both for the benefit of startups and the smooth functioning of internal departments.
- **Friendly payment terms.** Timely and specific payment terms are not just fair, but they attract startups, including those with the best solutions—and particularly the very best, who have the luxury to choose the client.
- **Intellectual property.** A transparent IP policy affects similarly to the previous point.

Integration and Scale-Up

Scaling-up is notoriously the most challenging step in any innovation pipeline,[6] independent of the source of innovation (i.e., it's not specific to startups—it also affects internal innovation). The function of the program in this respect can be:

- **Smoother path to integration.** The more known unknowns and unknown unknowns the program can transform into knowns, the easier it will be to greenlight the partnership and start the integration. Also, the integration itself can be planned more accurately. For instance, gauging the performance advantage brought by the innovation in terms of costs spared or extra revenues can help defend a business case for the integration and scale-up.

- **Take responsibility for scale-up.** The program could take responsibility for the scale-up phase during the follow-on stage (Figure 4.5). When it's too hard for one program to run the whole chain from initial engagement to scale-up, a system of programs could do it (Figure 4.6).

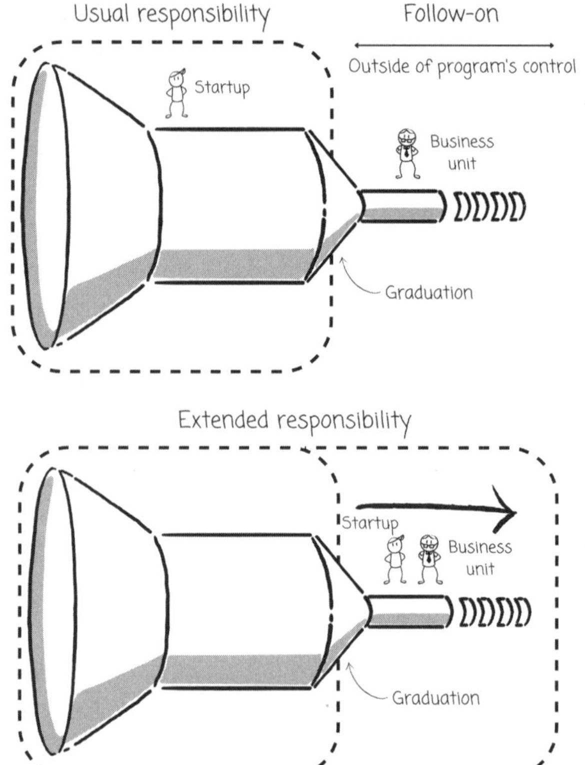

FIGURE 4.5 A first option is that the program extends its responsibility to the post-pilot phase (follow-on stage).

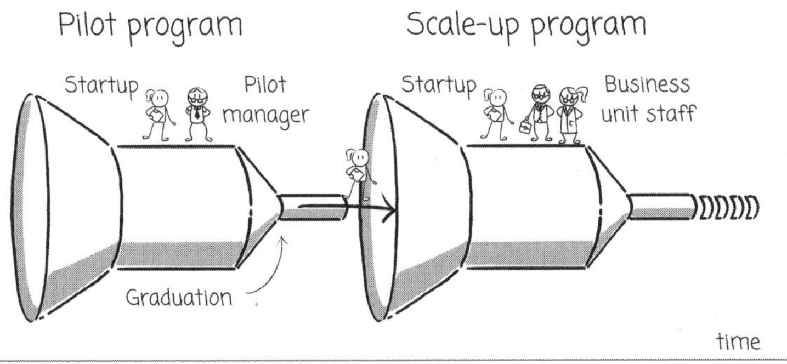

FIGURE 4.6 A second option consists of two programs in a sequence, one for piloting and the second for the scale-up.

From Venture Capital to Venture Client

In this chapter we have reviewed the challenges arising when an organization wishes to be a startup's client (remember Circle 2 in Figure 4.1). As we have seen in Chapter 3, when an organization is an investor it uses startup programs closely related to the private venture capital model. But when an organization plays the role of a client, venture capital becomes inefficient and new models have emerged to tackle the specific challenges of this situation: collaboration platforms, venture clients, commercialization programs, and others. The following case studies illustrate some of their salient features.

Collaboration Platforms—Unilever Foundry

The British multinational company Unilever launched its startup program in 2014 to attract startups that would partner with one of its 400 brands to expand markets and products.[7] Self-defined as a "collaboration platform" and not an accelerator or a challenge, by the end of 2018, the Foundry had channeled more than $20 million to over 200 pilot projects, scaling almost half of them, before entering a period of low activity.

Jeremy Basset, who spearheaded the Foundry creation, said, "We liked the idea of a competition, such as Mondelez's Mobile Future, but saw an opportunity for more than a one-off and PR-led initiative. When it came to corporate accelerators, there also wasn't much going on. We had analyzed the Nike+ FuelBand Accelerator, but that model seemed expensive and lacking the tangible impact that Unilever would need."

Unilever's approach focused on verifying a match with the organization's identified internal innovation needs, following a process of "brief-pitch-pilot-partner":

1. **Brief.** Unilever business units would provide a brief describing an identified internal innovation need; they'd also ring-fence budgets to run a pilot.
2. **Pitch.** The Foundry would publish the brief on its website and do proactive scouting, accepting applications on a rolling basis without a formal call for startups or cohorts. Selected startups would be invited to do a pitch presentation to the Foundry team and the brief owner.
3. **Pilot.** The two sides would agree on pilot implementation and set expectations for what the pilot would deliver.
4. **Partner.** Based on the pilot results, the Unilever brand unit would decide whether to move forward with a longer-term partnership.

The Unilever Foundry addressed:

- External and internal signaling: a continuous flow of challenges on the website.
- Internal pull: proactive requests for startups began to come spontaneously from the business units.

Collaboration Platforms—Multi-partner Programs

MobilityXlab is an open collaboration platform on future mobility solutions founded in 2017 and makes startups accessible to its six industry partners: CETV, Ericsson, Veoneer, Volvo Cars, Volvo Group, and Zenseact. According to Katarina Brud, the program director, "The partners attend the startup pitches and ask questions. If at least two partners express interest in a startup and can dedicate people to a potential project, the startup is invited to a six-month program. Each industry partner then contributes their competence, access to markets, customers, testing environments, and capital as they see fit."

Startup Autobahn is a similar program created by 15 founding partners, including the University of Stuttgart, Germany, and relevant players in the automotive industry, such as Daimler, to develop collaborations between startups and one of the many partners. The program is powered by Plug and Play, a Silicon Valley innovation firm replicating a similar "startup-to-many" model across the globe in other verticals.

These programs address:

- External signaling: more partners mean more options for applicants.
- Mobilization: pooling helps all partners with deal sourcing.

Venture Client—BMW Startup Garage

When setting up BMW Startup Garage in 2014, Gregor Gimmy, the program founder, realized that organizations could not benefit strategically from startups with the standard corporate processes or the standard venture models such as CVC or the accelerator model. "Engineers can't just look at startups in a demo day; they must use the product, test it," Gimmy said. "On the other hand, top startups do not have a consulting services business model to provide BMW engineering services. To be attractive to the best startups and solve BMW problems fast, we understood we had to position ourselves as a 'good' client."

A "good client" in Gimmy's mind is an organization with a fast-decision purchasing process that negotiates without outrageous demands such as up-front exclusivity, investment, or IP-transfer rights. The initial pilot should be purchased and paid with a commercial agreement, not extorted from the startup. The results of that initial pilot would provide data to possibly greenlight more juicy purchases. A good client also has the expertise and takes the time and effort to provide high-quality feedback. "Instead of the transfer of equity, we transfer the product," emphasized Gimmy.

This model was born out of considerations regarding corporate VC and accelerators and how they held a weak value proposition compared to their investor-driven competitors. In an interview in 2016, Gregor Gimmy and BMW Startup Garage cofounder Mathias Mayer shared their reasoning.[8] "Basically we asked, 'What can we offer to the best startups on Earth with the best technology, lots of cash, and the most talent to get them to come to us and not to someone else?' The best thing we could offer is to be their first—hence, venture—client. *No VC or accelerator out there would say they can achieve that value proposition because they are not clients; they are investors*" (emphasis added).

Gimmy coined this new approach, the "venture client" model. As a venture client, the organization becomes the early-adopting client of a startup's solution, even if its product, service, or technology is still in a prototype stage. It replicates a structure similar to the brief-pitch-pilot-partner of the Unilever Foundry. And do not call it procurement. "BMW Startup Garage is not a procurement model, it is a key strategic unit within R&D and Strategy of BMW," remarked Gimmy.

The exchange of value is based on the shared interest of reaching a commercial agreement. From the startup's perspective, any customization requested by BMW is a way of learning and validating the product and market. "If a startup understands how to tweak its product and business model to serve BMW, it goes a long way towards scaling with other potential clients in the same industry," Gimmy noted. BMW engineers, on their side, can access superior R&D funded by external venture capital.

Many other corporations have since followed suit. Bosch Group created Open Bosch within its CVC, LafargeHolcim created the LH Startup MAQER, and BSH Home Appliances made the BSH Startup Kitchen. The venture client approach has been adopted in various industries beyond automotive: telecom, insurance, e-commerce, and construction.

What these programs address:

- External signaling: the name declares the intent outside.
- Internal pull: the final user chooses the startup.
- Lowering risk and cost: selection speed or time-to-MVP (minimum viable purchase) are relevant success metrics.
- Likelihood of integration: pilots are designed to assess the benefits of scale-up.

Commercialization Programs—the Builders

"Many startups don't know how to sell to corporates," said Gabby Czertok, founder of The Builders in Tel Aviv, Israel. He created what he calls "commercialization programs" in

2014, which serve partners such as Coca-Cola, Warner Media, Mercedes, and Walmart. "When a startup CEO, who is also the head of everything from Business Development, Sales, and Marketing," Czertok noted with a smile, "meets with the Senior Director of Innovation and Product Ownership, in most cases, he has no clue of what this person's needs and goals are."

Czertok noticed a pattern similar to what gave birth to the Unilever and BMW programs: startups are often willing to accomodate the specific needs of large organizations as a means to refine their product and business model. "A corporate executive came to me and said they liked the startup, but they were going to say, 'no.' The reason was that the startup's business model was based on subscription, and they could only pay all-in-one to go in the yearly budget. 'What if they change the business model for you?' I asked. He seemed surprised, 'Really, would they do that for us?' 'Of course, you are their fifth or sixth client!' It worked." Another time, the startup's payment model was the obstacle, requiring different departments' budgets. They changed it so that only one department paid, and again it worked.

For mature startups (post A round), the Builders are giving help in presenting their specific technology to a particular corporation. The startups are introduced to key decision makers in the organization. On the other side, corporate managers learn how to deal with startups. The program educates each side and thus helps to build a "bridge" between them.

This program addresses:

- Cultural translation: training is included specifically for that purpose.
- Scaling and integration: the program has been evolving a strategy for post-pilot scaling-up of the solutions.

Challenges

In challenges, startups reply to a problem statement issued by the organization and suggest solutions. Unlike startup competitions, challenges are not always competitive: sometimes the organization might decide to follow up with more than one or even all the proposals.

Enel Challenges. In 2017 the multinational electric and energy utility company Enel implemented the crowdsourcing platform Open Innovability[9] (*innovability* is a fusion of two keywords: *innovation* and *sustainability*). Enel publishes challenges on widely defined specific problems on the platform, such as space applications for circular economy or innovative energy storage systems—some have a deadline, while others are open-ended.

Like with the Unilever Foundry, applications are considered on a rolling basis. Enel's corporate innovation unit supports the selected startups in creating pilots with the corporation. The challenges are inside a broader strategy that involves physical outposts called "hubs" immersed in global technology and startup ecosystems in the United States, Israel, Spain, Italy, Russia, Brazil, and Chile.

Comcast LIFToff Challenges. Alongside its accelerator and other startup engagement activities within its LIFT Labs, Comcast launches challenges for enterprise-ready startups to solve specific business innovation problems and awards a paid proof-of-concept pilot and hopefully a commercial agreement. Its targets are venture-backed startups already serving or piloting with Global 2000 companies, with a production-ready product and the ability to support an enterprise customer, ideally at scale. Topics include accessibility and inclusion and smart and sustainable environments.

These kinds of innovation sourcing challenges address:

- External signaling: like crowdsourcing and open innovation platforms.
- Mobilization: can fill a database of future options if proposals are enticing but not of immediate use.

Shared Features of Solution Sourcing Models

The previous examples showed how varied these models could be: from stable and internal units such as venture clients to external and independent initiatives such as commercialization programs and low-cost, light-touch programs such as challenges. Beyond the differences, there are several recurrent design parameters.

Equity-Free Agreements

Program managers report that requiring equity from startups can deter potential program participants' flow and quality. According to Gimmy, "An equity transaction is just an intermediary to a product transaction." A shareholder of a company does not automatically receive its products. Equity investments are capital intensive and illiquid, limiting a program's ability to scale the number of startups in a program. Coincidentally, they also raise the stakes for program managers by limiting opportunities and increasing the risk of failing the expectations.

Equity investments can be significant obstacles for corporates and startups (within the context of solution sourcing):

- **Limited pipeline.** A fixed corporate fund budget limits the number of deals, while the startup can accept only a certain number of strategic investors. Furthermore, the best startups' equity is often oversubscribed, so that a corporate often drives up costs having to face its industry competitors to seal an agreement.
- **Blocking other customers.** The startup may see other prospective customers reject its offer because one of their competitors is on the cap table (B2B startup). When industry competitors invest in the same startup, the fear that critical information could leak through the startup to competitors is always present.
- **Legal procurement issues.** There are legal issues connected to procurement from a startup where the organization is a shareholder or in public sector organizations due to possible conflict of interest and unfair competition.

With a commercial agreement, however, many of these problems disappear because startups can serve multiple competitors or an entire industry. "There is no limit," says Gimmy, "to having clients; everyone wants one more client."

Problem Sourcing and Curation Process

A unique operational feature of these programs is the internal preparation work necessary to discover and scope the innovation needs (i.e., the "brief"). Internal advocacy is often more time-consuming and intensive than the external promotion of the challenges.

While many program managers report strong internal inertia, early wins can start a domino effect once the program has established its internal brand with the other business units. "At the beginning, we were pushing startups to the lines of business, but now at our tenth cohort in North America, it's the lines of business that come and ask for startups," said Vanessa Liu of SAP.iO. This dual role—push and pull—requires that the program team is adept in both problem discovery and startup discovery.

Pilot, Proof-of-Concept (POC), Prototype

In solution sourcing, testing and customization of the startup's product are a must. Consequently, a pilot, proof of concept, or demo is an almost universal feature of these programs. Through it, the organization and the startup acquire information about the future integration, including projected benefits, foreseeable roadblocks, and a realistic timeline to obtain a financial or strategic return. In this way, everyone can more accurately plan the follow-up and increase the likelihood of long-term success of the collaboration.

Horizon 1 Supported

Solution sourcing programs typically tackle Horizon 1 goals (one to three years). The type of innovation is irrelevant—it can be incremental or radical, transformational or disruptive. What matters is a measurable return in the short term.

Target startups are typically post-validation and have enough operative capabilities to service an enterprise company—as a customer or as a distribution partner. Gimmy explained in our interview: "Our criteria are that a startup is selling products, it has intellectual property, and is pursuing high growth, which most of the time goes together with venture capital."

Although not a requirement, a venture-backed startup better fits these models. Gimmy continued, "From a corporate point of view, venture capital is like an innovation manager that has access to a lot of money. We leverage the VCs' capital, due diligence, and sorting while benefiting from their startups having us as clients. It's a win-win for everybody." In this respect, venture capital is seen as an external source of R&D funding.

Metrics of Efficiency and Margins

These programs tend to provide output metrics that are comparable with those of other execution business units. Program performance metrics that matter in this context include the speed of admission, speed to pilot, or engagement of other internal divisions. Additionally, the program should estimate post-pilot business case metrics: revenues, product or process performance improvement, or cost savings after scaling up the innovation, for instance.

Matching Schemes

Innovation sourcing programs may differ in the beneficiary of the innovation. While the interface toward the startup community is similar and consists of a call for proposals, whether the beneficiaries are one organization, many organizations, or the organizational sponsor's clients affects the matchmaking process and the program content.

Matching to one organizational sponsor. Often, a program is dedicated to the innovation of the sponsor alone. BMW Startup Garage sources startups to BMW's internal use, and so do the other venture client units, such as those inside LafargeHolcim or Bosch. Similarly, the Unilever Foundry was dedicated to Unilever brands only.

Matching to many organizational sponsors. The Builders, as noted, introduces startups to four companies, not just to Coca-Cola. Other programs follow a similar pattern, especially those formed by a partnership of sponsors who share the program's costs and do not mind sharing access to the same deal flow.

Matching to clients. A third model, popular with financial institutions and consulting companies, connects a startup with the organization's clients. These programs don't procure startups for internal use but benefit the organization's customer networks (numbering in the thousands in some cases). Mastercard Start Path, for example, a program initiated in 2014, connects later-stage startups with corporate partners seeking innovative solutions.

When It Breaks: The Pilot Trap

The success of these programs stems from the final adoption of the startup's solution. Therefore, all value is wasted after the initial pilot if an organization lacks the structure to capitalize on it.

We call this the "pilot trap": satisficing with the pilot instead of the integration and scale-up. "We have more pilots than Delta Airlines," noted Barry Simpson, SVP and chief platform services of Coca-Cola, to Czertok when they were reviewing and improving the program's post-pilot integration phase. Unfortunately, solution sourcing programs can generate more pilot projects than the organization's ability to scale them, sometimes due to a lack of capability or capacity, but often due to a lack of support from business units. "It's important to gain stakeholders' support in an early stage while defining the growth stage," pointed out Czertok.

In other words, the program managers become experts at implementing successful pilots but not at harvesting their outputs, that is, scaling them in the organization's business units. More mature programs have spotted this bottleneck and are taking action upstream. "Now we don't pay for any pilot unless there is an idea of what comes next," said Miguel Arias,[10] former entrepreneur and now global entrepreneurship director at Telefónica. "There must be full commitment from the brief owner [i.e., the business unit requesting the pilot] to scale."

The integration and scale-up phase deeply touches the execution business's internal cogs, and it is harder to manage in a scalable and repeatable way. Rather than a program, it demands a case-by-case approach. Like other models, you can push innovation sourcing models until they break. That's when someone evolves the model—not accidentally, but on purpose to address that specific problem. The Builders did, said Czertok, and Part Two of this book will help.

According to Brud, solutions to maintaining successful pilot programs' momentum include "partnership agreements, licensing deals, or commercial contracts." Measuring the value of a startup procurement program by the number of pilot programs is a vanity metric, not a measure of success, according to Czertok. "Now we don't just monitor the cost of pilots; we count the number of license agreements and the value of each agreement for the organization (anywhere from $20,000 to a million)."

KEY TAKEAWAYS

- **Commercial partnerships require superior technology.** In this second group of models, startups become relevant for an organization if a startup has a better solution than the organization can create internally or acquire from established partners. The value exchange materializes through a commercial deal whereby the organization becomes a customer or distribution partner for the startup, providing a use case, cash flow, and valuable early feedback. Archetypes of this group are challenges, venture clients, and commercialization programs.
- **Alignment through integration and scale-up.** The preconditions to success is that the organization (or its customers) can integrate and scale the startup's technology. The program's main task is to lower the transaction costs from both sides, organization and startup. Consequently, the problem owner (typically a business unit) is a key partner and should be tightly involved—from defining the problem brief to the selection, pilot deployment, and the post-program handover of the collaboration.
- **Pilots and improvement metrics.** Opposite to traditional startup engagement (CVC&A), equity agreements hinder solution sourcing and scare off the primary target—the most advanced or superior startups. A pilot or demo is a recurrent feature. Key metrics should be efficiency, performance, and potential margins provided by the startup's technology once deployed at scale.
- **A Goldilocks maturity stage.** There is a Goldilocks principle at play here. Startups cannot be so mature as to be inflexible and refuse to customize their product for the organization. But they cannot be too early, either, to a point where they don't have capacity to collaborate efficiently, and eventually scale the solution.
- **Mind the pilot trap.** The organization bears the cost of a divorce here: if nothing happens after the pilot, the startup has still received its payment. Additionally, these programs can incur what we call the "pilot trap": program managers often become experts at implementing successful pilots but not at harvesting their outputs. The number of pilots should not be viewed as a metric of success.

OBJECTIVE: ECOSYSTEM BUILDING

This chapter continues the exploration of how different contexts engender changes in the startup program model. Once again, we will show how every time an element of the context changes, all parts of a startup program must be adapted with intent.

More specifically, in this chapter, your organization becomes the *orchestrator* of an ecosystem, striving to pull in valuable startups and grow the value of the ecosystem for everyone (Figure 5.1). The ecosystem can be focused around the innovation produced or distributed by your organization (*innovation ecosystem*) or around the startup community of a region, city, or nation (*entrepreneurial ecosystem*). The startup programs used to build either of these ecosystems share many commonalities and will be discussed together in this chapter.

A key characteristic of startups in Circle 3 in this chapter will be their aptitude to proactively engage with and add value to other ecosystem partners. While the specifics vary from one ecosystem to another, the more involved the startups are inside the ecosystem and the longer they stay, the more benefit (value) they can add to other participants—including the orchestrator. Consequently, this chapter's programs achieve their return on

FIGURE 5.1 The anchor is the ecosystem and its platform (Circle 2), of which the organization is an orchestrator.

investment by increasing the retention of startups in the ecosystem while instigating an active engagement.

Nowadays, most startup programs of this family focus on the initial stage of the process, facilitating the *ecosystem's adoption*. While adoption is a time-bound and achievable goal, the lack of control in the retention phase can jeopardize these programs' success, at least in their sponsors' eyes—this can also happen with solution sourcing programs and integration. Nonetheless, the most common exchange of value pursued by the programs in this chapter is the following (Figure 5.2):

- **Circle 2.** The organization demands adopting an *ecosystem platform*—usually a technology platform for innovation ecosystems or a business platform for entrepreneurial ecosystems. The organization concedes marketing incentives such as discounts, subsidies, or fast tracks to incentivize adoption.

- **Circle 3.** The startup receives a business advantage from marketing incentives and, hopefully, from using the ecosystem platform. The thin distinction between the startups that join just for the incentives and those that also participate in the platform is one of the main issues affecting this chapter's models.

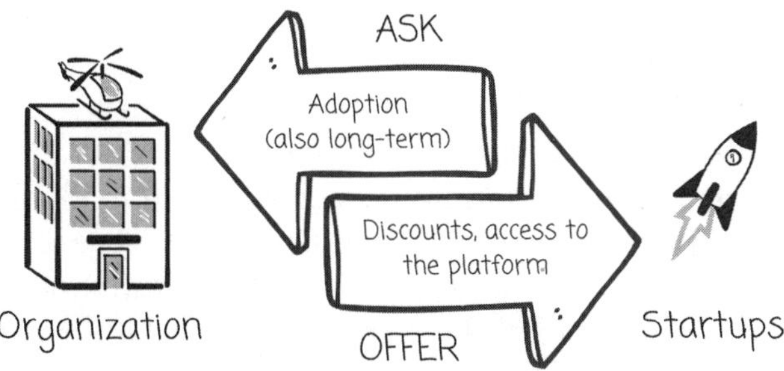

FIGURE 5.2 The value exchange is encouraging ecosystem adoption (also long-term) via discounts, perks, and facilitated access to the ecosystem platform.

Why Use a Program to Compete on Ecosystems?

In the era of platform economies and talent wars, the competition between corporations or regional economies has moved to the front line of ecosystems—innovation ecosystems for corporations and entrepreneurial ecosystems for regional economies.

Why Startups

Early in the second decade of the twenty-first century, corporate leaders recognized that managing their ecosystem was critical to market leadership. Organizations such as BlackBerry (formerly Research in Motion) lost their dominant market position in smartphones due to their failure to manage their ecosystem,[1] leaving an easy conquest of market share to Apple's iPhone and Google's Android.[2] Rather than attempting to build deep moats and obstacles to entry in terms of products or exclusive resources (the strategy of the large corporations of the past), today's successful market leaders create strong networks of partners and customers (*innovation ecosystem*) that revolve around the company and add value to all participants.[3]

Software technology such as Google's Android acts natively as a platform (through its app marketplace Google Play) and is a natural tool around which to build an ecosystem of independent software producers. But competition on ecosystems is not restricted to software businesses: digital platforms are nowadays in almost every other sector where they can open similar business models. In 2019, Amazon's "ecosystem partners," namely, the independent third-party firms selling their retail products through the behemoth's website, accounted for 53 percent of total sales, up from 3 percent 20 years before.[4] Attracting innovative manufacturers and brands to an ecosystem and retaining them on the platform will be increasingly crucial for Amazon—as well as for its competitors.

Innovative startups are a boon for innovation ecosystems. They inject new technology and enable new services that were simply not available before. They may contribute ideas, attract more customers, and indirectly help grow the organization's brand.

Governments are also competing for companies. At least until 2019, there has been fierce competition between nations, regions, and cities on the startup talent they could relocate to their territory. An *entrepreneurial ecosystem* is a network of partners who influence startup activity in a territorial area characterized by certain geographical features or shared cultural, environmental, or economic ties.[5] They comprise companies and talented potential hires, universities, investors, and institutional actors.

In this case, startups are the vessels of talent, technology, business opportunities, new or specialized jobs, and foreign investments from venture capital firms. Alongside attracting and retaining more consolidated firms, startups are naturally the target of mid- to long-term economic and social development policies.

Why Programs

Most startups demand an easy-to-understand and easy-to-use route to access new services or new opportunities. A dedicated startup program for ecosystem building provides precisely that: an interface, a gateway, and, often, a fast track for startups that intend to join an ecosystem.

Furthermore, a program can act as a marketing tool to market the ecosystem to the startup community, with a targeted offer consisting of specific incentives, free credits, or subsidies. The startups often receive guidance, consultancy, and training on how to use the platform:

- This generally consists of workshops for CTOs or technical employees or technical counseling on system architecture for technology platforms.
- For business platforms, it may include cultural workshops on how to sell in the new country, or counseling on national labor law and IP protection, for example.

Finally, a program establishes a single point of contact to enter the ecosystem.

A Closer Look at Two Types of Ecosystems

Since this chapter illustrates two cases in parallel—innovation and entrepreneurial ecosystems—it is essential to understand their differences and commonalities before going forward.

To start, they are two very distinctive objects. Innovation ecosystems are related to the concepts of customers, markets, and products.[6] They gravitate around one focal organization and contribute innovative products and services for its customers, which the other participants in the ecosystem also serve. Conversely, entrepreneurial ecosystems gravitate around a startup community, and their output is to foster entrepreneurs and entrepreneurship in general (Table 5.1).

TABLE 5.1 Distinctions between innovation and entrepreneurial ecosystems

Innovation Ecosystem	Entrepreneurial Ecosystem
Innovative performance. The ecosystem's output is to improve the performance in producing innovation to the advantage of customers.	**Productive entrepreneurship.** The ecosystem's output is to produce more and more productive entrepreneurial ventures.
Focal organization. As noted in Chapter 2, an innovation ecosystem is referred to and revolves around a focal firm.	**Focal community.** As noted in Chapter 2, an entrepreneurial ecosystem refers to and comprises a startup community.
Business ecosystem. The closest related concept is that of a business ecosystem.	**Startup-centered.** The concept is highly connected to startups, investors, and supportive institutions.

Notwithstanding these differences, both ecosystems benefit from high-quality and diverse participants. The most typical pattern for our purposes is that both types of ecosystems are built on one or more platforms of some sort:

- **Technology platform.** A software platform, such as Microsoft Azure or the Apple ecosystem enabled by iOS and the App Store; data streams or datasets, such as public open data and related applications; or other forms involving intellectual property. More common in innovation ecosystems.
- **Business platform.** An event or meetup, such as SXSW in Austin, Texas, or Web Summit in Dublin and later in Lisbon; a city or regional business network, including business associations and investor associations; a marketplace of ideas, opportunities, or contacts; and similar. Equally common in innovation and entrepreneurial ecosystems.
- **Operational platform.** A coworking space, a physical incubator building, a network of connected offices in different cities, and so on. More common in entrepreneurial ecosystems.

Although different in type, all platforms have similar functions—one or both:

- To provide business advantages in terms of cost savings, convenience, or time to market.
- To facilitate the interactions of ecosystem participants internally or to reach out to external partners or customers.

Active Participation and Retention as Preconditions to Win

In essence, this chapter's startup programs facilitate adopting the ecosystem platform by removing roadblocks, reducing costs, and increasing convenience. However, the organization generally wins only if the startup adopts the ecosystem long term and intensively participates. Active participation and retention on the ecosystem platform are two preconditions for a return on investment in most of these cases (Figure 5.3).

FIGURE 5.3 Although retention comes from the ecosystem itself and cannot be enforced by a program, it is a precondition to benefit from orchestrating ecosystem adoption.

The value a startup generates in an ecosystem depends on its intrinsic characteristics and how long and intensively it participates. To appreciate this concept, consider the difference between a unicorn and a pre-revenue startup. The unicorn can give immediate value, onboarding millions of users to your platform. However, its loyalty might be flimsy and swayed by a better offer. A pre-revenue startup might take longer to pay back to the ecosystem. Still, its adoption might be stickier and stay, eventually, until it becomes a unicorn—that's also a win.

Building on the previous examples, consider these two strategies to improve the health and value of an ecosystem:

- **Expand.** The first strategy consists of adding valuable startups inorganically, like in the case of the unicorn. With this strategy long-termism (L) is essential to winning; all short-termist startups (S) are rotten eggs (Figure 5.4). Among long-termist startups, the BL often carries the highest value. Because they are motivated by solid growth, generally speaking, they are more likely to be loyal and establish roots than the opportunistic (by trade) RL group.
- **Ripen.** Ripening means addressing the deficiencies of the current ecosystem and growing what it can offer organically. This objective can be pursued by "renting" external startups to help creativity, giving feedback on a technology platform (e.g., providing use cases), or educating and connecting with the local startup community. *Referrals*, in this case, are more important than retention: they keep fueling the program with fresh blood in future editions. Because a long-term relationship with the platform or community is not strictly necessary, PS and BS are also valid targets. Instead, the rapid-growth startups (R) may not prioritize giving back to the platform (Figure 5.5).

	short-term / to try	long-term / with intention
rapid growth	RS	RL
business growth	BS	BL
personal growth	PS	PL

FIGURE 5.4 When inorganically adding startups to an ecosystem, BL startups are a likely fit, with PL and RL in the second tier. S startups should be avoided.

	short-term / to try	long-term / with intention
rapid growth	RS	RL
business growth	BS	BL
personal growth	PS	PL

FIGURE 5.5 When organically maturing startups already inside the ecosystem, rapid growth startups (RS and RL) are worst because they are most likely to self-isolate and focus just on their goals.

In both strategies, PL can be attractive for talent hiring or technology development in innovation ecosystems or as potential connectors and hires in entrepreneurial ecosystem development—even if they don't end up starting a company.

Key Functions of Ecosystem Builders

To expand or ripen an ecosystem (Circle 2), any startup program in this family must solve the following goal-specific problems.

Marketing Funnel

These programs are akin to standard marketing endeavors of a product, asset, or region, or—in general—of an ecosystem and its cardinal platform. They must fuel a marketing funnel that runs from awareness to activation and retention inside the ecosystem. The model set forth by Ash Maurya for startups and traction[7] illustrates the various steps a startup program takes care of (Figure 5.6).

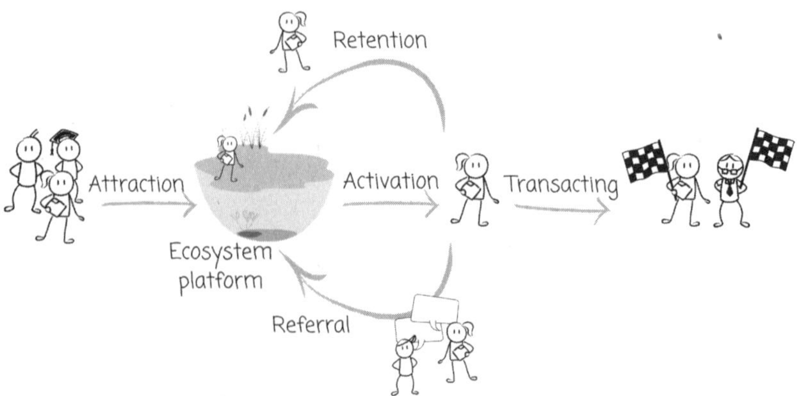

FIGURE 5.6 The ecosystem platform is the product: these programs implement a marketing funnel.

Figure adapted from Ash Maurya, 2016, *Scaling Lean* (Portfolio Penguin).

The marketing funnel combines a few functions that we have seen in other programs in previous chapters as well as others that are specific to ecosystem building:

- **External signaling.** Startups must be made aware that the organization seeks new ecosystem participants—for example, through a website or a call for applications.
- **Internal signaling (business platforms).** The current ecosystem participants may need to be made aware of the arrival of new startups. Think, for instance, of startup programs that relocate startups to a new city or country and how the program can signal to local companies and ecosystem players to help in the onboarding.
- **Acquisition.** Startups need onboarding on the platform; see below.
- **Activation, retention, referral.** As noted in the previous section, the real win for the organization occurs under these conditions.

Activation

This activity may range from opening an account (technology platform) to introducing the founders to the local associations (business platform), or to finding them accommodation and a local mentor:

- **Initial activation.** Enabling the startup to participate in the ecosystem fully and transact on it (e.g., sell the app on the app store). You may need to plan specific training.
- **Onboarding time.** Speed onboarding is often a large part of the value proposition of these programs.

Facilitate Transactions

Startup programs facilitate transactions between participants (in marketplace platforms) or with the organization's customers. Transactions demonstrate the ecosystem's value and incentivize retention. For instance, SAP.iO Foundries help startups sell through the SAP App Center. Destination programs, such as Start-Up Chile, support startups in raising local capital. Arch Grant St. Louis helps with local hiring. The assumption is that more transactions of value can increase both retention and referrals.

Operate the Platform

Some programs also operate the platform—for example, an incubator managing a coworking space or an annual event. It is not a general rule, however. Technology platforms are usually operated by separated technical teams; the startup program only takes care of marketing the platform and onboarding the startups (or not even that).

Startup Programs for Innovation Ecosystems

Digital platforms have emerged as central tools to build innovation ecosystems. For corporations offering digital platforms, startups may serve more than one purpose. They might become long-term, high consumption customers. Or they may rise to be *complementors*,[8] selling products and services to final customers while the platform pursues brand development. The following examples look at startup programs meant to create or nurture innovation ecosystems.

BizSpark / Microsoft for Startups

In late 2008, Microsoft[9] launched a worldwide experimental program named BizSpark—which now continues as Microsoft for Startups—set up to provide early-stage startups with free licenses for Visual Studio, SQL Server, and Windows Server products. Companies had to be privately held to qualify, less than three years old, with annual revenue of less than $1 million, and developing an online service or hosted application. Microsoft benefited from expanded use of the platform and first-hand knowledge of its integration with the startups' technology.

Entrepreneurs responded enthusiastically, especially those already building on Microsoft's stack, because of the opportunity to cut structural costs. "We're getting all the Microsoft software for free, so that's great for a startup like us trying to keep our costs low," said CTO and cofounder Nick Ganju of ZocDoc. "Some of these software packages can get pretty expensive, so it's great to be able to keep our software free for the first few years."

Microsoft's initiative was read as a defensive strategy to protect its market from new entrants in enterprise software such as Google or Salesforce.com. When a competitor aggressively markets to startups, organizations must proactively counter the strategy. Understanding the new environment, other corporate programs like the initial BizSpark model quickly appeared. Today, many major software corporations have programs (such as AWS Activate, Startup with IBM, Create @Alibaba Cloud, or Oracle for Startups), which offer guidance accompanied by discounts and free credits, from $1,000 up to $120,000.

Programs of this kind address:

- Marketing funnel: many of these programs essentially market a software product to startups. Technological lock-in is what generates the return on investment.
- Acquisition and onboarding time: training and customized support are frequent.

AppCampus

To better Apple's iPhone and Google's Android developer ecosystems, from 2012 to 2015 Microsoft, Nokia, and Aalto University (Helsinki, Finland) ran a startup program named AppCampus.

The program distributed equity-free grants in the range of €10,000 to €70,000 (approximately $12,000 to $84,000) to convince entrepreneurs to develop or port mobile apps on Windows Mobile. AppCampus also offered an accelerator-like educational program.[10] The startups had a global distribution channel for their apps through the Windows Phone Store.

The 305 AppCampus startups published 315 apps of higher quality than the application market average. For the Windows Phone ecosystem, AppCampus was successful in attracting developers. "The program allowed Microsoft to compete at ecosystem level against Apple and the others," said Paolo Borella, former AppCampus director. The program facilitated the launch of many new ventures locally, educated entrepreneurs, and enhanced Aalto University's legitimacy.[11]

AppCampus addressed:

- External signaling: the program was a massive awareness campaign for app developers of the relaunch of Microsoft and Nokia's smartphones.
- Activation and retention: activities included technical and business mentorship, allowing the apps to scale fast and produce attractive revenues.
- Facilitate transactions: the program team could mobilize free advertising credits to dedicate to selected apps to fuel their growth.

SAP.iO Foundries

A corporate digital platform can connect startups to the company's sales network. This offering is typical of large technology companies. SAP.iO Foundries, for example, are self-defined "startup accelerators" provided by enterprise software giant SAP. However, they have little in common with YC-style programs, except for the name. SAP.iO Foundries connect innovations from startups to SAP customers through integration with its products and availability on the SAP App Center.

"Customers were asking SAP for what were the breakthrough innovations that were making sense for them, and that they would possibly consume through the SAP investment they had made," said Vanessa Liu, vice president SAP.iO Foundries North America. "For startups, on the other hand, go-to-market is a very critical component, so doing that at scale with SAP can be very meaningful." Since 2017, about a third of startups supported by the program has invested in the integration.

The advantages brought by the program to startups mainly concern reducing the onboarding time. As Liu explained, "For startups, it's very tough to integrate with SAP because, like any other corporate, SAP is difficult to navigate. So, our program short-circuits what is typically a 12–18-months process into a 3–4-months process." Other benefits are orienting for internal collaborations with SAP and providing a channel to SAP's customer base—but not mandatorily. Liu continued, "Prior startup programs required all startups to integrate, but it doesn't work when you force startups to do something."

The accelerators are rigorously equity-free to decrease the barrier to entry to the ecosystem as much as possible and sign up new companies. "Being equity-free allows us to be stage agnostic; if we asked for equity, that would limit us to early-stage," said Liu. "This way, SAP.iO can work with startups up to Series C, such as meQuilibrium."

Diversity is often recognized as an enriching trait of a healthy ecosystem, and a noteworthy feature of SAP.iO Foundries is a focus on diversity (underrepresented founders account for 40 percent of all startups supported in the program, and 100 percent of those invested in New York for which Liu is responsible): "We believe that inclusion is a better strategy because it can be a game changer to support brilliant creators and entrepreneurs who historically have been overlooked, but who have the innovations to solve urgent challenges."

This program is complete and supports many of the functions discussed earlier:

- Marketing funnel: Acquiring partners that sell on the App Center was the initial goal. However, selling through SAP is now optional.
- Internal signaling: Specifically, the Foundries collect briefs for calls from the internal business units—a practice that is increasing spontaneously, said Liu.
- Onboarding time: This is a key performance indicator.
- Facilitate transactions: The program coaches the startups 360 degrees on go-to-market, technical integration, and operations to participate.

Other Programs from Big Tech

Such programs are not just for startups. In 2017, Microsoft understood that independent software vendors were increasingly looking to Microsoft for help with technology and growing their business. It then launched a program for all those who deployed their applications on Azure to make them available on its AppSource marketplace.[12]

Startups remain a frontier for the business ecosystem battle. Microsoft and Amazon have seen accelerated adoption of their cloud services during the Covid-19 pandemic as companies embraced remote work tools. Recently the race has leveled up to late-stage startups. Successful alliances include:

- **Microsoft and Abnormal Security Corp.** agreed to include the startup's email security software in Azure Cloud. Microsoft's sales force would sell the software to its large enterprise clients. Abnormal's chief executive, Evan Reiser, said that selling its security service to enterprise customers with ties to Microsoft was so attractive that it outweighed the downside of switching in cloud providers from AWS.[13]
- **Amazon and Apptio** agreed that the latter would expand its use of AWS Cloud Services while AWS would begin to market Apptio's services to AWS Cloud customers. AWS's outreach to later-stage startups is primarily through its APN Global Startup Program,[14] adding the new value proposition of facilitating go-to-market.

FIWARE Accelerator

Governmental bodies or NGOs, too, have used startup programs for ecosystem-building goals around new technology. In 2014, the European Commission committed 80 million euros (about $97 million) to the FIWARE Accelerate Programme to develop a European open-source alternative to private cloud platforms such as Microsoft Azure or Alibaba Cloud. Between 2014 and 2017 the accelerator funded more than 1,000 applications to use FIWARE technology.

After the European Commission's initiative, the software platform was transfered to the FIWARE Foundation, a nonprofit organization. As of 2020, over 170 cities and more than 8,000 developers from 1,000 startups had used FIWARE-based solutions,[15] including the Spanish farming animal welfare IoT platform Digitanimal, Italian mobility-as-a-service software Phoops, and a German company specialized in air quality sensors, data, and analytics.

The engagement of startups into the FIWARE ecosystem continues today with the FIWARE Accelerator, providing visibility and technological resources. "The solutions developed with FIWARE enable startups and young SMEs to enter the market in a short time in addition to becoming part of a large ecosystem," said Stefano De Panfilis, chief operating officer at the FIWARE Foundation. "Fresh blood in such an ecosystem allows the FIWARE Community, not only to strengthen its presence in the market but also to gain more ideas and directions on where to develop the FIWARE technologies further."

What this program addresses:

- External signaling: The program offers press coverage for the supported startups; this is only partially to attract more—describing concrete use cases is likely a principal reason.
- Acquisition and onboarding: The focus is on technical onboarding, whereas the program is less active on the other parts of the marketing funnel.

Growing an Entrepreneurial Ecosystem

From hackathons to ecosystem-building accelerators,[16] startup programs are often employed as tools to populate, educate, and connect an entrepreneurial ecosystem. More startups increase the local startup community's density and diversity for cities or countries, infuse entrepreneurial culture, create more local economic opportunities, attract fresh internal and external talent, and even act as bridges to other communities. Eventually, a healthy entrepreneurial ecosystem generates new jobs and taxes. Here are a few examples.

Start-Up Chile and Destination Programs

Start-Up Chile is a government program launched in 2010, attracting digital startups worldwide to spend six months in Chile's capital city, Santiago (Chapter 1). In 2020 the program marked 10 years, currently making it the longest-lasting program of its kind.

Other civic and government organizations have copied Chile's model in the last decade. Parallel18 in Puerto Rico, founded in 2016, is one of them. Other similar programs include Arch Grants, sponsored by the City of St. Louis, Missouri, and active since 2012, and TechPeaks in the Italian Alps, from 2013 to 2015. Recent programs have experimented with applying this model to digital nomads[17] without necessarily having a startup, such as Tulsa Remote, active since 2018 in Tulsa, Oklahoma, or 90-Day Finn,[18] run as a pilot in 2020 by the city of Helsinki, Finland. We collectively identify these programs as "destination programs" to highlight the binding *relocation ask* (undoubtedly aided by the allure of exotic or unusual destinations).

Retention appears to be the Achilles' heel of these models. "From 2010 to 2015, Start-Up Chile was meant to attract role models to educate and develop the Chilean entrepreneurial ecosystem. The retention of international entrepreneurs was 35 percent, and very often that applied to the founders, not to their business," explained Sebastián Díaz Mesa, former CEO of Start-Up Chile.

Mature programs understand this potential weakness and leverage the uniqueness of the territory and ecosystem they are in to select startups with a higher chance to stay in the long term. Start-Up Chile changed its model around 2015. It pivoted toward "startups that had a strong potential to create collaborations with corporations based in Chile, and to leave a business and not necessarily the founders," explained Díaz Mesa. The retention rate of businesses leaped to a whopping 65 percent.

Start-Up Chile implemented different functions before and after the pivot:

- Before 2015: The program pursued an ecosystem ripening strategy, renting startups from other ecosystems to support an internal cultural operation; external signaling, acquisition, activation, and referrals were more critical than retention or facilitation of transactions.
- After 2016: The strategy was rebalanced to a mix of ecosystem ripening and expansion, with the latter gaining momentum; facilitating transactions and retention became prevalent over the other functions.

Downtown Project in Las Vegas

The late Tony Hsieh, founder and former CEO of Zappos, was the impetus for the Downtown Project, a program to revitalize downtown Las Vegas and encourage digital workers to relocate there. The $350 million program includes investments in real estate, education, small business, and a tech accelerator. An independent analysis[19] of the project found that the community's recurring annual benefits encompassed 1,571 jobs, $70 million in salaries, and almost $210 million in economic output. This program included:

- Marketing funnel: relaunching a depressed area.
- Operating the platform: running events directly and other community engagement activities.

Techstars Startup Weekend

Originally a not-for-profit organization backed by various donors (including the Kauffman Foundation[20] for entrepreneurship, based in Kansas City, Missouri), Startup Weekend has been part of Techstars since 2015. Nonetheless, it still leverages a vast community of volunteer ecosystem builders across the world. Techstars Startup Weekend (TSW) is a 54-hour hackathon where founders or future entrepreneurs meet to explore new business ideas together. With more than 7,000 events in 150 countries and counting, this format is one of the most well-received and widespread ecosystem-building startup programs.

Learning and networking are the main benefits for participants. In this respect, it is a considerable tool for connecting a local startup community, creating collaborations, and eventually spawning joint ventures or new ventures. TSWs are generally organized and run by volunteers called "community leaders," but they receive sponsorships from private businesses and government agencies who seek access to the startup community.

The highest impact of TSWs is in creating and nurturing local communities. A TSW has a legacy of post-event meetups and social media groups or newsletters and sometimes also fosters educational pre-events in which would-be participants learn about business model innovation and investor pitching. The TSW team of volunteers in Paris, France, has averaged one event a month, each event gathering crowds in the range of

100 participants. The highest value comes from the long-term activation and retention of these crowds within the Paris entrepreneurial ecosystem.

TSW mainly addresses:

- Acquisition: TSW is vital in creating enthusiasm in undecided potential entrepreneurs, but it does not support the rest of the funnel (retention, etc.).
- Facilitate transactions: By attracting talents of different backgrounds, TSW facilitates the creation of bridges between tribes; also, the pitch night on Sunday is a showcase and a spark of negotiations for pre-seed investments.
- Ripening strategy: With a strong focus on PL founders, TSW is used as an educational format to improve the quality of entrepreneurs in the area.

Shared Features

Models capitalizing on ecosystem adoption share many features.

Platform or Community

Ecosystem-building models essentially promote a platform or a community to startups. They execute a marketing funnel similar to that of a business (Figure 5.6), and they must cater to retention and referrals. Sebastián Díaz Mesa agrees, claiming, "Behind the success of Start-Up Chile is the community that we created, based on trust, collaboration and win-win, something new in terms of a public policy." In many cases, transactions in the ecosystem make the platform or community more valuable, and thus they increase retention and referrals.

Platform/Community-Specific Knowledge

These programs may require technical or cultural expertise outside of the startup's capability, such as experience with a specific API or cultural adaptation to a different country. In such cases, sponsors should include training and coaching as part of the startup program. "The companies that are coming for the first time to Toronto need time to understand the culture of this ecosystem before they can start selling and hiring," said Miryam

Lazarte, CEO of LatAm Startups. This not-for-profit organization has helped over 100 startups from Latin America open offices in Canada. "We have a two-week bootcamp for market validation. If that goes well, startups enter a three-month program."

Strong Incentives

Free credits, discounts, and subsidies are essential incentives for startups who might apply to an ecosystem adoption program. In effect, the incentives are "restricted" capital, as good as cash when used for certain expenses. Most of these programs are equity-free.

Fast Track

Most of these programs offer a fast track to enter the ecosystem, lowering the costs of testing the platform or community and subsequent adoption. Technology platforms provide guidance and training, while destination programs offer visa support, relocation services, and local business development.

Permanence-Related Business Models

Whether it is revenue sharing, rent, or taxes, the business model (and so the return on investment) of many of these programs heavily depends on the permanence and retention of the ecosystem's startups. The common challenge is to entice retention after the end of those incentives (incentives evaporation problem).

Engagement Metrics

Beyond the metrics of monetization mentioned above, these programs may address the mindset shift, skills, or cultural aspects of the ecosystem to improve its health and maturity. In this respect, exceptional importance goes to metrics of engagement, such as the number of attendees to events, the number of active local partners, the number of users served, user feedback scores, media, and press coverage.

When It Breaks: Incentives Evaporate

These programs bestow funding, free credits, office space, and other perks to incentivize startups to dip their toes and facilitate access to the platform or community.

The hard truth is that most startups that join these programs do it for the benefits. When a startup needs an enabling technology marketed by one of the cloud computing tech giants, even better to get it for free; and if a startup team can work remotely from anywhere in the world, staying in an amazing new destination for a few months can be received as part of the appeal of the startup lifestyle.

Joining an ecosystem adoption program with its benefits and perks is usually a no-brainer for startups. But will it be a win for the organizational sponsor? After all, startups can grab the loot and flee as fast as they flocked to the honeypot. Some startups will leave; others will stay.

What is critical to understand is that free credits and other incentives are not the centers of the exchange of value; they are just a means to foster adoption. Without stimulating retention, the whole effort may end up being a form of charity for entrepreneurs without any return on investment. The startup electing to enter the program is essentially a "buyer" with the power to return the purchase after the discount expires so that the organization bears the risk of a divorce. If a startup leaves when the lure of incentives and subsidies ends, little of any value created stays with the organization.

To build long-term partnerships, an organization needs to provide reasons for retention. Startups seek increased revenues, profitability, or access to valuable resources, such as talent or local partners. "Startups need to access the core of the ecosystem," said Lazarte. Successful ecosystem adoption programs aim from day one to link a startup to customers, business partners, universities, or trusted suppliers and distributors.

KEY TAKEAWAYS

- **Ecosystems are a competitive advantage.** Today, competition has moved to the front line of partners and suppliers for corporations (innovation ecosystems), or networks of founders and investors for regional and national governments (entrepreneurial ecosystems).
- **Ecosystems always use a form of platform.** This third group of startup programs pushes the adoption of an ecosystem platform, which could be a technology platform (e.g., an enabling software), a business platform (e.g., a regional economic network), or an operational platform (e.g., a coworking space). These programs are akin to standard marketing endeavors of a product, region, or asset.
- **The common denominator is platform adoption.** Advantages for startups revolve around removing hurdles, reducing costs, and increasing the convenience of adoption. The organization may monetize the engagement through platform fees, rent, jobs, taxes, and so on or as fast-reactive safety networks against potential competitors.
- **Continuous participation is crucial for success.** Incentivizing the adoption is not enough, though. Programs must also stimulate active participation and retention (preconditions for success). The value for the organization gets higher the more a startup actively interacts and the longer it stays engaged. Like for solution sourcing, the organization bears the cost of a divorce: the startup has still gained the adoption incentives.
- **Rooting a startup from day one.** Convincing reasons to retain a startup are increased revenues, profitability, or access to valuable resources, such as talent or local partners. To that end, successful ecosystem adoption programs aim from day one to link a startup to customers, business partners, universities, or trusted suppliers and distributors.

6

OBJECTIVE: ENTREPRENEURSHIP FOR IMPACT

In this last chapter of Part One, your organization (Circle 1) becomes primarily a mission-driven *benefactor* (Circle 2) that uses entrepreneurship as a transformational force in society and economy to pursue a mission, often related to Sustainable Development Goals.[1] The startup program recipients can include under-resourced founders, students, particular social groups, or impact scale-ups that could be life-changing for millions of people (Circle 3).

Once again, Circle 2 is the anchor for all the programs presented here (Figure 6.1). It is dialed in to affect sustainability, climate change, social development, diversity, poverty, accessible healthcare, equal opportunities, and so on. This chapter's programs use known templates (such as venture fund, accelerator, incubator, challenge, or hackathon). Still, the impact-related context always gives a twist to those models, sometimes changing their nature profoundly (e.g., reducing or canceling the equity toll). Furthermore, in impact-driven programs, the educational component surges to an even more central role than in other models.

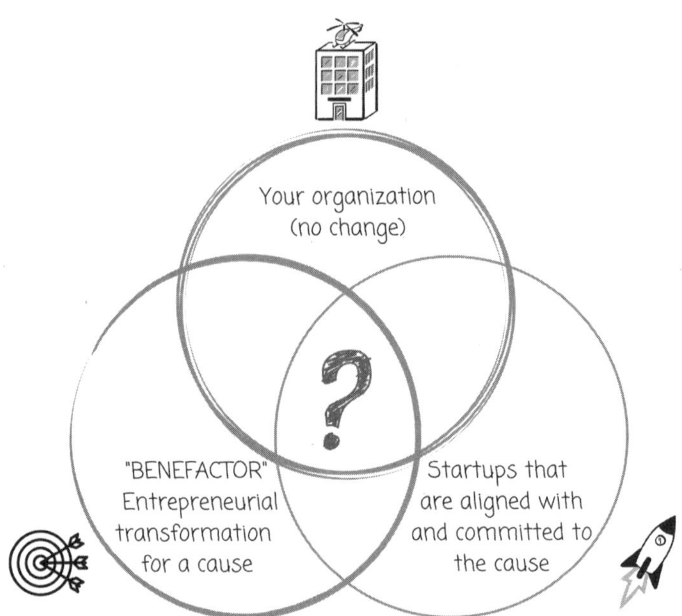

FIGURE 6.1 The anchor is causing an impactful entrepreneurial transformation (Circle 2). The organization plays the role of a "benefactor" (at least metaphorically, even if paid) with respect to being mission driven.

The exchange of value here is (Figure 6.2):

- **Circle 2.** The organization wants to instill an entrepreneurial transformation that impacts a social, environmental, or economic context.
- **Circle 3.** The startup wants the organization's resources, knowledge, and networks to have that entrepreneurial transformation. It is selected for participation because it falls in the measure's targets (alignment) or because it shares the core values and mission (commitment).

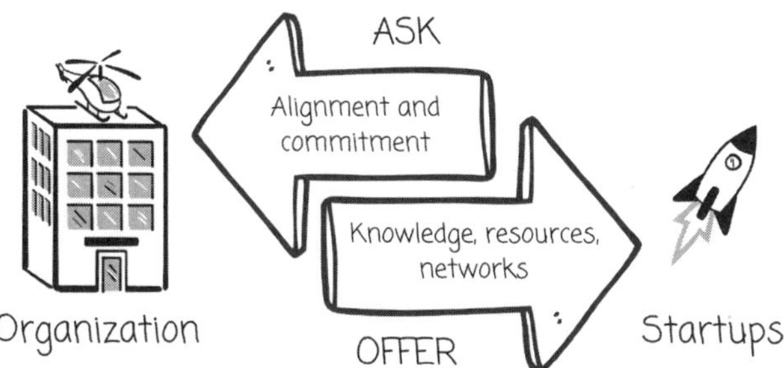

FIGURE 6.2 The value exchange revolves around the adherence and commitment of participants to the organization's mission.

Entrepreneurship as a Transformational Force

> *We want to democratize entrepreneurship. Everybody should have access to it without having to go to college. We create experiences and educational content to support young people in gaining the skills of entrepreneurship and innovation, and in some cases helping them pursue those entrepreneurial ideas through an acceleration program.*
>
> —Joanna Buczkowska-McCumber, Executive Director, League of Innovators

Why Startups

Civic and community leaders are always on the lookout for ways to stimulate the economy, and many view entrepreneurship as a potential source of self-empowerment and job creation. Evidence is on their side, suggesting that young firms are the most substantial contributors to new job creation. Once adjusted for survival, startup champions remain the major gross job contributors for the following years.

In the United States, startups contributed only 3 percent of employment but nearly all net new job creation and almost 20 percent of gross job creation in any given year up to just before the Great Recession.[2] State, regional, and national studies show similar patterns, including in more recent years. In Missouri, first-time employers created an average of more than 40,000 new jobs each year from 2014 to 2018.[3]

The same holds true in other geographies. In Nairobi, Kenya, 1 percent of entrepreneurial software firms produced 40 percent of the job creation in 2016. In Bangalore, India, 6 percent of the tech startups generated over 90 percent of jobs and capitalized most venture funding.[4] In developing countries, up to 16 percent of net job creation can be attributed to young small firms.[5] Young firms everywhere seem to contribute massively to the labor market's dynamism, and the champion startups that reach scale become the protagonists of new employment.

In the startup and investor community, entrepreneurial capital is never lost. Even if a startup fails, the entrepreneur will not. Entrepreneurial capital lives with the innovator, and it can blossom and produce an impact in the future. When a founder is successful, the experience and capital can be an engine of growth for the next generation of entrepreneurs in the same region or industry.

Startups are also seen as sources of innovative solutions for global challenges, such as the 17 Sustainable Development Goals set by the United Nations for the 2030 Agenda.

Technology, automation, new materials, new drug discovery, and other IP-intensive and research-intensive new products and services can solve challenging problems in ways that nothing else can. In this respect, the expectations put on startups by impact-driven initiatives are similar to those of client organizations sourcing solutions to complex problems that Chapter 4 reviewed.

Why Programs

An organization may launch a startup program to identify, raise, and accelerate the next generation of founders and innovative startups in a given region or social context. The underlying assumption is that entrepreneurship can be a driver for social and economic development and a positive force to fix individual and collective shortcomings. The advantages of running structured programs for these aims are the same as those reviewed in

Chapter 1. In the context of social and economic development, the benefits are primarily:

- **Framework.** Programs provide a framework to repeat and scale, at least to some extent, the same action over time or across different geographies.
- **External signaling.** Programs have a strong signaling power, catalyzing attention to reach the intended targets widely and efficiently.
- **Neutrality.** Programs create standard and neutral rules for all and exception zones with more entrepreneur-friendly terms than those applied to other businesses.

These impact-driven programs are operated by organizations worldwide, from the government to universities and even private investors. An example is the startup accelerator initiated by the United Nations World Food Programme (WFP), the recipient of the 2020 Nobel Peace Prize. More examples are the innovation prize for university students run by the Guyana Economic Development Trust or a private investor such as Y Combinator with its free online YC Startup School.

Programs in this chapter generally fall into three broad subcategories of goals:

- **New entrepreneurship.** Human capital acceleration and transformation, creating new entrepreneurial ventures and spurring technology transfer and societal impact of scientific research.
- **Scaling up impact.** Identify entrepreneurs and products that possess the mindset and capability of impacting tens or hundreds of millions and create the right conditions to scale.
- **Give first.** Voluntary pro bono work from successful entrepreneurs, professionals, or investors who love to work with entrepreneurs and wish to foster their positive impact.

Starting from recognizing that entrepreneurs as individuals, distinct from small businesses, learn by doing and interacting with others, successful public or impact-driven programs take a long-term focus on fostering connections and learning.[6] Both of these functions gain from a cohort- or class-based approach, both in efficiency and efficacy.

Commitment as a Precondition to Winning

Impact-driven programs are truly effective when they can select and support founders and startups with the capability and commitment to contribute to the cause. When entrepreneurs only take the offer as an embellishment to their CV or for reasons unaligned with the cause, no matter how well the program supported them, the impact metrics would not be high (Figure 6.3).

FIGURE 6.3 The startup's commitment to stay on course with its vision and mission is a precondition for the program's impact.

For example, if a government program supports local entrepreneurs, it assumes they will drive local economic development. Instead, if they leave to Silicon Valley, the resources employed are lost to the local ecosystem (at least temporarily, until they return). In this respect, long-termist (L startups) motivations are a requirement that the organization should enforce during the selection process for the goals of (a) fostering new entrepreneurship, and (b) scaling up impact (Figure 6.4).

Rapid growth may not be essential to have an impact. Steady-growing businesses can still scale solutions even if they don't land a big hit on the stock exchange. First-time entrepreneurs interested primarily in personal growth can still help their communities by becoming ecosystem supporters or teaming up with existing startups. However, if your organization is pursuing healthy and dynamic economic growth, it should target high-growth startups. Economic research consistently shows that a minimal number, from 1 to 6 percent of all ventures in a region, account for the lion's share of net job creation and other spillovers from entrepreneurship.[7]

An exception is pro bono work for a good cause or hacks for good deeds (such as creating a website for a hospital in need). In

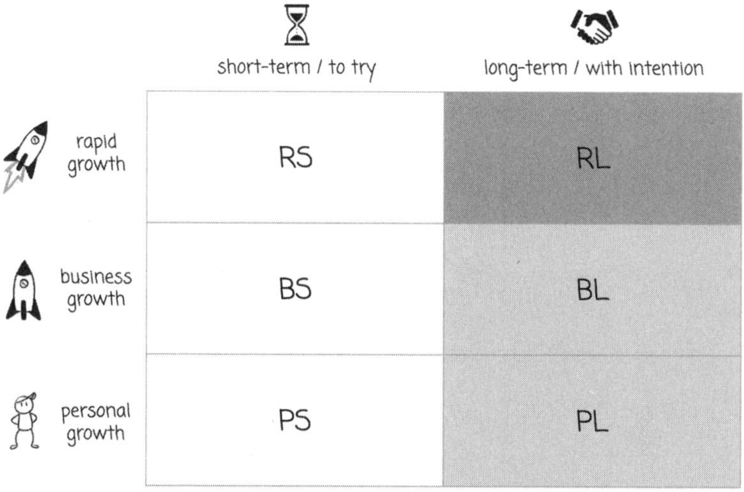

	short-term / to try	long-term / with intention
rapid growth	RS	RL
business growth	BS	BL
personal growth	PS	PL

FIGURE 6.4 Impact is potentially more considerable when startups are committed to rapid growth, but any individual or business with a long-term commitment is a match.

these cases, casual helpers or short-termist contributors are as good as any other type (Figure 6.5).

Key Functions of Transformational Impact Programs

Overall, these programs pursue a transformation with long-lasting effects on the recipient in line with the mission and cause they support.

External Signaling

Reaching the intended participants of these programs may be more costly than in other cases because some targets may not be looking for an entrepreneurial career or to scale their solutions.

Inspire

Publicizing entrepreneurship and making innovation a career choice in people's minds is critical for early-stage programs of this type. Generating and promoting role models enriches the

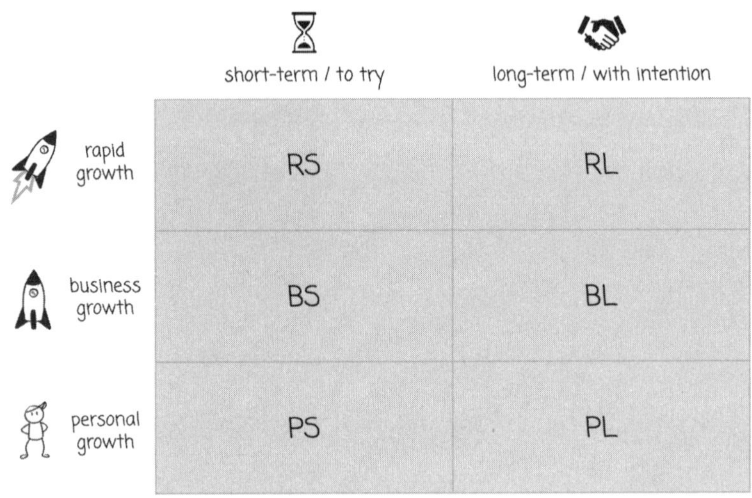

FIGURE 6.5 In one-off events such as hacks for good, any startup can contribute independently of motives.

external signaling function of future editions, and in the long run, it can produce a mindset and cultural shift, fueling a positive feedback loop. Opposite to other programs, where inspiration and role models might be ecosystem side effects and not deliberate outputs, this chapter's programs may have them as the primary goal.

Educate

> *We bring communities together or build them where they don't exist; to inspire and educate young generations to build entrepreneurial global businesses. Our first program was launched in high schools and universities, pro bono.*
>
> —Vlad Gliga, CEO of Rubik Hub

Educational modules are core in these programs but not of the kind seen in traditional business schools that are based on conducting a long-term market analysis or weighing various alternative scenarios. They use an approach called "effectuation," which resolves to take action based on the resources at one's disposal, using the world as a living lab, and giving precedence to learn-by-doing while avoiding "analysis paralysis."[8]

Facilitate Connections

What entrepreneurs find difficult, reportedly,[9] is to find fellow entrepreneurs and to reach investors. Connections are supported by the typical approach of working with a class or cohort of founders and startups. Like in MBA schools, programs provide room for peer-to-peer aid and camaraderie and many-to-many catalytic events and introductions to investors or partners.

Remove Roadblocks

This function tackles structural costs, initial financial backing, cultural skepticism, and lack of social mobility. It may include cutting costs, such as providing office space and secretarial support (e.g., in traditional incubators), or providing a stipend to reduce opportunity costs (e.g., a sabbatical for researchers turned startup founders). It also applies to programs addressed to less fortunate social segments, discriminated groups, or underrepresented founders.

Smart Scalability

The economic sustainability of impact programs is often based on philanthropic donations or public funding, limiting scale or continuity, encouraging programs to experiment with new ways to enable scalability and cost-efficiency.

Startup Programs for New Entrepreneurship and Impact Growth

Startup programs that engage with entrepreneurs for impact goals multiply and take on many different forms. They use all sorts of templates that are also common to other objectives.

Women in Cleantech Challenge

Some programs are explicitly designed to remove roadblocks to the entrepreneurial endeavors of underrepresented founders. After working with over 200 cleantech startups and scale-ups across Canada, the MaRS Discovery District in Toronto discovered only 4 percent of them had female founders. Upon a call to action from the government in 2018, MaRS teamed up with Natural Resources Canada (NRCan) to improve that number.

The result was the Women in Cleantech Challenge (WICT), a program for a cohort of women including a stipend for two and a half years, mentorship, introductions to key investors and customers, access to world-class NRCan labs, and a $1 million prize to the entrepreneur who made the most progress. The six finalists were chosen, in part, based on whether they could optimally benefit from working with the national labs. These features considered that growing cleantech companies, with the deep science and physical products involved, take more time and more money than a typical software startup—therefore, a traditional accelerator model was not a good fit.

The finalists tackle the planet's most intractable environmental challenges, such as energy-efficient large-area production of graphene nanofilms; sustainable extraction of green lithium for batteries from a by-product of oil and gas production; or biodegradable lipids for remediating oil contamination. To top it off, they have come together as a team, supporting each other through their challenges even though they are competing for the prize. "I would never have started a company without WICT support; the technology would still be on a shelf at a university," said a finalist.[10]

At the end of the program, the six companies—none of which was incorporated at the start—won a total of 21 independent prizes, grew to dozens of employees, began building production plants, raised several additional millions in nondilutive funding, and began preparing for Series A rounds.

WITC addressed:

- External signaling: The program's title and focus were instrumental in reaching an underrepresented target and reassuring possible candidates of the intentions of program financiers in their favor.
- Facilitate connections: Participants were connected to relevant national labs and investors they would not have been able to contact.
- Remove roadblocks: The stability of a guaranteed salary for two and a half years allowed the group to offset the risk of freezing or leaving their nonentrepreneurial careers.

Guyana Innovation Prize

Another example is the Guyana Innovation Prize, an annual competition and monthslong startup bootcamp for students, faculty, or alumni of Guyana's tertiary institutions living in Guyana. Lecturers and PhDs from the University of Guyana (UG) and highly experienced professionals based in the United States volunteer to teach the course. Promising research ideas are selected based on a competitive application process. Selected applicants are then paired with mentors, both in and outside of Guyana, over 12 months to help develop business plans and revenue models for commercially viable, scalable businesses.

"Our strength is the diaspora from our home country," said Oslene Carrington, CEO of Guyana Economic Development Trust (GEDT), the philanthropic initiative that coordinates the program. "Essentially, we all give because of the potential we see in compatriots back home and because we see it as our duty."

The program has been operating for three years. It counts its success in new ventures created and unique intellectual property produced by the country's scientists, technologists, researchers, and product developers from Guyana's tertiary institutions. Past projects supported by the program include fighting against fungal infections with leaves from coconuts and okra plants, using beeswax and cassava starch to retard fruit waste, and transforming sugar cane into ethanol for a sustainable fertilizer.

Guyana Innovation Prize by GEDT is only one example of a startup program driven by members of a particular community. Another example targeting Africa and the African diaspora is Tiphub Accelerator,[11] based out of Washington, DC.

This program fulfills the following functions:

- Inspire: The diaspora mentors act as role models that encourage students and researchers to exit their comfort zone. Allowing calculated risk is per se impactful for the target audience.
- Educate: Courses done in collaboration with experienced professionals and higher education faculty help fill the gaps.
- Facilitate connections: Creating bridges inside the country and with the United States.

WFP Innovation Accelerator

The World Food Programme (WFP) Innovation Accelerator was launched in 2015 to pilot new solutions and scale promising innovations to disrupt hunger. It has supported more than 100 projects worldwide, with 14 innovations scaling up to reach 3.5 million people. The WFP Innovation Accelerator comprises a portfolio of programs, including a six-month mentor-based program for proof of concept (POC) with an initial funding of $100,000 and the Scale-Up Enablement Programme for more mature companies able to significantly disrupt hunger by improving the livelihoods of over 100,000 people.

The WFP program seeks to:

- Facilitate connections: Support from a UN agency can open many locked doors.
- Remove roadblocks: Initial funding and mentorship can speed up both the POC and scale-up phases.

Youth Co:Lab's Springboard Programme

Cocreated in 2017 by the United Nations Development Programme (UNDP) and the Citi Foundation, Youth Co:Lab aims to empower the younger generations across Asia-Pacific by developing their entrepreneurial skills and supporting social innovation startups. Its Springboard Programme is an incubator targeting young SDG entrepreneurs, and especially young women, indigenous youth, and youth with disabilities.

The program runs an online directory of free courses for entrepreneurs and partners. Not everyone has access to the internet, though, and Youth Co:Lab strives to overcome the digital divide and bring educational startup programs to those who need them the most through the Youth Empowerment Alliance network.

"The toughest part is to reach certain villages where it's all pen and paper," explained Cynthia Cheung, a UNDP consultant.

The network comprises over 180 regional partners in 25 countries in APAC, national governments as leading partners, and private sector operators and investors. Youth Co:Lab seeks scalability through clear "asks" for partners while providing benefits such as free research and data to help build each partner's credibility.

This program tackles:

- Education: through online courses for both entrepreneurs and partners.
- Facilitating connections: acting as orchestrator of relationships in the region.
- Smart scalability: using online and recorded material and organizing a network of local partners.

150 Startups

The program collaborates with Alberta's 26 publicly funded colleges, universities, and polytechnics to expand regional entrepreneurial capacity and help students build potential unicorn companies across Alberta. Each year the most entrepreneurially promising postsecondary students are selected by their institution to participate in a program designed to turn an idea into a revenue-generating business in less than six months.

"Our primary measure is whether or not we turn someone into a role model, someone that inspires students by sharing their story during some public or private format on campus. It's amazing how just one role model can help many others also aspire to become an entrepreneur," explained Craig Elias, the program founder.

After completing a kickoff weekend that helps students build a team around their idea, students are given three phases of Lean Startup challenges. The first phase has them complete problem validation interviews with a budget of Can$750. In the second phase, if they apply technology to help scale their validated business idea and spend at least Can$2,000, the program reimburses 50 percent of these expenses. And finally, to encourage a focus on sales, the students receive an additional 50 percent for each Can$1 of revenue generated during the third phase of the program. Successful participants have raised six-figure investments and are now running companies that have customers like Boeing and NASA.

This program seeks to:

- Inspire: creating role models as a goal is per se a way to make a positive loop.
- Educate: effectual teaching and a system of incentives to stimulate entrepreneurial solutions and learn-by-doing.

- Promote scalability: teaming up with colleges around the province helps fill the funnel of applications (researchers are now admitted too).

Laudato Sì Challenge

Inspired by His Holiness Pope Francis's encyclical letter *Laudato sì: On Care for Our Common Home*, Eric Harr cofounded a startup program in 2016 to deal with climate change and the social hardships of forced population displacements. The program, supported by a collection of venture capital firms, tech companies, and organizations worldwide, recruited and financially supported startups intended to impact its issues significantly.

"Like a three-legged stool, we are connecting the private sector—startups and corporations—with the public sector and the faith sector," explained Harr. "Our unique value is that we connect chosen enterprises with the on-the-ground intel, trust, and distribution of the Catholic church and other faith leaders, so that we all may rise together."

In its first edition, the program adopted an accelerator model. Selected applicants received $100,000 in seed funding in exchange for a 6 to 8 percent equity investment and eight-week expert mentorship. The peak was the first-ever Silicon Valley–style demo day in Vatican City in late 2017, which generated extended press and social media coverage—beyond what the Vatican was expecting.

Abandoning equity investments, the Laudato sì Challenge dropped the accelerator model in 2018 and switched to a "commitment model," consisting of a call for interest and an invite-only networking event in Rome. During the event, startups, corporations, and government agencies pledged to pursue philanthropic investments within their reach.

"I respect VCs, but as soon as you accept money from them you are committing to a liquidity event," said Harr, "But we are building this program with an organization [the Catholic Church] whose timeline is eternity; that's why we moved into the venture philanthropy model."

This program seeks to:

- Inspire: Set the example and drive commitment to act.
- Facilitate connections: Bring together players that are not used to collaborating and make it possible to use faith institutions' networks for impactful causes.

Endeavor, Seedstars, Unreasonable, Village Capital

With a type of mission pioneered by Endeavor in 1997, many entrepreneur-led philanthropic startup programs and impact funds appeared in the vestiges of the Great Recession: Village Capital in 2009, Unreasonable in 2010, Seedstars in 2012, among the most prominent. They employ program models spacing throughout the range—from pre-accelerators, challenges, and competitions to accelerators, expansion programs, and venture funds.

The level of commitment they successfully extract from the supported entrepreneurs is commendable. For example, Unreasonable alumni willingly donated equity back to the organization after completing the program. Village Capital spearheaded an investment model in which the decision makers are the peers in the same cohort.[12] All of them can count on a highly involved and connected alumni network. Initially focused on emerging economies, some organizations are now creating alliances with corporations and governments to address diversity, inclusion, and underserved social segments in more developed countries.

At different levels and each with its peculiarities, these programs perform all the functions mentioned in the previous section, namely:

- External signaling: call for applications.
- Inspire: mentors and creating success cases in pristine ecosystems.
- Educate: entrepreneurial training and mentorship.
- Facilitate connections: inside the local ecosystem and also across different ecosystems.
- Remove roadblocks: provide office in dedicated coworking spaces and provide capital at friendly valuations and investment terms.

Hacks for Good and Reciprocal Education

Most of the programs reviewed in the previous section have long-term goals and require alignment and commitment from participants after graduation to achieve an impact. Some types of impact-driven programs can deliver a return during the program itself, such as hacks for good and programs based on reciprocal education, involving all types of players, as shown in Figure 6.5.

The term "hack for good" literally describes the act of using hacker skills for a good cause. As an extension, it indicates startup programs that involve entrepreneurs and startups to solve tough challenges with a high impact on society. XPRIZE is an example of a challenge format used to this end.

The second type of in-program results is reciprocal education programs, when both sides learn and teach simultaneously. Google pursued this kind of educational program in at least two initiatives:

- **Google.org Fellowship.**[13] Google employees spend up to six months with nonprofit grantees working in education, criminal justice, or economic opportunity. They use their skills to help grantees solve some of their toughest technical challenges. In 2019, Google spent approximately 50,000 hours in pro bono work.
- **Google for Startups Fellowship.**[14] Partnering with Atlas and American Underground, transitioning military veterans enroll for a three-month immersive experience at one of the startups in the Google for Startups Partner Network, a set of company-sponsored accelerators worldwide.

In programs like these, startups profit from new full-time team members at no cost and learn from them. Staff members of large organizations or the military bring industry knowledge or skill sets out of startup hires' average reach. From the startups, they receive back a culture conducive to innovation.

Shared Features

The formats and models used by impact-driven programs vary widely, but they share some characteristics.

Online Resources

Technology platforms are incredible enablers for these programs. "After a few iterations, we understood that all good content is already online," explained Terry Rock, president and CEO of Platform Calgary. Junction, the platform's nine-week residency program for early-stage startups, employs recorded content from Steve Blank (Stanford University) and other sources that it curates for founders.

Such content, however, does not substitute for peer-to-peer learning, says Rock's colleague David Yiptong, Platform Calgary's director of programs. The rigor of one-on-one work with mentors helps participants prioritize and focus on business activities to establish a 12- to 18-month growth road map. So, Junction replicates an accelerator's batch style to make people feel more united as a group.

Y Combinator (YC) also created a fully online, free course—YC Startup School—in 2017 that has impacted over 140,000 founders worldwide. About 45 percent of startups selected for the YC accelerator in 2020 came from YC Startup School, reinforcing YC's commitment to the school for its valuable deal flow.

Since its beginning, Startup School evolved from individual classes every eight weeks to continuous rolling enrollment classes. Its scalability, beyond the recorded videos, is provided by peer-to-peer advice groups. YC is still experimenting, and the program changes a bit every year.

Focus on Education and Networks

Entrepreneurial education, including that for the scale-up and growth phase, and a vast network of external supporters, mentors, advisors, and alumni are standard features in these programs. Adopting a not-for-profit juridical status helps these organizations to create exceptional networks.

Soft Metrics

> *Fundamentally, the government agency and three corporations, our financiers, wish to bring the new educational and economic trends to our region. They did not give us any KPIs, but they monitor what we do: if we get press, attract foreign mentors, and create new businesses.*
>
> —Vlad Gliga, Rubik Hub

For transformational impact programs, hard-financial success metrics are often out of scope. They must rely on softer measures, such as the level of engagement of participants and stakeholders (e.g., participants in events or courses), or leverage intermediated success metrics regarding the supported startups, such as growth metrics. A popular metric for these programs is the number of people impacted (usually estimated through the number of customers of the supported startups).

Beyond the specific metric set used by impact-driven programs, tracking their post-graduation metrics is even more fundamental than for other programs. Many rely on the relational ties built with participants during the activation stage for the tracking, but these ties can weaken if the program leader changes. Thus, these programs should always plan a system of incentives, such as access to alumni services, to encourage the founders to share vital data for program metrics.

Stories of Individual Progress

A distinction from programs with other objectives is that personal progress stories may count more than aggregated startup metrics. Programs that accelerate human capital must measure success at the level of individuals: their career developments, the role they take in an entrepreneurial ecosystem (e.g., as facilitators or investors), or the other startups they go on to found after the one supported. Especially for programs in the idea-team stage or the pre-seed stage, these stories (and associated metrics) might be even more significant than startup-related metrics.

When It Breaks: Sustainability

The Achilles' heel of these models is financial sustainability. As noted, impact-driven programs frequently rely on donations, sponsorships, or public funding. This dependency may make their economic sustainability more precarious than that of corporate programs. However, since self-sustainability would guarantee continuity in the mission, many organizations strive for it.

Organizations activate a mix of financial resources to reach self-sustainability. They may complement their main activity with ad hoc startup programs in collaboration with corporations, as a comanagement or consultant role, or use equity instruments to acquire monetization options.

For instance, Endeavor created an impact fund named Catalyst in 2012 with three goals: not just to support Endeavor entrepreneurs and provide a return to investors, but also to make Endeavor financially self-sustaining. At the end of 2020, Endeavor Catalyst had returned approximately $800,000 to Endeavor Local Offices and Endeavor projects to help achieve the goal of self-sustainability by 2030.

KEY TAKEAWAYS

- **Alignment around a mission.** This last group of startup programs leverages the long-term commitment to a cause (personal or societal) that some entrepreneurs might have, to impact the economy, society, or environment. The program instills a positive transformation (e.g., personal or business growth) in the startups to increase their impact potential. This is typically accomplished via education, networking, and grants.
- **Entrepreneurship as a means of transformation.** Governments and nonprofits view entrepreneurship as a potential source of self-empowerment and job creation. Evidence is on their side, suggesting that young firms are the most substantial contributors to new jobs. And, once adjusted for survival, startup champions remain the major gross job contributors. Startups are also seen as sources of innovative solutions for global challenges, such as the 17 Sustainable Development Goals set by the United Nations.
- **Select for commitment.** The startup's commitment to stay on course with its vision and mission is a precondition for the program's impact. For example, if a government program supports local entrepreneurs, it assumes they will drive local economic development—not leave for Silicon Valley. Thus, the startups' long-term motivations need to be carefully assessed in the selection process.

- **Donations or complementary funding.** Often lacking any possible revenue stream from participants (who, being the recipients of such measures, don't usually pay either in fees or equity), these startup programs must rely heavily on their sponsors. To soften this situation, they use scalable online resources (e.g., prerecorded courses) or they get associated with other for-profit programs, such as impact investment funds.

PART TWO

CREATING YOUR OWN STARTUP PROGRAM

7 DESIGN YOUR PROGRAM

Curious people break things to understand how they work and put them back together—chefs, comedians, computer hackers, and designers challenge the assumptions about how things were made by others and strive to improve them. This second part of the book provides tools to understand, modify, and, ultimately, create a program template or model. Part One reviewed several examples implementing four specific scenarios that require complex startup programs. Those models were mainly for accelerators and incubators, portraying a vast spectrum of solutions for investing, innovation sourcing, ecosystem building, and transformational impact. Part One helps you start with the end in mind.

Part Two gets your hands dirty in building a configuration of parameters that fits your needs and goals. Frequently, good design is key to successful execution. If, before opening this book, it may have appeared safe to pick a tested model and execute to the best of your ability, the earlier chapters should have clarified how risky that option can be. A model, even when proven, needs to be fitted to your context. Three contextual forces impose requirements on a program's parameters: your organization, the program's objectives (the initiator's or yours), and the target startups' characteristics. Your task as a designer is to ensure that the template you use stands at the point of equilibrium, or the ikigai (Figure 7.1).

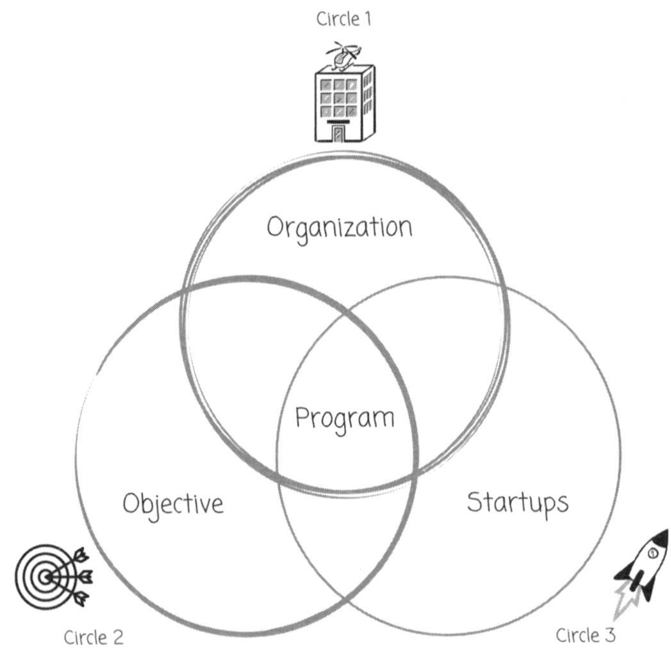

FIGURE 7.1 The designer's task is to balance the program at the Intersection of the organization's assets, program's objectives, and target startups.

How It Starts

> *Why are you doing an accelerator? Some do it to give back; others think it's a good strategy to be an investor without money. What assets do you have? A booming industry, talent, government support, local ecosystem. What result do you want to achieve with this particular program? And from these three answers, decide what you need like mentors, and education, etc.*
>
> —Marius Ursache, Metabeta

Why should you design and implement a startup engagement program? We covered that in Part One. Either you, your boss, or your client have decided it is time to renovate a startup engagement process or create one anew. You and your stakeholders have elected to work with startups, possibly in parallel to other alternatives, such as internal R&D or different suppliers (Chapters 16 and 17 will revisit this point); or it might be your only innovation action. You have opted to go beyond one-off collaborations—and while you can keep the door open to exceptions deserving of a tailored approach, you feel the need for a more standardized startup engagement process. You have a baseline: a history, some internal processes, a given team, and some experience. It is now time to formulate the blueprint based on where you already stand.

You may simply copy your peers and replicate their programs—for instance, an accelerator. But every model is filled with assumptions and ambiguity. "Accelerator," for example, is a term loaded with all different types of objectives, startup targets, and organizational context. Not all "accelerators" are startup programs, either. The term may also indicate an internal accelerator where the "startups" are all full-time employees. Even though many of the design implications and educational curricula are similar, engaging with internal innovators changes everything (internal partners are rarely as entrepreneurial as external ones).

An alternative to consciously or unconsciously jumping directly to an archetype model like a generic accelerator, CVC, or venture studio is to design a new program or adapt templates based on your context. Specifically, you may be facing one of the following situations. You are:

1. Starting with a similar context
2. Starting with the model (or a preexisting program)
3. Starting with the objectives
4. Starting with the recipients
5. Starting from chaos
6. Starting with a blank page

Starting with a Similar Context

You have identified a startup program that runs in an identical or very similar context to your own, and you intend to copy it. Government agencies around the world have indeed copied

Start-Up Chile almost down to the letter. Technology corporations have copied Microsoft or Google accelerators, just as angel investors have copied YC or AngelPad and community leaders have copied Techstars Startup Weekend or Junction.

If your Circles 1, 2, and 3 match those of the model you are copying, this strategy is safe. If you are copying YC and have access to a comparable network of mentors, have as strong a brand, have the same or superior backing of follow-on investors, foreground financial goals, focus on tech, and so on, then go ahead. Since YC tested the model in your same context and proved it works, it is just a question of execution.

But wait a minute. You need to ask: Do you have comparable assets and goals to YC? The first thing that happens when you don't is that startups (Circle 3) will not flock to you as they do to YC. In general, when you copy the Intersection but one of your Circles is different (in this example, Circle 1, that is, your assets are not the same as YC), then at least one other Circle slips out of control (in this example, Circle 3: you will attract different startups). Copying the Intersection when you don't have Circles that exactly match the original context will push your program out of balance, so to speak. If you don't make sure that Circles and Intersection are aligned, you will likely fail.

For more straightforward programs such as hackathons or challenges, the chance is that copying is safe. They fill negligible gaps in startup development, fit a nonselected audience, and their structure is simple to manipulate. That doesn't mean that running them is always a good idea, all things being equal, but copying them is bound to yield high fidelity and is less likely to throw you into a design tailspin.

For more complicated programs such as accelerators and incubators, instead, double-check the context before proceeding (Chapters 8–10).

Starting with the Model

> *The challenge is that clients often dictate the program design and come with a fixed mindset. This can make meeting the objectives tough or even mean the wrong objectives are sought.*
>
> —Charles Graham-Brown, Seedstars

You are already executing a model X, or your boss wants you to execute on a model X—where X could function as an accelerator, a venture fund, a hackathon, and so on.

If you are flexible about the model, you'll find yourself in good company. Many successful designs have resulted from taking an existing model and making targeted adjustments to adapt it to your specific context/requirements. The key here is to:

1. Stay flexible about the model and its parameters, taking into careful consideration the context that generated that particular configuration.
2. Study the fit of your context with the model's implicit assumptions and original context (Chapters 8–10).
3. Adapt the model just where the fit is missing (rest of Part Two).

Being rigid about the model is a bad start: Part One clarified that the model must be the ikigai inside three contextual elements. If possible, negotiate more room for change with your boss and stakeholders. If that fails, or if you are already irreversibly committed to a specific template, you can only optimize the structural and content features (Chapters 13–15). We understand this is often the scenario corporate programs are faced with, but we also must insist that it is a suboptimal position to find yourself in.

Starting with the Objectives

While starting from the objectives (Circle 2) may sound ideal, the caveats here lie in clarity and whether the internal environment (Circle 1) and external ecosystem (Circle 3) support the hidden preconditions implied by those objectives. Typically, the initiator is a senior executive with the clout to drive such an initiative, and their continued support is dependent on coming up with results they consider satisfactory, so when your boss mentions "an ambitious financial goal," does that mean a 3x return in 10 years (i.e., the performance of a good VC fund)? Or does it mean a revenue stream or cost cut in two years that positively impacts the group's P&L? And, in the latter instance, will your salesforce push the startup's solution enough?

Starting with an objective (Circle 2) heavily affects the choice of targets (Circle 3), especially for what concerns the maturity stage. For instance, if you aim to solve a technical problem, you will need startups with at least a testable prototype (i.e., more mature startups). On the other hand, if you intend to generate new ideas, you will want startups that are still flexible (i.e., at an earlier stage) or otherwise they'll just try to sell you. The maturity stage, in turn, has a domino effect on program content (Intersection): later-stage startups will want more customer feedback, integration, and commercial contracts and less entrepreneurial education or lean startup mentoring.

When the program's general objective is solution sourcing, it's critical to dissect the specific goal on a case-by-case basis with the problem owners (e.g., an internal client such as the engineering department or an external stakeholder such as a charity for the blind). You must engage problem owners to write a clear problem statement before you scout for startups, and, later, have those problem owners participate in every testing process and every selection gate. Without the problem owners, solution sourcing is bound to underdeliver or fail. After all, who is in a better position to determine if a solution is meeting their objectives?

Sometimes the objectives are simply too ambitious for your current baseline, and you will have to lay the groundwork using another program (such as an ideathon to generate ideas to be later accelerated), or with some ecosystem activities (such as fostering university entrepreneurial education or opening a coworking space to catalyze the local community). You can still read Part Two to devise the fertilization program (most likely a hackathon, bootcamp, startup competition, or similarly cheaper programs).

Starting with the Recipients

Your goal may be solving the participants' problems, not your own. Think of a government, university, or impact-driven organization fostering economic and social advancement—for example, for fresh graduates, PhD students, under-resourced entrepreneurs, social innovators, minorities, or people in poverty.

The objective is usually some transformation (cultural or of skill set) of a given group or demographic (Circle 3). You still need to assess the state of the reservoir, but the only outcome would be to tweak the content—not to change the target. The deliverable to the program's sponsors and supporters is improvement of the participants' business or career. Here, user-centered design is even more critical than in other cases. All of Part Two is relevant here, but you may focus on Chapters 13–15, as they will help you understand which program features (mentorship, training, the selection process) will have the most impact.

Starting from Chaos

Your organization has some ad hoc efforts for collaborating with startups in flight, but they are enclosed in silos, disorganized, unaligned, and not in sync. Results are lagging or unsatisfactory, internal politics are killing innovation, and the startup program manager is expected to end all this chaos with the next bulletproof initiative—the one that *cannot* fail.

Don't worry; you are in good company. This situation has been described to us on several occasions, in organizations large and small.

Every mess is different, and innovation governance at the organizational level is beyond the scope of this book. However, Chapters 16 and 17 will provide hints on how to frame a startup program within your other R&D and innovation activities, as well as on whether to hire an external company or use an internal team. You may want to read those chapters first and later apply Part Two to one initiative for a test run. Start small, gain early successes, win internal allies, and plan for more ambitious editions later on.

Starting with a Blank Page

Starting with a blank page is rare but possible in two subcases:

- **Independent founder.** You may want to invest in startups, grow a reputation in the community, or solve your corporate clients' specific innovation problems. In essence, you have an objective (Circle 2). You may also need to prepare a business case to find financiers (if you do not have a sponsor in Circle 1). The interesting stuff for you starts with Chapter 10 (read Chapters 8 and 9 last).
- **Entrepreneurial employee.** You may want (or be requested) to develop an idea of what to do with startups. It might be a dangerous situation: "Working with startups" should always be a means and not a goal; partnerships are sought and created for a purpose. You need to start from your organization's strategy and involve senior leadership from day one to identify an objective (start with Chapter 9).

In similar situations, it's natural to look for inspiration from other startup programs. That's fine, but remember to read other program designs through the lens of the three Circles. In successful programs, hardly any feature is left to chance. Part Two will help you avoid the most insidious pitfalls.

Your Task

> *When we started Pilot, I went to all VCs and said we were running an anti-accelerator; no mentorship, no investment, no demo day. Just a pilot, because that's what startups and enterprises really want.*
>
> —Chris Kay, CEO of Multiplicity

When you design a startup program, your task is to create a platform for startups that dovetails their development and your organization's goals. You must identify a *value exchange proposition* whereby the *offer* flows to startups and they can agree on an acceptable *ask*, that is, the terms and conditions set to capture value for your organization. A fair exchange is one in which simultaneously the participants' assets (technology, talent, etc.) serve the organization, and the organization's ready and unique assets (networks, capital, etc.) assist the startups' development (Figure 7.2).

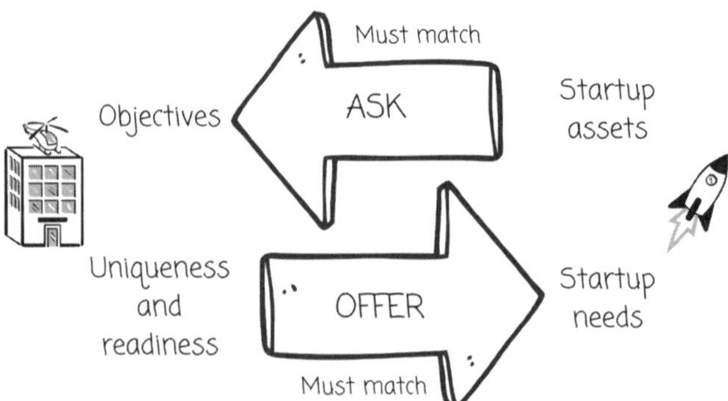

FIGURE 7.2 You need to create a simultaneous match between the startups' needs and organization's unique and ready support, and between the program's objectives and startups' assets.

To accomplish this task, you will have to identify a suitable configuration of features, including:

- **Content:** funding, mentors, training, community activities, etc.
- **Structure:** duration, location, intake process, schedule, selection gates, etc.
- **Terms and conditions:** equity, revenue sharing, relocation, exclusivity, etc.
- **Managerial aspects:** program team, metrics, governance, etc.

The context analysis of the three Circles will provide the requirements for that configuration, but you need to discover them (Figure 7.3).

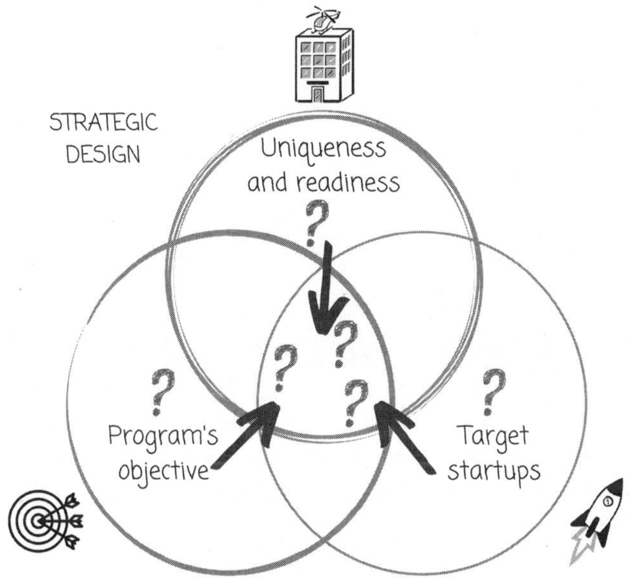

FIGURE 7.3 All three Circles provide explicit requirements for the program, but you need to discover them.

> *After discovering what our ecosystem missed, I asked people who had done it. I would not say we were innovating; we were just adapting great products to our local needs. Techstars was a reference for the early stage, YC for the later stage, especially for our educational programs.*
>
> —Vlad Gliga, Rubik Hub

You can start from an inspirational template or, much more rarely, from a blank page (Figure 7.4). Everyone copies in this industry. And while copying is acceptable, doing so without intent is a mistake. After choosing one or more templates (for adaptation/hybridization), you must test and refine the initial parameters until you are confident the configuration works in your context.

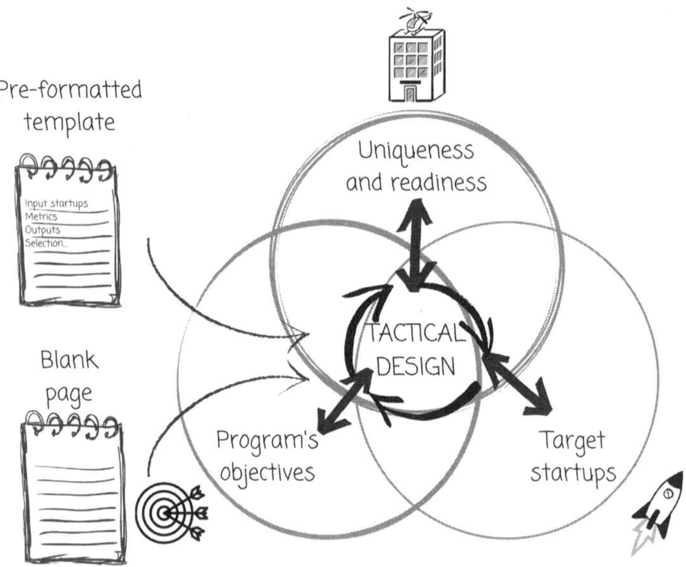

FIGURE 7.4 You can start from a program template or a blank page, but you have to iterate the configuration until you reach a match with all three Circles.

Mind Value Creation and Value Capture

The context analysis should focus on how value can be created and captured for both sides. The program's function as a platform is to smooth the dysfunctions in value exchange depicted in Figure 7.2.

On the startups' side (Circle 3), value capture is seldom the problem. Typically, startups act opportunistically and grab as much as possible—if they perceive the value, of course. A workshop might go deserted if the topic has become common knowledge (e.g., just another business model canvas workshop), or funds might stay unutilized if they are overloaded with bureaucracy—but generally founders use the resources offered. Of course, not all startups can create the same value for the organization. But the organization can gather a good mix of participants with different potentials and skills through targeted signaling and a balanced selection process—together with some wild cards.

The situation is generally reversed on the organization's side (Circle 1): it's more challenge to capture value for internal stakeholders than to create value for the participating startup. Value capture, as noted in Chapter 2, often occurs outside the program, and so beyond the program team's reach. Organizations need to ask the following questions: What happens to the ideas created in the new hackathon? Who will take care of extracting value from a pilot? Who will sit on the startup's board to guide it toward a fruitful exit in future years?

On the internal value creation side, the issues stem from unready processes, uncoordinated departments, internal rivalry, and politics. The program's task is to remove these roadblocks or simply assess what is possible and guarantee an honest service level to the startups.

Have a Vision for Future Editions

During context analysis, you may realize that a problem exists:

- **Unready organization** (Circle 1 is broken). The organization will not be able to deliver what it wishes to. Possible reasons: insufficient leadership endorsement, untrained program team, lack of a general culture of open innovation, bureaucracy, silos, or turf wars.
- **Overambitious expectations** (Circle 2 is broken). Given your baseline, the program will unlikely attain the set objectives and metrics in the desired time horizon. Possible reasons: fierce external competition (e.g., YC or local competitors), fierce internal competition (e.g., politics, budget wars, or turf wars), or inexperience in working with startups.
- **Dry reservoir** (Circle 3 is broken). The startup community of reference (i.e., the *reservoir*) cannot produce enough quality deal flow. Possible reasons: immature entrepreneurial ecosystem, insufficient referral network, or weak industry.

In mathematical terms, this would be called an over-constrained design problem, meaning that the context is not fertile for any startup program, no matter the design (Figure 7.5).

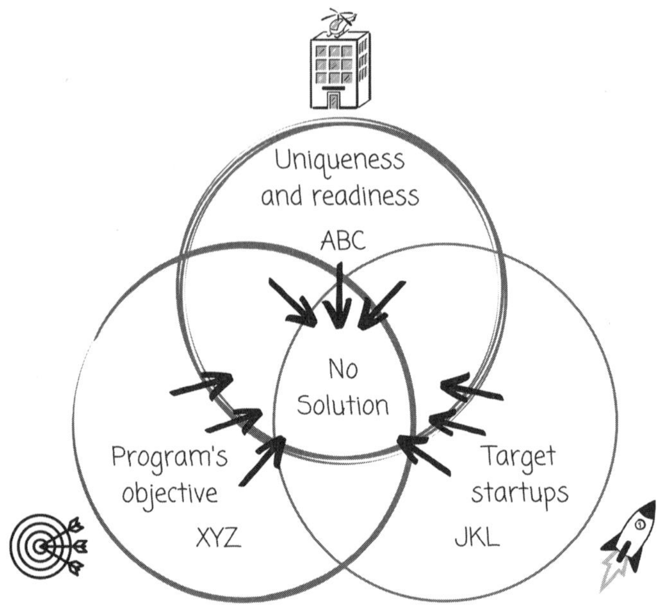

FIGURE 7.5 The requirements coming from the three Circles may over-constrain the design problem to the point that no program can satisfy them all.

By envisioning a continuation of the program through several editions (or years), you might develop an intermediary plan to first *fertilize* before proceeding with the original plan. For example, if you intended to open a vertical accelerator on blockchain technology in your state but have found there is not enough deal flow, your option is to freeze that intention, focus on deal flow generation activities (e.g., a series of hackathons on blockchain coding), and postpone the accelerator by one or two years.

The initial steps of a new incubator, accelerator, or venture fund might be better made, in fact, through more manageable programs such as hackathons, challenges, or startup competitions. Their lower complexity, lower budget, and shorter cycle time (from call to graduation) allow for quick iteration and learning for the organization or the program team.

In his book *The Startup Way*, creator of Lean Startup methodology Eric Ries illustrates how he and his colleagues applied agile, adaptive, and experimental methodologies to introduce entrepreneurial practices in institutions as large as the US Department of Health and Human Services or General Electric.[1] Ries advocates for a start-small approach in the initial phase to build a critical mass of internal supporters and champions in cross-functional teams and to involve senior leadership before scaling up to include the entire organization.

Startup programs should plan a similarly gradual approach, especially those pursuing post-graduation partnering, when metrics materialize outside the program's duration. Many such programs hand over the startups to execution business units or other downstream programs (for example, when corporate accelerators filter deal flow for their corporate venture fund). They also depend on external partners, investors, and referral networks for higher-quality deal flow (inputs) and more post-graduation opportunities for the startups. If you have more detractors than allies, focus first on turning foes into friends, and competitors into partners. Innovation thrives in collaborative environments.

From edition to edition, the program could grow internal buy-in, fine-tune processes, achieve standardization, accrue external recognition and partners, and improve the overall quality of deal flow. Any improvement to the program itself will ultimately benefit its stakeholders as well.

For example, the following looks at an ex post reconstruction of what a three-year look-ahead for TechPeaks would have been. The strategic objective was to create or attract 100 startups to the Italian Alps region. Table 7.1 shows the tactical goals that the TechPeaks team set for 2013 and 2014. For 2015, instead, it shows the plan even though the accelerator closed before its full actuation.

What Changes with Less Complexity

Part Two has accelerator and incubator design in mind. But designing a hackathon or a challenge is not as complicated as creating an accelerator or an incubator. While everything about

TABLE 7.1 Ex post reconstruction of multiyear evolution of TechPeaks design

	2013	2014	2015	Notes
Internal buy-in	Gain senior leadership support—both internal and of delivery partner.	Reinforce senior leadership support. Research units from local universities to provide technology and ideas.	Governmental department for innovation.	Internal senior leadership was aligned, whereas political turf wars required more work than expected with local delivery partners and senior leadership (government, university).
Process readiness / standardization	Legal docs (NDA, grant legislation, grant agreement), visa sponsorship, lodging, and office space infrastructure	New lodging and office space infrastructure (failed tactical objective in 2013), a new process for grant approvals	Long-term incubation process (up to 18 months) to increase retention	In 2014, the team overcame delays due to bad planning in 2013: in second year all processes were already standardized.
External partner network	Investor network of 50+ angels and accelerators	Local network of 20+ established businesses	Regional network of 100+ established businesses	External partnerships started with national and global entrepreneurial ecosystems to fuel deal flow. The team pivoted focus during 2014 toward local partners, in line with the retention value creation mechanism.
Deal flow quality / reach	Minimum 5 partner accelerators that would provide their immature deal flow (but mature enough for TechPeaks)	Intensify partnership with best sources, extend international reach	Intensify partnerships in verticals of interest for the region: digital tourism, smart city, foodtech	Initial partner network of 7 accelerators, including Founder Institute and six others in Southeastern Europe, was precious for deal flow

(continued)

TABLE 7.1 Ex post reconstruction of multiyear evolution of TechPeaks design (continued)

	2013	2014	2015	Notes
Output	New teams, traction, and pitch (growth)—showcase in a classic investor demo day	New teams, traction, and pitch (growth)—showcase in a closed-door investor demo day	Relocation, business is done locally or local hires	Mistake in 2013 in using a growth output when the program was using a value creation mechanism based on retention. Kept in 2014 to avoid a total pivot on brand. Pivot on output done in 2015.
Positive ecosystem effects	Share of voice, impressions, press coverage. Narratives / success stories to establish reputation and attract deal flow	Same as the previous year, plus local hacker community and researchers using the accelerator as a basis of operations	Same as previous year, to be intensified	
Outcome	At least 20% startups raising seed funding	At least 25% startups relocating locally for the next 12 months (program assigned special resources to incentivize retention)	At least 75% startups relocating locally for 12 to 18 months (program assigned special resources to incentivize retention)	Again, a mistake in 2013 in betting hard on startup growth to establish a reputation at the expense of retention. Corrected partially in 2014, and fully in 2015.

the context (Circles) will also apply to hackathons or challenges, we recognize that on the configuration side, these simpler programs entail:

- **Easier copying.** If you decide that a hackathon or challenge fits your Circles after context analysis, copying is viable.
- **Less costly mistakes.** One edition is short and inexpensive compared to other formats, so iterating and correcting the course is less expensive.
- **Less content.** The design parameter space is minimal: hackathons are a tiny container (two days versus several months), and challenges do not have content save for the prize.
- **Easier structure.** Challenges have an almost immutable composition (a call and a gate), while hackathons can be a bit more challenging to plan.
- **Less political encumbrance.** Hackathons or challenges might slip easily under the political radar. Their lower budgets and limited intrusiveness in organizational processes make them ideal for testing the water, learning, and preparing for more activities.

Big design mistakes in hackathons or challenges may have less severe consequences than in accelerators or incubators, but designing with purpose remains critical. Even though these models might not solve all the needs of organization-startup collaborations, intelligent expedients can still dramatically improve their results.

Iterative Design Process in Startup Programs

Startup program strategy can be locked into a long-term view. Once the three Circles are defined and the context within the organization is known, the strategy and the place within the ecosystem does not change much from cohort to cohort.

Startup program *design* however is never done. It is instead an iterative process—for each new edition the designer learns from what worked and what didn't in the past, and adjusts the offer, ask, structure, and managerial features to maximize the value for all parties involved. One of our most in depth case studies, with more than 10 cohorts and 20 unique programs is still asking for feedback, making changes, and learning—even in the middle of cohorts.

This concept of iterative design process is also applicable to iterating over a system of programs (as discussed in Chapter 16), with an extension: in systems of programs, iterative design concerns not just the individual programs but also the synergic interactions between them.

This iterative process makes sense for startup programs for many reasons. A startup program is a connector of multiple dynamic systems, internal and external. As the conditions, goals, needs, maturity, and accessibility of the organizational ecosystem (internal) and entrepreneurial ecosystem (external) change and evolve, so must the program strategy (and a startup program system, by extension). Also when at the strategy level all the Circles fit together on paper, those strategic choices are just hypotheses that need to be tested—just because you identify the right startup segment does not guarantee they will apply! New program teams almost certainly have an imperfect understanding of their surrounding ecosystems when they start, and consequently they undergo a learning curve through trials and errors. The TechPeaks case study (Chapter 2) provides an example (see the Notes column in Table 7.1).

The good news is that there are now a few ways to check the theory with the Strategy Canvas and even ways to test the actual assumptions. One of them is by doing pretests and smaller experiments. You can test Circle 3 with a challenge, hackathon, or even a social media contest—and you can even test Circle 1 with internal events and innovation workshops. Minor startup programs can be means to prepare the stage for an accelerator or incubator.

Likewise you can use edition 1 to test feature assumptions for edition 2—as long as you have the right investors/sponsors, just like with digital startups. Some founders get a big budget and trust to experiment upfront, others need to show traction and market justification early on. It is up to you to know your sponsors as well as your customers.

Iterative design is not exclusive to startup programs. It is actually the norm across many other situations characterized by unknowns, uncertainty, and dynamic environments. Innovative startups are themselves the beacons of iterative design. The very essence of the Lean Startup movement is exactly to ship an imperfect product as early as possible to observe how customers use it, learn what works, and then repeat based on real customer needs and validated learning. Airbnb had the quintessential minimum viable product[2] story when the two founders rented out an airbed in their loft-space in San Francisco in a matter of hours. The website was pieced together, launched, and tested with customers as quickly as possible. Later it was iterated based on learning from real users. Even restaurants, comedians, and authors use an iterative approach. Testing things with small versions, limited menus, open mic nights and first drafts—seeing what works, making changes, and so on.

Some tips specific to startup program design iteration:

- Features are easy to change from edition to edition—they are harder within the same edition. Plan carefully and explicitly which features you want to test in each edition.
- Agile management mid-edition is just good and sensible management: solve mentor mismatch, add a workshop on a missing topic, or cancel an investor meeting if a startup is not ready.
- Usually you cannot change impactful parameters such as structure (e.g., duration, location, or selection) or managerial features (e.g., governance) until the next edition (save for extreme examples like during Covid-19).
- Never run an entire edition just to test a feature—instead use the Startup Program Strategy Canvas to make sure that the pieces fit together, and if you need to test something in real life, you can pretest with a simpler program (e.g., a bootcamp, a hackathon, or a challenge).

Part Two will discuss only one design cycle, but that doesn't imply that we don't recognize the need for iteration—we're assuming that you will iterate later.

The Don'ts of Designing a Startup Program

Here are some red flags before you begin.

Don't Rush into Execution Before Defining the Context

Goal-driven design helps you avoid building the right program to serve the wrong need. Understand the context before you start. "But this is never what happens," said Lesa Mitchell, managing director of Techstars. "What happens is that the corporation signs a deadline that they want to do an accelerator—and there we go, open an application." Her advice is to do more prework, such as interviewing people, building a financial model, understanding who's on board, and how the program will deliver value to the organization before you even announce the program.

Don't Compete Directly Against Top-Tier Programs Without a Strategy

Avoid operating in a winner-take-all market unless you are disrupting that market. Take accelerators, for instance. Top-tier programs attract the best deal flow from all over the world, and for other generalist equity-based accelerators, it's hard to become profitable from exits. Sure, even the top-tier accelerators' business can be disrupted, but if you are playing by their rules without having access to their deal flow, it's a lost cause. Leverage your organization's uniqueness to differentiate the offer and attract talent that is laser-focused on your niche.

Don't Overlook the Follow-on Stage

If you have a post-graduation objective or you feel at risk of facing the incentives evaporation issue, focus your design effort on the follow-on stage. Remember the principle of "start with the end in mind"—look first at how you will capture value. Unless your objectives are limited to trend discovery, impact-driven education, talent hiring, or reputation, the post-graduation is when your KPIs will materialize. Make sure you have your nets in place to catch the fish when it comes.

Don't Add Features That Don't Aid Your Objectives

Features like demo days or equity requirements have a precise role in the context of for-profit accelerators. But they aren't their secret sauce. They aren't just "the language of startups." You may *not* need them in your program. Each feature that you insert should be functional to your objectives. Don't copy blindly.

Don't Conceive the Program as If It Was in a Vacuum

Planning your startup program in isolation from others, inside and outside your organization, may unconsciously create frictions and even damage the program. Think in systems. Connect the program with other initiatives, look for synergies and gaps in the ecosystem, and anchor on them.

Don't Let the Program Become the Solution

Whatever your objectives, the program is never the solution. The solution is the impact generated by the program on the startups and your organization. The program's task is to fill in the gaps to obtain that impact. You must plug the program's output into your organization's or your ecosystem's innovation strategy. Never let the program per se become the solution, or you will be slipping into "innovation theater."[3]

KEY TAKEAWAYS

- **Design is key in more complex programs.** For more straightforward programs such as hackathons or challenges, copying from an existing model is generally safe. They fill small gaps in startup development, they fit a nonselected audience, and their structure is simple to manipulate. For more complicated programs such as accelerators and incubators, double-check the context of the model and make sure it is close to yours before proceeding.
- **Program model iteration is normal.** The development and growth of startup programs are rarely linear. They go through an evolution where the first or second editions make many mistakes and may appear to be a big waste of money. In a sense, that is the cost of learning and growing the internal infrastructure. Just like startups, the journey of startup programs looks more like a scribble than a straight line.
- **Play a game you can win.** Avoid operating in a winner-take-all market unless you are disrupting that market. Top-tier accelerator programs, for instance, attract the best

deal flow from all over the world, making it hard for other organizations to compete. Instead, focus on leveraging your organization's uniqueness to differentiate the offer and attract talent that is laser-focused on your niche.

- **Focus on how to capture value.** Remember the principle of "start with the end in mind." Look first at how you will capture value. Unless your objectives are limited to trend discovery, impact-driven education, talent hiring, or reputation, the post-graduation is when your key performance indicators will materialize. Make sure you have your nets in place to catch the fish when it comes.
- **Innovation theater happens when you don't think in systems.** Whatever your objectives, the program is never the solution. The solution is the impact generated by the program on the startups and your organization. You must plug the program's output into your organization's or your ecosystem's innovation strategy. Never let the program per se become the solution, or you will be slipping into "innovation theater."

CIRCLE 1: UNIQUENESS AND READINESS

Every organization is unique. The people, culture, industry, networks, processes, resources, and assets make every organization different from every other organization—even its peers.

Your organization can leverage its uniqueness to engage with startups in a meaningful way. Startups might have more opportunities today than ever before. Still, most will not turn down a unique deal based on what only your organization can offer to their innovation or entrepreneurial ecosystem.

> *To thine own self be true.*
>
> —William Shakespeare

But are you "startup-ready"? Do you have the processes in place to handle a startup collaboration or investment? Do you have enough internal support? Will you risk prior relationships with your suppliers to switch to a new partner that might go bankrupt tomorrow? Just because you have those unique assets doesn't necessarily mean they are on the table and available for startups to use.

Most importantly, can you integrate value back into the organization? Can you really handle a startup collaboration?

Designing the program to operate is half the battle. It's an important half, but half, nonetheless.

This chapter looks at Circle 1 and how it can influence the other two Circles and the program (Figure 8.1). It will address four challenges:

1. How to achieve internal buy-in and alliances (either internal to the organization, or internal to the surrounding ecosystem—with partners other than startups)
2. How to make *your organization itself* a value proposition for startups by identifying the internal features that distinguish you from every other organization
3. How to prioritize the features for the incoming program and determine what features can be delayed, based on the manageable complexity
4. How to identify all the corollary boundaries imposed by your context on the design dimensions (location, duration, etc.)

All of the previous considerations follow the analysis of how much the program's value proposition and operations will be dependent on the organization, its internal units, and its external institutional partners.

There will be many connections to the other two circles. As noted in Chapter 7, this is an iterative process that we unbundle here just for the sake of exposition.

Can the Startup Program Create and Capture Value Alone?

> *The hard thing is how the corporation will adapt to work with startups: they have so many things going on, this is just one more project. Instead, for startups, this is a big opportunity; they work faster and invest a lot.*
>
> —Jose Deustua, UTEC Ventures

Often, startup programs are just one more project for a large organization. They usually sit at the intersection of core and new

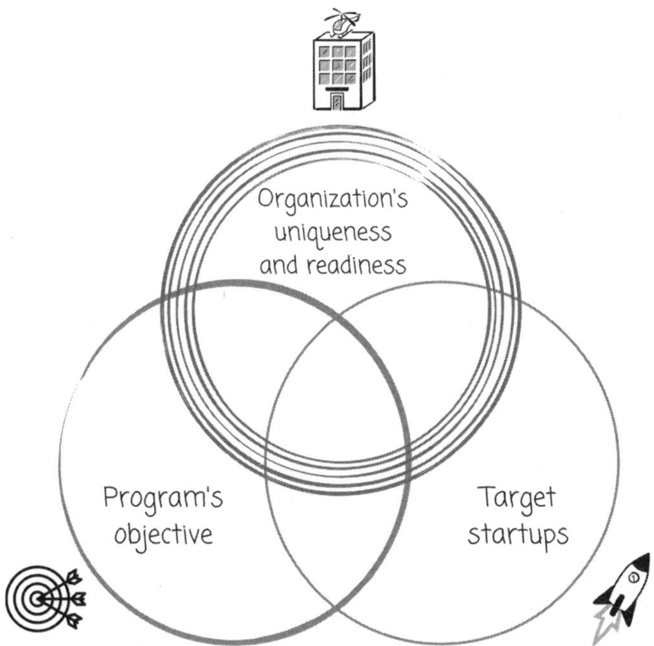

FIGURE 8.1 This chapter is about Circle 1, the organization's uniqueness and readiness.

business, or even outside the core. The rest of the organization continues on with its daily priorities as the program team takes care of engaging with external innovators.

Like any organ of a larger organism, the program is (or should be) in a symbiotic relationship with its parent company and its ecosystem. It can catalyze the opportunities created by startups, but it often depends on other units or partners for aspects of its value proposition or sustainability. And if the program does not deliver on its promises, it is the startups that pay the highest price. The cost of failure for the core business might be so negligible (in a short-termist vision) that the other units may not feel the urge to deliver their part. That attitude may just decree failure for the program and a net loss for the startups (of time, at the least). Ultimately, even though the cost of failure in the short term is high for startups, over the long term it can alter the entire ability of the parent organization to attract the right startups.

How can you avoid falling into such a vicious cycle? Each new program needs to understand how deep that symbiosis must be. Can the startup program create and capture value alone, or will it depend heavily on others? The answer sits at the overlap of what your organization is and how it operates (Circle 1), and the program's objectives as set by its initiator or manager (Circle 2).

Independent Value Creation

Securing the resources you need (budget, office, etc.) may not be enough to separate your value proposition. CVC funds, for example, often rely on the parent company for added value to compete for deals with financial VC funds, even when they are separate legal entities operating on a precommitted fund.

In truth, brand association with the parent organization is sometimes one of the central values a corporate or government program can provide to startups. Some other features inherently involve internal collaborations, such as access to customers or internal labs (see Challenge #2 later in this chapter).

Features that could be independent of your organizational sponsor and other internal allies are training, mentorship, and funding. In some cases, they might be sufficient to drive traction in the external entrepreneurial ecosystem and build a trusted network of external partners.

However, as in the cited example of CVCs, that also means your program is competing head-to-head with its private alter egos without leveraging the exclusive benefits of being part of a larger organism.

Independent Value Capturing

Self-isolation can cripple value capturing even more. You might be able to plan independently of internal or external alliances *only if* your program pursues pre-graduation goals, as discussed in Chapter 2 (Figure 8.2).

For those goals, your output could be as simple as a survey or report. For instance, if your goals are trend analysis, press coverage, employee mindset, or validated use cases for your proprietary platform, the program can crunch a report detailing the demographics, technology, or advancements of participating

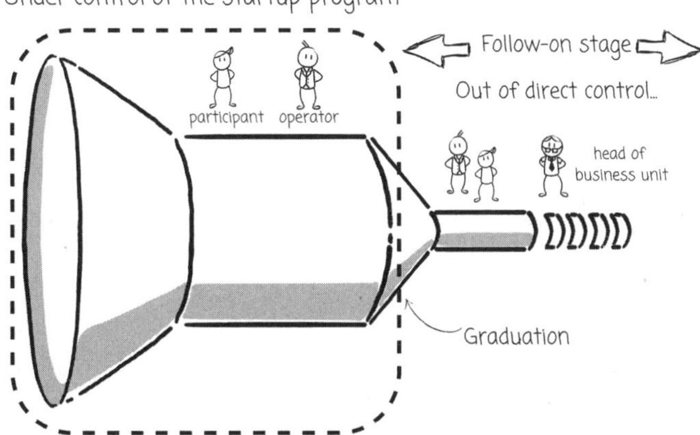

FIGURE 8.2 A program is independent in capturing value for pre-graduation objectives, during the recruitment or activation stage. Alliances become necessary when objectives and metrics are achieved after graduation.

startups, a report on media engagement, or a report on the improved innovation skills of internal employees.

If a report is an acceptable output in your context, to capture the value you simply need to create a process to collect that information. For instance, you may rely on the following:

- **Application form.** Include questions about the demographics. Use closed questions to classify the technology, state of development, or current funding of the startup population of your interest. Open questions might be inappropriate because they involve too much disclosure.
- **Participation tracking.** Counting the entrepreneurs or internal employees that show up, shake hands, learn, or build something together. Active participation can also be tracked and scored, as MBAs do.
- **Satisfaction tracking.** You could include NPS®[1] surveys or similar tools to measure participants' satisfaction in workshops, mentorship, and other program activities.
- **Progress tracking.** Tracking the startups' progress (milestones, metrics) can be easy while startups are in

> constant communication with the program team during the activation stage. However, progress tracking *after* graduation requires a careful design of incentives, tight alumni-program relationships, and a system of surveys, reports, and information collection.

If a report is insufficient, or if your goal requires a long-term partnership (Figure 8.2), then a robust internal or external partner network is usually the only way the program can achieve its metrics.

A commercial YC-style accelerator, for example, depends on the network of follow-on financial or industrial partners and investors for its business model. A venture client unit depends on the internal network of engaged business units and its ability to identify compelling use cases and innovation needs.

For objectives that cannot be delivered with a report, startup programs face similar problems as internal innovation and R&D: the scale-up or long-term adoption of a new product, service, technology, or business model must pass through the integration and handover of the project (in this case, a startup collaboration) to the execution business. And this phase is the hardest of all in most established organizations.[2] Yet without an infrastructure harvesting the results, a startup program will end up in innovation theater.

This problem also impacts ecosystem programs run by governments or corporations (Chapter 5)—but with a nuance. The question here is whether the ecosystem is healthy, easy to access, and receptive to new participants. Those preconditions will encourage startups to stay in the ecosystem even after the program ends. "Retention is a condition for ROI in ecosystem programs, but to achieve it, you need to check your services or the quality of your ecosystem, not force startups to stay directly," underlined Sebastián Díaz Mesa, former CEO of Start-Up Chile.

It takes an entire innovation pipeline to successfully scale up new products or services and a whole ecosystem strategy to shape a region into a startup hub. A program can be just a part of the solution, not the whole. You need internal support to capture the value the program will create. The more buy-in, the easier it will be to overcome unforeseen obstacles.

Change is complex, and its implementation conflicts with daily goals. Detractors are rarely incompetent, stupid, or contrarian; they simply abide by different rules—those of their job or role within the organization. For them, it's a tug-of-war between helping the program and helping themselves, without any sort of malice.

Challenge #1: Build Internal Alliances and Processes

The following paragraphs are a list of sources of internal support. Who can you convince? Have they accepted their role? How can you use the following sources to create the conditions to capture value? It usually takes more than one source of alignment to gain enough allies. Use the principle of starting small and growing as consensus grows discussed in the previous chapter.

Senior Leadership Buy-In

> *Top-level buy-in is crucial because if the CEO does not care, nobody cares.*
>
> —Alberto Onetti, Mind the Bridge

Accenture points to the CEO or managing director as the essential patron of startup engagement activities.[3] A startup program is among those initiatives that spend money and produce little cash flow for a comparatively long time, to the point that the rest of the organization is instinctively driven to starve its annual budget.[4] Senior leaders have the power to overwrite the natural short-termism of middle managers with longer-term strategic objectives. You can obtain senior leaders' involvement from day one through:

- **Investment committee.** Participation in selection or graduation boards.
- **Transparent reporting.** Regular data on progress can keep the pulse.
- **Direct sponsorship of a startup.** For example, in Stora Enso Accelerator, each startup is assigned an internal sponsor

chosen from top-level executives, sharing the responsibility for the collaboration's success.

Choose one of these options or devise your own method to obtain senior leadership support.

Champions

> *Finding internal champions supporting the program is key.*
>
> —Daniel Twal, ISDI Accelerator

Passion is necessary because managers take more risk in supporting a startup program and buying a startup product than in running the business as usual. As a corporate mantra goes, "No one ever got fired for buying IBM." Champions can help evangelize innovation inside the company and break the ice by example. Several corporations, such as Bayer,[5] organize internal programs to identify and multiply innovation champions. An anonymous government agency we interviewed has a coalition of volunteers responsible for bridging the gap between startups and problem owners.

Cocreation or Comanagement

Involving unit leaders and corporate functions early in a cocreation workshop or creating a comanagement governance (Chapter 11, Challenge #4) increases the sense of ownership and participation and helps prevent conflicts with existing procedures (Table 8.1).

For example, LG NOVA, the South Korean electronics colossus' innovation center in Silicon Valley, employs Entrepreneurs in Residence to orchestrate innovative solutions combining multiple partners, including internal units and startups. Another example: QVC NEXT™, a startup procurement program created in 2016 by retail sales television network QVC, initially encountered hostility from critical parts of the organization, especially buyers and legal. It took two years and a new cocreation process before the program could overcome internal resistance and take off.

TABLE 8.1 Different program objectives typically involve different internal stakeholders.

Unit Affected	Objectives	Example
Human Resources	Mindset shift (internal), talent hiring	Stora Enso Accelerator
Marketing and Communication	Brand positioning	TIM WCAP (2009–2014)
Corporate Development	Strategic investing	IBM Ventures
Business lines	Solution sourcing, innovation ecosystem building	Open Bosch
Ecosystem partners	Entrepreneurial ecosystem building	TechPeaks

Ambassadors or Points-of-Contact

> *We have created a cross-organizational team, like spiders in the web. These are knowledge and need bearers who operate from inside their units, through whom we can reach the whole company.*
>
> —Gabriele Molari, formerly Tetra Pak

To be pervasive and continuous in every relationship, an organization can activate stable points of contact or ambassadors between the innovation unit and other units. Enel, the Italian electric utility company, for instance, created a matrix structure around the innovation team. Each unit has an innovation manager reporting directly to the head of the innovation unit and the director of the business line.[6] The ownership of scouting and testing startup solutions is shared between the corporate innovation unit and geographical and vertical lines. A similar structure was reported in Seguros Bolívar[7] and Tetra Pak.

Internal Business Developers

Another tactic consists of dedicating a part of the program team to liaison with startups and internal units. For example, Robert Bosch Venture Capital has introduced the position of "implementation manager," an employee dedicated to originating new deals between portfolio startups and the parent organization.[8] Many government agencies are starting to implement a similar strategy.

Fertilize Corporate Innovators

> *To support corporations with startups, we have created an internal innovation program in which we engage the employees to generate ideas outside their expertise to create new business growth opportunities with our combined knowledge.*
>
> —Dan D'Souza, L Marks

If, at any stage of design, you judge internal alliances as inefficient or insufficient for capturing value, freeze Plan A momentarily and consider fertilizing first with simpler, stand-alone programs such as hackathons or challenges. Note the word *fertilizing*: you are running these smaller programs not simply as a placeholder or as a stalling technique but as a learning opportunity.

An increasingly popular way of building internal consensus is to create an entrepreneurial gym for employees to experience a startup venture firsthand, real or in vitro. Internal idea challenges or intrapreneurship programs use methods similar to those employed by startup programs and can be complementary sources of innovative ideas while at the same time educating internal staff about entrepreneurial needs, processes, and how entrepreneurs make decisions. Such programs can bridge the cultural gap and provide a proactive mindset for future collaborations with external startups.

Incentives and Rewards

> *It's not just program design that matters. It's the motivations of the participants. Getting the incentives right for corporate entrepreneurs is what has the highest impact.*
>
> —Franck Debane, CEO at Tango

Incentives and direct rewards on startup performance or program metrics can be difficult to introduce in corporations, and even more so in government. Most corporations with a CVC have failed to create an effective incentive system to encourage their employees to work with startups.[9] However, research by Mind the Bridge has shown that corporates that qualify as innovation leaders have an incentive system related to innovation objectives. Over a third of innovation leader companies extend innovation metrics to all employees.[10]

Advisory Board

A world-class advisory board can significantly aid a startup program. Beyond opening cross-organization partnerships, it provides credibility and a sense of direction, as well as helps prevent the program's premature death following a leadership change in the organization.

"Data and trusted partners are key to move fast, pivot, and protect the program. Start-Up Chile also formed an advisory board, mainly out of Stanford University. They helped us make better decisions but also backed the program, protecting it from political discussions," said Díaz Mesa.

Involvement Process

A dedicated process can help uncover innovation problems inside your organization or external partners (e.g., other corporations, or local small and medium enterprises) and convince directorates to work with you. The process may include an internal call for applications and an internal problem pitch with a selection committee or internal engagement managers that work with business units.

Many of the sources of internal alignment listed above, from senior leadership to stable points of contact, can generate acceptance of such a process and run it smoothly.

Challenge #2: Aces up Your Sleeve

> *We know you have your choice of airlines when you fly—thank you for choosing Alitalia.*

What can your organization do for startups? This issue occupies the overlap of Circle 1 and Circle 3 and directly affects how to emerge from the clutter, signal differentiation, and compete for startups against other programs. You can use any of the following strategies to stand out from background noise.

Opening an Asset or Network

One recipe for creating an enticing offer is to leverage a high-value asset or network and open it to the startup community. You must be pragmatic and remove all possible roadblocks that would hinder startups when using that asset or network.

In its BREW Accelerator, the Water Council in Milwaukee, Wisconsin, leverages its relationship with large water consumers such as Apple or PepsiCo to offer valuable introductions to startups in water technology. Illumina Accelerator provides startups with access to the corporation's sequencing systems, reagents, and lab space, which are some of the most advanced in the sector. In both examples, startups gain unique value that would otherwise be out of their reach—at a low marginal cost to the organization.

Higher Stakes

Few competitions and challenges offer prizes in the range of millions or tens of millions like XPRIZE. Higher rewards, investments at above-market valuations, or rich government subsidies may work—but it's a costly strategy.

Brand and Credibility

Brand association provides a vetting stamp to startups, which they can capitalize on through their website or during sales pitches. The flip side is that some startups may apply just for the badge, especially if participation is cheap (e.g., in equity-free programs).

Specialization

The value networks that your organization owns within an industry (suppliers, distributors), its customers, special facilities (e.g., test labs), standards, industry knowledge, and so on are all factors of differentiation that can interest everyone gravitating around the program. Mentors benefit from networking with peers within their sector; investors can access specific deal flow; and startups have more in common to make fruitful exchanges (not only expertise but also suppliers, distributors, joint prospects, etc.).

At the same time, specialization might not be negotiable. GV (formerly Google Ventures) invested in a nondigital business, the coffee chain Blue Bottle, but it's an exception. It would likely be controversial for the Water Council in Milwaukee to invest outside of water technology, for Airbus BizLab not to specialize in aerospace startups, or for the SETsquared Partnership to support startups outside Southwest England.

Beyond strategies related to an organization's location, there are also cases of specialization deliberately aimed at building the future. The Tribe Accelerator, funded by Singapore's government, specializes in blockchain to boost its still-young blockchain ecosystem. Bayer's G4A looks at digital health as an adjacent emerging opportunity for the pharmaceutical multinational.

The downside of specialization lies in limiting the quantity of deal flow (not necessarily the quality). If you specialize, you need to monitor your startup sources continuously and possibly engage directly in deal flow generation activities.

Destination

If a startup can work remotely, why not do it from a stunning or exotic location, maybe in the mountains or seaside? From Cape Verde to the Dolomites, from Finland to Miami, Florida, destination programs of all sorts are on the rise.[11] Corporations or government agencies proudly portray their fancy program offices on the application website. Whether that attracts a significant number of startups is unknown at this point.

The strengths should lie not in beauty or comfort, but in the entrepreneurial support system around the destination. For instance, Arch Grants in St. Louis provides a job board and local meetups for grant assignees. Start-Up Chile after 2016 encouraged the over 200 multinational companies based in Santiago to do business with its portfolio startups.

Fast-Tracks

Unique access routes to a commercial deal with the parent organization can be another differentiation source. Contracting speed, payment or disbursement speed (funding, invoices, grants), or admission speed are all performance metrics that can make a program manager proud. This is especially common in solution sourcing programs, as discussed in Chapter 4.

Many governments make regulatory exceptions for startups, such as the Startup Visa processes that have been introduced by

19 countries worldwide since the early 2010s. If governments put the startup community at the center of their political agenda, they have the potential to accelerate the pace of business and job growth.

Partnerships of Multiple Organizations

Organizations are increasingly forming clusters with other partners in the same industry or supply chain to create more comprehensive offers. For example, some programs function as one-stop shops that provide startups with the opportunity to interact with various players at different points in the value chain.

Free Electrons operated by Beta-i in Portugal gathers 10 energy utilities from countries as diversified as the United States, Japan, and the UAE, thus increasing the chances of matchmaking. The Agrofood BIC accelerator operated by Gellify in Italy integrates one of the largest national dairy companies, Granarolo, with value chain partners from production to packaging and corporate restaurants. Other examples of partnerships that run similar programs are Startup Autobahn, MobilityXlab, F10, or Flow Maritime Accelerator.

Trusted Brand or Partner

Governments, universities, and NGOs can use their institutional position to their advantage. They are often perceived more favorably than business organizations, and they can command trust and deploy vast actions, much like UNDP Youth Co:Lab does in the Asia Pacific.

Access to Talent

Since the dot-com boom, fresh graduates or even talented dropouts have contributed to a great many startups that have helped to revolutionize entrepreneurship. Local startup communities or universities rich in these resources can be very enticing to new startups.

A List of Value Proposition Features

From the cases we surveyed in our research, we have compiled a list of other assets, resources, and networks that organizations provide to startups that may serve as a starting point for internal analysis and brainstorming (Table 8.2).

TABLE 8.2 Assets an organization can use to support startups and create a program offer

Offer	Description	Examples
Venture capital	Funding reserved to acquire a minority equity position and hold it for several years	Y Combinator, Techstars, Wayra, Intel Capital, GV
Capital (non-venture)	Non-dilutive funding, such as a commercial deal, research subcontracting, or grants	EIT Climate-KIC Accelerator, BMW Startup Garage
Access to customers	Introductions to B2B customers, market tests on consumers, or access to distribution channels	SAP.iO Foundries, BREW Accelerator, QVC NEXT
Technology platforms	Free credits for own SaaS technology, or similar perks from other partners	Google for Startups, Microsoft for Startups
Operational facilities	Office space, warehouses, transport fleet, logistics, etc.	Cambridge Innovation Center
Testing facilities and labs	Prototyping labs, test labs, chemical materials, electronics, etc.	Illumina Accelerator
Prototyping or engineering support	Specialized internal support for product design and engineering, access to labs, etc.	Hybrids of accelerators and company builders
Access to supply chain	Direct access to own suppliers or partners with special deals	BeLeaf by Philip Morris
Production and manufacturing	Dedicated production or manufacturing line for small batches, either internal or through partners	Tetra Pak
Intellectual property and know-how	License agreements, access to own patented technology, knowledge transfer	NGA Accelerator, university-driven programs
Talent	Opportunities to find cofounders or hire top talent, student internships, or job boards	Entrepreneur First, Antler, Arch Grants St. Louis

(continued)

TABLE 8.2 Assets an organization can use to support startups and create a program offer (continued)

Offer	Description	Examples
Access to external funding opportunities	Support in preparation of grant applications for public funding opportunities	FundingBox
Access to investor network	Investment brokerage, introductions to private investors, investor readiness training	Y Combinator, Sting Accelerate
Advisory and mentorship	Entrepreneurs, investors, corporate managers, or technical mentors sharing their expertise	Techstars, most others
Market intelligence	Business intelligence, market studies, industry analysis, and market research support	PwC Scale
Brand, reputation, vetting stamp	Association with corporate programs or top-tier accelerators to win investments and customers	All major programs

Challenge #3: Select the Features for This Edition

Of all the cards in your hand, which do you play? All features come with an associated cost: venture capital investing requires expert selection and portfolio management; access to labs might conflict with normal business use of those labs; commercial deals may require exceptions to procurement rules, and so on.

At this stage, you are analyzing what is possible, not what is best to offer. Even when your organization can potentially provide a feature, it might not be willing or able to do it today without handling it as an exception. For example, many corporations, including Enel, keep investments out of their startup programs, reserving the option to follow up on a case-by-case basis.

There are three aspects to consider when selecting features to distribute equally to an entire cohort: (a) how ready your organization is to deliver a feature, (b) how strong your foothold is in the reservoir and the type of startups that will find your program, and (c) what your current program team can actually do (or how you can expand your team and capabilities).

Readiness to Delivering the Offer

> *I am still figuring out how to work better with our salespersons, they have limited bandwidth, and that's the bottleneck for startup collaborations at the moment.*
>
> —Monica Obogeanu, Orange Fab Romania

We spoke earlier of readiness for value capturing. You cannot overlook the internal readiness level of offer features either. Your ability to deliver value to the startup will influence the collaboration's outcome and the bond you create for future relationships.

Some features can be outsourced to an external supplier, of course (a classic build or buy dilemma; see Chapter 17). Still, any program should continuously check if the organization has all the processes, budget, and people to deliver what it claims in the launching campaign.

However ready you believe you are, optimism can be blindfolding. Prework on processes, legal frameworks, point-of-contact, and so on are not a walk in the park. Short-termism and power struggles are the norm.[12] It's unlikely that you can make the unique offerings available all at once. Even a simple traffic light indicator for each feature will provide guidance when you devise the offer (Figure 8.3).

Readiness	In this edition?
Venture Capital	✗
Capital (non-venture)	✓
Access to customers	✓
Technology platforms	✓
Operational facilities	✗
Testing facilities and labs	✗
Prototyping or engineering support	✗
Access to supply chain	✓

FIGURE 8.3 A readiness profile can be as simple as a list highlighting the readiness level with a traffic light system, where green means available for delivery to startups, yellow means at risk, and red means not yet available.

Outreach and Reservoir

Accessing quality deal flow can be critical for some objectives, such as financial investment, solution sourcing, or technology trend analysis. Having an established brand (*inbound search*) or a vast partner network in the entrepreneurial ecosystem (*referrals*) can complement your scouting efforts (*outbound search*). These factors affect how you can tap into the reservoir. Project what startup segments will find you attractive and decide which features and objectives to activate now, and which to delay to future editions.

When Start-Up Chile opened its doors in 2010, Chile was not a startup destination. In 2015 after years of brand building with pre-seed digital companies (the most mobile startup segment), the program pivoted to focus on attracting more mature companies who could adopt Chile as a business and operational platform.

Do You Have the Right Program Team?

> *My background is as an entrepreneur, and I only hire other entrepreneurs as collaborators in my team. You need to have done it, to have felt vulnerable.*
>
> —Andrea Welling, Futurpreneur Canada

The leading operator and the program team are pivotal figures in a startup program, acting as a liaison between the sponsor, startups, contributors (i.e., internal units or external partners), and beneficiaries (i.e., final customers, or other units) (Figure 8.4). "They are kind of the glue that holds it all together and drives it forward," said Charles Graham-Brown of Seedstars.

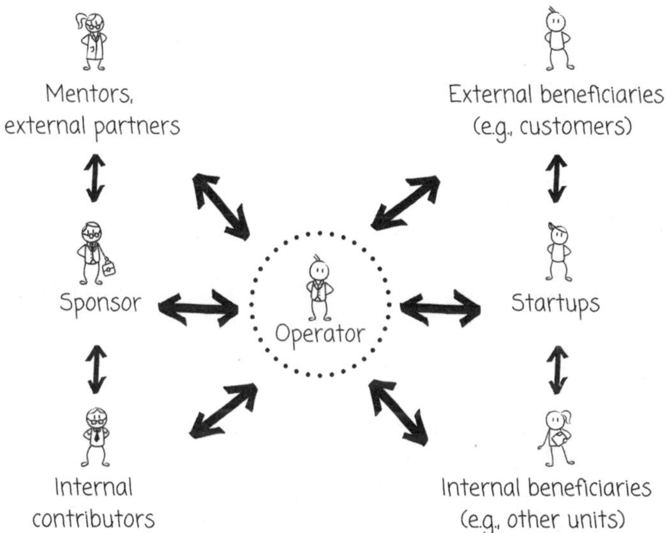

FIGURE 8.4 The program team is not just doing project management; it is at the center of a complicated relationship network.

Operators with good project management and community skills can manage pre-graduation objectives (e.g., trend monitoring, ideation, or mindset shift) with less dependence on the performance of internal allies.

Objectives requiring long term partnerships (e.g., solution sourcing and integration) and those that compete on deal flow in challenging markets (e.g., financial investing), however, often require an influential leader at the wheel who can drive solid alliances and participation throughout the organization and entrepreneurial ecosystem.

It takes credibility to lead a cohort of startups, manage senior mentors, and build relationships with business unit leaders, university deans, partner CEOs, or high-ranking government officers.[13] Having experienced startup life may be a plus, but understanding entrepreneurs does not strictly require an entrepreneurial past.[14]

Additional skills depend on the type of program (Table 8.3). For instance, a CVC investment team may not be best at managing the community aspects of an early-stage corporate accelerator.[15] Such program-dependent skills include, among others:

- **Ambidexterity.** The ability to understand startups and, at the same time, customer pain points and the execution business. Multitasking between two worlds dominated by different cultures is essential for innovation sourcing or ecosystem building goals.
- **Navigating the organization (or ecosystem).** Knowing and moving through the organizational charts and politics and reaching out to the right person. It may refer to a corporate environment, a community (e.g., blockchain developers), or a local business ecosystem. "My reputation in the startup ecosystem indeed helps the program's reputation," said Monica Obogeanu of Orange Fab.
- **Investment management.** Investment-driven programs need people with an investment or financial background. For the other objectives, internal technical or industry experts can run the selection and relationship management.
- **Entrepreneurial skills.** An ex-entrepreneur as lead operator has the advantage of understanding startup needs better and providing firsthand mentorship beyond performing the other operator's tasks—especially useful in programs such as company builders or growth accelerators. However, an Entrepreneur in Residence can easily supplement these skills if the operator lacks them.[16]
- **Domain expertise.** Specific programs may need domain knowledge regarding, for instance, technology, regulatory

frameworks, company internationalization from a given country or to a given destination, and so on. Also, these skills can be supplemented by a hired domain expert.

TABLE 8.3 Skills the program team should have, depending on the program's objectives

Type of Program Objective	Needed Skills (Beyond the Basic Skill Set)
Financial and strategic investing	Investment management Optional (early stage): Entrepreneurial skills
Solution sourcing	Ambidexterity Navigating the organization
Ecosystem building	Domain expertise (e.g., of software platform) Navigating the ecosystem
Mindset shift	Ambidexterity Internal: Domain expertise (human resources)
Trend discovery and market intelligence	Optional: Domain expertise (market or technology analyzed)
Talent hiring	Optional: Domain expertise (human resources)
Ideation and validation	Optional: Domain expertise (ideation methodologies, design thinking)

Challenge #4: Identify the Boundaries

Not all design dimensions are free. An organization might have nonnegotiable demands on specific program parameters. For instance, take the budget: higher management may impose it, making it a *bound variable*, or the designer can suggest it as part of planning, in which case it is a *free variable*. Another example is location: it can be bound, for example, if the program must occur in the city of the organization's headquarters, or free if it can happen anywhere.

Determining which variables are free and which are bound should be done as soon as possible (Table 8.4) because it may affect both objectives (Circle 2) and startups (Circle 3), as well as program configurations (Intersection).

Boundaries can be essential elements of the value proposition. A bound location, for instance, is necessary for destination programs. Or a part-time schedule (i.e., bound intensity) might be the only solution to entice specific profiles of participants, such as when Antler's Executive program aimed to recruit Fortune 1000 managers to cocreate startup teams with researchers from the National University of Singapore.[17] After doing customer research, Antler understood that these managers would only commit to a part-time program until they felt confident that the idea and team could work.

TABLE 8.4 Examples of design variables frequently bound by the context and not free for design

Variable Name	Examples of Bound Variable
Budget	The program must be deployed within a previously approved budget and cannot be altered.
Location	A real estate asset must be utilized as a coworking space (e.g., become newly available or underperforming). Or there is a destination program to attract startups to a city or country.
Duration / intensity	An international program including onsite physical presence is limited by the duration of a tourist visa (generally three months) or the venue's availability.
Cohort size / maximum number of participants	In hackathons or other startup events, the number of participants is constrained by the venue size. The same may occur for an incubator with a limited number of desks.
Expected payback period	In the public domain, it may be constrained by the duration of a funding scheme for entrepreneurs. In the private sector, by three- or five-year company planning.
Target startups	The investment thesis of a venture fund is centered around underrepresented founders only. Or a university only supports founders who are PhD students or postdocs.
Program activity or feature	The organization's unique value proposition is centered on a stay in Silicon Valley, or startups must use technology, such as in software adoption programs (e.g., IBM Watson).
Specialization	The program must look only for health startups with solutions for respiratory diseases or for blockchain-based personal finance—in general, any technology or industry sector.

Special Mention: Expected Payback Period—Two Years

A special mention goes to the expected payback period, namely, the time frame of when results are expected to appear. It happens all the time with innovation actions: the program starts with considerable press coverage and photos of a smiling executive on social media, just to end two or three years later when someone from the organization, attentive to performance and bookkeeping, knocks at the program's door to ask for return-on-investment metrics (ROI). Innovation metrics seldom appear that fast, unless the program is designed to produce some in that time frame.

The sentiment among innovation operators and consultants is that innovation is never given enough time. Operators even mock corporate short-termism. In a guide on the common mistakes corporations make in innovation practices, one is: "Expect returns within 12 months—Talk nonstop about the long-term but measure every forward-looking, somewhat risky partnership, investment, or acquisition with as short of a time frame as possible."[18]

The reality is that short-termism is rooted in the job duties of corporate executives and government officials. One can try to fight against short-termism or roll with it.

To roll with it, you should understand how long your stakeholders will allow the program to prove itself. You should plan to produce results or at least robust leading indicators by that time. As a rule of thumb, your stakeholders will assume a startup program will pay back in about two years. And two years are just about what detractors will need to kill the program if you don't show any result. If your model needs more time to deliver, it's important to make it clear upfront with the senior leadership and other internal stakeholders.

KEY TAKEAWAYS

- **Start with how you will harvest results.** Many startup programs face a similar problem as internally generated innovation: the new product, service, technology, or business model must be passed on to the execution units of the organization and integrated into the business. This phase is the hardest of all in most established organizations. Without an infrastructure that can harvest results, a startup program will be stuck in innovation theater.

- **Build alliances beyond senior leaders.** A startup program is among those initiatives that spend money and produce little cash flow for a comparatively long time, to the point that the rest of the organization is instinctively driven to starve its annual budget. Senior leaders have the power to counter the natural short-termism of middle managers, and it is critical to obtain their backing from day one. However, that is seldom enough, and you must also devise other tactics to win internal support, such as establishing incentives, cocreating the program with other vital units, activating internal ambassadors, or building an influential advisory board.
- **Offer only what you can deliver.** A powerful method to create an enticing offer to startups is to leverage your organization's high-value assets (e.g., test labs, standards, industry knowledge) or value networks (e.g., suppliers, distributors, customers). However, don't overshoot, and check your readiness. Any overpromising would damage startups first, but your organization's reputation would eventually take a hit as well. Two other essential factors to double-check are your current outreach in the startup community and the program team's experience.
- **Mind the boundaries of the design space.** Discover the limitations to the design dimensions you can use, set intentionally or unintentionally by your organization. For instance, location or duration might be fixed. Pay particular attention to the expected payback period—the general rule of thumb is that you have two years to prove the program's value.

9

CIRCLE 2: OBJECTIVES

This chapter discusses Circle 2, the objectives set by the program initiator, team, or sponsor. The program objectives are the north star of strategic design and cannot change on a whim. Usually, they descend from a senior leader and fit into the general organizational strategy. If there is space for change, it lies in clarification and refinement—rarely, if ever, in pivoting.

Confident leaders skilled in strategic design, however, are able to evaluate Circle 1 and the startups they know they can and should get into Circle 3, and then choose specific objectives that startup programs can solve while considering other internal and external alternatives, such as R&D, intrapreneurship, or traditional outsourcing (more in Chapter 16). In some cases, you might have to temporarily freeze a goal and prepare the ground for it with another program, driven by a *fertilization* goal (i.e., adopt a bridge goal in Circle 2).

Financial goals are what they are: money in, money out. They are defined by clear metrics, how many dollars you receive for each dollar invested. You can use ROI, IRR, breakeven, or payback period as metrics.

Strategic objectives are where the trouble begins, starting from their definition: a strategic goal is anything that is *not* a financial goal. A definition by negation is always hard to interpret—it is too vague. These goals often require clarification. Popular frameworks to express objectives and metrics associated with them are BSC (balanced scorecards), RBM (result-based management), MBO (management by objectives), OKR (objectives and key results), or V2MOM (vision values methods obstacles measures).[1] However, this chapter deliberately leaves the choice of the specific framework to you and your organization. We will tackle five challenges here:

1. How to position a program in the organizational strategy
2. How to clarify objectives in an actionable way
3. How to handle strategic and lagging objectives
4. How to derive asks from objectives
5. How to embed failure into the design

This chapter is interconnected with Chapters 8 and 10. Together, the three chapters reflect the search for the program's ikigai, or "reason to live" (Figure 9.1).

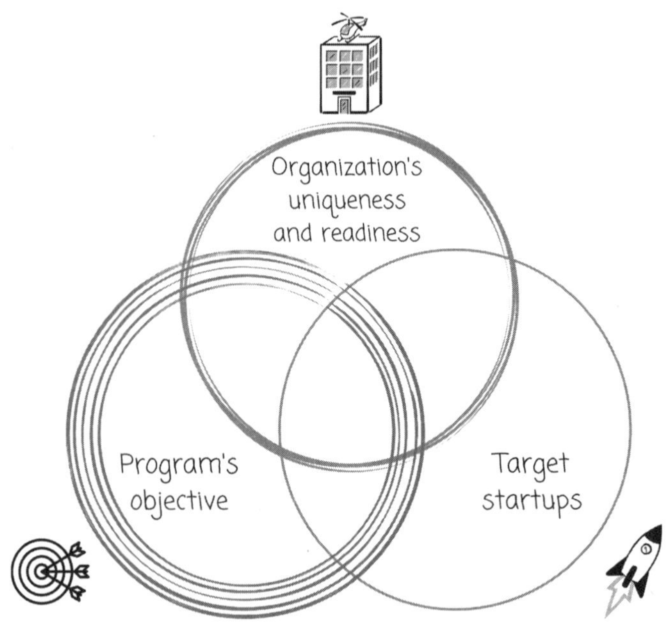

FIGURE 9.1 This chapter is about Circle 2, the program's objectives.

Objectives, Outcomes, and Metrics

When an organization creates a startup program, objectives may be as diverse as financial investing or cultivating an internal culture of innovation (Chapter 2). The expected outcomes might be, respectively, a financial return on investment (ROI) or more progress on transformational technology projects. The expected outcomes might also be very different: Financial investing could just aim to create a portfolio of hedging options. Cultural change could pursue the creation of new internal businesses. When you manipulate objectives, for clarity, you should also include the expected outcomes.

Outcomes are better understood when associated with a metric, although that is not a general rule.[2] For instance, the target can be a 2x or a 10x ROI. The real, measured ROI will be compared to those numbers to determine success or failure. Most frameworks like OKR, V2MOM, and so on make all three elements explicit: objectives, outcomes, and metrics.

Note that "working with startups" is neither an objective nor an outcome in and of itself. Working with startups is a means, not an end. If your objectives and outcomes are just to work with startups, beware.

Challenge #1: Strategy Fit

> *Our company is not ready for any type of disruption. It's very difficult to exit from our core, and innovation in new business models did not go well. Now we are very focused on startups innovating in our core business.*
>
> —Anonymous manager in a multinational public company

What should the program do for your organization? The only constant in innovation is change, and startup programs are a way to manage innovation whiplash and smooth the curve. A program, being a solution, should always respond to a need for corporate innovation or economic development (government, ecosystems).

How far can startup collaborations stray from the core strategy? Your organizational planning should determine whether the program approaches startups in H1, H2, or H3 of the three McKinsey horizons, or core versus transformational areas (Chapter 2). If you, your boss, or your client are attempting to change the general strategy with a startup program, prepare for a lot of political pushback and arm your David for battle against Goliath.

The Explore, Exploit, and Fertilize Framework

> *Start with strong links with strategy, don't follow a momentary fashion. Look for seeds of a plant that can grow on its own, and seeds that complete other plants.*
>
> —Gabriele Molari, Tetra Pak

Within the current strategy, the question may become: Will the program seek to explore or exploit[3] (Figure 9.2)?

- In **exploration**, the organization engages with startups to assess the expected returns of a new idea or technology (or economic specialization—for governments) and reduce its innovation risk, namely, its desirability, viability, and feasibility.
- In **exploitation**, engagement is motivated by the profitability of the current business (or economic sector) and controlling competition or risk of disruption.

Exploration is often better conducted outside of the execution business's gravitational field, but then it risks crashing when it reenters the orbit. Exploitation, on the other hand, requires an alliance with other internal units from day one, and it benefits from staying near the core.

In terms of time horizons, exploration is traditionally associated with H2 or H3, and exploitation with H1 or H2. This situation is changing in some fields, such as digital transformation, in which exploration of new ideas can be conducted as fast as core innovation.[4] However, exploration does entail tapping new competencies and creating new processes, whereas exploitation generally uses preexisting knowledge and organizational artifacts.

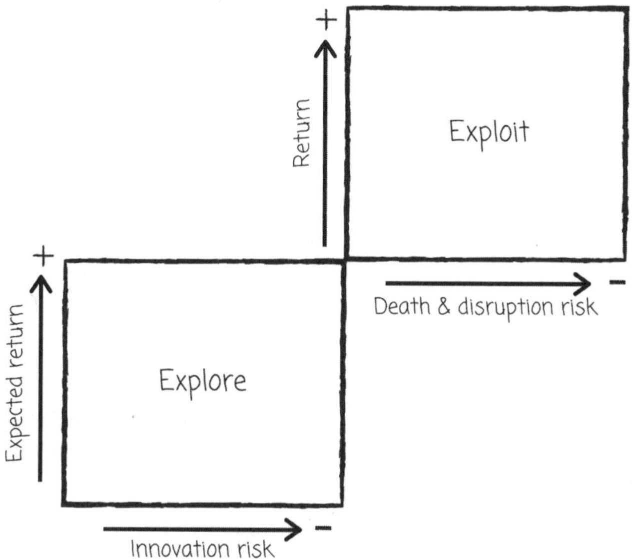

FIGURE 9.2 Strategyzer's Portfolio Map illustrates the explore and exploit portfolios in two spaces, mapping risk versus gain.

Adapted from Osterwalder, A., Y. Pigneur, A. Smith, F. Etiemble, 2020, *The Invincible Company* (Wiley). Copyright: Strategyzer.com. Strategyzer

A third option is to use the program to fertilize the internal or external ecosystem. Fertilization is more related to background preparation rather than developing any specific idea. It affects people, a culture of experiment-driven learning, connections, diversity, and bridges between different worlds. A fertilization program can provide ideas to either or both the explore or exploit portfolios (Figure 9.3).

The objectives reviewed in Chapter 2 can be related to one or more of these strategies (Table 9.1). Understanding which strategy framework the program operates will affect:

1. **Signaling and positioning.** The communication for deal flow generation.
2. **Selection criteria.** How participants are selected (Chapter 14).
3. **Outcome metrics.** How you measure success (this chapter).

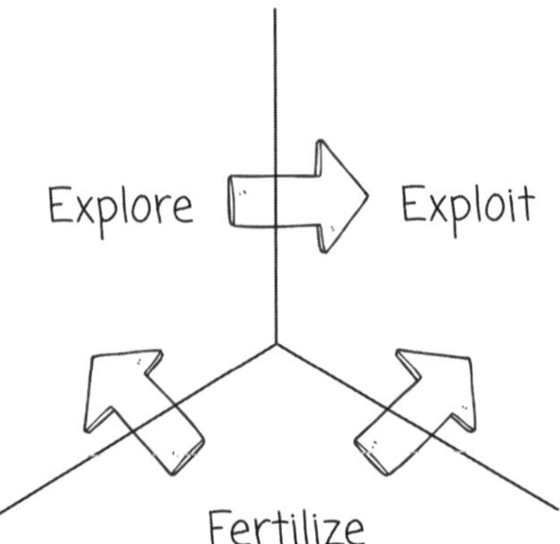

FIGURE 9.3 Three-partitioned map to represent the fertilize, explore, and exploit program portfolios. Fertilization programs can develop ideas for further exploration or exploitation.

TABLE 9.1 How objectives from Chapter 2 map on the three strategies. Multiple Xs indicate that the specific mapping depends on the goal's implementation.

Objectives	Fertilize	Explore	Exploit
Financial investing		X	X
Strategic investing		X	X
Innovative solution sourcing			X
Innovation ecosystem building	X		X
Entrepreneurial ecosystem building	X		
Mindset shift and organizational culture	X		
Mission-driven transformational impact	X		
Ideation		X	X
Validation		X	X
Trend discovery and market intelligence		X	X
Talent hiring	X		
R&D capital		X	X
Press and media coverage	X		
Brand positioning and reputation	X		

Challenge #2: Clarify Objectives and Outcomes

You should not plan the program blueprint until the objectives are crystal clear.[5] Whether it is about a need, an opportunity, or a learning path to achieve clarity for future programs, you have to convene your stakeholders and agree on what the program should accomplish.

We intentionally refrain from giving any advice on what objective framework to use (e.g., OKR or BSC) or how to drive the conversation with your senior leadership, beneficiaries, allies, and detractors. Our concern is about how to put those objectives to use for design.

The rest of this section describes a visual language to map objectives and outcomes in a way that can be actionable for agreeing on metrics and activity planning. The notation visualizes goals in correspondence to the stage that likely generates them, adding possible metrics in brackets (Figure 9.4). Other notation rules will be introduced via examples.

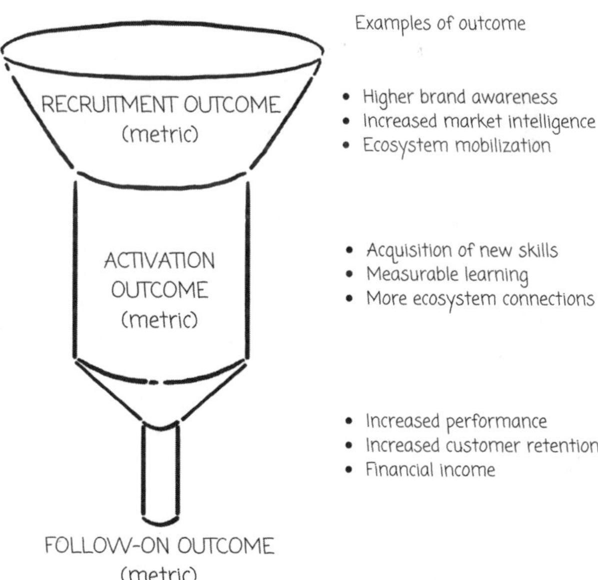

FIGURE 9.4 Objectives are annotated over the funnel stage that enables them.

Multiple Objectives

The Unilever Foundry was conceived to create commercial opportunities between a startup and a Unilever brand. The program would produce a pilot (output), but the desired outcome was a long-term commercial partnership, through either direct procurement, codevelopment, or comarketing. Multiple objectives can be represented with *branching* after graduation (Figure 9.5). In exceptional cases, Unilever would also acquire equity shares in the company down the line, even though that was openly not a target outcome[6] (not represented). If one objective is prioritized, it can be indicated with a square (the one shown in the figure is an example, not illustrative of the actual case).

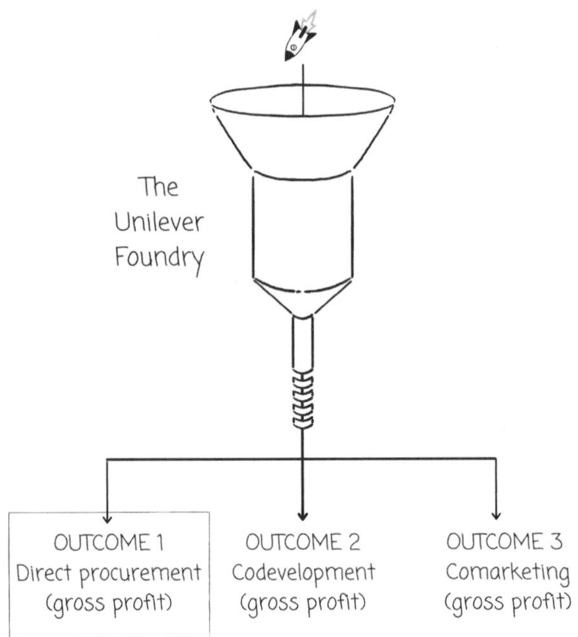

FIGURE 9.5 The primary objective or outcome is indicated with a rectangle.

Branching can occur at any stage, not just after graduation. Consider Conception X, a British educational company builder that supports deep tech researchers in understanding technology transfer and starting new companies. PhD students are admitted to the "training stream" and, after a few weeks, some are promoted to the "startup stream." The decision occurs in an intermediary gate before graduation, and in either case, all participants receive the same training. The envisioned outcomes are two. The first is a default outcome that entails upskilling and providing an innovation mindset to all participants. The second outcome is the creation of a new deep tech startup. After the split, the educational and mentoring activities follow two different courses (Figure 9.6).

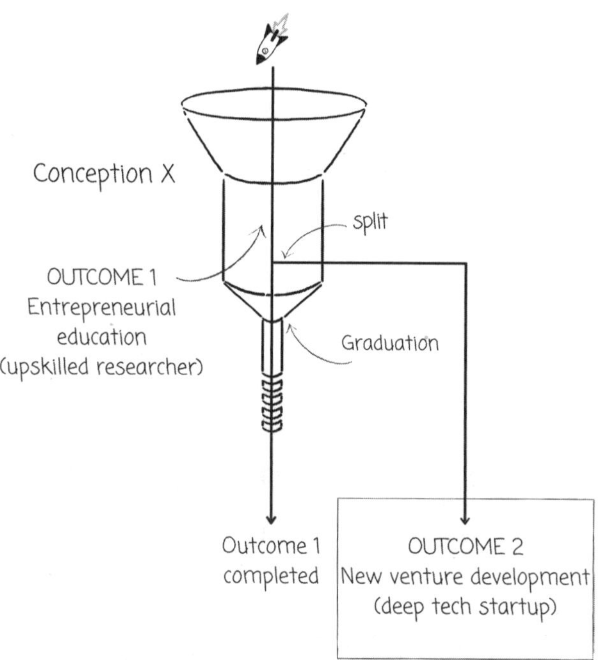

FIGURE 9.6 Branching indicates that startups are routed toward different objectives; the branching is noted in the stage where routing happens.

Multiple objectives are generally the result of two situations:

- **Accidental multiple objectives**, when the program manages numerous stakeholders at different stages of commitment, or when planning is lacking and the program is vague about its role in the general strategy.

- **Intentional multiple objectives,** when the deal flow is channeled in various streams, such as in Conception X.

A different approach to intentional diversity is to create a system of programs, each specialized on one purpose, which interacts in synergy to build a pipeline or alternative paths (see Chapter 16).

Proxies

Startup programs may introduce proxy objectives as leading indicators of lagging outcomes. For instance, YC-style equity-based accelerators track traction growth (*momentum*) during the activation stage as a leading indicator of a successful financial exit sometime after graduation (Figure 9.7). The primary objective is still the financial exit, but aiming for a high momentum as a proxy catalyzes the efforts during the program—more in Challenge #3.

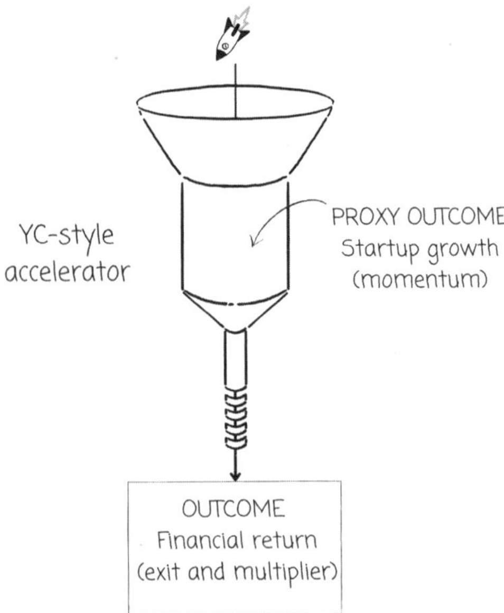

FIGURE 9.7 YC-style accelerators have an exit as primary outcome after graduation, but also pursue traction and startup growth during the activation stage as a proxy.

Ecosystem Effects

Beyond its commercial objectives, the Foundry also had another purpose: bringing a startup mentality and approach to Unilever "to help the company become more agile, more responsive and more ready for the digital world."[7] This objective would not affect the startups directly—it was a positive by-product or ecosystem effect. It stemmed from the interactions that Unilever executives and managers had with startups during the activation stage. Ecosystem effects can be represented with a backward dotted arrow pointing back to the ecosystem they affect—the company in this case (Figure 9.8).

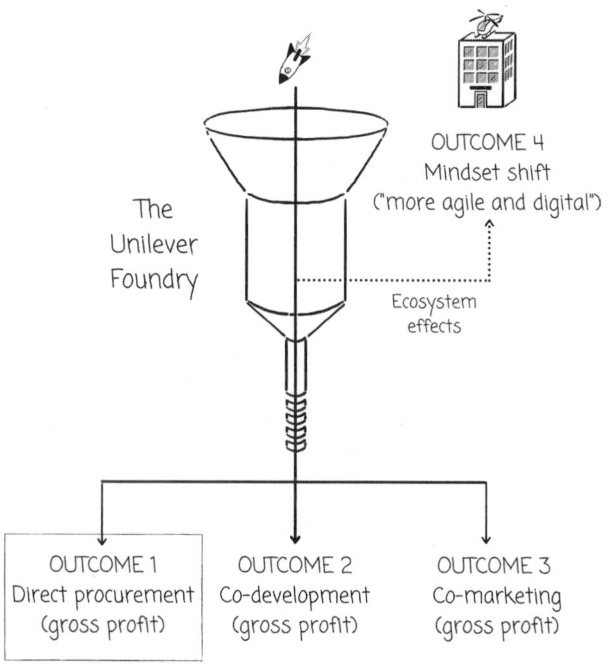

FIGURE 9.8 Dotted lines indicate ecosystem effects and externalities; they point toward the beginning of the funnel to signify a feedback loop.

Primary Objective

Start-Up Chile went beyond just producing some ecosystem effects as by-products, like in the example of Unilever Foundry above. In its initial editions (2010–15), SUP Chile was purposely designed around ecosystem effects—it was "primarily a cultural program aimed to educate Chileans in entrepreneurship."[8] In other words, the ecosystem effect is a deliberate objective pursued by means of the so-called return-value activities(as discussed in the Start-Up Chile case study in Chapter 1), and until 2015 it was a primary objective (represented with a box around it Figure 9.9).

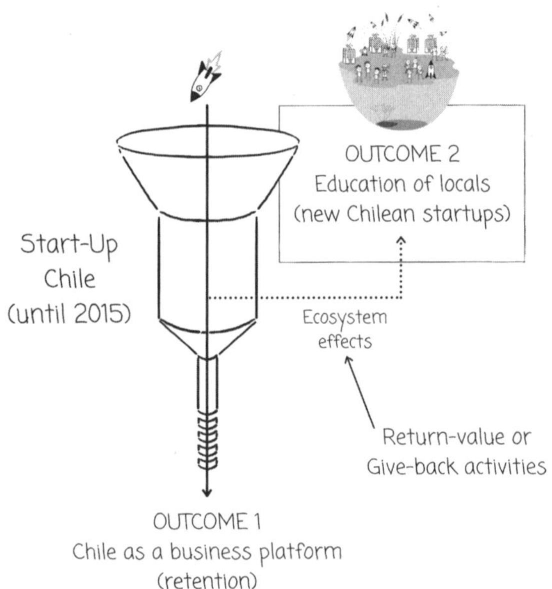

FIGURE 9.9 Start-Up Chile deliberately pursues ecosystem effects through the return-value activities.

It can be instructive to note the usefulness of highlighting the primary objective. Consider Sting Accelerate, a Swedish non-profit accelerator cofunded by the City of Stockholm and KTH (Royal Institute of Technology). While it follows the equity-based accelerator model illustrated above, this accelerator's primary objective isn't profit, but simply startup growth to the benefit of the founders, in line with its impact-driven mission (Figure 9.10).

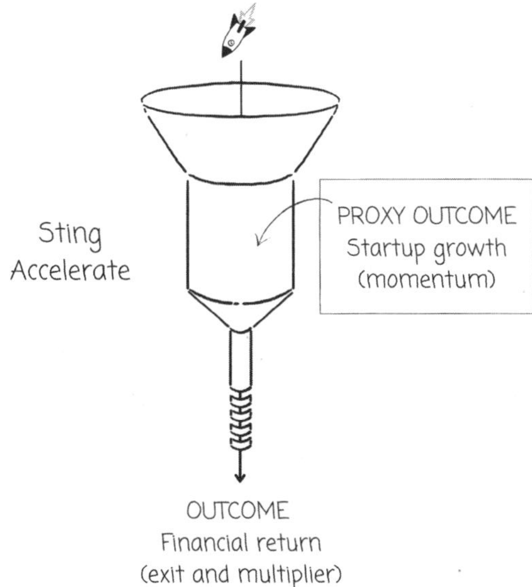

FIGURE 9.10 The proxy objective can be the primary goal, such as in nonprofit Sting Accelerator. Compare this image with Figure 9.7.

Even though Sting still acquires equity from startups, the organization is committed to reinvesting any successful exit in the fund itself without any personal profit for the managers. "If something is for free, it does not have value" is reported as a company motto. Taking equity, even without any intention of making a profit, puts pressure on the Sting team to deliver value to the accelerated startups.[9]

As a last example, consider accelerator programs sponsored by companies such as Techstars Detroit in Michigan or Startup Autobahn in Germany, both in the automotive sector. Ford was a sponsor in Techstars' Detroit continuously from its inception in 2015 until its end in 2020, mentoring all its 54 startups. Ford used its participation to survey industry trends while postponing any decision on what kind of partnership to establish with startups until after the program—closing a commercial deal being the primary possibility, while not precluding a strategic investment[10] (Figure 9.11). If you follow this model, make sure deal flow is not another blanket term. Deals should have an objective list, in the same way as startup programs should in Circle 2.

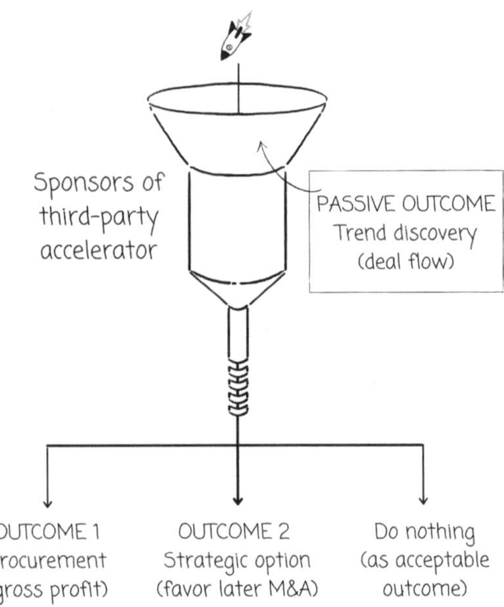

FIGURE 9.11 Organizations may sponsor a third-party program with the primary goal of accessing the deal flow, as Ford did with Techstars Detroit.

Challenge #3: Metrics and Leading Indicators

> *Our venture incubator started as a fund with financial gain. Later we understood that ethical results were more important to our bank and shareholders.*
>
> —Francesco Baruffi, former Head of Open Innovation at Emil Banca

Organizations often utilize startup programs for strategic goals, across the whole spectrum from government to for-profit businesses too. Some examples are strategic investing, internal cultural change, or fertilization of the external ecosystem.

The problem with strategic objectives is that no one has yet devised a universal way of measuring them. This makes it difficult to build benchmarks and agree on the right metrics.

To prevent such vagueness from degenerating into innovation theater, many organizations have deliberated to stick with financial indicators (e.g., revenues, cost savings, ROI) even when their program prioritizes strategic goals over financial goals. However, this approach can cause a distortion, because a program optimized for strategic objectives is not necessarily good at generating financial returns.

Even when a program adopts financial metrics, measuring results can be tricky. For equity-based models, return is a lagging indicator taking several years to appear. For models based on commercial partnerships, the contribution of startup technology can be watered down in another business unit's profit and hard to connect back to the program.

Our recommendation is that you assign at least one metric to every outcome on your chart (Figure 9.12). A process without metrics does not survive in most organizations. When you cannot find a metric that is measurable in due time to be useful or actionable, use proxy metrics—also known as leading indicators. Understand that metrics relate to objectives and models, as we lay out in the following paragraphs. When you benchmark your program against competitors, remember there is no holy grail in metrics—you must compare your metrics with those of programs pursuing your same objectives, or the comparison would always wrong one of the contendants.

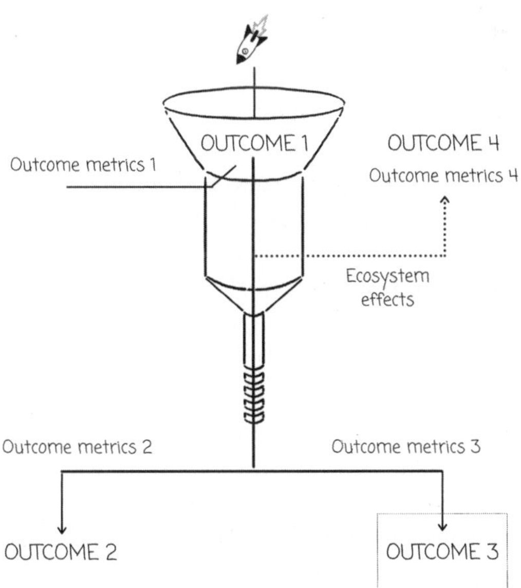

FIGURE 9.12 Every outcome should be associated with at least one metric.

Leading Indicators

To cope with post-graduation objectives and lagging indicators, you can introduce a *proxy objective* and associate a *leading indicator* with it. A leading indicator is a measurable phenomenon that helps predict the future value of another phenomenon. In startup programs, it is a metric that is measurable in the short term (in some cases even during the program) and helps predict whether you are on track with your objectives, and by how much. Table 9.2 illustrates some examples of leading indicators used for different objectives and outcomes.

Leading indicators should have all of the following characteristics:

1. **Possible correlation.** You can at least imagine a correlation with the outcome metric that it predicts. Even better if you can prove it.
2. **Continuous measurement.** You should be able to measure it at any time.
3. **Comparability in time.** Measuring the same indicator in time should be able to show trends and suggest a correction if you spot a negative direction.
4. **Accepted by the client.** Your senior leadership or organizational sponsor must explicitly accept that metric as a proxy.

Because there are no general rules and correlation is hard to demonstrate, the last aspect (acceptance) is fundamental. Without an agreement on the proxy metrics, they become useless. It is part of the design process to identify what stakeholders should participate in the metrics definition.

Leading Indicators for Financial Investing

For financial investing, leading indicators of startup growth are *traction* metrics such as revenues, users, valuation, employees, and funds raised, and their change in time, or *momentum*. It is not random that these are the dimensions monitored by YC-style accelerators and CVC funds: a hockey stick in those proxies is a good omen for a satisfying exit.

Notice that the value predictor in accelerators is not the investor pitch (see again Figure 9.7). A pitch is just a means to present that predictor. Many first-time accelerator managers, instead,

TABLE 9.2 Examples of leading indicators for diverse objectives and outcomes

Objective	Outcome Metrics	Possible Leading Indicator	Why It Can Work for You
Financial investing	ROI (exit value)	Valuation or other traction metrics	Valuation increase can help estimate the exit value of your shares.
Solution sourcing	Cost savings	Performance	Can be used to estimate the cost savings if the solution was scaled (for a business case).
Solution sourcing	Extra revenues	Traction	Like with startups, traction can be used to predict growth (for a business case).
Innovation ecosystem adoption	Increased platform value	Platform usage, business transacted on platform	Activation on the innovation or technology platform can be an indicator of business reasons to stay after the incentives dry up.
Entrepreneurial ecosystem adoption	Ecosystem economic growth	Local business volume, transactions with local customers / partners	Participation and transactions in the entrepreneurial ecosystem platform can be an indicator of business reasons to stay after the incentives dry up.
Mindset shift	Change acceptance	Self-assessment of cultural shift	Surveys filled before and after the stimulus can show its impact.
Trend analysis	Customer satisfaction	Applications or startups met / screened	A report can be compiled from all startups screened.
Brand and reputation	Brand value	Share of voice	Compare the program to a communication action and measure it with similar means.
Validation	Customer engagement	Interviews performed or MVP tests done	Like with startups, it provides learning that, in turn, can inform decisions to grow revenues.

mistakenly use the pitch as a focus and pitch improvement as proof of results—paving the way for innovation theater.

Leading Indicators for Solution Sourcing

For solution sourcing, the leading indicators can be deduced from a pilot as a *percent improvement* in performance, margin, or customer satisfaction. If it is a new product or product innovation that you are pursuing, then the value stems from the *opportunity costs* of doing the same product development internally.

The results of the pilot really become useful if and when scaled to predict the impact of the startup innovation on the organization. In other words, just making a qualitative demo is useless—a pilot should always provide quantitative information that can be later used to estimate the effects of a scale-up operation. As for the pitch, it is not about the pilot, but about the insights it provides.[11]

Leading Indicators for Ecosystem Building

For ecosystem building, the leading indicators are *platform usage* and *stickiness*. You need proof that the platform is delivering value to the startups, in a way that they will be incentivized to stay for long. For example, good indicators of retention could be a quick use of all credits on a technology platform, or that a founder moves all of his family to the city, like it happened for an Indian entrepreneur during the first edition of the InsurTech Hub in Hartford, Connecticut.[12]

Leading Indicators for Transformational Impact

Impact-driven programs have disparate leading indicators, depending on the type of impact. For instance, programs creating new entrepreneurship, such as 150 Startups,[13] may use the number of new *role models* (new founders who proactively speak at conferences and are an example for others). Another program supporting very early teams, such as Seedstars or FutureWorks NYC, may employ the *survival rate* of teams and startups in a given period after the program (one year, three years, etc.). EIT Climate-KIC Accelerator estimates the *carbon footprint* reduction brought by the portfolio startups with LCA methodologies.

Challenge #4: What to Ask (or Not)

Asks are actions the startups have *to do* for your organization, or assets they have *to give*. For instance, equity is something startups give; customization is something they do. Asks come from three sources: objectives, bound variables, and deliberate ecosystem effects. A list of common asks is presented in Table 9.3.

Asks Derived from Objectives

Objective-related asks are highly correlated with the program stage that achieves your objective. As a general rule, the later the program stage needed by a goal, the more demanding the requirements put on startups (Figure 9.13).

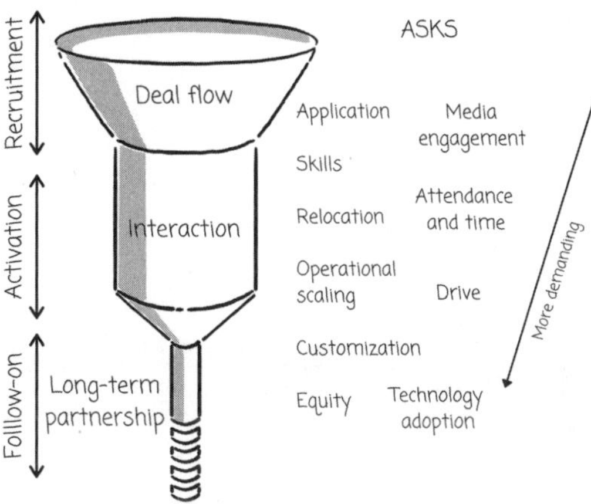

FIGURE 9.13 The *asks* will pay back to the organization in different program stages. An application form repays the organization with information early on during recruitment, whereas equity or customization return value after graduation.

The application form is the first type of ask, required by all the program formats that use an admission gate. If information gathering is a part of the goal, such as for trend analysis, then you want to employ longer and more complete forms; otherwise, the later selection steps will fill in any missing information (YC uses a relatively lean application form, for instance).

For objectives that are fulfilled by interactions (e.g., ideation, validation, mindset shift, or talent hiring), logistic asks such as

TABLE 9.3 List of asks that organizations often require as terms and conditions in startup programs

Ask	Description	Example
Application form	Fill in an application form with information about the idea or business.	Any but hackathons
Media engagement	Give rights to film or photograph and share interviews or social media posts on official or personal accounts.	Any
Advanced skills	Demonstrated knowledge of a specific technology, industry, market, or (at least) ability to test and validate an idea.	Incubators, JD AI Accelerator
Attendance	Presence (physical or virtual) to workshop, meeting, bootcamp, lecture, etc.	Junction
Relocation	Physical relocation of one or more startup team members (founders or employees) to a specific city or place.	Parallel18
Time dedication	Feedback, ideation, product testing, pilot development, and other extra time dedicated on top of that for attendance.	Comcast Lift Lab
Drive	Motivational ask. Strong commitment and achiever drive to reach ambitious business goals.	Antler
Product / Technology / IP	Having ownership (intellectual property, mastery) of an exclusive or rare technology or product.	Conception X
Standardized deal	Ability and willingness to accept a standardized deal (investment, commercial) with minimal or null negotiation.	Techstars Accelerator
Exclusivity rights	A form of exclusive rights (license, etc.) for a limited (6–36 months) or unlimited time.	TIM WCAP (up to 2016)
Technology adoption	Ability to modify the product stack or architecture in order to include a technology owned by the organizational sponsor.	Oracle for Startups
Business or product readiness	Ability to deploy the product or business model with relatively short notice in a real-world pilot.	LH Startup MAQER
Operational scaling	Ability to scale up production or distribution fast, including own budget to cover (at least partially) the incurred costs.	QVC NEXT
Customization	Ability to dedicate time, focus, and resources to customize the product or service to the needs of the organizational sponsor.	BMW Startup Garage
Equity	Direct concession of an equity share, or of investment rights (e.g., discount, first refusal, convertible), at present or in later rounds.	Intel Capital

attendance, relocation, or time dedication become imperative. Another frequent ask is about possessing particular skills (e.g., knowledge of a technology that should be validated or for which the organization wants use cases) or a drive and commitment to acquire those that are missing.

Objectives fulfilled by post-graduation partnerships must request the most demanding commitments: equity, revenue sharing, customization, business or product readiness, operational scaling, architectural reshaping for technology adoption, drive, and so forth. These asks enable the most advanced partnerships and create value-capturing mechanisms for the organization in the long term.

Table 9.4 summarizes the most common relationships between objectives and asks.

TABLE 9.4 Mapping of asks on objectives they frequently assist (not prescriptive)

Objective	Possible Asks
Financial investing	Equity Drive
Strategic investing	Equity Exclusivity rights
Innovative solution sourcing	Customization Business or product readiness Product / Technology / IP Operational scaling
Innovation ecosystem building	Technology adoption Business or product readiness Product / Technology / IP Time dedication
Entrepreneurial ecosystem building	Relocation Time dedication
Mindset shift and organizational culture	Attendance
Mission-driven transformational impact	Attendance Drive Time dedication
Ideation	Advanced skills Attendance
Validation	Advanced skills Attendance Time dedication

(continued)

TABLE 9.4 Mapping of asks on objectives they frequently assist (not prescriptive) *(continued)*

Objective	Possible Asks
Trend discovery and market intelligence	Application form
Talent hiring	Attendance
R&D capital	Product / Technology / IP Time dedication
Press and media coverage	Media engagement Attendance
Brand positioning and reputation	Media engagement Drive

Asks Derived from Bound Variables

The second group of asks is connected with the bound variables originating from Circle 1 (Chapter 8). For instance, destination programs such as Start-Up Chile or TechPeaks are bound to their reference location (by contrast, Techstars, SAP Foundries, and Wayra offer several locations). A target payback period puts constraints on the level of business or product readiness—immediate or reachable during the program—obliging startups to commit resources and focus to that end (Table 9.5).

TABLE 9.5 Asks derived from bound variables—variables imposed by the context and not free for design

Bound Variable	Possible Asks
Location	Relocation Attendance
Duration / intensity	Attendance Time dedication
Payback period	Business or product readiness Operational scaling
Specialization	Advanced skills Product / Technology / IP

Asks Derived from Deliberate Ecosystem Effects

> *A university program here in Beijing doesn't demand equity, but if you raise funds, they will ask for a donation, 2–3% of the round. If you are successful, then why not? I like it.*
>
> —Jelte Wingender, Innoway

A last group of asks regards the ecosystem effects and by-products that you are planning to deliberately produce (e.g., Figures 9.8 and 9.9).

Fertilization activities often require asks of relocation or time dedication directed to corporate managers or the local startup community, depending on what ecosystem you intend to fertilize.

Also, consider publication rights for data, logos, photos, videos, and anything else you may need for press releases and other media.

What Not to Ask

> *If you don't have an investor's mindset, either it's gambling, or greed, or you shouldn't take equity.*
>
> —Marius Ursache, Metabeta

First of all, always double-check if an ask is really necessary because it will restrict the reservoir, possibly compromising the deal flow (Chapter 10, Challenges #3 and #4).

Second, coercion does not work with startups. For rapid-growth startups especially (RL or RS), boundaries in logistics, technology, or operations bring a high opportunity cost that not many would be willing to pay—or that could damage those who inconsiderately agree to them. Late-stage startups might look for loopholes or workarounds in the terms, or they might back off and not even apply. For instance, corporations sometimes oblige startups to relocate to their corporate building during an accelerator, in hope of revitalizing the internal culture. But founders of a late-stage startup would rarely agree to such a long absence from the mothership, and they'd send some junior hires instead. Is junior staff going to provide the same spirit and network the founders would? Hardly so—and the program would suffer for it. On the other hand, those same founders would likely fly in for an immersive two-day meeting with top executives from the firm. Requiring mandatory participation in such a case is sensible, and has much higher chances of getting the founders to actually show up.

Lastly, startups can usually bear just one exacting ask at a time. Too many might discourage the most interesting startups from applying.

Challenge #5: Embed Failure into the Program

Embedding failure management into a startup program is like taking your own medicine. Innovation inherently relies on attempts and failures in unchartered territory, but this is the only way of learning. And startup collaborations make no exception.

"It's very important to embed an infrastructure that reframes failures as learnings as a regular part of the program," said Lisa Besserman, former head of Global Incubator at Indeed.com and previously the founder of Startup Buenos Aires, an educational accelerator in Argentina.[14] At Indeed.com, they prepare among other things, a learning deck after each failed innovation project and share it internally with other units that might benefit from this knowledge. "It's a way to save time, resources and provide a knowledge base to other people," she added.

The practice of reframing failure into lessons learned is also beneficial for the organizational culture. Enel, for instance, in 2015 introduced an online board entitled "My best failure" where employees are rewarded for sharing stories of unsuccessful innovation.[15]

To reframe failure as learning, add failure as a possible outcome and design a process to handle failed projects (Figure 9.14).

Figure 9.15 shows an example with multiple failure handling scenarios: a learning deck presentation, like at Indeed.com; a prolonged incubation period to allow additional experiments; or a marketplace to sell "failed" technology to other units. Christopher McLachlan, head of Company Builder at EnBW, a German electric utility company, successfully experimented with the latter tactic when a "failed" technology and project team received three offers of "buyout" from other business units.[16]

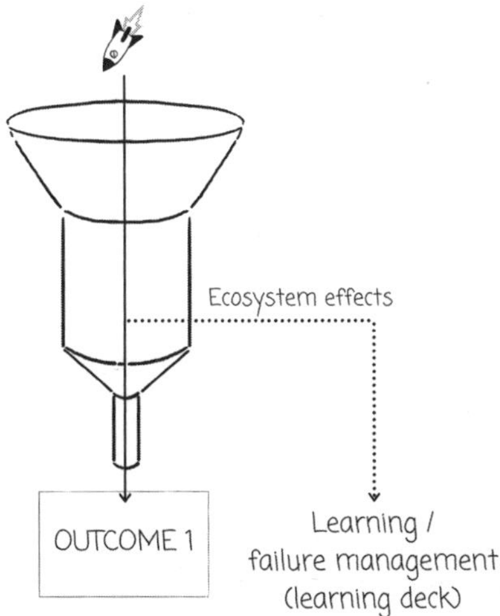

FIGURE 9.14 Dotted lines can represent learning scenarios as ecosystem effects or by-products instead of failure. The arrows point toward the funnel end to represent their similarity with unwanted evolutions.

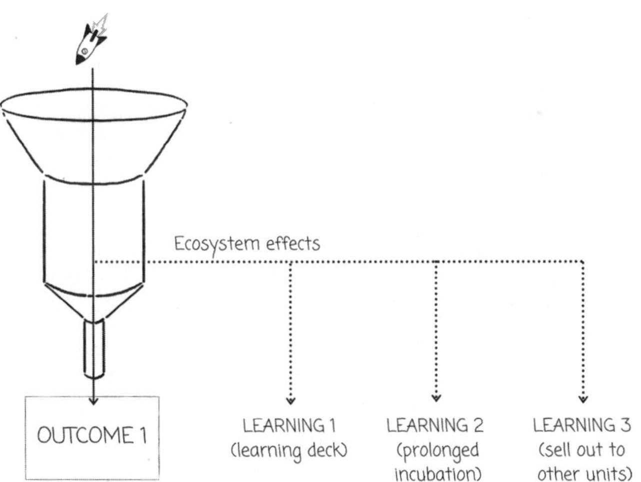

FIGURE 9.15 Alternative learning scenarios branch in the same way as outcomes.

Failures can also generate positive ecosystem effects or unintended by-products. Anecdotes of positive spillovers abound, but they are seldom tracked. "A participant to Pioneers of the Balkans reached the final with a crappy idea," reported Marius Starke, senior project manager of the namesake World Bank project, "but since then he joined a US VC-backed startup where he became a team lead, and later founded his own new startup. What is incredible, is that on the bus to our final in Belgrade he met his later cofounder, and at the event he met his life partner."

We applied the mapping tool to measure the positive ecosystem effects of a government-led accelerator[17] from 2013 to 2018. It turned out that over 15 percent of what were considered failures had in fact generated a positive impact: some founders had revamped another idea and started anew, others had joined existing startups as key employees, and a few more had been excited by the program so much that had decided to pivot their career toward innovation (Figure 9.16). Setting up such a map from day one encourages keeping track of ecosystem benefits.

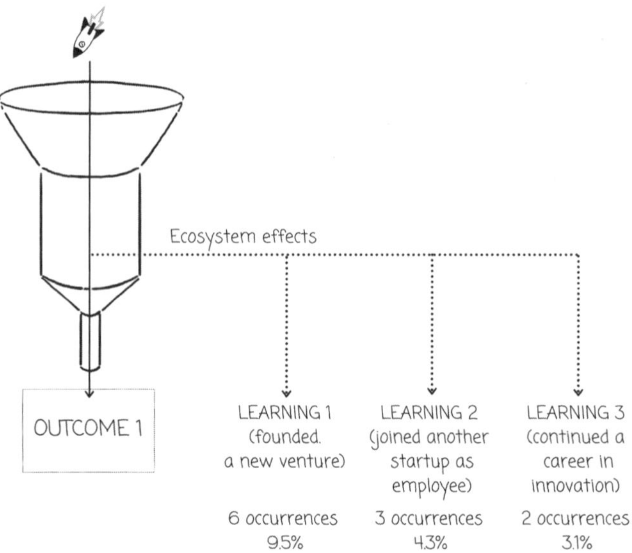

FIGURE 9.16 Explicit mapping of learning scenarios can later be used to account for alternative outcomes.

KEY TAKEAWAYS

- **Set the program's framework.** Fertilization, exploration, or exploitation are three different strategic frameworks, implying different features. For example, exploration is better governed outside the core business, whereas exploitation should be highly integrated with it. Fertilization is useful to build up readiness because it prioritizes ecosystem effects. Your chosen framework should be consistent throughout outcome metrics, selection criteria, and program positioning.
- **Never renounce measuring.** Even when a program has financial objectives, measuring results can be tricky. For equity-based models, return is a lagging indicator taking several years to appear. For models based on commercial partnerships, the contribution of startup technology can be watered down in another business unit's profit and hard to connect back to the program. While there is no holy grail for these problems, a process without metrics does not survive in most organizations, so you must assign at least one metric to each outcome on your chart—and use proxies when necessary.
- **Define proxy metrics.** Leading (or proxy) indicators provide actionable information even when results are lagging. For financial investing, use traction metrics and their change in time, or momentum. For solution sourcing, measure a percent improvement in performance, margin, or customer satisfaction during a pilot, and project the impact of a full-fledged solution. For ecosystem building, platform usage and stickiness are predictors of retention. In transformational impact programs, you need to reason on a case-by-case basis. For instance, the number of participants who become role models can be a leading indicator for educational programs, or carbon footprint reduction can work in environmental accelerators.
- **Reframe failure into learning.** Because many startups will fail, creating an infrastructure that captures value also from failures is critical. Failure can be reframed as learning, or unsuccessful projects can be reintegrated into other paths. For instance, the technology can be planned in a way that it can be reused, or teams can join existing units and be given more time.

10

CIRCLE 3: TARGET STARTUPS

The success of an engagement program always depends on the quality of the startups in the program. However, quality is context-specific. Many players in the startup community believe Silicon Valley sets the golden standard for what a quality startup looks like: a high-growth company disrupting an industry or reinventing an entire category, which will provide high returns from an exit. We strongly disagree that this predetermined standard is applicable to everyone and everywhere. Indeed, it works well for VC investors. But for a regional government in a developing country, high quality may be more likely identified with outcomes such as high survival rate of new startups or increased employment. An exit doesn't count as much, or it might even be detrimental because the new owner could decide to eradicate the startup from its ecosystem. The concept of startup quality hinges on the objective and the organization, and it emerges from the Startup Program Strategy Canvas. For example, solution sourcing programs are strongly dependent on the high quality of participants (the popular saying "garbage in, garbage out" applies there). By contrast, transformational impact programs not only can afford accepting unexperienced participants, but even seek them because they aim to elevate their entrepreneurial skills with loads of high-level education and mentorship.

If you think all startups are alike, then the only problem your startup program is solving is branding and promotion—and it is probably not solving that efficiently. Startups can differ in several aspects: what space they play in (industry, geography, technology, etc.), what stage they are at (maturity), who the founders are and what ambition do they have (motives).

In any case, can you get the startups you want? It is crucial to assess the state of the *reservoir* you can access by considering your serviceable market on the startup side and a segment's specific needs to craft an ad hoc offer.

This chapter completes the triplet about the three Circles analyzing Circle 3 and its implications, as part of an iterative process (Figure 10.1). It will address the following topics:

1. What startups are right for the problem you are solving?
2. Can you get them? Consider the targets' needs and what can convince them (or discourage them).
3. How big is the market? Assess and manage the *reservoir.*

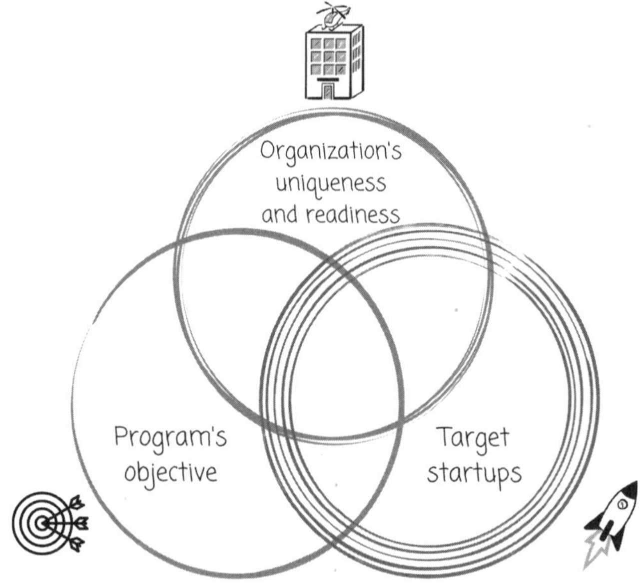

FIGURE 10.1 This chapter is about Circle 3, the target startups.

Startup Community Segments

The startup community is your external market, containing anything from informal teams still in search of a business idea, to scale-ups with over $1 billion valuations (the so-called unicorns). Exactly like other markets, the startup community can be segmented. Our research surfaced four relevant broad categories of segmentation:

- **Demographic segmentation.** Dimensions such as geography, industry, technology, business model, or time since incorporation. These dimensions are objective or almost (for instance, the industry might sometimes be debatable).
- **Innovation type.** Horizontal dimensions such as product or business model innovation, frontier research or application-driven development.
- **Maturity stage.** From early to late stages of the startup journey, startups walk their way from informal teams without an idea to international expansion (Figure 10.2).

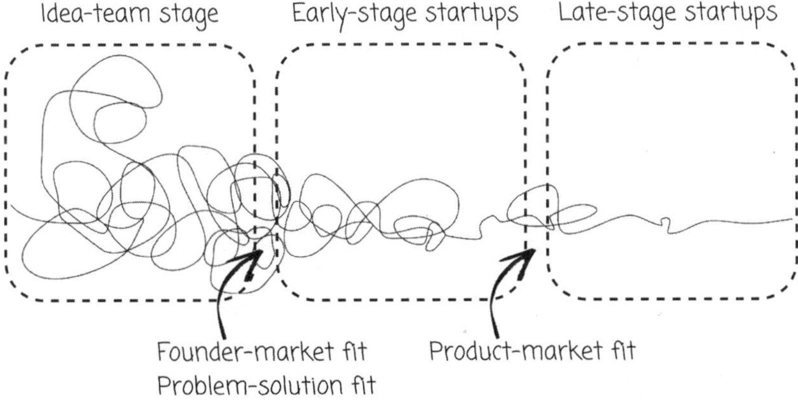

FIGURE 10.2 The startup journey goes through three maturity stages (by convention in this book): idea-team, early-stage, late-stage. The passages are marked by the problem-solution fit / founder-market fit, and the product-market fit.

- **Motives.** Chapter 2 introduced a classification in two axes resulting in six categories (Figure 10.3): short-termist (S) versus long-termist (L); and personal growth (P), rapid growth (R), or ambitious growth, but not as a black or white bet (B). The distinction between B and R is crucial for investor-driven accelerators and venture funds. Entrepreneurs must aspire to an exit in a time frame of five to seven years to be compatible with the VC business model (R).

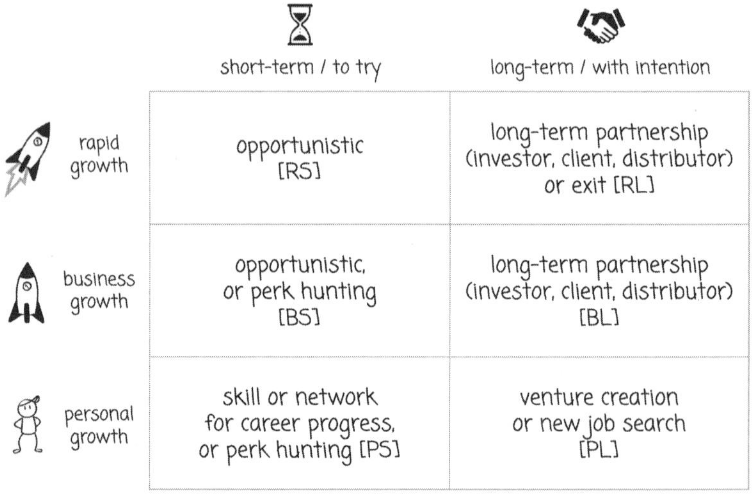

	short-term / to try	long-term / with intention
rapid growth	opportunistic [RS]	long-term partnership (investor, client, distributor) or exit [RL]
business growth	opportunistic, or perk hunting [BS]	long-term partnership (investor, client, distributor) [BL]
personal growth	skill or network for career progress, or perk hunting [PS]	venture creation or new job search [PL]

FIGURE 10.3 Startups' motives contribute to defining the startup community's segments.

Challenge #1: Identify Your Target

Corporations have an unclear understanding of what they mean by "startups."

—Mahdi Shariff, Slush China

Many large organizations struggle to achieve an internal alignment on what startups they want and why. All startups are not alike, and an offer (Circle 1) that sparks the interest of one segment might not fit another's needs. Furthermore, some startups will be able to work toward the initial goal (Circle 2); others will not. As noted in Chapter 9, objectives imply a set of terms or conditions that startups are required to comply with (asks), and not all startups can. Identifying a target means understanding precisely what startups your organization needs to work with, not just in general.

Demographics

Demographics depend on the industry, innovation problem, or investment thesis that you are targeting. They are generally more straightforward to define than other aspects, mainly because corporate and government programs often receive explicit directions from the parent organization—they are all "known knowns."

For example, Wayra seeks candidates with a strong connection with Telefónica's core business (telecommunications) in the geographies of its hubs. YC, instead, is industry agnostic and accepts worldwide applications (even though in its beginnings it focused on US national applications only to ease operations). 150 Startups targets students and researchers from Canadian colleges and universities to develop entrepreneurial role models, assuming that locals will have a more durable and visible cultural impact in the local ecosystem.

Demographic requirements are among the most accessible factors to scrutinize when you select a startup (*eligibility check*) and later on during the activation stage. You just check the startup's website, a pitch deck, or public data (e.g., incorporation date).

Innovation Type

Startups differ widely for the type of innovation they pursue, even within the same field or industry. Take artificial intelligence startups, for instance. Some use simple, almost off-the-shelf technology and focus on business model research. Others, like DeepMind (founded in 2010 and a part of Google since 2014), push the limits of the technology—in its case, it was machine learning applied to videogames.

From Circle 2 (objectives), including time horizons of the desired innovations, you should derive two crucial aspects:

- Whether you seek technology or business model innovation
- How experimental that innovation should be

Essentially, you need to translate any goal you identified in Circle 2 into a set of requirements (or lack thereof, if they are not critical in your case) on technology or business model for target startups in Circle 3.

If you are pursuing startup engagement for financial investing or ideation, for example, you would lean more toward extreme experimentation in an attempt to anticipate the next innovation wave and monetize when it moves more mainstream. On the other hand, if you are pursuing solution sourcing or validation of your technology platform, you would typically prefer products with immediate application to current use cases.

Be aware that some programs can target more than one innovation-related segment, for instance, when an incubator targets either new sustainable energy business models in Horizon 2 or disruptive sustainable materials in Horizon 3—both can profit from similar mentors, networks, partners, and industry knowledge. Other times you may want, instead, an entirely different program, connected in a system of programs (Chapter 16).

Maturity

Segmentation on startup maturity depends on various, often interconnected factors, among which are:

- **Expected payback period.** Later-stage startups are likely to deliver earlier on particular objectives, such as solution sourcing of mature innovations, or ecosystem adoption and benefits (e.g., job creation). They tend to be more business-ready, have sales and delivery processes, and have the ability to scale faster (Figure 10.4). However, fast-moving early-stage entrepreneurs (the R ambition type) could surpass a slower later-stage competitor.
- **Your general strategy.** Early-stage is a quantity game. Late-stage shifts toward proven track records and picking the champions. For example, seed accelerators invest in higher quantity and lower maturity startups than VCs, but can function with smaller funds (Circle 1) and longer horizons (Circle 2).

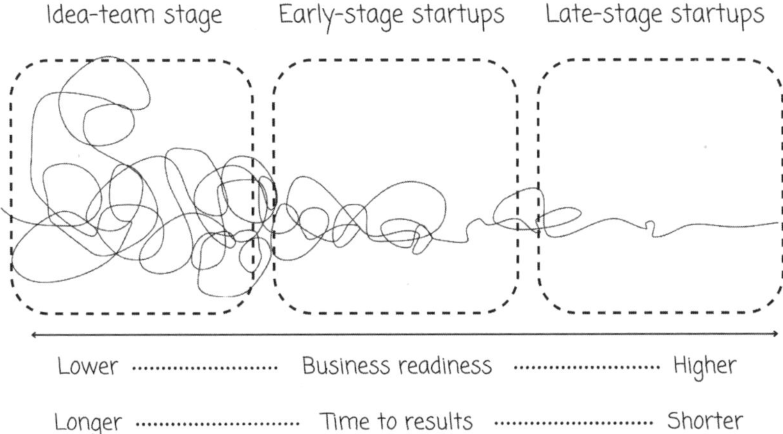

FIGURE 10.4 The ability to deliver results and scalability increases with maturity.

- **Your readiness.** What level of startup complexity can your organization handle? Fund size (or budget), team experience and skills, internal allies and buy-in, as discussed in Chapter 8, are some of the factors at play.

Early-stage startups are flexible and can be molded but need time to define and pivot the product. They are more suitable for pre-graduation goals of ideation, validation of your technology (e.g., your proprietary AI platform), cultural and mindset shift of your employees, and so on. Founders are also more likely to relocate to your destination—and away from it.

As startups mature, they become more business-ready, with higher reliability and capability to scale up. Solution sourcing is best served by them. They also provide a more reliable pulse of new technology and market trends. They tend to have superior technology, more market experience, validated customer data, and a beachhead in an emerging market with a stronger brand. The flip side is they are more "expensive": terms must be more tailored, valuation more flexible (and higher), and founders harder to relocate. All but nimbleness tends to improve with more maturity (Figure 10.5).

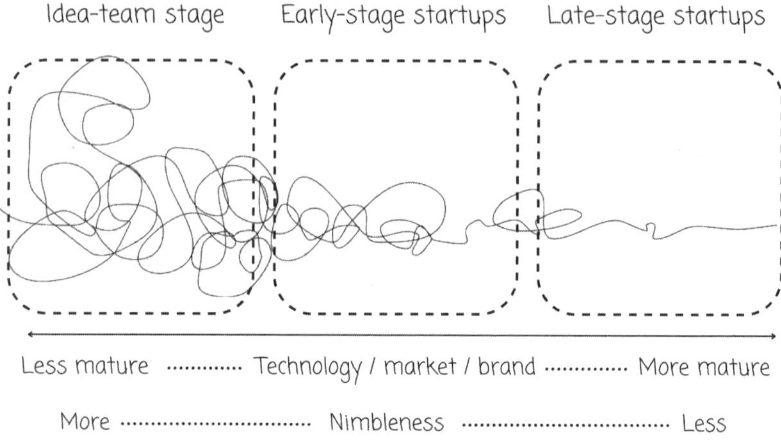

FIGURE 10.5 Relationship between startup's assets and maturity stage.

Motives

Motives depend on your objectives, investment thesis, and business model. Chapters 3 to 6 reviewed the relationship of the startup's ambition and four long-term goals:

- Financial investing requires RL startups—entrepreneurs committed to a rapid and high-value exit.
- Solution sourcing is less tied to rapid growth or long-term commitment, but cannot accept solely personal objectives (i.e., all but PS or PL).
- Ecosystem building favors long-termism without hasty exit goals (BL), such as in destination and regional development programs. PL or RL are still interesting.
- Transformational impact manages equally well many motivations, including personal (i.e., P accepted or sometimes the main focus, such as in 150 Startups).

Pre-graduation objectives can accommodate more short-term ambitions and motivations. For ideation, for instance, you may even profit from short-termist participants (S) because they would likely be less emotionally attached to the idea they produce in the program. For culture and mindset shaping, you may benefit from startups with less ambitious trajectories (B or P) because they are typically more patient and available for educating others.

Challenge #2: Targets' Needs and Minimum Viable Proposition

> *You need to clearly communicate the value of why a startup should join.*
>
> —Joanna Buczkowska-McCumber, League of Innovators

Startups from different segments often require a tailored value proposition. For example, the Women in Cleantech Challenge reviewed in Chapter 6 lasted two and a half years and provided a stipend based on the specific needs of women entrepreneurs in that sector.

To foster the interest of startups in your target segment, you must understand their needs, and which of them are underserved in your ecosystem. While crafting the offer will come in Chapter 12, the analysis of Circle 3 will expose a sort of *minimum viable proposition* that can potentially move a startup to apply (yes, the acronym is "just another" MVP, just like the one standing for minimum viable product but with a very different meaning).

Startup Needs

Startups typically exhibit gaps or needs in seven areas:

- **Knowledge.** Information or methodologies on market, industry, technology, trends, business administration, sales, business planning, intellectual property, or investor pitching, for instance.
- **Mindset.** Founders sometimes need to overcome cultural preconceptions about the entrepreneurs' role in society, failure reframed as learning, how corporate sales work, the value of diversity, and so forth.
- **Resources.** Capital and talent are sovereign resources for startups. Capital (in the form of investment, grant, debt, or revenues) can be used for exploration, research and development, and expansion. Early talent is vital to foster growth.
- **Operations.** From prototyping to manufacturing, distribution, logistics, or immigration bureaucracy—they are all important for allowing the founders focus on the business model and product exploration.

- **Networks.** Introductions to investors, access to industry leaders, access to supply chain or distribution partners, or institutional partnerships.
- **Recognition.** Building a brand and signing up new customers are universal business needs. Brand association and a vetting stamp may contribute to opening new gates and are also synergic for networking.
- **Strategy.** Advisory and guidance on product and market strategy, expansion, competition, and so on.

Programs generally concentrate on just a few of these gaps. If you think of CVC funds, for example, they primarily focus on one: resources. But as the context changes and the industry reorganizes after a bubble, sometimes overcoming one gap only is not enough to differentiate yourself. Yet "too many" also causes you to stumble. Challenges and competitions, for instance, mainly address recognition and resource needs (with awards and cash prizes). Incubators focus on operational and networking needs. Mentor-driven accelerators prioritize strategy, knowledge, and networks, with just enough resources to support founders through the program. Each kind of proposition attracts different startups, and this is how the MVP for your target influences the program template (Intersection).

Needs Dependence on Segment Characteristics

> *Hire people on the program team with customer service skills and simply listen to the startups' needs.*
>
> —Lisa Cashmore, Communitech

Demographics can greatly affect a startup's needs. Industry and gender, for instance, are among the main elements that shaped the Women in Cleantech Challenge's concept. Nothing short of customer discovery and research can provide insights into a specific segment you are targeting. Customer interviews, focus groups, and customer-centered design or codesign are the elective tools for this analysis.

Maturity has a high correlation with needs too, of which we have a more general understanding (Figure 10.6). Early-stage founders are generally more in need of guidance, industry

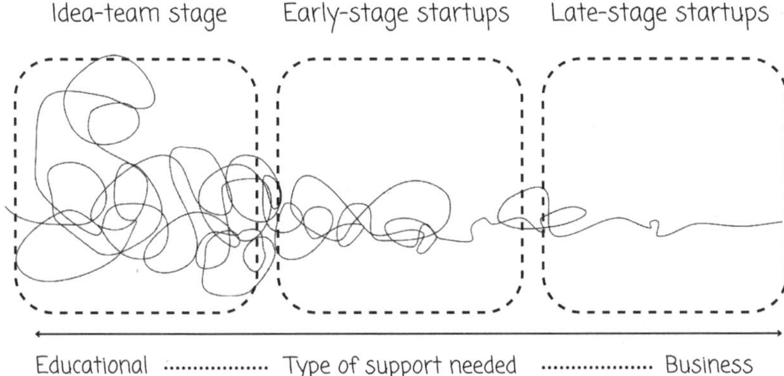

FIGURE 10.6 Earlier-stage startups tend to need more educational support, whereas more mature startups demand business development and customers.

knowledge, market intelligence, and, if first-time entrepreneurs, also of developing new skill sets. Mentors should be skilled in exploration and apt at coaching. Talent for the management team needs to be entrepreneurial.

When they mature and accumulate experience, learning, and networks, startups' demand shifts toward business development. Mentors and prospective management team members should be industry experts experienced in scaling up. Introductions to potential partners or clients are more valuable than pitch training.

Motives, finally, may impact the balance between offer and ask that the startups will support. Rapid-growing, ambitious startups value time and speed over everything else, so the program should focus on what can accelerate their business growth trajectory: cash, resources, customers, new hires, and networks. By contrast, participants driven by personal career motivations may need more counseling, new skills, and recognition, and may trade relocation and dedication to obtain them.

Competition and Underserved Gaps

Your ecosystem might include other active players serving one or more needs of your target segment. Map existing gaps in the ecosystem to understand your target's uncovered needs. This analysis will provide information on how tough or expensive it can be to drive participation to your program against competitors for the MVP.

Like for other markets, an underserved need in your ecosystem can offer an excellent opportunity for a startup program. Specifically, new entrants are generally successful when they target verticals that are unsupported but have many entrepreneurs working on related ideas—such as it could have been the case for blockchain and cryptocurrency startups in many regional ecosystems around the world in 2015–20. Even a program with a rather basic offer (i.e., a low MVP) would have good chances to succeed in that situation. And not just that: it would help develop the local startup community, even when "social impact" and "ecosystem development" were not explicit objectives in your Circle 2.

On the other hand, if a vertical is already occupied by another program, you can still devise smart tactics without needing to go head to head. For example, if a leading accelerator such as Techstars already operates a food tech program in your city, attracting good startups to another food tech accelerator could prove challenging. However, you can boost cluster effects, especially if you can also leverage the local supply chain or business community—for instance if you operate in a region particularly renowned for the food sector such as somewhere in Italy or France. Or you can look for synergies with the existing program (in the sense discussed for systems of programs, in Chapter 16): You can go upstream and create a pre-accelerator for less mature startups which can provide deal flow to the existing accelerator; or you can go downstream and create a commercialization platform or a fund for follow-on investments for accelerator graduates.

The bottom line is that, because the alternative offer highly influences needs and gaps in your entrepreneurial ecosystem and reservoir, you should always conduct a competitive (or synergic) analysis before executing on a new program.

Minimum Valuation

Any offer inherently implies a startup valuation, and how the startup feels about that will determine its participation—an insight that many programs seem to ignore. Equity asks are a straightforward example. If an accelerator demands 10 percent for $100,000 in capital and $200,000 in services (e.g., office space or mentorship), is the implied post-money valuation $3 million or $1 million? For the accelerator it might be $3 million because it accounts for the services as part of the investment, but the startup's previous investors may disagree and induce the CEO to refuse the offer.

The implied valuation does not concern equity investments only. Another example comes from the logistic asks of relocation and attendance. To gauge the implicated value, you can take the average price of a Big Four consultant for the time of onsite presence requested to founders (adjustable if remote). For a two-day hackathon, that easily amounts to $3,000 to 5,000 per founder; for a three-month accelerator, that could surpass $100,000 per founder. A lower reward will appeal only to less-than-consultant-grade founders.

When estimating the MVP, you should look at the average market valuation for the segment you are targeting and check if you have the internal resources (Circle 1) to approach that segment with the asks you intend to require from the participants.

MVP and Iteration

The MVP for your program looks like a set of minimum offers along the seven categories of startup needs listed at the beginning of this section, from knowledge to strategy needs. They describe what the program must offer given the target that you want. They will be useful in Chapter 12.

Like for other assumptions, there is no way to validate a minimum value proposition without talking to customers, running a pilot or scaled-down version of your program, and collecting validated learning. It is challenging to get the offer right at the first attempt, so iteration is crucial.

Challenge #3: Don't Implicitly Discourage Your Target

Some aspects of your ask have a more evident effect than others on how different segments will react to your MVP. This section is at the crossing of Circles 1, 2, and 3 and gives a sneak peek at the final solution (Intersection). Yet, for relevance with targeting, we include it here.

Ask: Standardized Deal

Startup programs often work with standardized term sheets because they allow more replicability and quicker decision processes. A standard deal always encodes a fixed implied valuation, the same across all participants. However, that may cause issues with startups of any stage that have already received an investment round. The later the stage, the higher the likelihood that a fast-growing startup has raised venture capital, and the harder it is to sell a standardized term sheet (Figure 10.7).

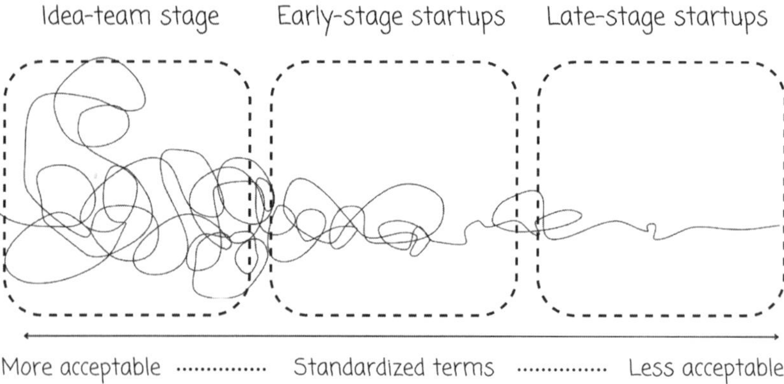

FIGURE 10.7 Acceptance of standardized deal terms depending on maturity stage.

To reduce this friction, programs targeting later-stage startups often introduce a semi-standardized deal: the ticket is fixed (e.g., \$100,000) but the valuation is negotiable, or both are negotiable but other terms are preset. Exceptions exist: many startups are ready to accept more onerous terms for the advantage of being associated with an exceptional brand, for instance.

Asks: Product Stack, Business Architecture, or Logistics

When ecosystem adoption is the objective, startups may be requested to integrate a technology (e.g., for software platforms), relocate or hire specific staff (e.g., for ecosystem platforms), or expand into a particular market (e.g., for business platforms).

Contrary to other parameters, maturity does not generally correlate with more or less flexibility: it alters the aspects that a startup can renegotiate. Earlier-stage startups, having more operational flexibility, adhere more easily to such terms, also agreeing to relocating founding members or restructuring their product stack. Later-stage startups become a good fit when they are ready for product diversification and international expansion. In this case, however, they would often relocate hires, as opposed to founders, or start a new line of business, as opposed to modifying their core product (Figure 10.8).

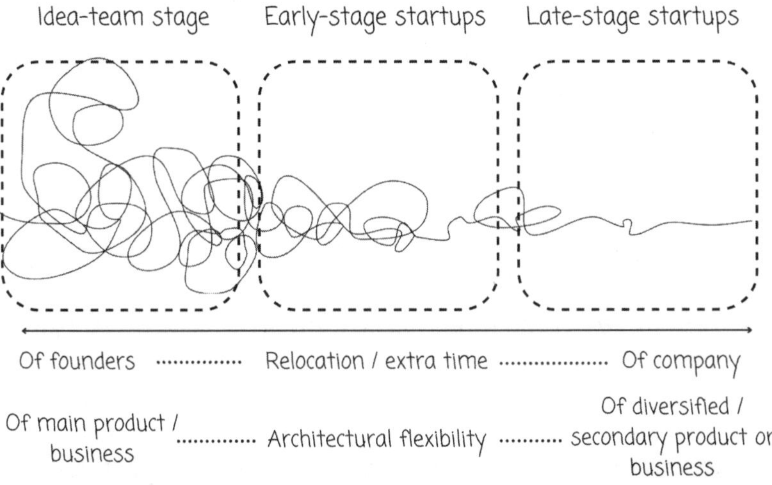

FIGURE 10.8 Contrary to other parameters, maturity does not generally correlate with more or less flexibility: it alters the aspects that a startup can renegotiate.

Logistic and architectural asks incur the risk of attracting short-termist, hit-and-run opportunists who grab the rewards and abandon the platform as soon as the program ends (the incentives evaporation problem). Startups without growth ambitions (PS and BS) could fill the pipeline because they are less sensitive to taking a diversion, even at the cost of losing ground to competitors (Figure 10.9).

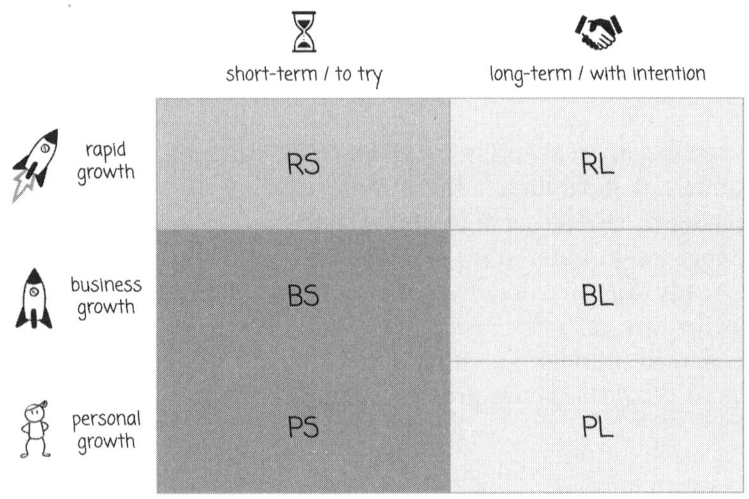

FIGURE 10.9 Asks about flexibility might fill the pipeline with S startups, who are more open to renegotiate their business because they know they will not commit long-term.

Consequently, handle these asks with care. You can mitigate this problem in two ways:

- **Include pre-graduation objectives** (Circle 2). Involve PS and BS participants in ideation, validation, technology testing, trend analysis, mindset shaping, or talent marketplace. These activities will extract value from their presence during the program. If those are your goals, S startups are your clients.
- **Use staging** (Intersection). Participants may comply with asks such as relocation, dedication, or technology experimentation during the program, but they rarely stick to those asks for long (e.g., they relocate back at the end of the program). To incentivize more stickiness, you can stage the rewards over both the activation and the follow-on phases—i.e., distribute them in time, subject to reaching milestones connected to those asks (see also Chapters 12 and 13).

Challenge #4: Assess the Market Size

How large is the serviceable obtainable market (SOM) of your program? The SOM is the market you can capture based on your operational model, channels, and partners. In this book we call it *reservoir*. A startup program searches for startups in the ecosystem much like a fisherman catches fish in a lake, via scouting (like with a harpoon) or a call for applications (like with a net). The reservoir, in this metaphor, is the smaller area of a lake where a fisher can hunt, given a boat and equipment, partners, or competitors (Figure 10.10).

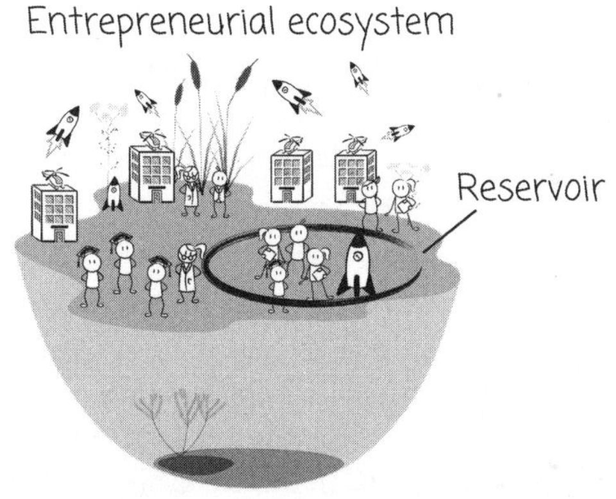

FIGURE 10.10 Your program's reservoir is the subset of the startup community that you can reach. It depends on structural features (e.g., location), your partner network, your brand, and so on.

The reservoir size may increase with the promotion you make (online or offline, in partner universities or other programs, etc.), and it is limited by the bounded variables of Circle 1 and 2 (Chapter 8). TIM WCAP, for instance, only admits Italian digital startups—non-Italian, nondigital startups are outside its reservoir. Onsite hackathons have a reservoir geographically limited to one or two hundred miles radius.

A program's reservoir contains diverse segments, but startups of a particular type may not be in its reservoir. For instance, if a program in a peripheral town accepts only local startups, the chance that a unicorn health startup is among that number might be null.

What startup segments does a program's reservoir contain? Does it provide enough quality deal flow to achieve the program's goals? These questions can be answered through market research, probe events such as pitch nights, databases compiled by specialized firms such as Crunchbase, PitchBook, or DealRoom,[1] referrals from your partner network, surveys in the startup community, and so on.

If the reservoir in Circle 3 does not provide enough quality deal flow, consider the following options, both of which affect the other two Circles:

- Lift some of the boundaries imposed by Circle 1 and 2.
- Pivot to a fertilizing action that increases the quality and quantity of your segment of interest.

Lifting the Boundaries

If you have a narrow strategy with many requirements on startups (*bound variables*), there may just be no startup that fits your ideal champion. You must accept a trade-off between quality and quantity. If you specialize in one aspect, you may have to lift the boundary in another (Circle 1 or 2).

For instance, if you restrict the innovation need, you could release the geographical constraints—as did Open Accelerator, promoted by pharmaceutical group Zambon. When the focus shrank from generic therapeutics to brain and respiratory diseases, "the number of proposals dropped by almost 40% and those that came had to be actively scouted internationally," reported Federica Destro, "but the quality was higher."

Logistics asks such as relocation or dedication are among the costliest for fast-growing startups because staying close to their customers and speed are two of their key advantages. Consider carefully what people you need in the program. Founders are only required if the program delivers coaching and mentoring that can affect the startup's strategy, such as what happens in YC or Techstars (e.g., to secure a course of action toward an exit, or the founders' professional growth).

In solution sourcing or innovation ecosystem building, a non-founding manager or even a technical sales account could be sufficient. If founders are essential, consider founder-compatible schedules such as Tuesday dinners in YC, or concentrating meetings every two or three weeks.

Sometimes lifting a boundary will collide with the program's mission (Circle 2), displeasing your stakeholders. On the other hand, politics could jeopardize results if those boundaries deprive the program of deal flow. For example, universities may face internal opposition when extending their programs outside of their students or researchers. When Velocity, the University of Waterloo's incubator, was about to open up its admission requirements, many questioned why it should use its dollars to subsidize non-alumni. "The hardest thing sometimes is just to win stakeholders' alignment," Jay Shah said.

Pivoting to Fertilization

If Circle 3 does not provide enough quality deal flow, you may be facing an over-constrained context. You will have to improve the organizational outreach in the ecosystem (Circle 1), or temporarily change focus on your objectives (Circle 2).

To improve the organization's ability to attract startups (Circle 1), you can use one or more of the following tactics:

- **Make your offer more enticing.** This may involve adding a content feature in the pipeline but not ready yet, or unlocking more budget for higher rewards.
- **Brand exposure in the startup community.** Put your brand out there by giving first to other programs, before asking for participation to your programs. Sponsor other organizations' events or programs or offer free mentoring and consulting to startups. Tactically (and temporarily) redirect focus on receiving press coverage.
- **Acquire a trusted referral network.** Referrals are reported to be the best source of startups. Partner with universities, venture funds, and other programs, or sign up mentors to refer startups to the program.

As a tactical goal for the initial editions (Circle 2), you may temporarily suppress or deprioritize your leading objectives in favor of deal flow generation:

- **More but shorter.** Temporarily prioritize objectives that require shorter programs, such as ideation hackathons, do many of them, and later build on their outputs.
- **Fertilize universities.** Accelerators and incubators sometimes organize free courses or hackathons for university students to generate new early-stage deal flow. 150 Startups is an example.
- **Create a system of programs.** Add one or more programs at earlier stages, such as a pre-incubator or a pre-accelerator, that prepare your deal flow (see also Chapter 16). Examples of this tactic are F10's threefold offer from an ideation workshop to an incubator and an accelerator, or Concept, Velocity's pre-incubator.

KEY TAKEAWAYS

- **Four market segmentation categories.** Our research surfaced four relevant broad categories of startup segmentation: Demographic segmentation, such as geography, industry, technology, business model, or time since incorporation. Innovation type, such as product or business model innovation, frontier research, or application-driven development. Maturity, which ranges from the early to late stages of the startup journey. Motives, which comprise six categories based on short-term versus long-term viewpoints and the growth ambitions of the startup.
- **Assess the entry price.** The minimum value proposition (MVP) is the minimum set of features (offers and asks) that appeal to a given target segment. Each segment has different needs, so you must conduct market research to define the MVP for your case. You can see the MVP as the entry price to collaborate with the startup segment you want. That also means that you must avoid features that implicitly discourage that segment.

- **Mind your competitors' offers.** Because needs and gaps are highly influenced by the competing programs in your entrepreneurial ecosystem, you should always conduct a competitive (or synergic) analysis before executing on a new program.
- **If your reservoir is small, expand your outreach.** If you determine the size of your reservoir (i.e., your SOM) is too small, you can make your offer more enticing (provide more resources); stay in the backline for a while and build a brand and network by sponsoring other programs; or acquire a trusted referral network by partnering with universities, venture funds, and other programs.
- **Alternatively, ripen your reservoir.** In addition, as a tactical goal, you may temporarily suppress or deprioritize your leading objectives in favor of deal flow generation by (1) prioritizing objectives that require shorter programs, such as ideation hackathons, (2) fertilizing universities by organizing free courses or hackathons for university students, (3) adding one or more programs at earlier stages, such as a pre-incubator or a pre-accelerator, to attract more participants.

CAPTURING VALUE

This chapter opens the tactical design phase. Tactical design and feature configuration rarely follow context analysis (Chapters 8–10) in a one-off waterfall process. Instead, strategic and tactical design alternate in an iterative cycle until you find a formula that works (Chapter 7). In the three previous chapters we analyzed the context—in Circle 1, 2, and 3, respectively. Now it is time to discuss how to configure the features of your solution (Figure 11.1): its managerial features (in this chapter), as well as its structural and content features (the following four chapters).

Reminder: Don't get ahead of yourself. Make sure the Startup Program Strategy Canvas looks right and passes the smell test before moving on to tactical design.

Start with the end in mind, and first focus on how you are going to capture value from the program. Of course, that depends on your objectives and metrics, as discussed in Chapter 9 (Circle 2). Here we will discuss what program stage produces your success metrics—recruitment, activation, or follow-on. Only after identifying the stage and output of value can you judge if and how your organization can capture it. And only once you know what startups you are working with can you really lock that in, which is why you want to look at strategic versus tactical design as two separate activities. Governance and performance metrics

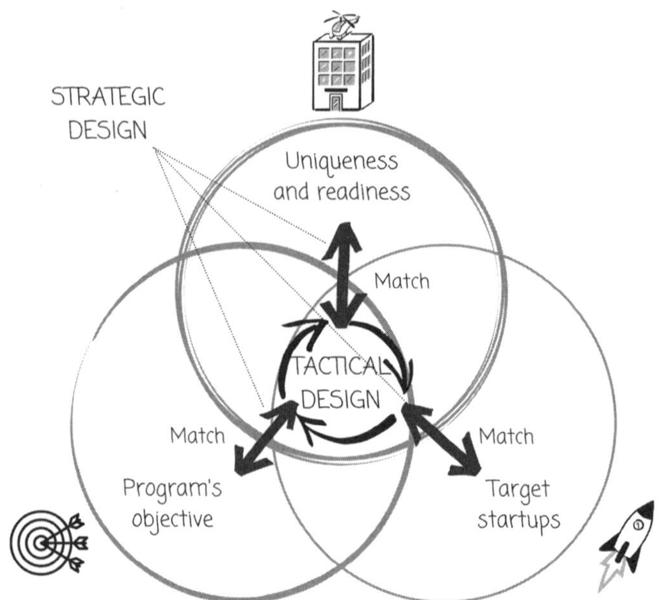

FIGURE 11.1 This chapter and the following four discuss tactical design and the configuration of program features.

derive from value considerations. This chapter will address the following challenges:

1. What stage creates value for your objectives?
2. What functions do you need to design for?
3. How do you intend to capture value?
4. What kind of governance should you put in place?
5. What performance metrics do you need?
6. How to pursue economic sustainability beyond/without internal sponsorship?

Challenge #1: What Stage Creates Value for Your Objectives

Objectives (Circle 2) determine what program stage is the most valuable for you, since each stage enables different kinds of goals (Figures 11.2 and 11.3):

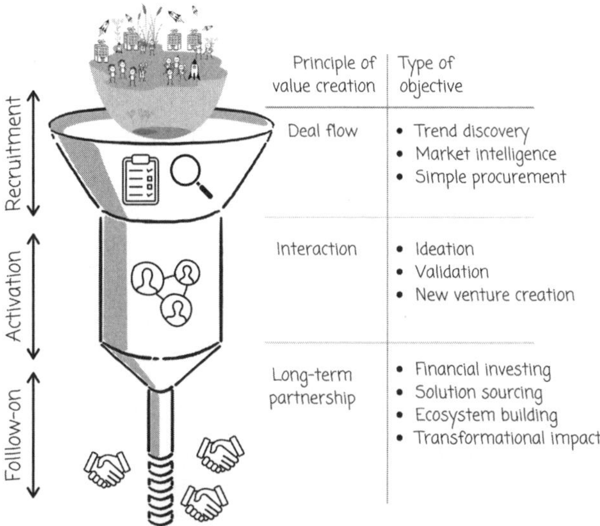

FIGURE 11.2 Each stage contributes to specific objectives. Some need long-term partnerships, and thus can be achieved only after graduation. Others can be obtained in either the recruitment (deal-flow based objective) or activation stage (interaction-based objective).

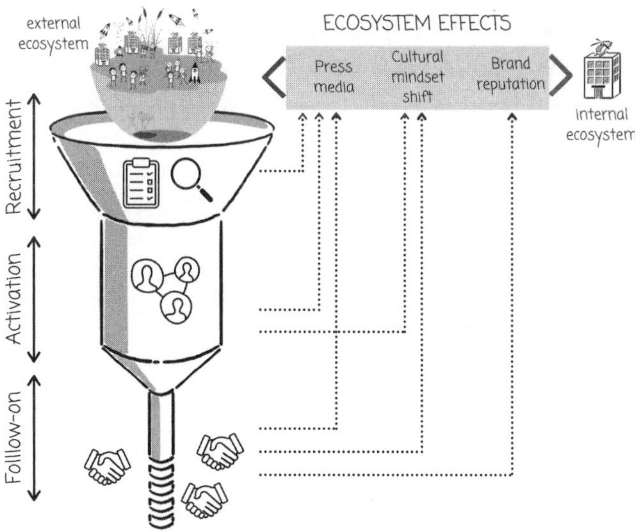

FIGURE 11.3 Ecosystem effects follow a similar principle and stem from one stage or another. They may affect either the external or internal ecosystem, or both.

- **Recruitment stage.** This stage is all about generating and capturing deal flow, in quantity and of quality. As such, it contributes to many objectives, but specifically it satisfies those that rely just on receiving a lot of applications, such as trend analysis, market intelligence, and idea proposals. Also, it generates press and media coverage (an ecosystem effect, in our framework). If those are your goals, then design a program that accentuates this stage, execute recruitment well, and you are mostly done. A call for application or startup scouting can generate all the required information and the hype you desire. Your output can simply be a report containing intelligence (e.g., trends or technology mapping) and communication metrics (e.g., share of voice or social media impressions).
- **Activation stage.** Interactions among the participants (or between participants and your employees) happen in this stage. During this time, participants (and employees) connect, network, understand, try, fail, and learn from failure. Interactions are a necessary stepping stone for objectives such as ideation, validation, talent hiring, new team formation, initial ecosystem adoption, or minor transformational goals. Entrepreneurial culture, new knowledge, and new skills are formed in this stage.
- **Follow-on stage.** This stage affects objectives only when they require a long-term partnership with the startup for post-graduation objectives (Chapter 2). In those cases, the program has two proxy objectives: (a) creating a long-term partnership that will enable the real goal, and (b) accelerating the startup toward that goal (e.g., increasing its metrics). Financial investing, solution sourcing, long-term ecosystem adoption, and long-term transformational impact demand continuation of the startup's engagement after graduation. A program's reputation is also built up over time in the follow-on stage (with spillovers to its parent company) through a track record of successes.

Figure 11.3 illustrates how the different ecosystem effects are produced at different stages: press and media coverage in all stages; culture and mindset starting from the activation stage; and brand and reputation especially stemming from the program's track record of successes (follow-on stage). You can design the program to direct these effects toward either or both the entrepreneurial and organizational ecosystems.

Create a map of the program stages with your objectives and desired ecosystem effects, and use it to guide your attention during design. Seriously, go sketch it out using the methodology of goal mapping illustrated in Chapter 9, Challenge #2. We will still be here when you return. Magic happens when you write seemingly obvious assumptions down on paper and observe causation. The next chapter will discuss how this affects your choice of template.

Note that objectives in later stages necessitate the support of previous steps. For example, a program cannot produce investor-ready startups for a post-graduation objective of financial return without functional recruitment or effective activation. Thus, the map is essentially suggesting whether you can ignore later stages (e.g., follow-on stage) or not.

Challenge #2: Identify the Internal Functions

The program fulfills a set of functions in the organizational pipeline dedicated to startups.

The relevant functions for your program derive from Circle 2. But even within the tasks defined by your objectives, there can be different priorities. For instance, BMW Startup Garage favors transaction risk management, whereas The Bridge favors cultural translation (Chapter 4). The respective programs will contain different features. A program prioritizing cultural translation might focus on joint workshops between startups and corporate managers, whereas one prioritizing risk management might add more pilot project meetings.

Chapters 3 to 6 showed how models directed at different objectives implement key functions for those objectives. For instance:

- **External signaling.** Communicating that the organization is open to partnering with the startup community (recruitment stage, outcomes).
- **Internal signaling.** Catalyzing and organizing the involvement of internal allies, including pulling innovation

needs that can be redirected to startups (activation stage, outputs, outcomes).

- **Information gathering.** Surveying the technology and emerging market trends in the startup community to inform organizational strategy (recruitment stage, activation stage).
- **Cultural translation.** Educating each side to the nonnegotiable needs of the other side to make the partnership happen, such as decision speed or bureaucracy (activation stage).
- **Cultural fertilization.** Producing ecosystem effects for maturing the internal innovation ecosystem or the external entrepreneurial ecosystem (activation stage, outcomes).
- **Mobilization.** Ensuring a pipeline of partnership options for the organizational sponsor, with many relevant startups willing and able to partner (recruitment stage).
- **Sorting.** Identifying startups with the highest match with the organization's strategy and program's goals (recruitment stage).
- **Onboarding.** Facilitating the initial steps of the partnership or, in the case of ecosystem building, streamlining the adoption phase (activation stage).
- **Gap filling.** Arguably among the most important if not the quintessential program function, this is about removing roadblocks to startups, to advance them toward the program's objectives, such as improving team formation, skill set, or capital (activation stage, follow-on stage).
- **Transaction risk management.** Lowering the costs and risk of participating in the partnership for each side, enforcing timing, payment terms, IP rights, and so on (all stages).
- **Follow-up warranty.** Addressing the preconditions for a durable partnership, including portfolio management, integration, and scale-up (activation stage, follow-on stage).

Program stages contribute to functions in different ways, and some stages cannot contribute to some functions. Figure 11.4 gives you the map of functions (right) to stages (left). Look up your priority functions in the right column, and the left diagram will show which stage is the first one (in order) that can contribute to them. If a function appears near the recruitment stage, it means that stage and the following can contribute to it. If a

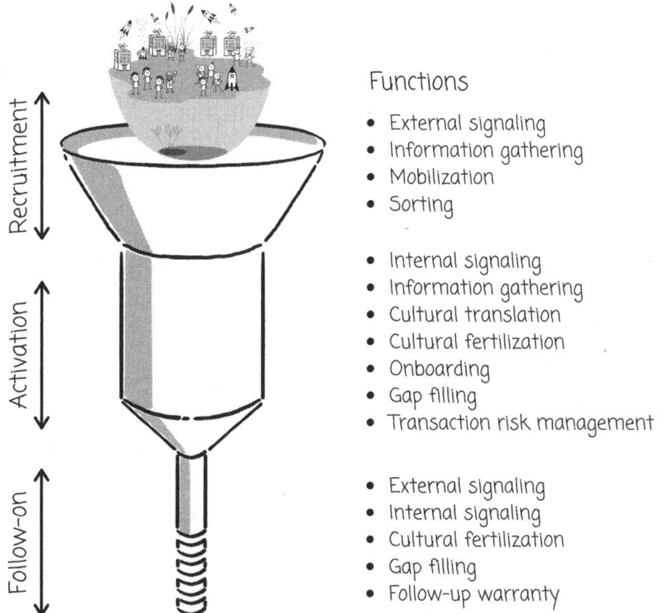

FIGURE 11.4 Look up the functions you are prioritizing: the left of this map will tell you what stage implements them first (later stages can also implement them).

function appears in a later stage, it means that earlier stages can contribute to it only partially or not at all. The distinction is not net, and a function can be executed in more than one stage.

For instance, information gathering (which we map in the recruitment stage) can be done during startup interviews for admission (i.e., in recruitment), but it could continue also in the activation stage, for example, with tests and demos. Instead, cultural fertilization (mapped in the activation stage) cannot be achieved in the recruitment stage if not in a very minor form, through the limited interactions between startups and the employees in the admission jury (and it would be limited to the few employees involved in that jury).

You should use this map in conjunction with Figure 9.13, which maps the program stages to the asks described in Table 9.3. Many functions are made possible by introducing specific asks. For instance, an application form can be used for the information gathering function (both appear alongside the recruitment stage in the two figures). You can use the two maps together to double-check that you have identified all the asks for your priority functions. Also, you can drop or simplify some asks that do not map to any of your priority functions. For example, if information gathering is not a priority, you could decide to simplify the application form.

Challenge #1 in the next chapter will complete this reasoning about what stages count most for you, as we will finally connect functions to the most well-known templates.

Challenge #3: Define How You Capture Value in Each Stage

Once it is clear which stage or stages generate your objectives, you have to put into place a structure to capture that value. Here are the issues to solve:

- **Identify the necessary partners.** This step is usually intuitive—it could be a business unit, customers, follow-on investors, or the same startups. What is important is that the partner is willing and able to help you capture value. Wayra, for instance, selects a startup only if an internal client has already committed to going forward if the initial pilot is successful. Start small and grow later. Identify the readiest partners and go with them for the first or second edition. A program can always sign up more partners as it builds a track record and gains more internal traction.
- **Keep the partners engaged.** This task is possibly one of the most challenging, particularly in the context of post-graduation partners. You can review the internal buy-in strategies illustrated in Chapter 8 and choose a set to start the engagement. Then, devise a process to keep that engagement alive. For example, you could create an innovation board for your senior leadership or set up a tracking system to show progress on internal pilots.
- **Collect data for measuring the program's metrics.** Often, designers overlook the data collection issue until it is too late. Startups might stop responding to surveys after graduation; internal allies might focus on their metrics

and not on those associated with the program's outputs; or external partners might never put a system in place to collect the data you need from them. Whatever the cause, you want to prevent it by design.

- **Define the output.** The form of output should be defined beforehand, possibly together with the partners or stakeholders who will use it. What will enable your partners to capture value? It is not just about deciding between a pitch, a pilot, or a demo, but rather about the details of what that output should contain: what information, what performance metrics, what features, and so on.

Capturing Value in the Recruitment Stage

When your objectives are generated solely in the recruitment stage, you generally just need to design how to collect information efficiently (e.g., application form or database). If you use the activation stage for extended due diligence, you may need additional tools (e.g., progress tracking). The output is generally a report, a showcase, or an equivalent document or event summarizing information for a selected public.

You are most likely able to capture this information independently of other business units or allies (Chapter 8). There may still be some minor dependencies when identifying trends and interesting startups during the scouting phase or selection process, but partner relationships should not be an issue when recruitment is your main value-capturing stage.

Metrics such as number of applications, social media engagement, number of impressions of your ads, and similar process and output metrics focusing on the recruitment stage are all relevant measurements. They can act as a proxy of the depth of your scouting action, or the loudness of your communication activities.

Capturing Value in the Activation Stage

In the activation stage, a program can pursue interaction-based objectives. To capture value from these interactions, you must focus on fostering meaningful participation. Depending on who should participate, this task can be accomplished independently or may have to involve the support of other units or partners. For instance, if you just need external lecturers, you can procure them autonomously with your budget. But if your program intends to cross-fertilize corporate culture with startups HR will be a fundemental ally. Or you may need mentors from a specific internal unit (e.g., R&D or top-tier business sales) if the participants need advice, contacts, or information that only that unit can provide.

To document the progress on objectives such as validation or mindset shift, you need to determine a *baseline* at the program's start and then *final status* when the program ends. For validation, for example, you document the inputs given to participants (e.g., a problem brief, a technology to test) and the results of any test performed. For mindset shift or skill set learning, you can distribute a self-evaluation survey before and after the program and register how people perceive their own changes.

You may want to continue tracking the change for some time after the program. For example, you can monitor how employees have altered their behavior one year later by distributing a follow-up survey. Possible metrics include increased attendance to innovation activities, the number of employees joining an incubated spin-off, or the number of ideas that actually take-off. Of course, such continued monitoring entails creating an information collection system in the follow-on stage. These same metrics can keep your partners engaged by demonstrating results.

Capturing Value in the Follow-on Stage—Data Collection

The objectives that are most difficult to capture are generally those involving the post-graduation stage, because the program always depends on other partners or participants to score its metrics.

Collecting data from startups and partners can be a problem in itself. Once startups leave the program, their obligation of transparency and reporting might end, or it might slip into secondary consideration. However, data can be a critical output, for example, to assess impact objectives (on startups, or on the entrepreneurial ecosystem) or to track the economic upside of a startup innovation introduced in a core business process.

Data collection/sharing (from startups to the program management team) must be incentivized by design. Some strategies include:

- **Automation.** The best way is to enable your partners to produce data as part of their everyday operations. For example, you could endow the startups with an accounting platform to keep track of their progress seamlessly. Or, you could require only documents they would produce anyway (such as their income statement). For internal units, you may leverage an internal reporting software, or add a personal KPI linked to innovation that they would feel like part of their duty to report on. Of course, make sure they are aware of this parameter early in the recruiting stage.

- **Relationship management.** A program can keep active relationships with startups through a well-managed alumni program—ranging from a newsletter to a regular alumni reunion or an exclusive online platform with additional services. Such relationships can then be used to solicit timely data disclosure. Similar engagement tools can be used, with changes as needed, for internal units.
- **Use staging.** Delay part of the benefits for startups to the follow-on stage and unlock them only when startups disclose their updates. These can be alumni benefits, such as participation in alumni meetings, or standard program benefits, such as tranches of funding. Of course, make sure this delay and its reasons are clearly communicated to startups.

At the end of this analysis and planning, you want to create a table similar to Table 11.1, where for each objective you have at least one hypothetical path ahead (the table gives just two lines as an example).

TABLE 11.1 Example of planning needed for post-graduation objectives

Objective	Post-graduation Partner	Continuous Engagement Strategy	Metrics Collection Strategy
Strategic investing	Corporate development	Biannual updates on startup status, senior leadership involvement	Pull data from shareholder documentation prepared by the startup
Solution sourcing for customer care	Sales unit X	Champion X inside the unit, revenue tracking	Tracking number of calls to startup's SaaS solution
. . .	. . .	. . .	. . .

Capturing Value in the Follow-on Stage—Partners

Planning the partner engagement process is important in general, but crucial for post-graduation objectives. The program will "hand over" the startups to other partners, so their role in capturing value is decisive. Planning their involvement in the follow-on stage implies planning the entire program, including the previous two stages. You want to design partner-related actions inside each step that contribute to the final output. When organizing partner engagement, answer these questions:

- **Who are the key partners, those without whom the KPIs are at risk?** External follow-on investors and leading customers are key for financial investing. Corporate development, often, is crucial for strategic investing. Internal execution units are critical for solution sourcing. Internal operation units are important for ecosystem building around technology platforms. Local businesses, institutions, and associations are vital for ecosystem building around a regional business platform. And so on.
- **How will they be engaged, through what process?** Cocreation workshops, meetings, matchmaking events, and demo days are popular options. Shared governance is also a possibility (see Challenge #3 below).
- **How will you keep them engaged, through what process or data?** For post-graduation objectives you have to play a long-term game. One of the program's assets is the network of follow-up partners it can offer to startups. Signing up a new partner is typically more expensive than keeping an existing relationship alive. You want to spend design time to make sure you have an internal process to build your internal and external partner network.
- **When will they be involved, at which stage?** Internal and external partners should be treated in two different ways, as the following paragraphs will discuss.

Many programs involve internal partners from the beginning, or even before the program starts—during the design phase. Key business units, for example, could participate in codesign or coownership of the program or its interactive parts—for example, coordination meetings with the client unit, feasibility studies, or intermediary demos (see also Challenge #3 later).

For solution sourcing programs, even more than for others, internal business units are engaged in all phases, from problem definition (they are often the problem owners), to selection, to planning meetings defining a pilot project, pilot evaluation (graduation), and pilot implementation or scale-up. Designing a specific engagement process for internal partners is a necessary condition to success.

There is a debate around the best time to involve external partners, such as investors or customers. Some programs favor interactions distributed throughout the the activation stage. Others concentrate them at the end in a graduation event (e.g., a pitch session in hackathons, or a demo day in accelerators). The latter approach (concentration) seems to be more effective,[1] as we will discuss in Chapter 15.

However, fans of the earlier approach repeat the adagio that "investors invest in lines and not in dots," meaning they prefer to see startups several times, at different stages, and to track progress before deciding an investment. These programs include intermediary pitch events and interactions. Not just accelerators, but also short programs such as hackathons sometimes have halfway pitch sessions with the sponsor or its associates. This practice provides the participants with feedback about two or three alternative ideas startups are exploring and guides the idea they will develop in the second part of the event.

Meaningful Outputs

Outputs are the proxies of the desired outcomes that are under the program's direct control. They should procure the most reliable leading indicators of outcomes (and, in turn, of objectives), as shown in Figure 11.5. Defining the form of outputs is, in itself, a critical design task. You want to identify an output for each outcome in your mapping from Chapter 9 (including for ecosystem effects).

The most common forms of outputs, depending on the objectives, are:

- **Reports** for deal flow and interaction objectives. Reports specifications should include a table of contents, metrics, and questions a report should tackle. Content depends on who will read and use the report after the program.

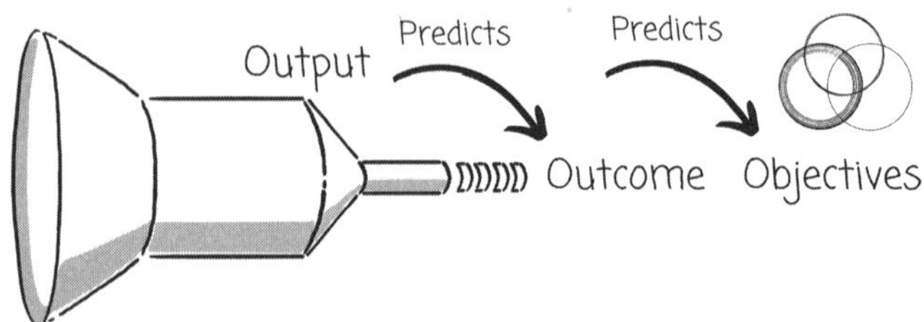

FIGURE 11.5 Outputs should be proxies of the desired outcomes, and those should be proxies of the objectives.

In a sense, a live showcase using pitches or demos can be considered equivalent to a report. Reports or showcases are extremely frequent outputs in hackathons, matchmaking events, or recruitment stages.

- **Pitches** for financial or strategic investing, ideation, validated learning, or new venture creation. A pitch typically contains business information including market size, competitive analysis, financial projections, traction and momentum, and other items of a classic business plan in summary form—the kind of information that investors (external or internal) will need to decide their involvement.
- **Demos or pilots** for solution sourcing, or ecosystem building when a technology platform is involved. Not all pilots are equal, though. Good pilots should demonstrate the value generated when the startup's innovation gets deployed at scale. Projections of a pilot's financial impact (a business case) are fundamental for greenlighting the follow-up.
- **Tailored outputs.** In some programs the type of output could be negotiated case by case, although this is rare. It may happen in programs pursuing impact goals centered around the participant's transformation (as opposed to society, the environment, etc.). "A leading indicator for the cause-effect analysis we are doing is whether the founders think the program is transformational," said Charles Graham-Brown of Seedstars. "The meaning of 'transformational' is going to be different for each one, and that is why in our programs there is a foundation which everyone benefits from, but then there is absolutely individualization."

In many of these instances, the startup program should include a step to negotiate the output with the intended post-graduation partner. While the general form of output can be standardized (e.g., a pilot), the specifics of each case are essential to using the output value later. Some programs instruct participants on how to produce the output, such as with pitch training in many hackathons or accelerators. Other programs, such as venture client, include moments of detail negotiation, where the startup and follow-on partners (e.g., the internal client) discuss the expected parameters and features.

Challenge #4: Governance

Together with identifying outcomes and outputs, you should determine the most favorable governance framework to achieve them since governance issues can be decisive for long-term success, especially in more durable programs such as venture funds, incubators, or accelerators. So let's take a look at the pros and cons of each governance framework.

Startup Program as an Independent Entity

Chapter 1 pointed to the concept of a startup program as a neutral ground for collaboration, like a sandbox where the standard organizational rules can be partially suspended to give room for exploration.

Startup programs, especially incubators and accelerators, have indeed been allowed to bend corporate rules, creating the premises for startups to actually do what they are expected to do, to make things happen without the sticky friction of the parent organization. The very reason for startup engagement sometimes lies in leveraging this gray area where more corporate freedom stems from delegating exploration to startups.

Generally speaking, it is easier to bend organizational rules in independent units than inside the organizational structure. Some programs operate in a separate company or nonprofit created ad hoc for that purpose. This arrangement is used in corporate venture capital (CVC), accelerators, or incubators (rare for other programs). CVC funds in particular have seen waves of spin-out and reaggregation, with the current wave seeing more CVCs being shifted to financial goals and independent units.

In CVC, independence from the parent company goes together with being free to embrace the venture capital model and pursue financial goals or self-disruptive opportunities with a higher degree of autonomy from the parent's strategy. In independent CVCs, such as Sapphire Ventures or GV, the parent organization's strategy might still influence the investment thesis and sectors, but the fund management takes all decisions. The separation may allow CVCs to structure employee incentives around the VC model (i.e., with carried interest) according to market standards, and attract talented fund managers at market rates.

Independence also signals to startups that their exit strategy will be less dictated by group logic, increasing the odds of closing deals with faster-moving startups. By contrast, sometimes strategic selection criteria reward slow-growing startups—and their low financial performance then affects the overall fund performance.

In general, an independent unit combines full accountability of its results with complete control of its budget and means. It has to grow its own brand and foothold in the entrepreneurial ecosystem, but it can have a head start thanks to the resources coming from the parent organization.

The main drawback is the risk of detachment and lack of integration with the parent. Execution business units may perceive the program as a separate entity, thus at the same level as any other external startup program. Shortcuts or fast-tracks for the program's startups might be harder to obtain. The independent entity's staff may lack sufficient leverage to activate the execution business units and new on-demand resources based on the specific needs of a given startup.

These characteristics seem to make independent units more apt at pursuing financial goals, or goals that entail only minor strategic wedging with the parent organization.

Startup Program as Part of the Execution Business

It is not uncommon that the program is run by an existing unit, different from corporate innovation, such as marketing and communication (MarCom), human resources (HR), research and development (R&D), corporate development (CD), or a geographic division.

The most direct consequence of this governance option is that outcome metrics mirror those of the immediate parent unit. Whether or not explicit metrics are identified for the program, the operators will feel the pressure of their most proximate managers. Program managers will be preoccupied with doing their job well, or in other words to maximize the unit's output.

The consequence of this pressure may reverberate in many aspects of the program. To exemplify, taking selection as an example:

- **MarCom wants stories.** MarCom sees an upside in brand visibility. Hence the number of applications and the best stories from a communication standpoint might get priority. One of us was once part of the selection committee for a startup program sponsored by a TV channel, and the selection process prioritized the prime time appeal of the startup's story/storytelling rather than its actual innovation.
- **HR wants employee development.** HR prioritizes employee engagement; thus, it might steer operations and startup selection to what appeals to employees, or to those founders who have more time or patience to grow the employees' skill set.
- **R&D wants technology.** R&D, in the best scenario, sees efficiency, cost reduction, and time-to-market as good outcomes. In the worst scenario, it might select only technology not in conflict with internal projects (as a consequence of the "not invented here" syndrome).
- **CD wants M&A targets.** Corporate Development might only consider candidates for M&A, hence startups that are very close to the core business—perhaps neglecting emerging markets and H3 or transformational bets.

The pro side here is that the program is highly integrated with at least with one execution unit. If the program rightfully pursues objectives in tune with the unit, there is no internal conflict.

The con side is the risk that corporate quicksand could sink the startup. Given the general skepticism of the startup community toward corporate and government sponsors, the program may end up with a pipeline of hit-and-run, short-termist startups that are simply interested in the perks (and a rapid passage).

Startup Program as a Cross-Unit Project

In this instance, the program is run as a joint project of more than one unit or function (for example, QVC NEXT® was led by MarCom and Procurement in close collaboration with Legal). The governance is thus shared between two or more units.

This kind of direct involvement may help prevent internal conflicts and organizational quicksand. Accountability for program delivery may stay with each department for what falls within its competence (e.g., payments with the CFO office, social media coverage with MarCom, etc.). Accountability for orchestration and project management, on the other hand, usually goes to the appointed leading operator.

Startup Program as a Dedicated Internal Unit

Sometimes an organization creates a dedicated unit that centralizes all startup-related activities—what the rest of the organization would deem "the startup folks." It may be a corporate innovation unit, such as Open Bosch or Enel Innovability, or an ad hoc unit for startup relationships, such as it was for TechPeaks inside its parent government agency. EnterpriseUp calls this team a startup engagement outpost—a separate or virtual platform with a startup engagement thought leadership and a corporate-startup cultural ambidexterity.

While the mandate may be explicit, the means of how to make it actionable might not be as clear. Autonomous decision power and resources would allow such a unit to execute relatively free of internal politics while still holding it accountable for results. For example, the team could control a budget to directly allocate to startups, or a cofunding to allocate to internal departments who commit their budget to a startup collaboration.

Compared to the independent entity, this governance option might more easily obtain a tighter integration with the execution business. A common practice is to engage in startup projects only if the collaborating unit contributes its budget and resources to the collaboration.

Multi-partner Programs

In multi-partner programs (Chapter 8), several organizations pool resources to run the program under a unified brand.

Often, the program is run by a third party, such as a specialized external innovation firm like MassChallenge. The partner organizations act as sponsors and receive benefits such as scouting services, access to deal flow, right of first refusal for collaborations or investments, brand visibility, or training opportunities for their employees (e.g., as temporary team members or mentors). Startup Autobahn powered by Plug&Play or Hartford InsurTech Hub powered by Startupbootcamp are two examples.

In other cases, the governance may be assigned to an ad hoc neutral entity or to one of the partners, who runs the program on behalf of the others. F10 seems to fall in this category.

Challenge #5: Process Performance Metrics

It's hard for stakeholders to assess an early-stage idea without a clear traction road map.

—Ash Maurya, CEO at Leanstack

Beyond the outcome metrics and their leading (or proxy) indicators discussed in Chapter 9, any large organization requires process monitoring in the form of performance indicators. You can define such metrics only after clarifying the internal value creation and capturing processes and the governance. Performance metrics are those on which program team members are judged and, possibly, receive their incentives (e.g., management bonus). Research conducted by Tree in Italy revealed that performance metrics are the most common metrics used by 30 corporations interviewed—primarily because they are influenceable by the program team. If anything, the problem was that many did not have outcome metrics in place.[2]

Performance metrics include three categories, logically moving backward from outcomes to the recruitment stage:

- **Output metrics** describe the quality and quantity of outputs.
- **Process metrics** measure the quality of processing the inputs into the outputs.
- **Input metrics** (or activity metrics) capture the quantity of work or participants introduced into the process.

Note that outcomes are more important than outputs. Inputs + program = outputs. Outputs with intentional design = outcomes. Outcomes with proper strategy up front = objectives.

Metrics as Alignment Tools

Like for any other metrics, the definition of performance metrics should be a choral endeavor involving higher management and strategic decision makers or stakeholders. We mapped over 100 of such metrics,[3] but each program uses only some of them, usually 10 or less. Too many metrics may distract and confuse the program management team and induce erroneous optimizations.

When selecting metrics for a program, you should keep in mind the first and foremost goal of measurement in this context: alignment. Startup programs generally involve many stakeholders, including the initiator, the sponsor, the program team, the startups, internal business units, external partners, ecosystem players, financiers, and others. Updated data about the program and its performance are the elective tool, in most societies and organizations, to keep the diverse agendas of such stakeholders focused on the program mission.

As a first logical consequence of this realization, the process of metrics identification should involve all the relevant stakeholders. Self-imposed or top-down metrics will not work in this context. Performance metrics should be understood and approved chorally, not just identified from a minority of stakeholders.

A second consequence is that any set of metrics should be correlated with the desired outcome metrics because you want to align the stakeholders with the mission. However, establishing a correlation or, better, a cause-effect relationship between indicators is complex. Therefore it is natural that metrics can be modified and iterated as the program evolves.

Output Metrics

Output metrics are part of the value-capturing strategy and were discussed in Challenge #2 above as proxies of outcomes. Examples include traction/momentum metrics and completeness of final pitch, if you have financial investing goals; volume of potential impact of piloted technology, if you have solution sourcing goals; platform usage, level of technology integration, or level of regional presence, if you have ecosystem building goals; documented change from a pre-program baseline, if you have transformational impact goals; and so on.

Note that the output metrics are often dependent on the startups (their quality and hard work) and the partners' involvement (e.g., the collaboration of client execution units). In some organizational environments, metrics that are not controllable by the program staff may get pushback. How could a government incubator manager be held accountable for the low traction metrics of the incubated startups? Focusing on output metrics may also create distortions, such as embellishing results to receive a salary bonus. Consequently, while corporate programs may monitor these indicators, they might not be linked to the program team performance assessment (although they likely should be).

Process Metrics

These indicators monitor how the process is working. Organizations frequently employ these metrics to assess the program team's performance because of how closely correlated they are to the team's work and output. Process metrics may include:

- **Speed of processing.** Time to pilot (from initial engagement), time to admission (for the selection process), etc.
- **Funnel health.** Startups promoted from substage to substage, number of drop-offs, progress tracking for each startup, milestones achieved and their quality, etc.
- **Internal engagement metrics.** Number of internal allies mobilized, client-unit budget mobilized for pilots, number of attendees at startup-corporate workshops, etc.
- **Leverage of organizational networks.** Number of introductions made, number of partners meetings organized, value of third-party agreements signed by startups, etc.
- **Leverage of organizational assets.** Utilization of office space, use of labs, technology platform usage during the program, API calls made by participating startups, etc.

Correlating these metrics with outcomes and outputs can inform adjustments and iterations of the program's offer for future editions.

Input Versus Output Metrics

Input metrics are the activities, hours, and efforts that enter the system. However, something that is rarely understood is that meaningful input metrics depend on objectives as much as other metrics do.

For example, most operators tend to consider the number of applications as an input metric to the program funnel, but it might be considered an output in some contexts. If your objective is financial investing, the number of applications is a process metric, measuring a necessary intermediate step of the whole process. But if you aim to generate press coverage and brand awareness in the startup community, then inputs are the number of hours and advertising budget spent; outputs are social media engagement, the share of voice, and the number of applications generated by your promotion campaign (i.e., the recruitment stage is what creates value in your case).

Input metrics should monitor the activity level of the program team, startups, and partners. They might include the number of working hours (i.e., timesheets), the amount of budget spent, the attendance and dedication of participants or partners, the number of matchmaking events organized, and so on. For example, cheese, tomatoes, olives, and bread are inputs. Delicious pizza is an output. Happiness is one outcome. But the outcome is only contributing to the objective if happiness was the *intent*! If the intent was the economic development for the South of Italy, and a new market for organic olives, that might be a different story. Once again, it's crucial to involve stakeholders in metrics identification and to monitor the correlation of metrics with outcomes.

Challenge #6: Economic Sustainability

When startup programs cannot rely on sponsorships alone or aim for self-sustainability independently of the main sponsor, they also look at alternative revenue streams.

Figure 11.6 uses Strategyzer's Business Model Canvas[4] to visualize a business model for a YC-style accelerator. Some of these programs cover operational costs with management fees, if a fund and limited partners back the accelerator.

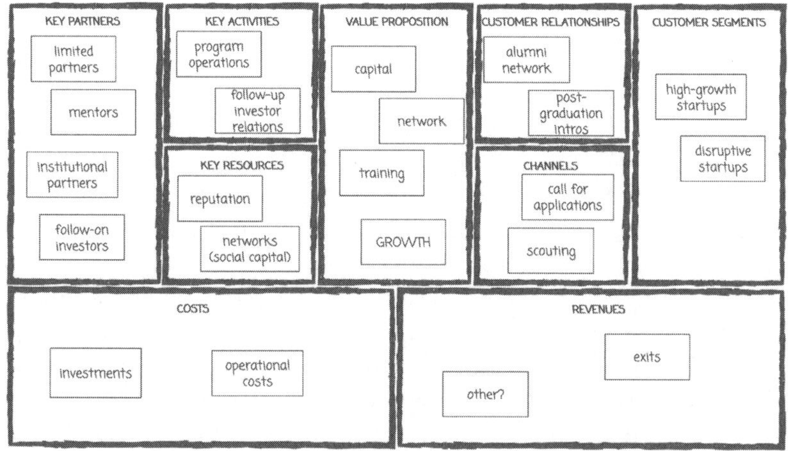

FIGURE 11.6 Business Model Canvas of a YC-style accelerator

However, most YC-style accelerators or related programs must activate additional sources of cash flow until their portfolio is mature enough to produce exits (particularly, if they don't have limited partners or a fund). Paul Sturrock of FastForward, a London pre-accelerator offering a six-week part-time program, said, with a note of British sarcasm: "We have a terrible business model." "We receive sponsorships from some of our partners plus we ask each team to pay a small amount, just enough to make sure they show up. The traditional accelerator model is not going to work for us. Until some time ago, we were taking 25 percent equity, but even with that, there is no cash flow coming in."

The early-stage equity accelerator space is very competitive, and it has the dynamics of a winner-take-all market. If the equity thesis is flawed or does not work in your specific market, then you must build your program's sustainability thesis on other revenues.

Alternative sponsorships. Diversifying the backings beyond the program's parent organization is a common strategy, but it implies complex relationship management. Multiple corporate sponsorships may create a conflict of interest or just be hard to get. Government funding, on the other hand, loads up with bureaucracy. If you finally decide to sell sponsorship packages, hire someone to do that full-time because you will need it.

Other revenue sources. Beyond equity and sponsorships, programs resort to one or more of the following revenue streams:

- **Event tickets.** Organized inside the program (e.g., a well-known mentor in the startup scene participates in a public event) or in side events.
- **Education fees.** Billed directly to participants, such as in FastForward, or billed to outsiders who participate in occasional seminars or workshops.
- **Scouting fees.** Searches paid by third parties, based on the databases and networks grown through the program.
- **Engagement fees.** Monetize the opportunity of accessing a cohort or alumni network, including an occasional hackathon sponsorship within a more extended program.
- **Consulting fees.** Consulting projects carried out by the program team as an extra-program activity (e.g., innovation strategy, internal coaching, etc.).
- **Rent.** Rent part of a coworking space used by the startup program or other similar revenue streams based on real estate or facilities.
- **Networking fees.** Some programs monetize their networks with business development, marketing, or investment opportunities for third parties or participants (e.g., via retainer, transaction, or success fees).
- **Access to grants.** Redistribution of subsidies provided by government bodies, foundations, or similar players, retaining a management fee or a grant application fee.
- **Management fees.** Direct on the program's fund, or indirectly if your program de-risks an associated investment fund.

A note: Some of these revenue streams may not be compatible with the legal framework in a corporate or government environment, so double-check with your legal and administrative departments.

The Math of Exits

Venture capital (including also early-stage accelerators) competes based on proprietary deal flow. Persistence is substantial; successful firms tend to be successful in later funds, and vice versa for unsuccessful teams.[5] For small to mid-range funds, fund size directly correlates with returns[6] (smaller funds experience fewer returns). And earlier investors, in the acceleration range, have smaller returns compared to top-tier programs.

The payback period is often too long to work for corporate or government programs, faced with the inevitable short-termism of quarterly reports and elections, respectively. Consider the example of a YC-style accelerator investing $50,000 for 10 percent of each company in a cohort. If that company sells for $50 million without any further dilution, the program cashes in $5 million. That sounds like a good deal, right? And in fact, it would be. The average YC exit is less than half that, just above $20 million dollars,[7] dropping our estimate to $2 million.

Top-tier accelerators have divested between 14 and 24 percent of their portfolio so far.[8] Now, suppose that a second-tier program accessing weaker deals would perform below that range, for instance, 10 percent. That would virtually value each startup from $200,000 to $500,000 (10 percent of $2 million or $5 million). It would be a 4× to 10× the average return on investment when compared to $50,000—in line with the reported target for business angel deals (our simulation is thus not far from industry standards).

The real question is: When will the startup program receive that return? The average time to exit varies from industry to industry, from 4 years for digital payments to 14 years for research-intensive hardware startups.[9] If you compute the investments and operations for 6 to 10 years, the costs will accrue. The IRR is still decent to outstanding (from 15 to 52 percent in our simulation), but is it feasible to endure 6 to 10 years without cash flow?

Equity or Not

Perhaps also for these reasons, many corporate or government accelerators or seed-stage programs are equity-free.

Our speculation about equity so far has concerned accelerators or seed venture funds, but similar math holds for incubators, too. Lesser programs not providing shortcuts in the startup journey have no leverage to ask for equity—see challenges, competitions, or hackathons. Later-stage, purposely built, lock-in venture funds have the equivalent math of private venture funds, with IRR around 20 percent.

Renouncing equity might introduce a distortion as program managers could become neutral to startups' future destinies. On the other hand, it may help deal sourcing because participation does not erode the founders' sweat equity (and does not dilute other investors). Plus, it does not overload the organization with micro involvement in dozens of small businesses.

Startup equity might be a diversified and uncorrelated asset class compared to other investments, but it does not seem to contribute to startup programs' economic sustainability. If your organization decides to pursue equity investments, it should be for the bigger picture, not just to attain a startup program's economic sustainability.

KEY TAKEAWAYS

- **Identify the most valuable program stage.** Your objectives determine what startup program stage is the most valuable for you. The recruitment stage contributes to goals connected with deal flow, such as trend analysis, market intelligence, and idea proposals. The activation stage hosts any activity that requires connecting, networking, understanding, trying, failing, and learning from failure. The follow-on stage includes objectives that that can be achieved only after the program, such as: creating a long-term partnership that will enable the real goal, and accelerating the startup toward that goal.
- **Create the value-capturing infrastructure.** After determining which stages generate your objectives, you must set up a structure to capture that value. The issues to solve are: identify the necessary partners; keep the partners engaged; collect data for measuring the program's metrics; and define the output.
- **Outputs should predict outcomes.** Defining the form of outputs is a critical design task. You want to identify an output for each outcome. Common forms include reports; pitches; demos or pilots for solution sourcing or ecosystem building when utilizing a technology platform; and tailored outputs when pursuing transformational impact goals centered around the participant's transformation.

- **The best governance is relative to the outcomes.** Together with identifying outcomes and outputs, you should analyze what is the most favorable governance framework to achieve them; the startup program as an independent entity; as part of the execution business; as a cross-unit project; as a dedicated internal unit; or as a multi-partner program.
- **Metrics are tools for stakeholder alignment.** While your leading metric is reaching your objectives, there is no general rule for outcome metrics. Goals inform outcome metrics; outcome metrics inform output metrics; and so on, all the way back to input metrics. What is essential is to choose measures that align your stakeholders and allies.
- **Financial sustainability without sponsorship.** When startup programs cannot rely on sponsorships alone or aim for self-sustainability independently of the main sponsor, they sometimes look at alternative revenue streams, such as event tickets, education fees, scouting fees, engagement fees, consulting fees, rent, access to grants, and management fees. The math of equity exits works against accelerators and incubators that are not in the global top tier.

12 VALUE PROPOSITION

A startup program is a platform for value exchange and mutual value creation between startups and organizational sponsors. The program's role is to facilitate the exchange (Figure 12.1). To the organization it provides access to startups in a structured way, with terms that allow it to capture value from the partnership (*ask*); to startups, it provides capital, mentoring, knowledge, networks, and other content features directly from the organization or through its indirect sponsorship (*offer*). Furthermore, the program also sets a schedule, milestones, and deliverables, this way managing resource allocation as well. In a sense, it acts as a warranty and enforcer of the value creation and exchange in regard to both sides.

The ask was discussed in Challenge #4 of Chapter 9. Structure and schedule, both integral parts of the offer, will be the topic of the next chapter. This chapter will focus on the content features of the offer and their balance with the ask, based on the feasibility analysis of Circle 1 (Chapter 8), and will address:

1. Identifying a program template or program category for benchmarking and ideas
2. Deciding the amount of content needed
3. Designing a mutual exchange of value
4. Balancing standardization and customization

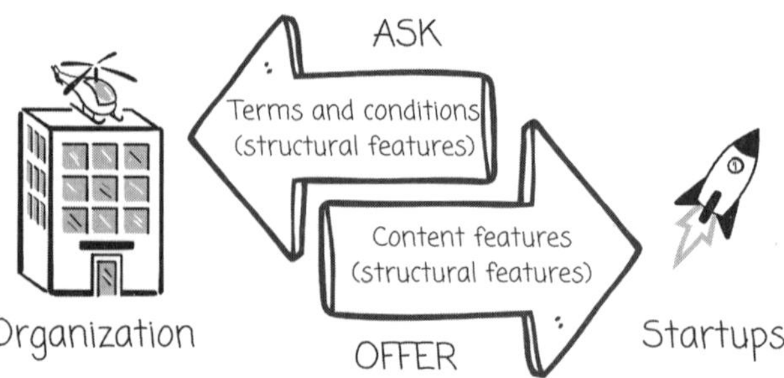

FIGURE 12.1 Content, such as capital, mentors, networks, and similar features, composes the offer; terms and conditions compose the ask; structural features enter both offer and ask.

Challenge #1: Now You May Choose a Model

The premise of Part Two is that many of the current program models (e.g., accelerator, CVC, or hackathon) are elastic, adaptable containers. The name of each model is a convention, and discussing the boundaries of each template is for academics, not practitioners (Chapter 1).

Yet, as argued in Chapter 7, in many cases, your organization or your boss has already committed to a particular "model." Don't worry; with what you've learned in the previous chapters about the three Circles, you'll find you can still change the configuration without renouncing a name, as long as you and your stakeholders agree to "loosen the definition" of the model. And while there is room for adaption within each model, you'll find that for your particular context, certain Circles offer more or less latitude within a particular model, and particular models, similarly, offer varying opportunities for stretching their definitions.

On the flip side, if you have not chosen a model yet, you now have the elements to pick a general category and look for inspiring configurations that have been tested by other operators. Once you consciously identify the current industry category that has more in common with your context, your search for reference models and a market benchmark will be more self-aware and precise.

There is also a second aspect to identifying an existing model category for inspiration, related to market expectations. Each template brings with itself a market standard for the offer, in terms of structure and content. The startup community has expectations about that standard. For instance, a hackathon lasts one to three days, while an incubator lasts one to three years. You can undoubtedly market a two-week hackathon or a two-week incubator, but such alterations would be better understood (and communicated to startups) in the context of a bootcamp or an accelerator, respectively. Similarly, if you name your program an "accelerator," startups and other stakeholders will expect to find mentors and funding inside your content offer.

Finally, once you identify your program in one of the existing buckets, you enter other people's benchmarks for that bucket. If you position yourself as a CVC, then everyone in the industry will look at your financial ROI even if that is not your goal.

This section will offer some guidance in the task of identifying a reference model, or models (for hybridization). The following tables illustrate how your context may call for one program template or another, respectively, for Circle 1 (Table 12.1), Circle 2 (Table 12.2), and Circle 3 (Table 12.3). Refer to the online companion to this book for more details about the templates. Remember that these tables are not prescriptive "if-this-then-that" rules; there is a reasonable amount of latitude here, and the templates can be adapted by changing the feature configurations.

Table 12.1 illustrates what templates are enabled by assets and resources that your organization can play (Circle 1). A capital X indicates a strong fit, while a small x is a weaker fit.

Table 12.2 shows the relationships between templates and objective types (Circle 2), including time horizons (McKinsey's model) and the fertilize/explore/exploit framework illustrated in Chapter 9.

Table 12.3 connects some characteristics of startup segments in Circle 3 to the templates (without being exhaustive). A small x here indicates a lower correlation, often related to specific cases (e.g., an accelerator for the idea-team stage such as Startup Boost is instead called a pre-accelerator).

TABLE 12.1 How Circle 1 influences the model: templates that employ organizational assets available for offer

	Accelerator	Challenge	Competition	Codevelopment	Commercialization	Course	Hackathon	Incubator	Matchmaking	Venture client	Venture fund
Venture capital	X										X
Capital (non-venture)		X	X	X			X	x		X	
Access to customers		x			X			x	X	X	
Technology platforms	X	X		X		X	X	X		x	
Operational facilities	X			X				X		x	
Testing facilities and labs	x			X				X		x	
Prototyping / engineering	x			X				X		x	
Access to supply chain	x			X				X		x	
Production / manufacturing	x			X				X		x	
IP / know-how	X	X	X				X	X		x	
Talent	X					X	X		X		
External funding				X				X			
Access to investors	X		X				X	X			x
Advisory and mentorship	X					X	X	X			x
Market intelligence	X			X	X	x				X	x
Recognition	X		X								X

TABLE 12.2 How Circle 2 influences the model: templates that may best contribute to the program's objectives

	Accelerator	Challenge	Competition	Codevelopment	Commercialization	Course	Hackathon	Incubator	Matchmaking	Venture client	Venture fund
Horizon 1		X	X		X		X		X	X	
Horizon 2-3	X			X		X		X			X
Fertilize	X		X			X	X				
Explore	X	X		X				X			X
Exploit		X		X	X				X	X	X
Financial investing	X										X
Strategic investing	X							X			X
Innovative solution sourcing		X		X	X				X	X	
Innovation ecosystem building	X		X	X	X		X		X	X	
Entrepreneurial ecosystem building	X		X			X	X				
Mindset shift and organizational culture			X			X	X				
Mission-driven transformational impact	X		X			X	X	X			X
Ideation			X			X	X				
Validation	X	X		X				X		X	
Trend discovery and market intelligence	X	X									
Talent hiring			X			X	X				
R&D capital								X	X		
Press and media coverage		X	X				X				

TABLE 12.3 How Circle 3 influences the model: templates that are best fitted for various types of startups

	Accelerator	Challenge	Competition	Codevelopment	Commercialization	Course	Hackathon	Incubator	Matchmaking	Venture client	Venture fund
First-time entrepreneurs	X		X			X	X	X			
Idea-team stage	x	x	X			X	X	X			
Early-stage (before product-market fit)	X	X	x	x			x	X	X	x	X
Late-stage (after initial product-market fit)	x	X		X	X				X	X	X
PS (personal, short-termist)			X			x	X				
BS (business, short-termist)		X	X	x	X		X		X		
RS (rapid growth, short-termist)		X		x	X				x		
PL (personal, long-termist)			x			X	X	X			
BL (business, long-termist)	X	X	x	X	X			X	X	X	X
RL (rapid growth, long-termist)	X			x	X			x	x	X	X

Finally, the functions summarized in the previous section are connected with possible templates, as shown in Table 12.4 (again, not prescriptively):

- Functions of signaling and information gathering are better associated with templates that push their brand, externally and internally, and are fine-tuned to generate deal flow at a lower cost.
- Functions that require educational formats have a stronger fit with long or intensive activation stages (more in the next section).
- Functions with long-term payoffs (in the follow-on stage) are best implemented by templates that can build lasting relationships.
- Lastly, if your only functions focus on ecosystem effects (e.g., cultural fertilization), you may want to avoid CVC or other costly programs.

TABLE 12.4 Templates that may best implement various general program functions

	Accelerator	Challenge	Competition	Codevelopment	Commercialization	Course	Hackathon	Incubator	Matchmaking	Venture client	Venture fund
External signaling	X	X	X	X	X		X		x	X	X
Internal signaling	X	X		X	X			X	X	X	
Information gathering	X	X	X				X			X	
Cultural translation	X			X	X			X	X	X	
Cultural fertilization			X			X	X				
Sorting	X	X	X	X	X	X	X	X	X	X	X
Onboarding	X			X	X		X	X		X	
Gap filling	X			X	X	X	X	X			X
Transaction risk management	X			X	X			X		X	
Transaction broker	X				X				X	X	
Follow-up warranty	X			X	X			X		X	X

Challenge #2: Select the Offer Features

The activation stage is when startups receive training, mentorship, capital, and other support. Some content may be delivered in the follow-on or recruitment stages,[1] but activation is where the bulk is concentrated.

The amount of content packed in the activation stage affects the program's overall duration and intensity. You will have to find a compromise between the amount of content you intend to deliver, the time that the target audience can dedicate, and the program's objectives.

For instance, the objective in Conception X is to create new deep tech startups from entrepreneurial scientists and PhD candidates, but without interfering with their scientific work until they are ready to commit to the business. The content is paced over nine months to create a synergic interaction between the PhD's career and the future startup.

More content in the activation stage—not just in terms of education, but also capital, operations, and so on—can potentially add warp speed to a startup journey. The absence of content in the activation stage, instead, does not alter the startup's advancement (Figure 12.2). Examples of templates with more content are accelerators and incubators, whereas challenges or matchmaking events have comparatively fewer activities.

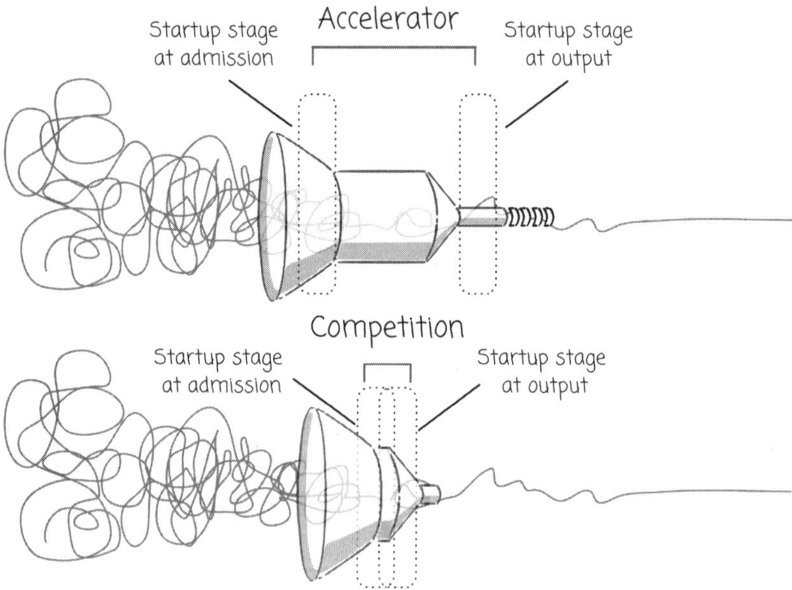

FIGURE 12.2 More activation usually corresponds to a shortcut in the startup journey (whence the name "accelerators"). Programs without or with little activation do not push the startup along its journey.

Table 12.5 weighs the pros and cons of a more content-rich activation stage. Longer and fuller activation stages (e.g., accelerators or incubators) create more opportunities for positive ecosystem effects on the internal and external ecosystems and act as containers to build more relationships with mentors and partners. On the other hand, they require more dedication from founders and the program team alike (costs) when compared to challenges or competitions.

TABLE 12.5 Comparison between content-rich and light-touch activation stages

Resource-Intensive Activation Stage	Light or No Activation Stage
Earlier-stage intake. Allows to tap upon founders that are not within reach of later-stage programs (what accelerators did with respect to venture funds), i.e., competes in a different segment.	**Less demanding for participants.** Since these programs require less commitment in terms of attendance and time, more startups can make space for the program (indirectly: a lower barrier to entry).
Opportunities for positive ecosystem effects. Educational workshops and inspirational talks can be extended to employees or to the surrounding entrepreneurial ecosystem to enhance positive externalities.	**Outsourcing alternative.** Startups provide their own means to achieve the program's objectives (e.g., to solve a challenge), and thus this is a form of innovation outsourcing.
Partner network. More activation generally means having more mentors, and more mentors imply a more extended partner network.	**Fewer operations.** Requires a smaller team to operate, and the most part of the operations is marketing and promotion.

Minimum Content Features for Internal Value: Gap Fillers

Chapter 10 introduced the concept of MVP—the minimum features that appeal to your target segment and make the program relevant in the face of competition. Mirroring what appeals to startups, you must identify a minimum VP that satisfies the organization's objective and the functions. We are still speaking of a proposition for startups, made of benefits for them. However, this time the features in the basket will be those that serve internal needs, not just the startups' plans—although they hopefully overlap. For example, FIWARE Accelerator offers technology mentoring on the FIWARE platform because its mission is to speed up technology adoption.

To determine this second minimum set of features, start from analyzing the *gap* separating the general state of target startups in *input* (Chapter 10), and the *output* necessary to produce outcomes (Chapter 11). Your program will have to educate, advise, develop relationships, or otherwise support the average input startup to deliver the output. It does it by filling the gaps (or removing the roadblocks) that metaphorically separate the startup from that end (Figure 12.3).

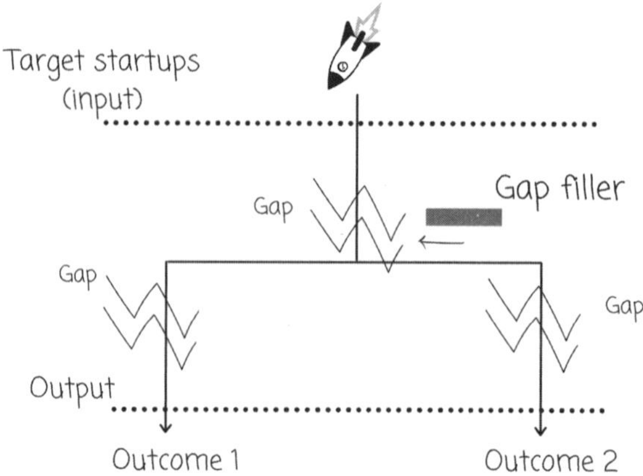

FIGURE 12.3 Content features can be interpreted as fillers for knowledge, capability, or networks gaps (among others) between a startup and the output and outcomes.

Gap fillers solve the organizational sponsor's problem: to get the job done (by the startups). Nonetheless, they target the same gaps experienced by startups in their startup journey, listed in Chapter 10: knowledge gaps, mindset gaps, resources gaps, operational gaps, networks gaps, recognition gaps, and strategy gaps. In this respect, gap fillers are activities, resources, or networks that cope with the same problems as MVP features—not anything different. However, the reason they are included in the offer is other: they are in the organization's interest, not (just) in the startup's interest.

In the ideal scenario, all of the content features benefit both sides. However, the ideal scenario is not always achievable, and sometimes a program feature ends up serving only one side. This depends not just on the feature or the program model, but also on who implements that model, why, and for whom (i.e., the context). Take the demo day, for example. In YC, the demo day advantages both startups (for fund-raising) and the program—in that it showcases its ability to select and prepare startups for investors. In more peripheral accelerators with a weaker investor network than YC, the demo day still provides visibility to the program and the its sponsors even though startups might fail to fund-raising because the investors are not a fit. In such demo days, startups are used more like trophies for the program, declassifying the event to innovation theater.

Table 12.6 summarizes the gap description from Chapter 10 and connects it to content features addressing each gap. Chapter 15 will further discuss some of the most prominent content features.

TABLE 12.6 Types of gaps experienced by startups that a program can help close

Type of Gaps	Description	Offer Features to Address Them
Knowledge	Missing information or a missing skill—examples: knowledge of technology trends, or financial planning skills, or sales skills	Education and training; mentors; coaching; peer-to-peer learning; professional counseling; and temporary management
Mindset	Missing entrepreneurial mindset, customer discovery approach, failure as learning	Education and training; mentors; coaching; peer-to-peer learning
Resources	Missing capital, missing human capital (needed talent: cofounders or hires)	Venture capital and non-venture funding; intellectual property; technology platforms; partnerships with universities (internships); engineering, design, or prototyping support
Operations	Missing operational capability or distracting operations (such as immigration bureaucracy, accounting or labor law)	Facilities; office space; labs; perks; bureaucratic shortcuts; professional consulting; production and manufacturing
Networks	Missing social or relational capital, i.e., connections with investors, potential customers, supply chain, distribution, or institutional partners	Brokerage and introductions (such as social mixes and demo days, for instance); and mentors, peer and alumni networks
Recognition	Missing brand, missing trust from prospective customers or investors	Brokerage and introductions; brand and vetting stamp
Strategy	Missing strategic direction and mission control	Mentors, advisors, and coaches

Examples of Gap Fillers

Consider a corporate solution sourcing program targeting post–Series A startups with a commercial deal as output. On average, Series A startups have a working prototype or even a rough product (or that might be an admission criterion), but they might be inexperienced in selling B2B (gap type: knowledge). At the very least, they must identify the internal decision makers who can greenlight the collaboration (gap type: network). Furthermore, startups might not have the resources to solve project roadblocks and manage bureaucracy internal to the organization (gap type: operational). Consequently, useful gap fillers, first and foremost for the corporation, might be:

- **Addressing the knowledge gaps.** Training on corporate strategy and its purchasing processes, including formats on how to sell to corporate units.
- **Addressing the network gaps.** Internal brokerage meetings with client units to agree on a pilot.
- **Addressing the operational gaps.** Project management to enforce progress on the pilot from both sides; fast-tracks to speed up commercial deal closing and payments.

By contrast, in this example startups don't need to change their strategy just for selling one solution, so activities addressing strategy gaps, such as strategic mentorship, are not necessary. If the program offered them nonetheless, the motivation should be to increase the appeal.

As a general rule, any feature that is not a gap filler should be included in the offer only if it belongs to the MVP discussed in Chapter 10. For example, you can offer industry mentors even when that mentorship doesn't directly benefit your organization, if that's useful to attract your target.

Consequences of Content Choices

Two consequences of content features deserve mentioning: the effects on structural features, and the type of startups you can attract.

First, more content features regarding education and, partially, networking opportunities imply a longer duration or intensity. More training, workshops, mentorship, events, or meetings make the program longer, or require more hours per day or week from founders.

Similarly, validation and customization activities (typical asks) require time and effort from the startups, with analogous effects on the overall duration and intensity. If the program's output is a pilot integration or demonstration, the program would have to possibly include time-consuming tests, customer interviews, and meetings with the client business unit. In general, such a program would last longer than one that just aims to create a compelling investor proposition for the next round of funding.

On the other hand, more content will allow you to target earlier-stage startups and still produce the same output. For instance, YC and its emulators' education in creating a pitch, refining the business model, and gaining traction metrics allows them to work with teams of techies with little entrepreneurial experience and make them appealing for YC's investor network. VCs cannot afford to work with teams at such an early stage, partly because of their business model and partly because they would have to set up a similar educational curriculum (Chapter 2).

Vertical Integration: Company Builders

> *Unlike most VCs which are passive and wait for founders to come to them, we come up with a lot of our ideas, and we also then look for the founders that map to those ideas or already have a company in those ideas. If we can find ideas that center around frictions and then map talent onto them, we can go faster.*
>
> —Jeff Schumacher, founder and ex-CEO
> BCG Digital Ventures[2] (BCGDV)

Company builders[3] exemplify the use of a longer and more content-rich activation stage to vertically integrate the startup journey. What is special in these models is that they also contain a team building substage in which they help assemble the founder team and associate it with a business idea (Figure 12.4).

Some company builders, such as BCGDV or NEC-X, accompany the new startup from zero to exit. The goal here is to produce new startups for the program's sponsor or its corporate partners. "We create like a fishpond where corporates can fish from," said Schumacher of BCGDV.[4]

Others, such as Entrepreneur First or Antler, go from no team to Series A. Batches of 50 to 100 individuals are paid a stipend for about two months to form investment-ready teams, of which the top 30 to 50 percent receive investment and are admitted

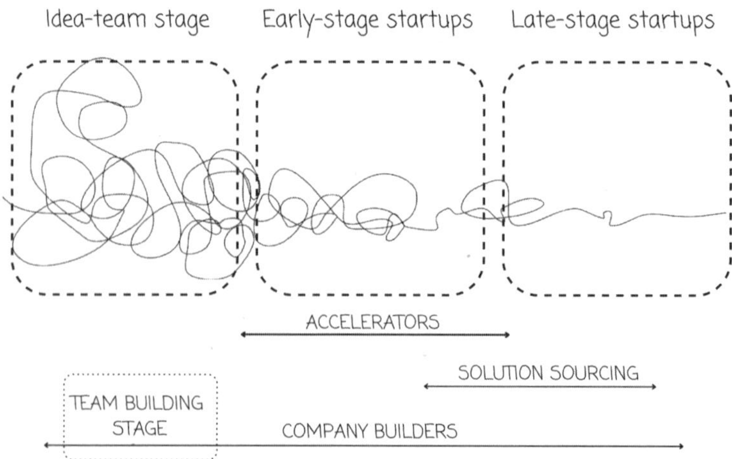

FIGURE 12.4 Company builders can potentially cover a long path on the startup journey. Their peculiarity is to include support for the idea-team stage.

to a follow-on acceleration substage. Adding the two substages together, the total startup journey is longer than what accelerators cover. "We are an early-stage venture capital augmented by a startup generator program to build our own proprietary deal flow," explained Dimitri Maroulis, formerly with Antler.

Finally, some pre-accelerators or even hackathons (such as Techstars Startup Weekend) only cover the team formation stage. The newly formed teams must join another program if they wish to continue (Figure 12.5). The duration of the three kinds of containers is proportional to the startup journey covered.

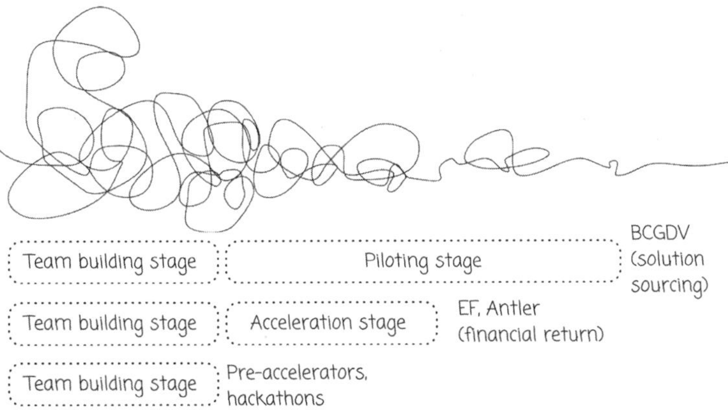

FIGURE 12.5 While all company builders start from the early beginnings, the different activation stages allow programs to reach a specific target maturity.

Challenge #3: Mutual Exchange of Value

Good startup programs produce a win-win for both sides. The minimum requirement is a fair quid pro quo, in which each side receives an equivalent value. Fairness creates the conditions for an initial engagement and, with time, for a long-term partnership.

As argued in Chapter 7, a program's task is to simultaneously match startups' assets with organizational objectives and organizational assets with startups' needs The offer and ask should derive from the considerations collected so far. Specifically, the offer (Figure 12.6) is at the crossing of the organization's unique and ready assets, the gap fillers (above), and the MVP or "market price" of startups (Chapter 10)—namely, between what is feasible (Circle 1) and what is desirable from both sides (Circle 2 and 3).

The ask (Figure 12.7) derives from three elements: (1) what value can be captured and used given the active internal allies (Circle 1); (2) the mechanism that captures value and the relevant stage that enacts it (Circle 2); (3) the acceptable terms and conditions given the maturity level of target startups that don't trigger a deal break (Circle 3). All of these elements have to match each other.

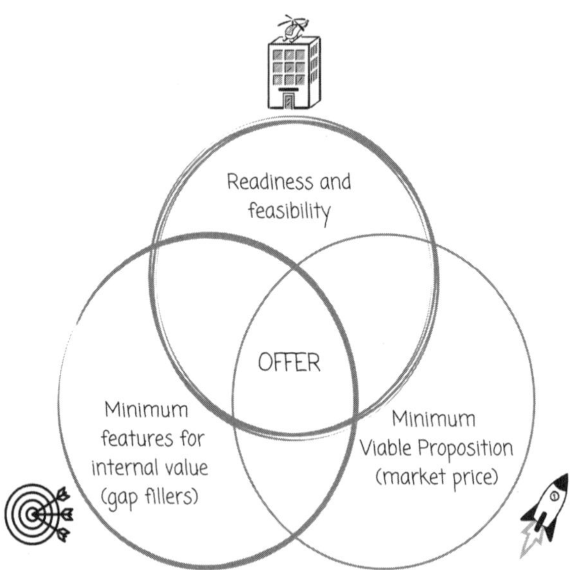

FIGURE 12.6 Three ingredients concur to the offer: the organization's ready assets (Circle 1), the gap fillers (what Circle 2 needs to succeed), and the MVP (startups' demand or "market price").

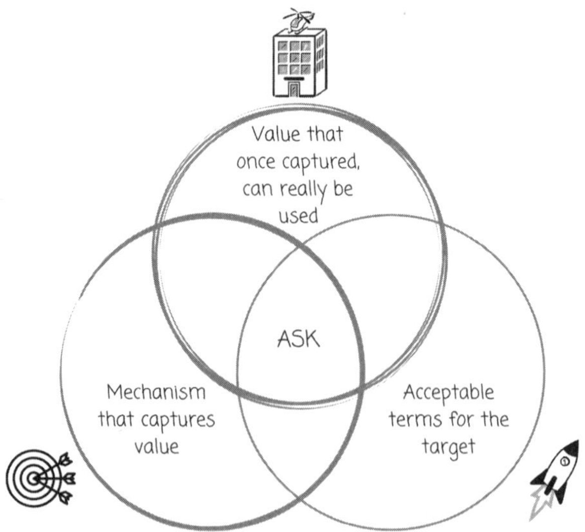

FIGURE 12.7 Three ingredients concur to the ask: what value the organization can capture (Circle 1), the mechanisms that activate the value flow (organization's demand), and what startups can accept (startups' deal breaker).

An Example of a Balanced Offer and Ask

A practical example of a successful and balanced value proposition design comes from the Stora Enso Accelerator in Finland, run by the homonymous worldwide leader in wood and paper products.[5] The company engaged startups to integrate a preexisting executive education program with more hands-on innovation experience.

Using startups to instruct corporate managers in entrepreneurial ways is not uncommon. Other companies invite founders to workshops or hackathons, create mixed teams with corporate executives, and launch toy challenges at them. In these instances, startups exchange time for business cards, and corporate managers get some sense of how startup founders make decisions. The value exchange might be mutual, but only if business cards convert into follow-up meetings—otherwise it was just a zoo for corporative executives, with startups on display like exotic animals.

Instead of just using founders as temporary teachers, Stora Enso created a concrete business opportunity for both sides. In their three-month-long codevelopment program, executives work as part of the startup team to advance a real integration project for the core business. The startups receive business development opportunities and direct access to the corporation's C-suites. Stora Enso, on its side, kills two birds with one stone: it reaches its educational objectives, and it starts concrete innovation projects (Figure 12.8).

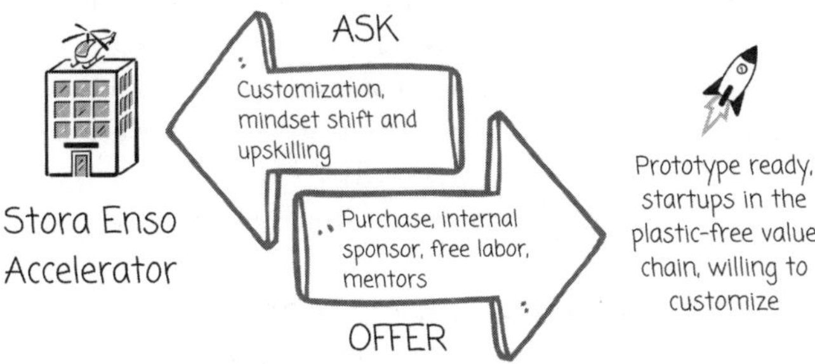

FIGURE 12.8 Example of value exchange in Stora Enso Accelerator

Step #1: Spot Win-Win Features

In Stora Enso Accelerator the executives are at the same time learners (a win for the organization) and navigators for the entrepreneur (a win for the startup). When you can match a feature with both the startup's needs and the organization's objectives, that is a perfect design feat.

As another example, take hiring services in destination programs. Arch Grants, the attraction and adoption program of St. Louis, Missouri, leverages its presence in the territory to offer hiring services to the participant startups. Meanwhile, startups that hire in St. Louis are demonstrated to be more likely to stay and grow in the region, thus contributing to retention at the same time. As a result, both win: about 85 percent of active Arch Grant recipients still operate in St. Louis.[6]

YC-style accelerators display several of these win-wins:

- Product strategy and pitching skills training are in line with growing the portfolio value (YC-style accelerators acquire equity shares before the educational programming starts).
- Introductions to investors and demo day are also in line with portfolio value. If a startup raises a new round, its valuation usually increases.
- Mentors are at the same time advisors and potential investors. There is a win-win here as well, because by serving as mentors they do due diligence for themselves, before demo day.

These mutual win-wins derive from the alignment induced by the precondition of growth: both the startup and the accelerator want the startup to grow (Chapter 3).

When you have features that encounter the aligned interest of both sides, you should factor them in first. Use your readiness profile from Chapter 8 (Figure 8.3) to prioritize what you can activate in the current edition and what needs to be postponed.

Step #2: Produce the Ecosystem Effects

When ecosystem effects are explicitly part of your objectives (Chapter 9), you need to factor in the activities that produce them—for example: open talks for the general public, mixed teams like in Stora Enso Accelerator, or the return-value activities of Start-Up Chile, Parallel18, or TechPeaks (Figure 12.9).

Although they might not be valuable for participants (just an ask), ecosystem effects can be part of the internal value proposition toward allies in the organizational hierarchy or the surrounding entrepreneurial ecosystem.

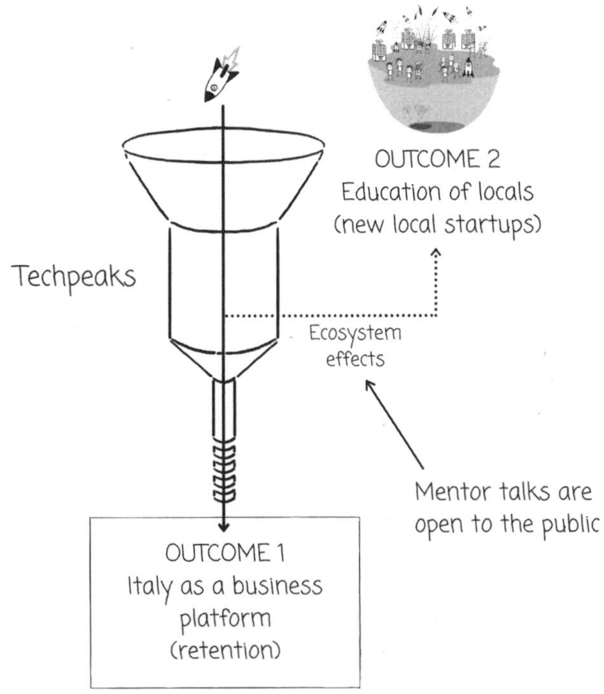

FIGURE 12.9 Return-value activities are an ask used to enforce an ecosystem objective in TechPeaks.

Step #3: Balance Asks with Incentives

Features based on alignment are automatic win-wins, and that's intuitive. Other features can still be a win-win even though the reasons for value are different on the two sides. In Stora Enso Accelerator, the executives' temporary participation in startup teams brings learning for the executives and company navigation for the startup.

Any other feature outside of a mutual win-win needs to be balanced in striving to reach a fair exchange, or a quid pro quo. This is also true when the logic may appear predatory at first sight. Many hackathons, for instance, literally exploit the free work of hackers and students, who get paid back in networking and perks (a quid pro quo). "Sponsors aim to benefit financially and operationally from the prototype APIs that participants create, but we propose to interpret computer coding at hackathons as both self-exploitation and self-investment," sociologists wrote in a study of six hackathons.[7]

To balance a value proposition, list the mutual exchange features. Then, list the asks and gap fillers on a balancing table. If you discover an unbalance, use additional features of your unique and ready potential offer to correct the fairness of the exchange (Table 12.7). As always in service design, this is going to be an iterative process of adjustments that will continue from one program edition to the next.

Incentives must be offered in good faith, however, if you have data that shows startups are unaffected by these even if they value them, be kind and wise.

TABLE 12.7 Example of a balancing card for asks and offers (gap fillers plus incentives)

Asks	Gap fillers + incentives
Mandatory coworking space	Organize meetings with corporate managers, startups. Organize investor tours in the space
Equity	Funding, credibility, access to follow-on investors

Note that programs with unfair offers do exist. An example is a challenge with a single prize of "up to" $250,000 to the best app developed for a corporate software platform.[8] Developing the app may cost months of coding, but some participants may still be lured by the prize notwithstanding the slim chance of winning the prize. And a challenge, not having any interactive activity with either mentors or peers, cannot balance out self-exploitation with self-investment, like a hackathon does.

Typical incentives to balance out unfair asks are:

- **Higher rewards.** You can at least pay well. Useful for deal-flow-based objectives.
- **Recognition and credibility.** A badge or public recognition is cheap for the organization, but it can be valuable for the startup.

- **Extra dose of benefits.** Beyond features that act as gap fillers, you can add more mentors, education and training, networking events, and so on.

Again, use your readiness profile (Figure 8.3) to guide the decision on what incentives to put on the table.

Step #4: Finalize the Follow-on Stage

Remember that, every time you have post-graduation objectives, content design should not stop at graduation. Chapter 11 discussed the cases and issues of keeping the commitment of allies and startups alive in the follow-on stage.

In practical terms, you must repeat the exercise of Step #2 also for this stage and plan appropriate alumni activities (Chapter 15). Even better, you could start planning from the end (the desired outcomes) and backpropagate appropriate actions through the follow-on and activation stages.

Step #5: Eliminate Redundant Features

Beware of inheriting redundant features when you use a template. There may be gap fillers, asks, or incentives that worked in the original circumstances but that, within your context, provide no gain to either the startups or the organization. Double-check and eliminate these as needed (Figure 12.10).

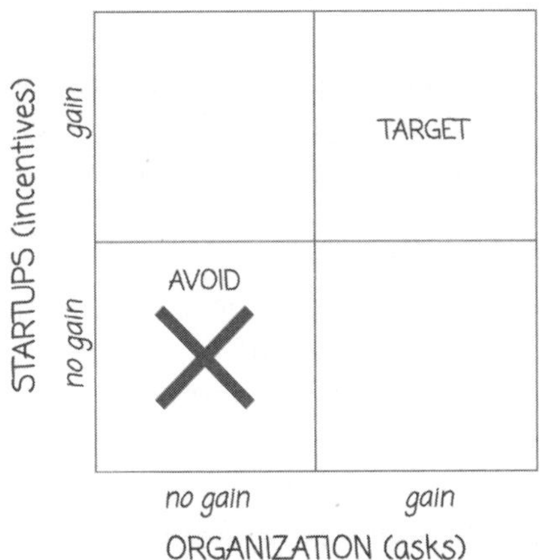

FIGURE 12.10 When you apply a template, remember to delete features that are of no value to anyone in your context.

An example: Equity asks in solution sourcing accelerators are a heritage of the original YC model, but they have no use in the new context. On the other hand, they might discourage the startups with the best solutions, because the best solutions also attract higher valuations than those commonly set by an accelerator.

Challenge #4: Standardization Versus Customization

Startups in the same cohort never have the same gaps. Even when they do, some may grow or catch up faster than others during the program, and so what was a uniform cohort at the beginning has all sorts of maturity levels at the end.

You must decide the level of standardization for an ample range of activities: mentors, seminars, workshops, peer community and collaboration, or social and networking occasions. It can be daunting, but you can boil it down to three options (Table 12.8):

1. **Standardized schedule.** A fully standardized curriculum that forces all startups to do the same activities.
2. **Opt-in activities.** A buffet style in which founders pick from a preset range of offerings.
3. **Custom.** Activities are tailored to each startup after assessing their needs (i.e., after admission).

You can apply the same option to all kinds of support, or you can differentiate by category: for example, mentors are custom but seminars are standardized (very frequent).

Standardized Schedule

Standardized curricula may cause pushback from more advanced startups or startups operating in niche markets or with a very specific technology. Founders might discount the relevance of: seminars or mentors because of a temptation to satisfice; industry-outsider or generalist mentors; or training that the startup received in a previous program (e.g., financials or business model). Standardization can feel like a loss of time for some founders.

TABLE 12.8 Summary of pros and cons of using standardized, opt-in, or custom content features

Activities	Pros	Cons
Standardized	Forces all startups into revising all aspects of their business, avoiding early satisficing. Easier to manage: all resources can be planned ahead (office, speakers, etc.). Avoids customization errors by program team.	Might look inappropriate or superfluous to more advanced startups in a inhomogeneous class (and get pushback).
Opt-in	Activities and perks are preset but optional: easy management but no pushback. Founders have control on trade-off between new opportunities and execution slowdown.	Some prebooked resources may remain underutilized. Founders may mistakenly discount the relevance of some features (especially affecting first-time or overconfident entrepreneurs).
Custom	Tailored to each startup after status assessment. Best value, use of time and resources for startups, at least in founders' perception.	Most difficult to manage: each startup consumes different program resources, and in a different way; more "runtime" improvisation. Does not force founders out of comfort zone, may indirectly encourage satisficing.

Yet research has shown that enforced sequencing of activities (e.g., from customer discovery to business modeling) can reignite search along dimensions where entrepreneurs have implicitly satisficed, independently of the specific sequence and content.[9] Rigid application of a sequence of tasks to the entire cohort can win the innate resistance coming from that sentiment of "losing time."

There are also managerial advantages of standardization: (1) it prevents the program team from making customization errors, e.g., indulging in all of the entrepreneurs' whims; (2) mentors, seminars, and other resources mobilized by the program do not go underutilized, entailing less relational costs (e.g., an empty room); (3) once the standardized blueprint has been tested and proven by more experienced staff, program execution can be more easily delegated to junior staff; and (4) internal allies such as corporate managers or mentors can access startups more easily, knowing the schedule. One program's leaders even confessed they enforced activities to ensure the coworking space was full in case a C-suite executive showed up—to justify its costs.[10]

Opt-in Features

When using the opt-in method, you create a range (or buffet) of preformatted opportunities and let the startups choose. Ideally, participants opt into a feature because they see the value, not because they are obliged. Examples are mentor sessions available on demand, or optional seminars.

Founders can self-regulate the workload, trading execution for additional exploration. Later-stage founders, busy with active customers, might accept this as the only possible pattern for their participation.

Mirroring the standardized option, opt-in requires judgment and experience from the founders. Startups might inadvertently discount the usefulness of certain mentors, when instead meeting with all mentors might generate serendipitous and unpredictable opportunities. First-time entrepreneurs might be overwhelmed with options, and if they do not learn fast, they may miss out.

Fully Custom Features

> *We review our content after the cohort is selected, and some of the content is then adapted to meet their needs.*
>
> —Joanna Buczkowska-McCumber, League of Innovators

It is undeniable that different startups require different types of support (e.g., knowledge, mentors, labs) depending on their industry, maturity level, current challenges, and the experience of the founders.

A fully custom approach entails an assessment of each startup after admission and a tailored activation of mentors, seminars, or introductions. The assessment can be done once or many times, even at regular intervals (e.g., at the end of two-week sprints).

Customization might be the winning move for value (at least, as perceived by founders), but it requires more effort and resources from the side of program management. Also, it postulates that you can activate resources on demand during program execution (or "at runtime," as software engineers would say). This may be tough in many large organizations because of yearly budget limits, prebooking of resources from other business units, or possible conflicts with the execution business. Hence, if you use this method, you must assess the readiness level of each service you intend to manage in this way even more thoroughly than usual.

KEY TAKEAWAYS

- **Value must flow in both directions.** Your value proposition toward startups must keep in mind the other side, the organization. You must design a mutual exchange of value rather than just a one-sided proposition. A program's task is to match startups' assets with organizational objectives and organizational assets with startups' needs at the same time.
- **Templates impose implicit assumptions and expectations.** Program templates can provide ideas and guidance to craft your value proposition, but beware: once you identify your program in one of the existing buckets, you enter other people's benchmark for that bucket. Each template brings with itself a market standard for the offer, in terms of structure and content. The startup community has expectations about that standard. For instance, if you identify as a CVC, then everyone in the industry will look at your financial ROI—even if that is not your goal.
- **Fill the gaps, then balance asks with incentives.** Good startup programs produce a win-win for both sides. To conceive a win-win value proposition, start with gap fillers—those features that help startups achieve the organization's goals. If they also help startups achieve their own goals, that's even better. Second, balance out the asks with incentives (e.g., higher rewards, a vetting stamp, or an extra dose of support or perks) until you achieve at least a fair quid pro quo, in which each side receives an equivalent value.
- **Conciliate standardization and customization.** Customized terms or content typically bring more value to participants because they account for each startup's specific needs. However, they also require a better analysis

of the startup's status and more mature founders. On the other hand, standardization makes the program more manageable, provides predictability and replicability, and induces the startups to avoid satisficing too early. These two practices need to be conciliated according to your objectives. You can also use opt-in features—a set of activities or benefits that are semi-standardized but optional.

13

STRUCTURE AND SCHEDULE

A program's *structure* determines the pace of stages and gates, and its *schedule* states how content and asks are arranged within that structure, both being integral parts of the value proposition and value creation on every side. The perceived value can change with different intake schemes (e.g., calls versus rolling applications), selection timeline (e.g., response time), or capital staging over the course of the program (e.g., funds distributed at start versus at end). It's easy to look at these things from your own point of view or from an accountability or punitive perspective for the startups. Challenge yourself to look at the value side from the startups' perspective.

Do you prefer founders self-finance their participation to show their commitment, or that they have enough funds to sustain themselves during the program? There is no wrong answer, they are just different. The important part is that you have a reason, and that you understand how those different startups view you and your offer.

Structure, schedule, and content are tightly interconnected. You may know the famous motto, "We offer three kinds of services: good, fast, and cheap. But you can only pick two." Paraphrasing that, in startup programs you must pick two from deep content ("good"), short duration ("fast"), and low intensity ("cheap"), as shown in Figure 13.1. More content in a stage or substage implies either longer duration or higher intensity. On the other hand, if duration is a bound variable, you either increase intensity or pack less content.

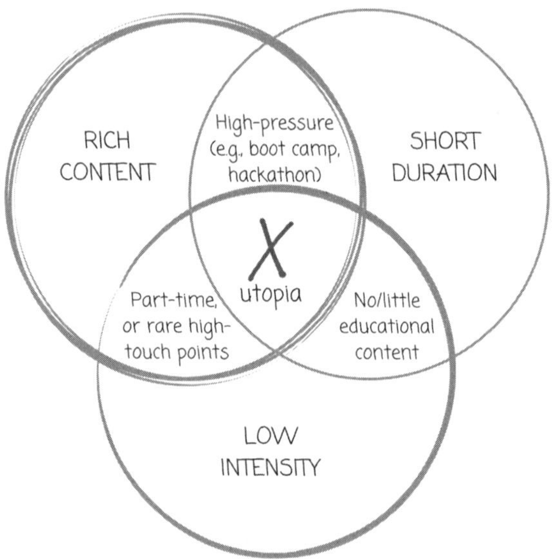

FIGURE 13.1 Your program can offer three kinds of services: deep content, short duration, and low intensity. Pick two.

This chapter will help you answer the following structural questions:

1. How to set the program duration?
2. How to structure the intake?
3. How to establish the cohort size?
4. How to choose between remote and physical location?

Finally, it will guide you in setting the schedule. Once you have drawn lines in the sand regarding total duration, cohorts, location, and once you have established the content (based on Chapters 9 and 12), the schedule develops organically—it is the careful output of thinking through and implementing all the previous steps. You are now building an optimization function from the intake to the stated objectives. There are only a few levers left to pull, and they are all "known knowns." You must strike a balance between optimization (e.g., founder's time, resource allocation) and an attractive value proposition. You can use substages and intermediary gates to provide a natural rhythm and flow to the program, more efficient distribution of content and resources, and a risk control mechanism (Figure 13.2). This chapter and Chapter 15 are the closest you get to product features, and any good product manager can make minor adjustments along the way. This is why it's more important to get the Circles lined up properly—those are nearly impossible to change mid-program, if at all.

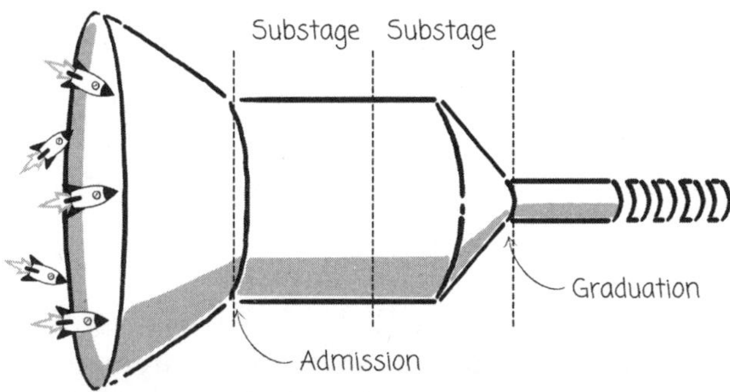

FIGURE 13.2 Gates and substages distribute the content throughout the program.

Structures, Substages, and Schedules

Think of the last time you attended a conference or another planned event with a timeline. At the registration desk, you were probably handed an event schedule specifying what speaker is in which room or venue and at what time. A similar practice finds application within startup programs, where an activity plan guides the startups from admission to graduation.

Techstars Accelerator[1] exemplifies such a scheduling practice, with its structure comprised of three four-week substages. The first substage is what insiders call mentor madness;[2] after one orientation week, the startups are stormed by more than 70 mentors and industry executives there to challenge their assumptions. The next substage focuses on product execution and traction (growing users, customers, and revenues). Business funding and the investor pitch come in the last substage, ending with an investor demo day (Figure 13.3).

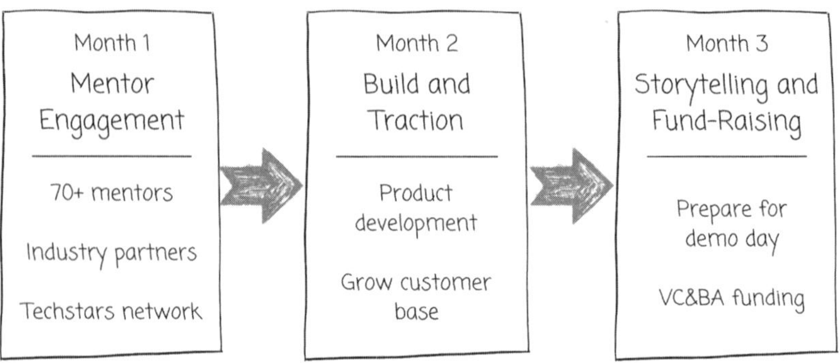

FIGURE 13.3 Overview of activation substages in Techstars Accelerators.

The purpose of concentrating mentor madness at the beginning is threefold: to reveal false certainties, direct founders to a better product-market fit, and match each startup with the lead mentors who will accompany them until demo day.[3]

Techstars employs substages to organize content and coordinate stakeholders like mentors. The passage from one substage to another is automatic, without any intermediary selection.

In Antler, in contrast, the program contains two phases, separated by a decision gate presided over by an investment committee (Figure 13.4). The two substages have a vastly different focus and pace. Phase One takes a batch of strangers as input and produces startup teams with a pitch as output (idea-team stage). It lasts 10 weeks and is filled with design sprints, team-building exercises, master classes, and inspiring speakers. The committee greenlights only half the teams on average. In Phase Two, which is 12 weeks, the newly formed teams build their product and gain traction before demo day.

Here, the function of substages is not simply to organize content but also to implement a staged investing strategy that distributes resources and capital efficiently, involving a stay-or-quit decision that cuts out underperforming teams.

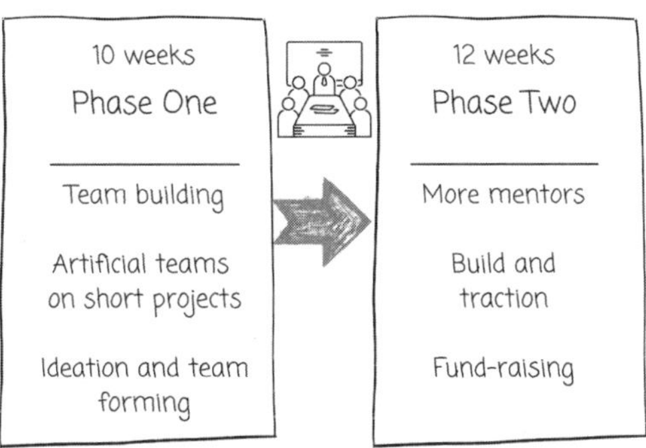

FIGURE 13.4 Overview of activation substages in Antler.

Space3ac, a commercialization program in Poland, uses three substages for its solution sourcing program: a preparation camp with training and meetings with an industry partner; a one-month substage to prepare a plan for a pilot, reserved for the best startups; and a three-to-six-months pilot, in which funding is released only upon hitting three pre-agreed milestones (Figure 13.5). "We provide a secure and effective platform for both parties. We cut out startups that are too immature for corporate partners, and for startups, we guarantee fair negotiations. Around 60 percent of our alumni continue cooperation after the program," said Wojciech Drewczyński, CEO of Space3ac.

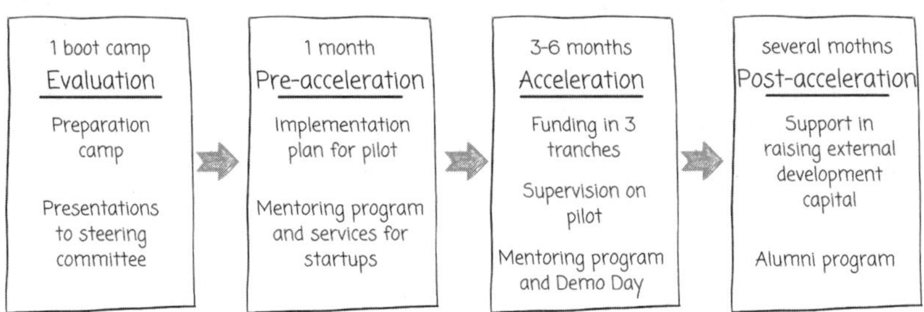

FIGURE 13.5 Overview of activation substages in Space3ac.

Note that substages can also exist in shorter programs, such as hackathons and startup weekends; and not just in the activation stage, but also in the recruitment stage (more in Chapter 14).

Challenge #1: Program Duration and High-Touch Points

The total duration can be as often a free variable as a bound variable. When it is a bound variable, you will have to compromise on content or increase the intensity. The binding conditions are generally external. For instance, a summer camp must last for a trimester only, or an international program must respect visa regulations.

When duration is a free variable, then you can let content drive and set a duration that achieves your target segment's educational needs (see Challenge #2 of Chapter 12). If you are imitating or improving a template, you may want to start from the template's structure and make minor adjustments. For instance, accelerators last between three and six months; hackathons between one and three days.

Alternatively, you can let intensity drive. For instance, you can start from postulating a part-time program that allows participants to keep their daily job or serve their customers.

Another aspect to consider is how long you make the *high-touch points*, the active parts of the program when the startups are required to spend time on it. Some programs are two years long in theory, but the high-touch points are two weeks in the beginning and one week at the end. Other programs are organized in bootcamps of two or three days every two or three weeks. These high-touch points can contain the bulk of the content in very intensive bursts and are structured to achieve a balance between duration and manageable intensity (when spread over the entire period). For instance, Pioneers of the Balkans, a program distributed over five countries in Eastern Europe, was organized in a series of four weekends of master classes, one per country, plus a final session to give entrepreneurs in each country easy access to training and mentors.

Challenge #2: Cohorts Versus Rolling Intake

In many models in use since before accelerators, the norm is to engage with new startups on a rolling call basis. Incubators usually fill their slots as interesting applications come by, while venture funds invest when an opportunity arises at any time during their investment period.

Accelerators popularized the cohort (or batch) concept, whereby a group of startups enters and leaves the program together. Accelerators also popularized the idea of a demo day. Now that you see how this book attempts to decouple labels like accelerator from startup programs, features like cohorts and demo days can still be used or even copied, if you make sure to adapt them when using them in a different context. Just as it is dangerous to copy an entire model without understanding its job, it is dangerous to haphazardly copy a feature as well.

The cohort-based intake model focuses the program's marketing and outreach around one or two critical dates per year. While YC now accelerates 200 to 250 startups per batch, the average size is 5 to 20 startups. Table 13.1 compares the pros and cons of cohorts and rolling intakes.

TABLE 13.1 Comparison of intakes in cohorts or on a rolling basis

Cohorts	Not
Peer-to-peer learning: Participants share tips and solutions to common problems or exchange expertise with their peers.	**Rolling application and processing:** No dependence around specific dates for application processing and admission. More timely matching.
Cross-networking: Exchange of networks among founders, especially useful when startups are from the same industry or use similar technology.	**On-demand call:** A new call can be opened on demand, even for as little as one startup. Timelier for solution sourcing objectives.
Alumni network: Cohorts create a sense of comradery that generates long-lasting relationships beyond the program.	**Noncompetitive:** Better for noncompetitive admission, when the program is at the service of incoming startups in need (e.g., public incubators).
Cost efficiency: Flying a mentor in for one startup or 10 has the same cost. Cohorts allow programs to impact more startups while also being efficient in the use of resources.	**Per-startup costs:** You renounce any economy of scale or scope for the program costs. Each startup has similar costs of processing. Customized features don't increase the cost of the program.

When to Use Cohorts

Cohorts are popular among programs emphasizing peer-to-peer networking, cross-learning, and educational activities (e.g., lectures or workshops). Cohorts spread fixed costs (such as flying a mentor in) over many startups, thus multiplying the impact for each dollar spent—a welcome feature, especially in government or social-impact programs. Cohorts might also serve as a comfort mechanism for participants, giving them an official excuse for interaction with mentors and investors whom they might not have been able or willing to approach otherwise. Being part of a cohort can provide founders with the courage to exit from their comfort zone, or with a shield against prejudice or discrimination, if these could be an issue.

Cohort-like intakes are in more models than you may think. Hackathons, being limited-number events, inherently re-create the all-in all-out effect of a cohort model. This kind of dynamic promotes serendipitous self-learning, cross-help, and interaction-dependent objectives. Startups might create alliances on specific problems or specific customers, or even joint ventures. The relationships built during a cohort-based program often continue after graduation, particularly if supported by an alumni program. In the activation stage, use a cohort model if the program aims at:

- **Creating new teams.** Cohorts or an event-like batch are necessary when participants are looking for cofounders, such as Antler or Entrepreneur First.
- **Ideation.** Allows an exchange and bridge-building across different worlds.
- **Inducing a mindset shift.** Not strictly needed, but it enables group learning.

From an organizational point of view, cohorts spread risk, not just operational costs:

- **Investment risk** on many parallel opportunities, especially useful in early stages. Cohorts also counter drop-offs.
- **Relational risk** toward partners such as investors at demo day or mentors. The likelihood of a match with at least one startup increases (quality being equal, of course).

To decide the size of your cohort, follow this rationale:

- The minimum size comes from risk management and peer dynamics; too few startups concentrate risk and limit peer-to-peer networking and cross-learning.
- The maximum size originates from resource availability and allocation, such as investment strategy, fund size, budget, venue size, or office space.

When to Use Rolling Applications

If you go without cohorts, you process a startup as it applies, and possibly run the program for that startup only. Rolling intakes are best for:

- **Noncompetitive admission.** For most incubators, access is first-come, first-served—or another noncompetitive logic.
- **Timeliness.** Without fixed dates, programs can seize opportunities when they come, with positive effects on deal-flow dependent objectives.
- **Individual startup.** When only one startup is needed (or two), such as for innovative solution sourcing.

Some programs, such as Wells Fargo Accelerator, use this approach to be more startup-friendly and adapt to a startup's timing and needs rather than vice versa. Others take a hybridized approach, opting for small cohorts and very frequent, fast-paced, short editions—look at the model adopted by DreamIt Ventures, for instance, which runs almost ad hoc accelerators as relevant startups knock at its door.

Challenges are sometimes open-ended (no deadline), to signal the organization's interest in startups of a given vertical or technology sector. In this respect, a rolling intake is essentially a doorway to access the organizational sponsor and a gateway for spontaneous proposals.

Challenge #3: Location Versus Remote

As noted in Chapter 8, location can be a bound variable. When it is not, it is worth considering carefully because this feature heavily affects a program. It is not about fancy colored walls or Ping-Pong tables in the office, but about how the location supports the mission or, vice versa, how it hinders participation.

A physical location can be of significant value in some circumstances, for instance:

- **Mentors.** Investors and industrial partners in the surrounding area may be more likely to start interactions with the startups if they are just a taxi ride away. Katarina Brud of MobilityXLab highlighted the advantage of running the program in Gothenburg, Sweden, where Volvo Cars and the other partners are based, saying: "This means it's easy to interact as all our offices are next door to each other."
- **Peer-to-peer interactions.** Fruitful exchanges between founders become more likely outside of sessions, such as in coffee breaks or on beer nights.
- **Ecosystem effects.** When spillovers into the local startup community are crucial, they can benefit from open events, educational workshops, or give-back programs such as in Start-Up Chile or Parallel18.
- **Real estate performance.** Location is, of course, a bound variable when the program's objective is to foster the adoption of a real estate asset (e.g., a coworking space) or to foster relocation of businesses to a destination.
- **Attractive destination.** Let's be honest, yes, there are trade-offs with cost and being away from family—but *if* a founder or mentor is already accepting these trade-offs—travel to a new and attractive location can be quite a feature for both startups and mentors.

By contrast, just sharing a common office is not enough to spark collaborations, especially without creating the right incentive system. A corporate program manager[4] said he doesn't "believe that sitting with startups in the same building will change anything. If you spend 20 minutes with a startup on a Friday, then you go back to your boss on Monday, and she asks, 'when are we launching?'—nothing changes. If your incentives do not change, nothing changes either."

Remote programming, on the other side, brings advantages such as increased access to global startups (a wider reservoir) and more cost-effective operations for both the program and the startups. It spares the logistics of managing a physical space for the organizers, and of relocation or travel for the founders.

With the availability of video conferences and high-quality video streaming, entirely remote programs have been a growing trend for a few years—at least for educational purposes and preparation for the main program, such as for YC Startup School. And the same is true for partially remote programs with a few high-touch points—for example, one program features onsite bootcamps at the beginning and the end, with the rest of the program running remotely.

Leaving the startups in their ecosystem can support validation and growth. Charles Graham-Brown, CIO of Seedstars, said, "Onsite acceleration is fine in ecosystems with a critical mass of ventures. But if you have a batch of startups from different countries, there is no point extracting them from their customer base for three months. They need to be on the ground, with their team, and close to their customers."[5]

When adapting to the new normal of the Covid-19 pandemic, Ocean Solutions Accelerator (OSA) had to renounce its Alaska cruise that had been its scenic opening theater in the previous edition and adopt a full-remote model. "The virtual accelerator has allowed us to support a more diverse collection of startups than ever before. Our remote program in 2020 removed some of the financial barriers related to startups relocating for the program," said Jon Letts of Sustainable Ocean Alliance.[6] "We will reinitiate an in-person portion of the program when it is safe to do so and will continue to offer virtual programming to our global community."

A virtual program can also turn out to be more engaging. "When Covid happened, we transferred everything online. Surprisingly, the demand and accessibility of the program increased massively," said Riam Kanso of Conception X, speaking of how PhD students from deep tech tracks showed a preference for remote interactions.

Table 13.2 summarizes the pros and cons of a physical or virtual program.

TABLE 13.2 Comparison between remote and onsite programs

Onsite	Remote
Ecosystem effects: Can involve the local population or partners' staff outside the program in open events, inspirational talks, and interactions.	**Wider reservoir:** Can serve startups from distant geographies without any need for costly relocations.
Easier peer-to-peer interactions: Can be casual and at easy reach. Instead, remote requires being intentional about interactions.	**More convenient participation:** Not having to commute to a venue can boost engagement and attendance.
Mentor engagement: Onsite presence can make local mentors more casually accessible.	**Access to own market:** Startups can stay close to their market of reference for validation and initial growth.

Challenge #4: Creating the Schedule

Structuring the value delivery in substages is meant to achieve a balance of three sometimes contrasting interests:

1. What startups need for advancing toward the program goals
2. What startups can absorb and process
3. A logic of staged investing that optimizes resource allocation

The problem is twofold: (1) to identify the transition points, and (2) to distribute features in substages (activities, resources, and other support). As with other design problems, this one may require more than one iteration to obtain a satisfactory balance—usually from one edition to the next.

Ideal Advancement

The Techstars and Antler examples above illustrate two ways in which substages transition from one to the next: a *content change* in Techstars, and an *intermediary decision gate* in Antler.

From a designer's standpoint, however, that distinction has a more subtle meaning. When a transition is purely content based, you are postulating that startups have reached an implicit milestone of some kind. At the end of the first Techstars substage, for instance, the assumption is that startups have figured out how to test their product-market fit. And at the end of the second substage, the assumption is that they have enough traction to raise an investment round. Simply, these two intermediary milestones are not formally checked with a gate—but they are still implied (Figure 13.6).

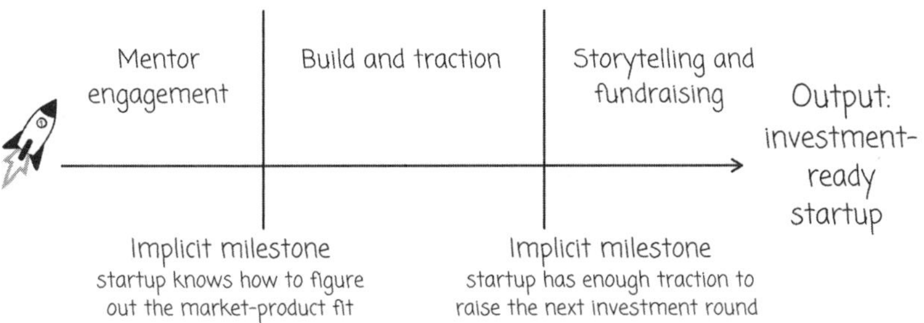

FIGURE 13.6 In Techstars Accelerators, implicit milestones mark the transition between substages (intermediary gates are absent).

In essence, when you plan substages, you are imagining an ideal advancement for the startup mixed with the reality of timelines—knowing that some startups will not hit the milestones, but life must go on. In some cases, you will check if they are progressing (with an intermediary gate or explicit milestone), while in others, you will postulate it without checking (with a content transition or implicit milestone). Figure out what steps or milestones mark the advances in this ideal schedule. Each of them will mark a transition; you then just need to decide whether or not to check each transition with a gate. These assumptions just serve the purpose of making a program standardized, more scalable, and repeatable. The ideal path does not need to be precise. What is ideal is not always real and each startup will follow a different journey, but you can handle those differences with the techniques discussed in Challenge #4 of Chapter 12.

Milestone Planning

The first step is to identify a set of milestones, explicit or implicit, that you should require from participants. Second, you will distribute resources to support participants to reach those milestones.

Each milestone will mark a transition point, and it can be embodied by one or more of the following options:

- **Learning landmark:** problem-solution fit, product-market fit, etc.
- **Deliverable:** demo, pitch deck, business plan, patent, etc.
- **Startup state:** team formed, product launched, revenue positive, etc.

For each milestone, you want to establish whether it should be:

- **Explicit,** i.e., formally verified; or
- **Implicit,** i.e., marking a content change without an intermediary gate.

Finally, you need to decide whether explicit milestones also entail a go/no-go gate, or they are just a formal stepstone. At the end of this design process, you will have a logical sequence of milestones, of substages (in between two milestones), and some filtering gates corresponding to explicit milestones (Figure 13.7).

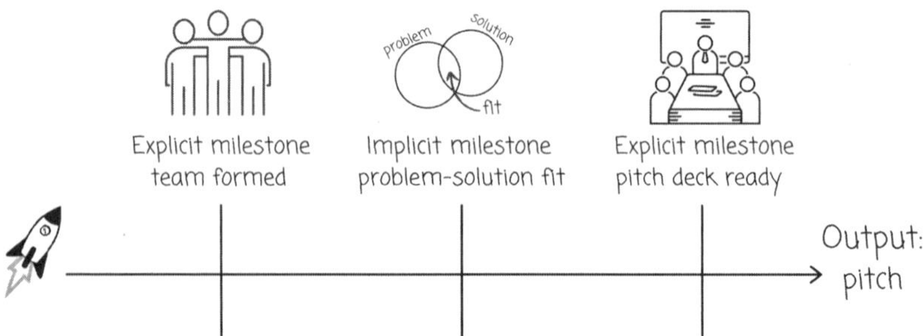

FIGURE 13.7 Milestone planning lays out a sequence of explicit and implicit milestones.

Explicit Milestones

There are two prominent reasons to make a milestone explicit and, possibly, use it for filtering part of the cohort. First, if the milestone is a must-have for the rest of the program, you will likely need a verification gate. For instance, in Antler, having a team and a pitch ready at the end of Phase One are preconditions to incorporate a startup and hence receive an investment. The investment committee at the end of Phase One provides the necessary verification gate.

Second, intermediary gates implement a resource-based version of staged financing or staged investing—the process venture capital firms follow when investing in a startup. Rather than funding the entire development and marketing cycle up front, they control risk by providing just enough funds for the startup to prove certain assumptions about the business model and product feasibility, viability, or desirability. When enough data validate the model, the firm may agree to unlock more money. Similarly, in a startup program, explicit milestones and intermediary gates optimize resource allocation, redirecting them only to a selected subset of participants.

Forward Planning Versus Backpropagation

How do you create a logical succession of milestones? The most intuitive approach is to follow an additional logic from the start of a stage onward—following the temporal order of the program, from the input state of startups to the desired output state, spacing out duration and content based on educational or operational gaps between one milestone and the next (Figure 13.8).

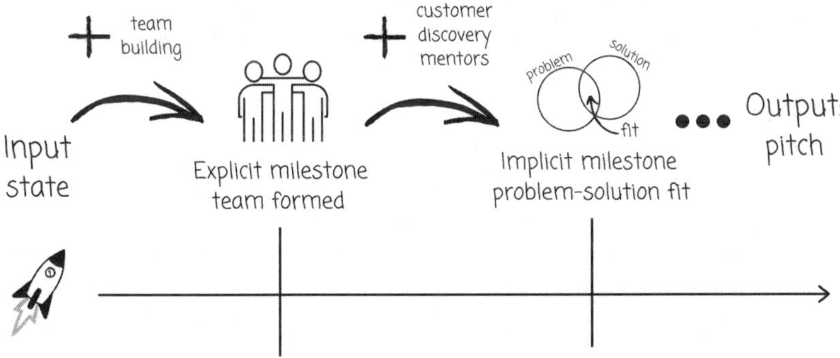

FIGURE 13.8 In forward design, the anchor is the input state.

The alternative is backpropagating the output through the necessary milestones to obtain the ideal input state, using a subtraction logic (Figure 13.9).

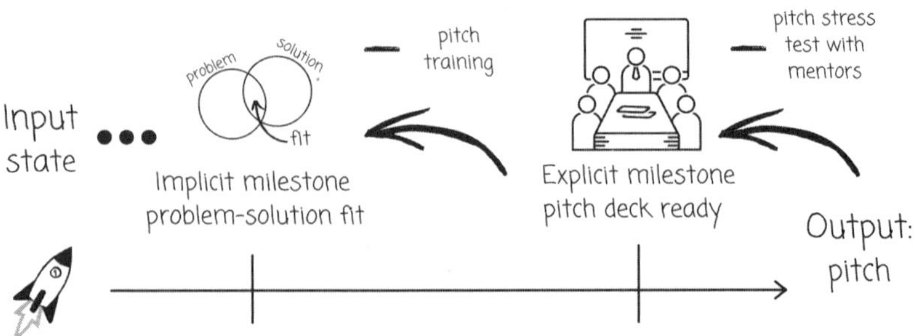

FIGURE 13.9 In backpropagation, the anchor is the output state.

While forward planning is anchored on the input state, backpropagation is anchored on the desired output. Forward planning answers the question, "How can we support the startups to reach the next milestone?"—and it adds a piece at a time. Backpropagation is about "What do startups need to achieve this milestone?"—subtracting the support you can provide, and thus deducing the previous milestones. For experienced and very meticulous designers, either approach will work equally. However, backpropagation can help you stay goal-driven and expose bottlenecks in the ideal advancement. Starting with the end in mind is a better design practice.

Backpropagation is even more powerful when you start propagating from the outcome, enabling the follow-on stage to enter the equation. Even though the program may have no control over the follow-on stage, spotting needs that arise in that stage can suggest backup plans for the activation stage.

For instance, suppose that your program ends with a pilot. If the pilot is successful, the startup will need to further integrate its software platform in a business unit's processes after the program. Seeking the blessing of that unit's IT engineers on the hypothetical solution can simplify the integration. Backpropagating the integration step might lead to adding a milestone ("approved software architecture") that might have been missed if one proceeded forward instead.

Using backpropagation might also reveal flaws in the target segment (Circle 3) if the average startup in that segment would hardly obtain your output given the resources available for support. For example, if you can only distribute $10,000 to startups for the said pilot, and the desired outcome is innovating a core business process, you are implying that startups have their own means of cofinancing that pilot—hence likely excluding pre-seed startups.

Remember to repeat the milestone and activity planning for the planned ecosystem effects too. You can use forward planning or backpropagation to introduce more milestones and activities (Figure 13.10).

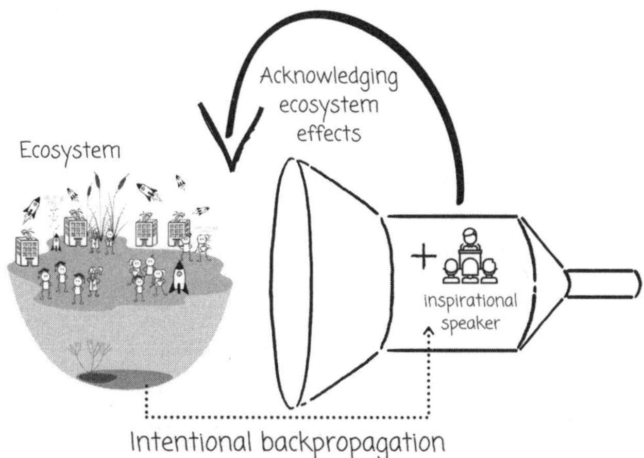

FIGURE 13.10 You can backpropagate the ecosystem effects to design specific activities for them.

Substage Duration and Content

Filling the substages with activities or resources is generally a consequential task. It's all known knowns: fill in the gaps between milestones with the appropriate support and activities (e.g., mentorship, training, or capital) needed to reach the next milestone. If your constraints are designed with intent and not just arbitrarily based on the CEO's yacht schedule, and the content is also chosen appropriately, then how those things are scheduled is ultimately less risky. In the example of Figure 13.11, after the team is formed, you can plan customer interview training and access to customers to let the startup get closer to problem-solution fit.

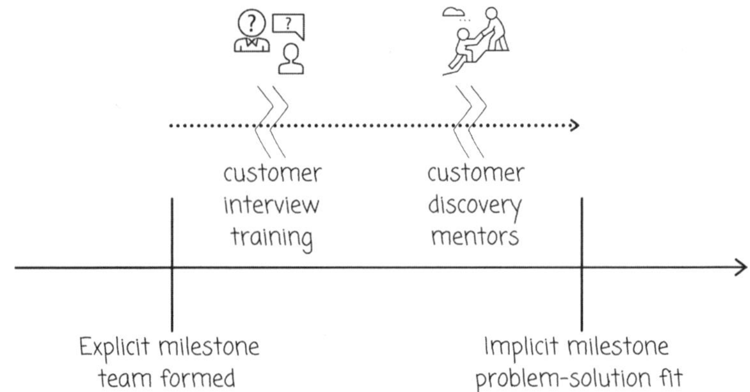

FIGURE 13.11 Add content needed between two milestones.

One sensitive point is the usage of the startup founders' time. Time is frequently the most precious resource a startup has (unless you are targeting pre-seed participants or just aspirants dipping their toes in the water, such as college students). First, speed is one of their exclusive competitive advantages against industry incumbents.[7] Second, startups must seize a window of opportunity before closing; timing might be the most critical reason for the startup's success.[8] A win-win value proposition, consequently, must be respectful of startups' and founders' time. Consider lower intensities whenever possible, so as to leave more time to founders to grow their business and cater to their customers.

Program Blueprint

At the end of the design process, you could craft a *service blueprint*[9] of the program, with both frontstage and backstage schedules, activities, booked resources, and milestones (Figure 13.12). The frontstage shows the startup's perspective, and the backstage describes how the organizational staff and resources get involved.

Interactions are among the most critical activities to plan. Their scheduling must be both timed to startups' needs and the gaps to be filled, and respectful of administrative staff and resources (including external partners such as external mentors).

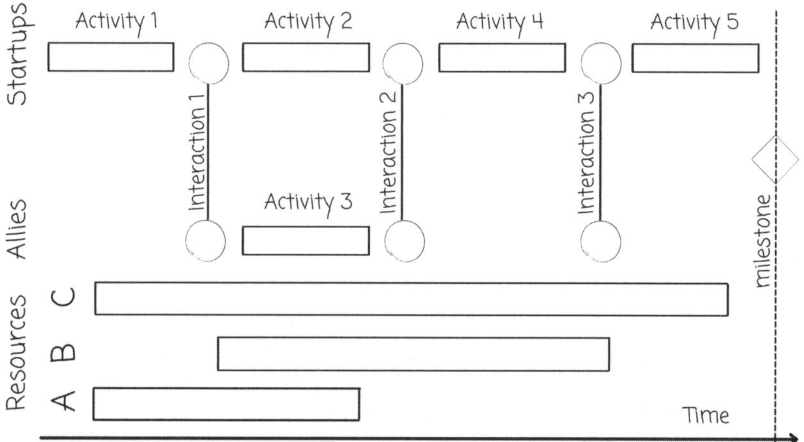

FIGURE 13.12 A complete service blueprint contains the customer journey (startups, internal allies), frontstage (touchpoints), and backstage (support actions and processes). It can be transformed into a manual for operators and internal allies.

Once you have a blueprint, you can generate a program manual or playbook to run the program. For instance, Techstars Startup Weekend provides a detailed organizer manual[10] with tips throughout the three months preceding an event. Antler's Dimitri Maroulis also reported having created a manual for program operators across the world.

KEY TAKEAWAYS

- **Choose two: good, fast, or cheap (for startups).** The structure and schedule are integral parts of a startup program's value proposition. You must pick two from deep content ("good"), short duration ("fast"), and low intensity ("cheap"). For example, more content in a stage or substage implies either longer duration or higher intensity. Or, if the duration is limited, you must either increase intensity or pack less content.

- **Use high-touch points.** When balancing the duration-versus-intensity trade-off, it's important to consider how long you make the high-touch points, the most time-consuming parts of the program. Programs do not need to be at high intensity for the entire duration. Some programs are two years long in theory, but the high-touch points are one week in the beginning and one week at the end, for example.
- **Pros and cons of cohorts.** The cohort (or batch) approach whereby a group of startups enters and leaves the program together is popular among programs emphasizing peer-to-peer networking and educational activities (cohorts spread fixed costs over many startups). Vice versa, rolling intakes, whereby startups enter and leave a program individually, enable organizations to seize opportunities when they come, with positive effects on deal-flow dependent objectives or on innovation sourcing needs.
- **Ideal advancement and substages.** Substages and intermediary milestones enable progress tracking and in-program filtering. Substage transitions can be content-related (implicit milestones) or marked by formal decision gates (explicit milestones), but they equally imply the same planning exercise: imagining an ideal advancement.
- **Backpropagation is rooted in outcomes.** To schedule program activities, look at the ideal advancement and project what education, funds, or other resources or support the startups will need from one milestone to the next. Backpropagation from the final goal or output is a more solid method of grounding the milestones and schedule, and it seamlessly includes planning for the follow-on stage.

14 SELECTION

The sourcing, curation, and selection of startups represents a key function of startup programs, and it is one of the main tasks that other parts of the organization usually delegate to engagement programs. These three functions are carried out in two phases: (1) during the recruitment stage, culminating in the admission gate; and (2) during the activation stage, with intermediary gates and graduation (Figure 14.1). Intermediary gates may also route startups toward different paths and desired outcomes, as discussed in Chapter 9.

Sourcing is a question of positioning (the Circles), reservoir management (Chapter 10), or good execution of scouting and promotional actions. By contrast, selection is specific to tactical design (the Intersection in the Startup Program Strategy Canvas). Selection is not always mission-critical, but when it is, design must first and foremost create the right conditions for it, including "good enough" procedures and selectors. A flawed selection process, in some cases, might jeopardize the whole program. This chapter will examine the following challenges:

1. How to source startups
2. How to identify selection criteria
3. How to compose a selection committee
4. How to soften rating bias
5. How to structure the selection process

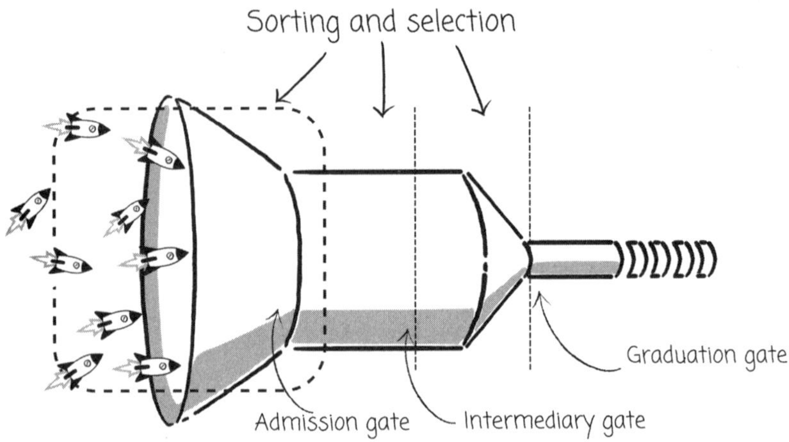

FIGURE 14.1 The sorting function is distributed through the different stages, and selection gates mark explicit milestones.

We start by providing an overview of a standard selection process and discussing its importance.

Selection Process

Selection processes differ depending on the stage at which they occur: admission, intermediary gates, or graduation.

In the latter two instances, selection is generally concentrated in just one event: the startups pitch to a committee to gain access to more resources, funding, perks, or to receive the final prize (Figure 14.2). For instance, Antler and Entrepreneur First hold a pitch session for the intermediate gate and another on demo day. Start-Up Chile organizes a voluntary pitch competition two months into the six-month program to assign perks such as a trip to Silicon Valley or higher-profile mentors.[1]

In contrast, the admission process often includes multiple steps, filtering startups progressively like a funnel. The reason lies in the high number of applications: YC receives 12,000 to 15,000 applications per class, calls 1,200 to 1,500 for interviews, and selects 200 to 250.[2] Although YC is undoubtedly an outlier, this tactic allows a program to shift the more costly selection resources (e.g., senior leaders, or the accelerator's partners) to later steps.

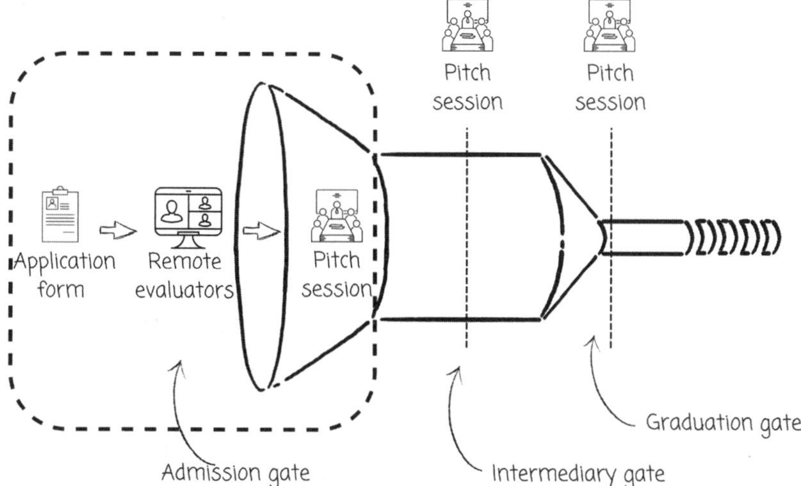

FIGURE 14.2 Intermediary and graduation gates usually comprise only one session (the pitch). The admission gate generally includes a sequence of steps.

A standard filtering sequence consists of:

- **Online application form.** Startups fill in a standard application form, providing data about the idea, market, team, and current state.
- **Eligibility screening.** Applications are filtered based on hard facts, e.g., whether a company is already incorporated or not, or whether it has at least one female founder, or similar requirements.
- **Remote evaluation.** Each application is screened remotely and asynchronously by two to four judges.
- **Live evaluation.** The most promising startups are invited to give a live pitch.

When Selection Is Mission-Critical

There is a trade-off with selection that cannot be understated. On the one hand, effective sorting of entrepreneurial proposals has an impact on resource allocation, matching of startups and program offer, and fit with the organizational strategy. But, on the other hand, selection might reduce serendipity and quench the unpredictable spark of innovation.

The actual contribution of the selection process to the overall success of startups after the program is still debated. For some, the sorting effect of top-tier accelerators is the key to their success. For others, that effect does not depend on how the selection process is structured. In a study conducted on over 60 organizations classified as "accelerators" (not just YC-style), researchers found no proof that better-performing programs are more selective.[3] Yet, the participation of experts has been demonstrated to play a critical role in selecting winning startups, and even more when scores are adjusted after accounting for some judges' generosity bias.[4]

When assessing the importance of selection process design in your case, the main factor to consider is the type of objective (Circle 2). If you aim for financial investment opportunities or innovative solution sourcing, and in general for long-term partnerships, then selection is likely to be critical (Figure 14.3). Here, quality is very important. It is not just about the business type, technology, and entrepreneurial skills, but also about motivations. Venture funds must bet on founders with rapid-growth vision and commitment, for instance (RL startups). Even with the right technology, an excellent team that wants to build a solid but not rapid-growing business (BL) is not a potential match for a VC.

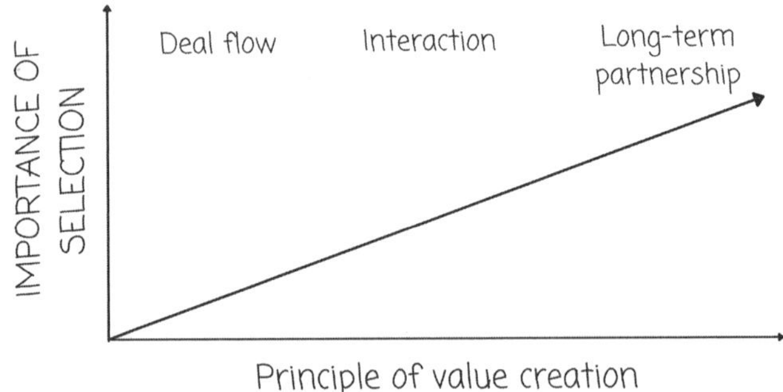

FIGURE 14.3 Selection becomes more mission-critical as objectives are related to later program stages, and selection is the most significant for long-term partnerships.

At the opposite end of the spectrum, objectives such as trend discovery, market intelligence, or brand positioning benefit more from quantity. Also, role model creation (e.g., 150 Startups) or entrepreneurial ecosystem building (e.g., Techstars Startup Weekend) can function with entrepreneurs with just a temporary drive (PS, BS, or RS). For these goals, sorting might be less mission-critical than a visible promotion campaign on a variety of channels.

Mission-Critical Paradox: Avoid Early Kills

> *We don't want to be only business-case driven because that would kill experimentation. Instead, we are creating a niche where it's acceptable to move by small steps and small results.*
>
> —Gabriele Molari, Tetra Pak

Corporate and government organizations, for a variety of legitimate reasons, are at risk of making startup collaboration decisions that are too conservative. This cautiousness is true about innovation and change management in general. Gregor Gimmy of 27pilots said, "In the venture client model the decision is always made by the end user, the client. The program unit has the function of supporting that decision, making sure that it happens, and providing the ability to avoid a 'no' when they should say 'yes' instead."

Almost paradoxically, sometimes the selection process should encourage the organization to be less selective than usual. Corporate managers and government officers may need a fresh, external perspective to help them take calculated risks with potentially game-changing projects even when they appear to underperform in traditional metrics. To this end, for example, Dawn LeBlanc of Hartford InsurTech Hub reserves two wild cards for herself to reinsert startups discarded by the program's insurance partners.

Finally, especially in the early stage, the human factor counts more than what seasoned corporate managers imagine. YC, for example, has been credited with investing in founders over the business idea and giving gritty and ambitious founders a chance with a secondary idea if the main one had flaws. The YC application form even includes a question about such a secondary option.

Challenge #1: Sourcing

> *Many leads are through referrals from our accelerator and investor network, or from our database—they have already been vetted. Others come from newsletters, calls, promotion. . . . If a company has lesser brand recognition, startups don't jump on the opportunity because they don't know how impactful the collaboration could be.*
>
> —Dan D'Souza and Alex Reynolds, L Marks

A program must first encourage startups to apply. Chapters 1 and 11 highlighted signaling as one of the key functions of a startup program: it communicates to startups (Circle 3) the intention of the organization to engage with them (Circle 1). Signaling is highly related to positioning the program in the market—a strategic design action that involves all three Circles.

Your organization (Circle 1) can be a magnet for startups, especially if it has a strong and recognizable brand as an innovator or ecosystem builder (or vice versa, it might discourage applications if it's not positioned or perceived negatively). People inside your organization (again, Circle 1) who have contacts with startups, mentors, or investors, can activate their personal network in the ecosystem.

The problem or the objective (Circle 2) can also contribute to attracting startups, in some circumstances even more than the organization's brand—for example, in sustainability, social, or other impact-oriented programs, or with problems related to edge technologies, such as artificial intelligence or blockchain. Startups that want to disrupt Google or Johnson & Johnson might still join a specific challenge if they believe it's relevant or interesting. This circumstance may be rare, but it happens, and good designers are able to use this causation to their advantage.

Finally, the abundance or scarcity of targeted startups in the reservoir (Circle 3) has obvious consequences on the ease of sourcing. Reservoir curation, fertilization activities, and partnering with ecosystem players are all tools to this end (Chapters 7 and 10).

Tactical Aspects: Scouting and Promotion

Beyond improving the program's positioning, you can act on more tactical aspects such as scouting (*outbound sourcing*) and promotional campaigns (*inbound sourcing*):

- **Outbound sourcing** is when the program takes an active approach to search through scouting and direct contacts to best-fitting candidates. The average pipeline quality tends to be higher because the scouts, in effect, operate a preselection before contacting the startups.
- **Inbound sourcing** is when the program signals its activity and waits for interested startups to show up. Inbound sourcing allows startups to self-qualify and raise their hand if they think there is a fit, overcoming any defiance or ignorance. A spot-on stealth startup might knock at the door, or an apparently uninteresting startup could surprise the selectors. However, missing any preselection, this approach typically requires more filtering later.

Outbound sourcing requires either a wide network of partners in the startup ecosystem, or databases and software tools to scrape and aggregate startup information that is available online (such as F6S or Leadspicker)—even better if you possess both. Furthermore, you need trained scouts—people who know how to pre-assess a startup in a reasonable amount of time. Although it's a brute-force job often delegated to juniors, scouts generally have at least some knowledge of the industry or technology they are scouting for. Depending on the internal availability of these resources (Circle 1), you may want to use more scouting or rely more on promotion.

Scouting is one of those activities that can be easily outsourced to an external supplier because it involves only minor participation of internal allies and decision makers (more in Chapter 17). Look for providers with a strong network in the industry or ecosystem you are targeting: referrals usually make the strongest applications thanks to the pre-vetting they receive from you or your provider's networks.

Inbound sourcing requires a bit more planning, because there are multiple channels. The program's visibility can be enhanced by:

- **Call.** A public call for applications or event promotion.
- **Promotion.** Online or offline campaigns and websites.
- **Startup platforms.** Call hosting platforms functioning as aggregators of calls for startups[5]: F6S, YouNoodle, etc.
- **Partner network.** Distribute the call to universities, investors, other programs, etc.
- **Alumni network.** Recommendations by alumni.
- **Deal flow activities.** Road shows, startup competitions before the main program, bootcamps to educate startups to apply, etc.

Some of these channels are available to any program, such as a call and its promotion, whereas others need to be built over time, such as a partner and alumni network. So, much of the inbound mix also depends on the readiness of your organization (Circle 1). Promotion and call management can be outsourced to external providers even more conveniently than scouting.

Generally, you will need a mix of both outbound and inbound strategies, so the main decision is how to distribute resources between the two. Your sourcing strategy will also be highly dependent on the health of the entrepreneurial ecosystem in which the program operates, and the reservoir maturity and extension that it can reach (its SOM, serviceable obtainable market). For example, proactive scouting in universities, tech hubs, or hacker spaces could be the only reasonable tactic in an immature ecosystem that has a low level of entrepreneurial activation.

Challenge #2: The "Best Startup" May Not Be Best for You

Defining tailored selection criteria can be important, especially to coordinate multiple judges. Judges score on a standard set of criteria defined by the program designer. Selecting for one objective using criteria optimized for another might lead to disappointing results. For instance, corporate accelerators employing VC-like criteria often fail if they then push the selected startups to business units; aspiring unicorns may not be willing to solve an immediate innovation need.

Choosing a representative set of criteria will guide evaluators in what to prioritize, something that counts when you employ several judges from outside the organization (e.g., in the remote evaluation of Figure 14.2).

Types of Criteria

Intuitively, selection criteria should be significant in evaluating the startups' fit with the objectives (Circle 2) and the value proposition (Intersection). They include (Table 14.1):

- **Objective factors** and hard facts such as: whether a startup is pre- or post-revenues; the number of clients or patents; industry; technology used; and so forth.
- **Subjective factors** regarding the founders' ambition, grit, personality, commitment, coachability, and ability to deliver. Also, the strategic fit of the team and idea with the program's strategy; and so on, depending on your objectives. They dominate in the early stage when startups lack any significant metrics. Because nascent businesses use projections instead of a track record, even numbers such as current revenues often require a more subjective interpretation.

Startups can be segmented along many dimensions such as demographics, innovation type, maturity stage, and motives. Objective factors are effective to verify the startup's demographics, and the basic aspects of its innovation type and maturity stage. They can be used in eligibility checks and delegated to junior staff or automated prescreening. Subjective factors assess the startup's motives; more advanced aspects about its innovation type and maturity stage; and the future potential of the collaboration. They must be evaluated by experts (until we have better artificial intelligence, of course).

TABLE 14.1 Frequently used selection criteria

Criterion	Description	Notes
Company demographics	Geography, year of incorporation, pre- or post- revenues, no. of team members, no. of employees, etc.	Can be used for eligibility.
Industry	Sector in which the startup operates.	Can be used for eligibility but may need an expert check.
Technology	Type of technology used (e.g., nanomaterials, AI).	Can be used for eligibility but may need an expert check.
Market	Addressable market, its dynamics, and trends, competitive landscape, emerging needs.	Can be less subjective than other criteria but needs expert judges.
Strategic fit	Consistency with the program's goals and the organization's mission. Could include ethical considerations.	Requires internal judges. Not always used for financial goals.
Team	Skills, experience, and quality of the management team. Missing skills and possible hires. Ability to scale.	Very subjective.
Motivation	Drive, commitment, where the idea came from, reasons to participate.	Very subjective.
Feasibility	Technical aspects related to technology and product, scalability.	Can be less subjective than other criteria but needs expert judges.
Viability	Business model and economic feasibility aspects, barriers to entry, market-related dysfunctions.	Can be less subjective than other criteria but needs expert judges.
Innovation	Uniqueness, disruption, degree of novelty, business model innovation.	Can be less subjective than other criteria but needs expert judges.
Competitive advantage	Patents, other intellectual property, first-mover advantage, other competitive moats.	Can be less subjective than other criteria but needs expert judges.
Traction	Measurable market success such as revenues, number of active users, ongoing pilots, user growth, churn, etc.	Depends on the market and industry so needs expert judges.
Financial performance	Performance in previous years (balance sheet, income statement, cash flow statement).	Objective. Could be used for eligibility in some cases.
Financial projections	Same as above, but pro forma. Breakeven analysis, payback period, projected NPV, or IRR. Funding needs.	Very subjective. Less so for costs (burn rate and runway).

Criteria for Eligibility Screening

Objective criteria find their natural use in the initial eligibility screening, to assess the fit of a startup with the target demographics.

If your only objective is trend analysis, market intelligence, or anything similar that is indifferent to the individual quality of a participant—then this is enough. For example, if you are surveying the market for new carbon neutrality technology, you just need to assess whether the startups in your pipeline produce any piece in that stack or not.

Likewise, ecosystem building events such as startup weekends might simply do a light filtering to guarantee enough software developers and diversity in the event (or they even let everyone in). Many governmental grant programs for entrepreneurs stop at eligibility as well. When the goal is to reach the target audience and attract applications, objective demographics are the main, and often the only type of criteria.

Criteria for Expert Evaluations—Pre-graduation Objectives

Non-demographic criteria are in the realm of subjective screening, for the most part, which implies expert reviewers.

Experts need guidance about what they are asked to judge, for at least two reasons: (1) Given the reviewers' limited time and dedication, you should focus their attention on what matters to the program; (2) you should establish a framework that maximizes the comparability of judgments across a large number of reviewers operating independently or semi-independently (e.g., in remote evaluations).

If choosing criteria for experts is so important for the human factor, it should also be highly connected to the objectives the experts are selecting for. For pre-graduation objectives, the participant's motivation can easily be compensated with a fair quid pro quo (Chapter 12). Consequently, selectors can almost ignore the participants' motivations and focus on their ability to contribute and interact to the level required to meet the objective. For example:

- **Ideation or validation** objectives rely on the participants' skills and knowledge. Elective criteria are the team's qualifications, its track record, and its ability to brainstorm and work in a group (e.g., with internal employees).

- **Mindset shift** objectives rely on the time spent together and teamwork. Selection should look for entrepreneurs who have time to give back (e.g., after a successful exit, or while still pivoting in the earliest stages), or who see a personal advantage in spending time with whoever is the recipient of the cultural operation. In this last case, motives count (i.e., what are they looking for?)—although not critically.

Criteria for Expert Evaluations—Post-graduation Objectives

For post-graduation objectives, the preconditions that determine the program's success become more diversified, and so should the criteria. Selecting for financial return is totally different than choosing someone who would set up business in Chile or Puerto Rico for the next 10 years. More specifically, let us look at the five most prominent post-graduation objectives.

Financial investing, being based on rapid growth, must select for market potential, team, motivation, and competitive advantage. Be aware that, for disruptive technologies, lower costs or the ability to open new markets are more important than current market size or financial performance. Focus on identifying opportunities ahead of the curve[6] and teams aligned with lucrative exits (RL). There might be other preconditions, depending on the specific industry. For instance, feasibility may be more of an issue in hardware products than in digital services. The strategic fit might sometimes be better ignored (a reason why CVCs are often spun out of parent companies).

Strategic investing: (1) When investing is just a hedging option against disruption, then the priority goes to strategic fit, feasibility, and viability. (2) When it pursues a mechanism to stimulate more revenues, for example, by complementing the demand for the core business,[7] the criteria are more similar to those of financial investing because the startup's success would drive the core business and its top line.

Solution sourcing is usually successful only if the startup's product goes through integration and scale-up. If the main expected advantage is cost efficiency, then feasibility, viability, and innovation are priority criteria. If, instead, the advantage is expected to be generated by a new revenue stream, then market potential and possibly team become also very important (even more so if you are considering an M&A down the line). Motives here might be clear if the startup is B2B and wants the organization as a client, or B2C and can use the organization as a distribution partner, as well as all other relevant combinations. However, if M&A is the final objective, motives should be inspected more thoroughly.

Ecosystem building is substantially different from the previous cases because here the precondition to success is that a startup has or can develop reasons to stay in the ecosystem (retention). Consequently, assessing motivation and strategic fit is the absolute priority. Parallel18, for instance, demands applicants demonstrate how they would use the local market opportunities in Puerto Rico. An exception, for which market and financials matter too, is when you ask for a revenue share, such as when building an innovation ecosystem on a technology platform, such as Google Android store or SAP's marketplace. Another exception implying market potential is when you are looking for mature startups that would hire massively in your region. More revenues generally bring more jobs.

Transformational impact, finally, postulates that the participant is committed to using the support offered by the program to pursue whatever cause the program is championing. Here, team and motivation are a priority. If your program is making impact investing, like Village Capital's or Endeavor's funds, then financial criteria are also important.

Payback Period

When choosing the target segment (Chapter 10), you should also consider the expected time for results, or payback period. In part, the maturity level of your target should already reflect the payback period, but it is wise to inform the experts of your expectations. Are you selecting for outcome metrics that must appear in one or two years, or do you have a more patient strategy?

Make sure you are providing guidance to experts, directly or indirectly, about this temporal dimension. Financial projections can be a clue, but only when the startup's revenues matter.

In solution sourcing, for instance, the expected time horizon of results is more tied to feasibility in the context of the organization's current operations. Strategic fit is equally important because it measures the chance to rally active internal allies (see also McKinsey's Three Horizons[8]).

Anti-patterns in Selection Criteria

To avoid mistakes in identifying selection criteria, three anti-patterns to think about are:

- **Too many criteria.** Three to six criteria are the industry standard. Too many criteria discourage a holistic evaluation and are time-consuming to score—possibly causing distraction and incoherency. Bad example: one program had 88 criteria, each contributing 0 to 0.25 points toward the total score. Good example: another one started with 27 overlapping criteria, but reduced them to just 5 after assessing the performance of its selection committee.
- **Ambiguous descriptions.** Criteria should be clear and easy to interpret. Bad example: one scorecard had both desirability and market potential—how are they different? Every expert will have their own opinion about how much they overlap or not.
- **Scoring ranges.** Wide ranges (0–10 instead of 1–5) may introduce imprecision as two judges are more likely to use the scale differently, hence adding to scoring noise. A group evaluation can help solve ties better than a wide scoring range (see Challenge #5).

Challenge #3: Committee Composition

> *In one multi-partner accelerator we manage, the scientific committee is the osmosis membrane, not a filter: that's when cross pollination happens between partners.*
>
> —Michele Giordani, Gellify

Selecting startups can be hard, especially in admission committees. Graduation committees can leverage the longer diligence done during the activation stage.

A committee can contain anywhere from two judges to several dozens, and members can come from the ranks of investors, experienced entrepreneurs, corporate managers, people with a role in the local ecosystem, business consultants, technology experts, academics, or program alumni. In massive government programs, such as the EIC Accelerator or Start-Up Chile, they can reach hundreds. An individual startup, however, is scored by two to four evaluators, save for pitch sessions, where up to 10 or 15 selectors might sit together.

In our experience, the identity and background of judges appear to be more influential than their number. The successful evaluation of subjective criteria depends on personal skills rather than headcount. One exceptional oracle might have the Midas touch that a committee of 10 experts lacks—the VC industry knows this well. Hence, selecting the selectors is no secondary task.

If you cannot hire a Midas, then a fair mix of competencies and backgrounds can be beneficial. "We used to involve junior people as well as senior managers to gather different perspectives," said Felix Wong, former Techstars community manager in Hong Kong.

Here, a measure of common sense and job-to-be-done play a role. If you are selecting for something highly technical, you must bring in your most trusted technical advisors. If you are including selectors to give them a voice and not necessarily to audit complex code—design for that.

Most of the time it's overkill to have a 20-person selection committee with representation from every business unit. On the other hand, sometimes this is an important peacekeeping and alignment activity. Know the difference and design for that. If your reservoir is strong and produces high-quality deal flow, over-resourcing the selection committee tends to have decreased marginal utility and is not worth the cost. In some cases, it even has negative marginal utility since over-resourced committees tend to screen out the wild cards that often round out the cohort.

Dependence on Objectives

Matching selectors' skills with program objectives is also a matter of design, not just execution. It would be a mistake to engage investors for solution sourcing, for example. Coping with a precise innovation need requires domain knowledge rather than VC skills. Involving internal engineers to judge long-term macro-economic or business trends might lead to a likewise undesirable distortion.

Discerning stars from rotten eggs cannot be easily ascribed to a selector's background. Yet, here are some very high-level considerations (Table 14.2):

- **Financial investing.** This objective can be independent of the core business and can rely solely on the startup's ability to hit the jackpot. Thus, venture capital investors or experienced entrepreneurs can contribute to the decision, even when they possess little knowledge of your organization. Conversely, corporate leaders might pollute the decision with overly conservative considerations.
- **Strategic investing.** By contrast, this objective requires a deep knowledge of your organization's strategy. You would need at least one senior leader on the committee or someone aligned with the top management's vision. The key is to spot synergies that can indirectly stimulate core business revenues or other core business success metrics (e.g., impact metrics if for government).
- **Solution sourcing, ideation, or validation.** The problem owners are likely the best selectors, or at least they should have a voice. Venture client units let the user pick the winning startups, as do Hartford InsurTech Hub or MobilityXlab. At least two of the accelerator's corporate partners must commit to working with a startup for it to be admitted.
- **Ecosystem building.** You need ecosystem leaders or alumni who can discern if the startup can be inserted and can profit from the ecosystem's opportunities. It is more about detecting a fit (which will foster retention) than scoring market or technology merits.

Distinct Committees for Distinct Criteria

Several programs separate the scoring into subcommittees for: business criteria, technical criteria, and strategic criteria. Dividing the judgment into specialized committees can help involve selectors on criteria of their competence in just the right committee. It can avoid unwanted imprecision or unaware ignorance of self-confident committee members.

TABLE 14.2 Different profiles of selectors in relation to post-graduation objectives

Objectives	Profiles	Examples
Financial investing	Selectors with skills in assessing the potential of future growth based on considerations on emerging market needs, disruptive technology, and team	Investors, experienced startup founders
Strategic investing	Selectors who can imagine synergic scenarios where the startup stimulates demand, revenues, or other success metrics of the execution business	Senior leaders, corporate managers
Solution sourcing, ideation, validation	Selectors who know the needs of the client (internal business unit, external customers) and can compare the solutions coming from startups with the state-of-the-art	Corporate managers, technology experts, customer experts
Ecosystem building	Selectors with a deep knowledge of the ecosystem platform (its pros and cons) who can assess the fit for its long-term adoption by the startup as well as cultural fit	Alumni, marketers, platform experts (technology or local business or ecosystem platforms)

Start4Big, for instance, a cross-sector open innovation initiative of five corporations in Spain, implemented a two-stage remote screening (before a final live pitch). The first step is evaluated by external judges more skilled at technology trends and emerging markets, and the second is done by internals who evaluate the feasibility of a pilot with one of the partners.

Case Study: Peer Selection

Since 2009 impact-investing Village Capital has experimented with an unusual system: at the end of each program, cohort participants elect who among them are the most promising ventures and deserve to receive an investment.

While program alumni are recruited as judges for admission in many other programs, the unique formula of VilCap's peer investment is based on a lengthy due diligence that lasts for the entire program.

Data from over 10 years of operations suggests that peer selection mitigates selection bias and fosters inclusivity.[9] This peer-selected investment practice has started to spread to other accelerators or programs, such as SheEO in Canada, which is centered on women and nonbinary diverse entrepreneurship.[10]

The Importance of a Lengthy Due Diligence

Beyond the selector per se, it is the diligence of the specific startup that really makes a difference. Observing a startup in its evolution provides more information than just one meeting or demo day. Hit-and-run judges are more susceptible to the founder's stage performance or a flashy business plan than those who have seen the startup at work out of the spotlight. A best practice, then, is to involve people who did more protracted due diligence during the activation stage: mentors, the program team, or peers (such as in Village Capital).

Challenge #4: Compensating for Rating Bias

During an evaluation process, different startups can be assigned to different judges (especially for the remote evaluation step), thus introducing incongruences in the scoring of subjective criteria. Subjective criteria imply personal bias. Research and our own experience show that some judges are more "brutal"—they consistently rate lower than average—while others are more "generous" and consistently rate higher.[11] Not less important, a diversity bias has also been proven in the investor community.[12]

While computing the average or median could mathematically mitigate bias over many judges, these methods may fail when committees consist of just two to four members.

The simulation in Table 14.3 illustrates this concept. Four selectors (Crazy, Dubious, Equal, and Funny—identified by their initials) scored five projects V–Z on a scale of 0 to 5. F is a generous judge, while C is a brutal judge. Projects W and Y win depending on whether we use the median (W) or average (Y) to aggregate the ratings. However, it is unclear whether we should trust the judgment of D (who scored zero on W) more than that ofF (who rated Y the lowest). It is possible that either of them possesses some information that the others do not have, or maybe one of them misunderstood a proposal. The only solution would be to ask them.

TABLE 14.3 Simulation of ratings of projects V–Z by evaluators C–F (the median and average select two different winners)

	Project V	Project W	Project X	Project Y	Project Z
Crazy (C)	2	3	1	3	3
Dubious (D)	1	0	3	4	0
Equal (E)	3	5	3	3	3
Funny (F)	5	5	5	4	5
AVERAGE	**2.75**	**3.25**	**3.00**	**3.50**	**2.75**
MEDIAN	**2.50**	**4.00**	**3.00**	**3.50**	**3.00**

Some programs use more complicated mathematical operators. For instance, one program discards any outlier and averages the rest. If that were applied to the example, W would be scored by averaging only 5, 5, and 3—without the zero.

Some researchers suggested a mathematical formula to detect generous or brutal selectors and to compensate their scores, although that requires fairly solid statistical skills.[13] Until better mathematical or artificial intelligence solutions are developed, bias limitation strategies will have to pass through the human factor:

- **Selector manual.** Train selectors with examples and with an evaluation manual before they start the review. For instance, the EIC Accelerator distributes detailed recommendations on how to score specific criteria.
- **Selectors' comments.** Ask selectors to write a comment to justify their score, then use those comments to make sure the mathematical method you are using reproduces their intentions.
- **Group evaluation.** Introduce a group evaluation (discussed next) after the scoring step in which judges can overcome any information asymmetry.

Challenge #5: Defining the Selection Process

The introduction to this chapter presented a blueprint of the selection process for the admission gate, reproduced in Figure 14.4.

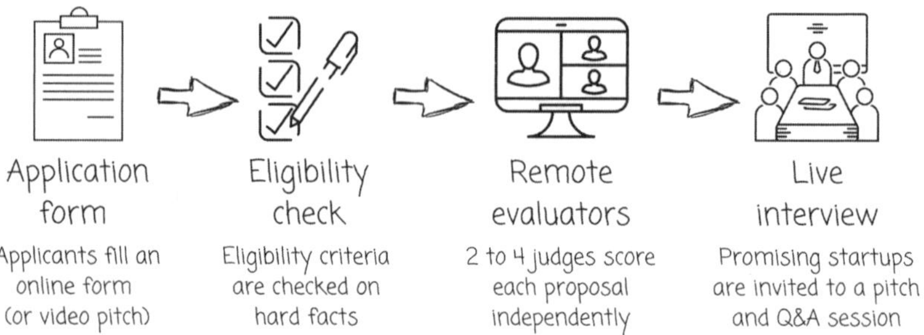

FIGURE 14.4 A basic admission process is composed of application form, eligibility check, remote evaluation (asynchronous, documentation only), and live evaluation (synchronous, Q&A).

Alternative examples are shown in the following figures. The YC process closely resembles the general blueprint. The online application is followed by independent scoring and ranked by the average score. If needed, an intermediate pre-interview clarifies the project. The top tier is invited to a 10-minute live interview with three to four YC partners (Figure 14.5).

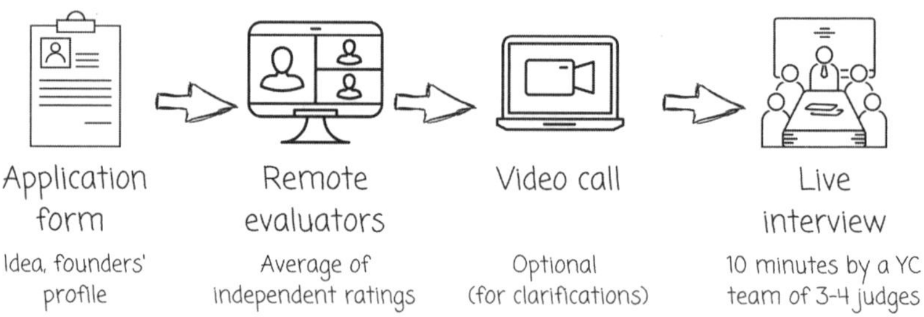

FIGURE 14.5 Overview of the selection process in Y Combinator.

In a WhatAVenture Startup Factory, a corporate program, the live scrutiny is in two steps: a pitch session followed by a three-day innovation camp where most of the corporate decision makers are invited[14] (Figure 14.6).

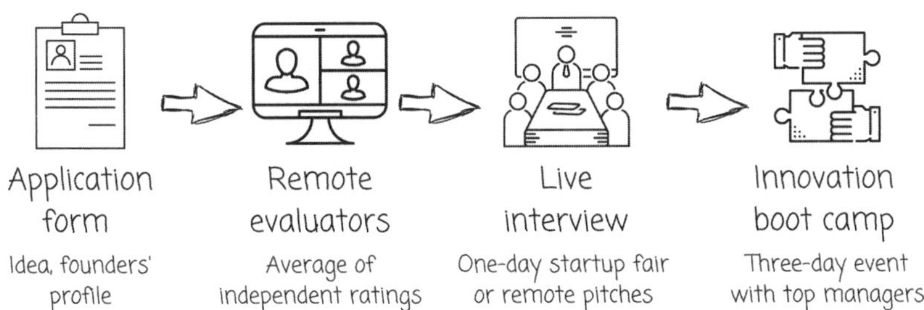

FIGURE 14.6 Overview of the selection process in WhatAVenture Startup Factory.

Antler, given its focus on unmatched aspirant founders, employs human resource screening: application is via résumé, followed by a cognitive test and an optional screening call. Successful candidates are invited to a first interview and assigned a case study to develop; the process ends with a second live review (Figure 14.7).

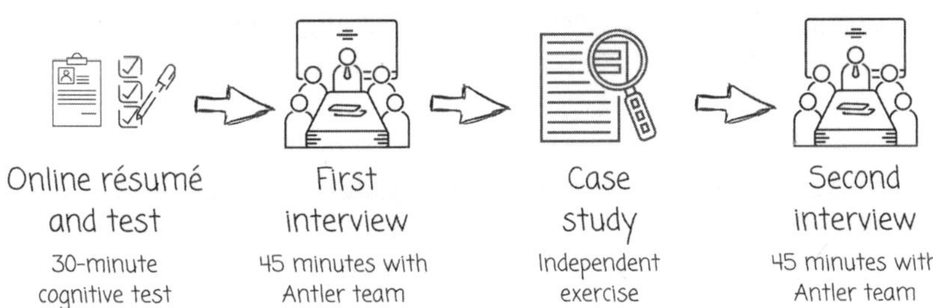

FIGURE 14.7 Overview of the selection process in Antler.

Parallel18, like many other government programs, has an eligibility check. After the online application (requiring a video pitch), the first screening round is dedicated to eligibility requirements. The judging round digs deeper into the fit with the local market and opportunities, possibly requiring up to two interviews. Finally, a local committee makes the final decision (Figure 14.8).

FIGURE 14.8 Overview of the selection process in Parallel18.

From our research, beyond the steps already illustrated in Figure 14.4, we identified additional building blocks such as:

- **Diligence events.** Bootcamps allow selectors to assess characteristics such as coachability, drive, commitment, and communication skills. Startup Wise Guys preselect up to 25 startups to be invited for the three-day Selection Bootcamp. Sony Accelerator in Europe used a five-day selection workshop.
- **Training sessions.** Sometimes less experienced teams need support to apply or to perfect their pitch (to soften the bias in favor of good stage performers). For example, Oasis500's selection process has a total of three pitch sessions, but before the final pitch day they provide a pitch practice workshop to level up the contenders. Zinc Catalyst offers a two half-day idea development and storytelling workshop for researcher-entrepreneurs, just before the final jury event.
- **Group evaluation.** Instead of independent rating, evaluators convene and openly discuss their opinions before ranking the proposals. Pros: discording scoring gets explained (Table 14.3); ranking can be used instead of rating; you can ask sponsors to commit to the startups they vote (e.g., Hartford InsurTech Hub and MobilityXlab, see above). Con: risk of overconfidence and leadership bias (one evaluator imposing decisions on the others by virtue of hierarchy, charisma, or personality).

Research is missing about what works best or what is superfluous. Vice versa, a study suggests that program performance is not correlated with different arrangements of the selection process, including also different forms of screening (remote evaluation, interviews, pitches, tests, or group exercises).[15]

Given this insight, the guiding principle, in our view, is that the process should be user-centric and tailored around the needs of applicants first, and of judges second.

Trade-Off: Completeness Versus Friendliness

In the search for a user-centric selection process design, a first trade-off is between a long and complete application form for the organization and a seamless application experience for the startups. A startup that invests its time in a lenghty application proves its commitment; but, on the contrary, it might instead be desperate for more runway and will do anything to raise funds or make an outside bet that a program will give it more time to exist.

A 2016 study run on 16 European government-corporate accelerators uncovered a tendency for bureaucracy that goes beyond the real needs of the selection process.[16] It is tempting to pack numerous questions in the application form, but that only matters if your program is pursuing a deal-flow-based objective (such as trend analysis or market intelligence). Consider alternative strategies (see also Table 14.4):

- **Staged information disclosure.** Divide the application process into two stages: a first form to check the eligibility criteria, and a second form where you concentrate the most time-consuming information input.
- **Standard pitch deck.** Ask for a pitch deck or a one-pager investor summary—documents that startups can reuse. You can solicit more information after a first screening.
- **Video.** Video presentations communicate body language, providing extra information that helps clarify ambiguous points or stop unfit candidates earlier, saving time. Also, a video can contain a product demo.

Trade-off: Speed Versus Diligence

A second trade-off is between response speed and sufficient analysis. The design problem stems from making "good enough" decisions in the shortest possible time.

The window of opportunity to catch a given startup may not be too long, as startups have abundant opportunities nowadays.

TABLE 14.4 Pros and cons of typical items requested during the admission process

Application item	Pros	Cons
Business plan	More complete information.	Requires a high investment of time from startup, can be distracting.
Application form (online)	Convenient and relatively quicker than business plan if the number of questions is limited.	Each program has a different form, so startups have to repeat the work (would not happen with a business plan or a pitch deck).
Staged information	Startups send only some standard information format at the beginning (e.g., a pitch deck, or website link) and add information only when approved after the initial admission step.	The selection process might be delayed if startups don't promptly provide the additional information.
Pitch deck	Most startups will have a pitch deck ready.	Not all first-time entrepreneurs know how to write an effective pitch. The show effect can give advantage to good communicators.
Demo	More complete information about the product and its current state.	Time consuming for both startups and selectors. Better in later stages of the selection process.
Video	Conveys body language that would otherwise be perceived only during live interviews.	Time consuming for both startups and selectors. Better in later stages of the selection process.

As a general rule, for accelerators a response time of up to one month is fast; up to three months normal; anything longer may discourage a startup from waiting.

A remote evaluation step with tens of reviewers in parallel can help shorten the evaluation time. Still, as discussed in a previous section, you must then manage imprecision and decision noise from generous or brutal evaluators or mathematical formulas.

KEY TAKEAWAYS

- **Selection is not always mission critical.** Your objectives should drive your selection process. If you aim for financial investment opportunities or innovative solution sourcing—and long-term partnerships in general—then selection is likely to be critical. At the opposite end of the spectrum, objectives such as trend discovery, market intelligence, or brand positioning benefit more from the number of applicants than a careful selection process.
- **Look ahead of the curve.** Almost paradoxically, sometimes the process should ensure that large organizations are less selective than they instinctively are. Investing ahead of the next curve while taking calculated risk is what provides a competitive edge, both in corporate innovation and regional entrepreneurial development. Give external experts a few wild cards.
- **Select the selectors and use group evaluations.** Subjective criteria (e.g., team, motivation, or market potential) are the most difficult to assess, and yet they are crucial to spot outlier opportunities. Consequently, selecting the selectors is no secondary task. One exceptional oracle might have the Midas touch that a committee of 10 experts lacks. However, she could lose her touch in a remote evaluation—unless judges operate from a clear reference framework, for instance, through selector training or a manual. Group evaluations, on the other hand, can help control the bias of mathematical rankings since the judges can explain their scoring.
- **Long due diligence matters.** Hit-and-run judges are more susceptible to the excellence of a founder's presentation skills or a flashy business plan. A best practice, then, is to involve people who did more protracted due diligence during the activation stage: mentors, the program team, or peers (such as in Village Capital).
- **User-centered design for the selection process.** While research about what works best in the selection process is missing, a study suggests that program performance is not correlated with different selection process arrangements, including all forms of screening (remote evaluation,

interviews, pitches, tests, or group exercises). Given this insight, the guiding principle, in our view, is that the process should be user-centric and tailored around the needs of applicants first, and of judges second.

CONTENT

Startup programs employ a wide variety of programming activities. This chapter highlights some of the ways to support startups, focusing on recurring content features used in the activation stage across many popular templates:

- Mentors (experienced entrepreneurs, managers, investors, etc.)
- Training and educational formats (workshops, lectures, etc.)
- Peer-community activities (community building, peer-to-peer learning, etc.)
- Brokerage and introductions (connections to investors, managers, partners, etc.)
- Funding (cash, a budget, reimbursement of expenses, etc.)
- Activities fostering ecosystem effects (return-value activities, open seminars, etc.)

From Strategic to Tactical Planning

The support offered to startups can take many forms: capital, mentors, training, educational formats, validation opportunities, matchmaking, coordination meetings with decision makers, recognition and visibility, peer community, introductions to investors or to partners, access to customers and business development support, office space, labs or other facilities, technology platforms, datasets, prototyping or production support, or access to cofounders and talent, among others.

The why and what of these features belong to strategic planning, and the how-to belongs to tactical planning. Yet, the how is an integral part of the value proposition and consequently of positioning. It makes a big difference for startups if capital is structured as equity, debt, or a non-dilutive grant, for instance. Likewise, the prevalent background of mentors (entrepreneurial, technical, or corporate) can alter the allure and usefulness of a program.

The space of possible content configurations is extremely vast. There are best practices and patterns but no rules. Keep in mind the general considerations presented in previous chapters:

- Spot the *gaps* that separate startups from achieving the outcomes. Gaps can be in knowledge, mindset, resources, operations, networks, recognition, or strategy (Challenge #2 of Chapter 10).
- Start with content features that are *gap fillers*, then add the *incentives* that make the offer appealing to your target (Challenge #2 and #3 of Chapter 12).
- Lay out these features according to an *ideal advancement* schedule (Challenge #4 of Chapter 13), distributing them in substages.

For good startup program design, content features should be added with purpose. When startups throw a million features at an app, they are usually insecure about what the customer or user actually wants. The same is true with startup programs.

Mentors

> *When you find smart people, who are respectful, who challenge you, who are as committed to growth as you are and are in the right systems of engagement with one another, it is something very special.*
>
> —Chris Heuer, Founder of Mentor Bureau

A universal definition of a mentor does not exist, but generally it is an individual with stature, experience, an ecosystem role, or even all three. Mentors provide industry knowledge, strategic advice, feedback, introductions, and occasionally also funding when there is a business angel or venture fund manager among their numbers. They can help with:

- Knowledge gaps
- Mindset gaps
- Networks gaps
- Strategy gaps; and occasionally
- Resources gaps

Accelerators take pride in being *mentor-driven*, with an average of 167 mentors in the Global Accelerator Network (GAN) community of 105 programs in 163 locations worldwide.[1] Hackathons too involve mentors in the range of 10 to 20 or more in each event.

A high number of mentors maximizes the probability of finding a match with a startup. However, one spot-on mentor is valued more than 10 unrelated ones. The actual transaction can be as short as an hour to several months. Advice flows without preparation—it comes on the fly from direct experience, seldom from a pre-study of the startup (save when the program provides pre-mentorship summaries). Mentors often give conflicting advice, especially if there is no presession coordination, as it is the most common practice. It is up to founders to make sense of mentorship, and inexperienced founders may struggle.

Who to Involve

Mentors have a variety of backgrounds, including founders with company building experience, business owners, academics, technology experts, professionals, investors, corporate managers, or government officials.

Ecosystems are full of amazing people that can make a difference for a startup, but convincing them to serve as mentors depends highly on the operator's own leadership and credibility as well as the program's brand recognition (many would be proud of being a Techstars or 500 Startups mentor, for instance). You may want to sign up a mentor with the purpose of:

1. **Strategic advice.** This can be on the business idea, marketing strategy, or entrepreneurial challenges in general. Divergent or convergent thinking are very different skills, and you want to understand which one a mentor is better at and assign them to the appropriate phase: earlier for divergence, later for convergence—or at alternate steps for more validation cycles.
2. **Project management.** Strategic mentors can also act as a clock for progress, keeping the startups on track.
3. **Technical advice.** Given by domain experts on the product, system architecture, technological roadblocks, or other technical resources. Best on an "as needed" basis, whenever a related problem arises.
4. **Internal ecosystem liaison.** Someone who can help navigate organizational mazes, bureaucracy, and hierarchy is crucial for solution sourcing, internal innovation ecosystem building, and other goals implicating the deep involvement of internal partners.
5. **External ecosystem liaison.** Mirroring the previous, but in the context of the entrepreneurial ecosystem: local partners, associations, universities, and so on. Crucial for business or regional ecosystem building.
6. **Prestige.** Renowned mentors can help attract the startups you want, directly thanks to their reputation or indirectly through referrals (from their own network).

As to geographical extraction, your mentor network will depend on how you structured the location features (Chapter 13); your target segment; and your reservoir (Chapter 10). In prepandemic programs, most mentors were local. For example, in the GAN community, 81 percent of mentors in 2019 came from within 100 miles of the accelerator. This locality was partially due to the logistics of meeting startups at the program venue, and partially to developing the program's presence in the local ecosystem. With the ongoing trend toward remote programs, the demand might shift to international and super connected mentors.

Internal Employees as Mentors

For corporate programs specifically, involving internal employees can contribute to reshaping the corporate mindset, gaining buy-in, and fostering internal champions (ecosystem benefits). "We encouraged all of our colleagues who wanted to help the other colleagues and startups; a corporation is full of these people but even our close colleagues don't ask for help. So, we created an academy where expert colleagues train our startups—so they get to know each other and start exchanging," said Christopher McLachlan of EnBW, a German utility.

Some programs use internal employees as technical mentors, mainly when a startup exploits the organization's technology or vice versa. This arrangement can work quite well—but make sure the employees know what to expect. While they are experts, some of them are not mentors by trade. Some will find it exciting and helpful; others will ask, "What am I doing here when I could be at work?"

Training mentors and startups on how to conduct a session is a best practice, although seldom employed. Corporate staff, not having experienced startup life firsthand, may require pretraining on how to pace the session, how to interpret the most common tools (e.g., the business model canvas), and how to challenge startups while not getting personal or defensive. If you are using internal employees as mentors, consider a preprogram academy to prepare them.

Mentor Matching and Management

> *Beyond the quality of mentors, matching and mentor management are very important, because otherwise mentors will stop answering your phone calls. This is the most difficult part, and you need a person who is respected.*
>
> —Paolo Borella, Vertical.vc

For a founder, mentorship can be game-changing, but the challenge is to match mentors with the right startup (and vice versa) and to keep them engaged. Mentor-startup matching can be designed in two complementary ways (Table 15.1):

- In a **pull** or "buffet" mode, mentors publish office hours and the startups book a session according to their needs.
- In a **push** or "fixed menu" mode, the program team operates the matching or the mentors pick according to their preference.

TABLE 15.1 Comparison between pull and push modes of mentor management

Mentors in Pull Mode (Buffet)	Mentors in Push Mode (Set Menu)
Self-regulated workload. Founders are free to choose how much time to invest in mentoring and networking versus execution on their business.	**Pre-regulated workload.** The program team can regulate the mentorship across different startups based on their stage or progress.
High numbers. Needs a higher number of mentors, to spread the mentorship workload and avoid concentration on the most notorious mentors.	**High commitment.** Needs highly committed mentors, not just hit-and-run—may include a reimbursement or payment (also common for Entrepreneurs in Residence).
Assigned with office hours. A credit system can be used to regulate access so that everyone has a chance to book a session.	**Assigned in pitch sessions** where startups pitch and mentors pick; in mentor panels or clinics; or in "all-see-all" speed dating formats for serendipity.
Issue: Risk of overbooked or underutilized mentors. The latter may be caused by lack of time, or lack of awareness of the mentor's value.	**Issue: Requires a deep understanding** of a startup's business in order to do a good matching, because the decision lies with the program team or mentors.

The typical implementation of pull mode is an online *booking platform* where mentors publish their free hours on a calendar and the startups choose when to see them. An example was the catalog of 141 mentors made available in Pioneers of the Balkans, where startups from five Southeast European countries could book online sessions at their convenience.[2] However, even a pull system needs active refereeing, to balance out the load among more and less famous mentors, or guide startups in understanding whom they need.

In an extreme implementation of push mode, many startup programs opt for making all founders meet with all mentors to leverage the unpredictability of personal chemistry and of serendipitous matches (e.g., Techstars' mentor madness, Chapter 13). This all-against-all pattern overcomes the issue of suboptimal matching—trading off mentors' and founders' time.

Other times, push-mode mentor matching is like cherry-picking. For instance, in Google for Startups Accelerator (GFSA), at each end of day in a bootcamp, the program team runs an assessment of weak points and opportunities exposed by mentors and by startups. From this process follows a handpicked match of startups and mentors for the next day. The GFSA team takes particular pride in this approach—which is the extreme opposite of what is used in Techstars. From anecdotal evidence, this agile matching system adds tremendous value—although at the cost of some late nights for the program team. Mentor matching can be facilitated on the fly with pitches (startups to mentors) or reverse pitches (mentors to startups), with a few sticky notes to vote for preferences on both sides.

Timing the Mentoring

There are two rationales when it comes to timing mentor sessions (Table 15.2):

1. **Space out.** Mentor sessions are either opt-in (pull mode) or they are spaced out to let teams iterate on product development between mentor sessions (e.g., in accelerators: once every one or two weeks).
2. **Concentrate.** Mentor and customer interactions are concentrated to accumulate feedback (usually up front), freezing product and business development during that time (pausing only for Saturday afternoon in startup weekends, or even for several weeks, such as in Techstars).

TABLE 15.2 Comparison between sparse and concentrated mentorship timing

Space Out	Concentration
Time to iterate. Founders have time to alternate mentoring and product development cycles, thus testing the feedback received from mentors.	**Information flooding.** Overabundant and independent feedback can build proof against the founders' wrong assumptions—if elaborated correctly.
Trial and error. Frequent iterations generate a chain of trials and errors in learning, which might be better for experimentation but slower.	**Avoid suboptimal solutions.** Accumulation of evidence up front can help spot misinformation or misguidance and identify patterns pointing to product-market fit.
One-coach approach. Can allow for one mentor to sit with the team throughout the program, to give consistency to feedback—at the risk of bias.	**Intensive mentor dating.** Must be implemented with intensive, full-time mentoring for a period (typically, at start)—from 3 to 10 mentor sessions a day.

Spacing out gives a startup more time to digest the feedback, experiment with the product, and iterate. The lower density of information can be a double-edged sword, however: while it is easier to process, it might be insufficient to make effective changes to the product or business model. Not stopping the development and operations may help serve present customers while iterating on new features. On the flip side, that postulates that the business model is already proven.

Research suggests that concentrating mentor sessions may accelerate learning and improve the product-market fit, as it avoids premature satisficing and settling on suboptimal solutions. Founders can compare conflicting feedback more easily, quickly spotting differences and patterns and avoiding misguidance. Finally, it forces founders to search more widely (including looking at competitors and alternatives) before converging on one idea.[3]

Crafting the Mentor's Experience

Giving a reason for mentors to remain active and engaged is crucial. Generally speaking, mentors are volunteers and cut out time for sessions from their busy days. They serve as mentors for one or more of the following reasons:[4]

- A genuine passion for mentorship, give-back, and helping others succeed
- Meeting and networking with other mentors
- Deal flow for their own investment activity
- Brand association with the program

Think of mentors as another kind of customer for whom you need to craft a captivating user experience. The more of these soft incentives you can activate by design, the better. Recognize their contribution by giving them a space onstage at events, demo days, or panels with invited speakers. Panels or "mentor days" with multiple mentors convening together are superior to isolated, one-to-one sessions because they provide mentor-to-mentor networking opportunities. Organize dedicated mentor pitch nights or startup community dinners. Keep them informed with constant data on the startups' progress that may facilitate some investments.

Consider paying programmatic mentors to guarantee more continuity and a higher professional commitment. In some programs paid mentors are called "coaches" to distinguish them from volunteers. They often advise the same startup throughout the entire program. In Conception X, for example, "Each PhD is assigned one business coach and one technology coach, and these are paid positions with a reporting duty, not pro bono mentors," emphasized Riam Kanso. "When you assign a technology coach who knows about the technology they are building, it is much more likely to get them on a technology road map."

Training and Educational Formats

Educational programming is at the heart of the activation stages that accompany the startup for a piece of its journey, especially accelerators (refer to Figure 12.2). Sessions such as seminars, workshops, lectures, or inspirational talks address two kinds of gaps:

- Knowledge gaps (direct skill training, information)
- Mindset gaps (through interactions and learn-by-doing)

They are cost-efficient means of one-to-many knowledge delivery or skill development, and an opportunity for fostering peer interactions.

However, the advantages of educational programming are also its limitation, because the main challenge is to achieve relevance across the entire class. Since each startup is different, operators struggle in selecting content that is equally engaging to all participants. Relevance can be improved in a number of ways:

- **Pre-courses.** Preparation classes for less experienced founders make the cohort more homogeneous toward the upper level. The best time to teach startups how to pitch is before you receive their applications. Pre-courses can be prerecorded and delivered online. For example, Antler Launch Academy is a free five-week online course full of preparatory tips for applying to Antler.
- **Opt-in training.** Make educational sessions nonmandatory, letting entrepreneurs choose (Challenge #4 in Chapter 12).
- **Customized training.** Topics and speakers are identified after assessing the knowledge gaps for each startup once the cohort is selected (again, Chapter 12).

- **Case-centered workshops.** A short lecture followed by guided application to participants' cases—essentially, a mix of teaching and mentorship.

Impact of Training

A massive randomized experiment conducted on a sample of 346 innovative SMEs, in which half were given investment readiness training and half not, revealed that educational formats positively affect the ability of second-tier startups to raise private funding, at least in the short term.[5] However, first-tier or third-tier startups seemed less affected or unaffected. The findings showed a significant impact in the likelihood of raising funds just for smaller firms (one to three founders or employees) with lower investment readiness scores before the program, and for up to six months after the program. Larger firms (likely at a later stage of development) were still affected by the training, but not to a statistically significant level. After two years, there was little difference between those who received the training and those who didn't.

In summary, education helps the ignorant more than the geniuses, and so it is best leveraged when directed to first-time entrepreneurs, such as techies, students, or researchers. The study reinforces the intuition that experienced entrepreneurs or salesmen already possess several of those skills, and their time in the program is better spent on other activities than just another pitch or business model training. However, some veteran founders anecdotally expressed appreciation for one or two days of intensive workshops in which they can zone out of their daily commitments and question their assumptions when guided by an expert. Quality of training might have a higher impact than what the study could grasp.

In conclusion, you may want to force participation only to top priority workshops, leaving the others as opt-in or custom.

Peer Community

You can activate peer community benefits when your program is cohort-based, is an event (e.g., hackathon), or has alumni activities. Peers can be an important source of information, knowledge, problem solving, and contacts, sometimes also providing opportunities for mergers, joint ventures, or cross-startup hiring. Peers can help with:

- Knowledge gaps (cross-learning)
- Mindset gaps (sharing)
- Networks gaps (introductions, sharing customers or suppliers)
- Resources gaps (talent from other startups)

Peer-to-peer learning brings advantages mainly in programs with interaction-related objectives such as mindset shift of corporate employees, education of entrepreneurial students and researchers, new venture development, or startup growth.

Highly successful programs such as Techstars Startup Weekend or Y Combinator make the peer or alumni community a central piece of the value proposition. Our research suggests that peers are often a surprising and sometimes unexpected cornucopia for founders. In our interviews of 63 startups of a government accelerator,[6] peer-to-peer learning was never indicated as a reason to apply. However, 27 percent of interviewees spontaneously mentioned it in an open question about an ex post evaluation of the most impactful program features. Anecdotal evidence from other accelerators (including YC and Techstars) suggests this is a widespread sentiment. To reinforce the importance of peers and fellows, one founder said that "just putting us together in the same room for some months would have made a great program without even bothering about training and all the rest. We bonded then, and we still help each other so much."

Forced Versus Serendipitous Interactions

From a design perspective, one major decision is between forcing interactions or leaving them up to fate (Table 15.3).

Forced interactions are notably employed in programs such as Antler or Entrepreneur First having the goal to create new founding teams from strangers. "We run 48-hour bootcamps in which temporary, artificial teams come together to solve a real challenge and deliver something concrete, for example: ideate a solution or product to reduce food waste and pitch for investment," explained Dimitri Maroulis of Antler. "We rotate the teams so that everyone is exposed to different potential cofounders, and repeat a few times in the first weeks." Forced interactions of widespread use are:

- **Public progress updates.** Some programs require founders to update others in stand-up meetings or keep track of target metrics on public boards.
- **Open demos and pitches.** Presentations to mentors and investors can be public since the first moment, to encourage exchanges, peer pressure, and cross-learning.
- **Bootcamps or internal hackathons.** Typically, on occasional challenges or toy projects and with artificial teams, as exemplified above.

Serendipitous interactions, instead, use less structured and tactical means: anything from a private social media channel for the cohort, to a colorful cafeteria with a hired chef that smells of innovation theater. The program just plants the seeds of interaction, leaving the initiative to participants. The idea is to give founders an opportunity to network, but to leave them in control of their time. Think of the almost mythological Tuesday-night founder dinners at YC Combinator putting together an invited talk and a meal, back in 2005 cooked by YC founder Paul Graham in person.[7]

TABLE 15.3 Comparison between enforcement and free initiative about peer interactions

Forced Interaction	Serendipitous Interaction
Guaranteed participation. Founders are obligated to participate in activities with their peers, such as team building, dinners, or challenges. Guarantees participation and interaction.	**Random participation.** Founders are free to interact in spare time, coffee breaks, networking events, without any scheduled activity. Random and serendipitous, no guarantee.
Moderated and synchronous. Done with scheduled events and synchronous, moderated activities.	**Self-organized and asynchronous.** Done with social media, coworking space, cafeteria, dinners, or other mostly nonmoderated meeting occasions.
Extra cost. Needed for new team formation, requires content preparation and moderation.	**Almost for free.** Left as a plus. Low-cost for the program team.

Disclosure Level

Research suggests that simply creating a social network among participants is not automatically conducive to more learning. Fostering a culture of transparency and cross-help is a decisive factor.[8]

Startup programs often state from the start what level of transparency they require, together with the level of protection granted to participants. Although only few formally adopt an NDA (nondisclosure agreement), many of those that foster peer transparency also recommend secrecy toward the outside world, thus increasing a sense of camaraderie and trust while setting the stage for transparent sharing.

Transparency can be achieved by a number of means:

- **Program culture.** The program team can set the example by sharing internal information or sitting with startups in the same office, for instance.
- **Location or schedule.** An open coworking space or clear and regular meetings help founders access others or set aside time for peer interactions.
- **Public pitches and updates** as described above.

Information secrecy, on the other hand, might be more appropriate in environments where patents or secrets more than customers and product-market fit are essential to a startup's competitive advantage (e.g., biotechnology or pharmaceuticals). However, it may also indirectly limit the amount of cross-help and cross-learning in the peer community.

Alumni Network

> *In every program that I run I've seen an opportunity to create a joint venture of two or more startups, particularly when we run a program in a specific category or an industry.*
>
> —Bill Barber, Innovation Ecosystems Architect

Alumni networks can be a powerful plus of any program with strong peer interactions, from accelerators to hackathons. Alumni create meetups, groups, alliances, and occasionally also joint ventures. In the absence of relevant research, our direct experience testifies how long-lasting the sense of camaraderie and the relationships created in cohorts through informal interaction can be. TechPeaks alumni still spontaneously meet eight years after the program.

Alumni engagement in the follow-on stage can be encouraged through:

- **Reunions.** Formally organized alumni reunions offer opportunities to catch up and mingle with mentors, investors, or current participants.
- **Online platforms.** Social media channels or forums enable the exchange of advice and contacts (e.g., YC's Bookface platform).
- **Job boards.** Aggregated job boards for portfolio companies are frequent in accelerators or incubators.
- **On-demand introductions.** Post-graduation brokering services can create custom connections for alumni to investors, customers, or prospective hires.
- **Collaborations or joint ventures.** Although it is uncommon for two startups to move toward a formal merger, collaborations on individual customers or projects are frequent. For instance, Bill Barber reported of three alumni startups from two different cohorts joining forces to create a unified farmer efficiency system, each contributing a feature for the final project.
- **Active role in the program.** You can involve alumni as mentors or selectors in later editions of a program; as beta testers for current participants' products; or as investors in demo days or closed-door pitch events.

Brokerage and Introductions

Brokerage and networking are at the core of most startup programs, and one of the main reasons startups participate. Brokerage services include ad hoc introductions and networking events such as demo days, industry events, or business speed dating. A program can lead to connections in days or hours that startups would otherwise take months to obtain. Brokerage specifically addresses:

- Network gaps (expand a founder's personal network)
- Resource gaps (indirectly, when introduced to new investors or new talent)

Introductions can be to investors, supply chain partners, distributors, customers, research and development partners, potential hires (e.g., graduates or researchers), and so on. Investors are the specialty of equity-based accelerators, since their business model postulates that startups raise follow-up investment rounds. Access to customer or supplier networks is a prerogative of companies that institutional financial investors cannot provide to the same extent. Governments or universities can leverage their institutional position to create a communication hub between startups and local businesses—incredibly impactful in ecosystem programs.

Sebastián Díaz Mesa, former CEO of Start-Up Chile, explained, "To anchor the foreign startups into the Chilean economy, in 2015 the program turned toward the over 200 international corporations headquartered in Santiago. Many, as it turned out, were eager to collaborate with our startups."

Networking Events

Brokerage events can be a climax in a startup program, independently from when they are held—for graduation or before. The possible formats include a pitch session in which startups present to attendees, a reverse pitch in which attendees present to startups, one-on-one business speed dating, or startup fairs (Table 15.4).

TABLE 15.4 Frequently used events for brokerage and networking mix

Event type	Description	Example
Pitch session	Classic setting in which startups pitch to investors or corporate partners in a timed window; Q&A and an informal mix follows.	Volition pitch nights connect startups with investors.
Reverse pitch	A reverse pitch is an event where organizations pitch entrepreneurs on a business plan. The organization attempts to sell the startup on a collaborative path forward.	In [RE]verse the City of Austin, Texas, and partners pitch their waste materials for reuse to social startups.
Business speed dating	Fast one-on-one sessions of 3 to 20 minutes. Can be all-against-all, moderated matching, or in office-hours style. Can be done in conjunction with the previous two formats.	Free Electrons uses this format during the opening stage, to match startups and partners for a pilot.
Startup fairs	Startups have a booth for business and demo; investors and corporate managers visit in search of opportunities (sometimes called "a zoo for suites").	TIM WCAP switched from demo day to startup fair when it turned from accelerator to open innovation program.

Demo Day

Demo day is the king of brokerage services, an event in which founders pitch their businesses to large audiences of potential investors. For YC-style accelerators, the investor demo day has even earned its place in some formal definitions as one of four distinctive features of this model.[9]

Even hackathons have their version of demo day: it is compressed into a one- or two-hour pitch session formally closing the event, when a committee assigns the prizes. In startup challenges, a similar format of *pitch-and-jury* might be used to select winners. The "demo day" sometimes lasts two or three days to give space for a more extended analysis or one-to-one meetings after the plenary pitch session.

Demo days have been often criticized for not being the innovation panacea they were supposed to be. But there is also an unconventional story behind demo days and pitch-and-jury sessions—their use going beyond just presenting the startups to investors. First, they have a *focusing function*, to artificially create a tension toward delivery. Kat Mañalac, head of outreach at YC, reportedly said, "We have experimented with a bunch of other programs at YC and found that if there is no demo day, there is a lack of focus."[10]

Second, they create hype and stories for the press. It is not by mistake that journalists are the only category beyond investors who can access the closed-door, invite-only YC demo day.[11]

Finally, demo days are a way to create artificial scarcity and dialog between startups and investors, corporate or government managers. Starting from 2017, TIM WCAP transformed the classic investor demo day into an internal event, entirely dedicated to creating connections between the startups and execution business units.

Matchmaking and Coordination Activities

Program objectives such as solution sourcing or ecosystem adoption usually require that startups coordinate and agree on an action road map with client units or ecosystem actors (e.g., business associations, local institutions, or universities). For instance, a startup and its client unit must negotiate the details of a pilot or a startup, and a university must agree on technology transfer and licenses. Only through specific agreements can a startup move forward in integrating its product with the corporation, or leverage the local ecosystem, respectively.

Coordination or matchmaking are often pursued by a mix of planned meetings and enforced advancement under the supervision of the program team, for instance with:

- **Events and demos** (Table 15.4).
- **One-on-one sessions.** One-off at the beginning or repeated throughout the activation stage.
- **Continuous reporting.** Boards or online project monitoring tools that display progress.

The program team often acts as facilitator or enforcer of the relationship. It may be present at meetings, check deadlines and quality of deliverables, or provide implementation support to one or both sides.

Funding

Capital fuels experimentation and growth—its usefulness to startups can never be overstated. From a design perspective, more than the sheer quantity of money, it's the funding structure that counts: in what form funds are delivered (e.g., debt, equity) and when—at the start, in a substage, at graduation, and so forth.

Funds Delivery

The alternative forms of funds delivery include (Table 15.5): cash or wire transfer; a budget on which startups have rights of spending decisions; reimbursement after presenting supplier invoices; a stipend for participants; vouchers for expenses from a preset list of suppliers.

Investor-driven programs favor forms such as cash or stipend that allow more spending flexibility—key in explorative search of new business models. Entrepreneur First or Antler, for instance, use both: a salary in the first phase, before teams are formed, and a cash-for-equity deal after the mid-program investment committee.

However, those same forms may be difficult to implement in government or corporate programs because of concerns about the possible fraudulent use of taxpayer or shareholder money. While that is understandable, you must pay attention not to overload a startup with red tape and create distractions. "We had to hire one person just dedicated to abiding by the accounting and reporting rules of the funding," an entrepreneur explained during our research.[12]

Staging

Staged financing is the practice of investing or distributing funds to startups in tranches rather than all together in one round. Venture funds invest in stages in subsequent rounds, called seed, Series A, B, and so on, with a growing amount invested in each step. This practice has been scientifically proven to be efficient,[13] not just an intuition of Silicon Valley investors.

Several startup programs use this practice as well. The cited Entrepreneur First invests around £2,000 monthly in stipend per participant in the "Form" phase, and grows that to £80,000

TABLE 15.5 Frequently used methods of funds delivery

Form of delivery	Pros	Cons
Cash (funds are transferred to the startup's account)	Most attractive for startups because of flexibility and adaptability to changing needs during exploration.	Organization has no control on spending. Fraudulent individuals could cash in and leave the program: such risk is often unacceptable for government programs.
Budget (funds stay with financier, but startup has right of spending)	Organization exerts a strong control over spending, can block fraudulent spending, can monitor expenses in real time, easy accounting.	Startups must pass through corporate procedures to spend. Spending constraints and bureaucracy may be cumbersome. Requires overhead for the organization to preapprove the expenses.
Reimbursement (startup spends first and presents the invoices or employee payrolls)	Organization has continuous monitoring on spending and can block fraudulent spending.	Startups need operative capital to cope with the expense-reimbursement delay. Spending constraints and bureaucracy may be cumbersome. Requires overhead for the organization to check and approve reimbursements.
Invoice for services (startup bills an invoice to the financier)	Startup can claim the organization as a customer. Freedom of spending. Easily accounted by both startup and organization.	Taxes involved. Procurement rules may apply, if not overwritten by a specific startup procurement policy. Payment terms may not be startup friendly.
Stipend (founders or startup employees receive personal income)	Freedom of spending. Can be used before formal incorporation.	Taxes involved. Recruitment rules and labor law involved. Does not provide any funding for new hires.
Voucher (can be spent only according to certain rules or with preset suppliers)	Organization exerts a partial preemptive control over spending when choosing the preset list of allowed suppliers/vendors, easy accounting.	The suppliers/vendors included in the voucher may not match the startups' needs. Only a subset of needs may be served.

of financing for those startups who enter the "Launch" phase. Considering two founders per startup, that's a 10x increase. Even YC-style accelerators, traditionally place their bets at the beginning of the activation stage, are more and more often raising follow-on funds to continue investing in the later stages.[14]

If copying the staged investment model of venture funds may look normal for investor-driven programs, corporate programs make no exception. TIM WCAP used to deliver the funds in two installments, one of 40 percent at the beginning of the accelerator, and the remaining 60 percent after graduation if the startup had delivered on the mutually agreed milestones. The rationale was to give founders enough funds to sustain themselves during the program and top up on winning horses after the business units had picked their champions for further collaboration.

Activities That Foster Ecosystem Effects

> *Our corporate partners see the content program as a tool to develop their own workforce, to the point that corporate staff are commanded to attend our training sessions and talks once a week.*
>
> —Andrea Landini of Gellify

Startup programs are a potential source of fertilization for the surrounding environment, both for the organizational and entrepreneurial ecosystems (Chapter 5). Content created for the program (e.g., inspirational speakers or entrepreneurial training) can be reused to generate spillovers in culture, mindset shaping, entrepreneurial skill set, brand positioning, press, relational capital, and reputational capital for the program and its organizational sponsors.

Relational capital building passes through creating networking opportunities between startups and the intended targets (e.g., corporate managers, local politicians, or scientific researchers), and it's the crucial step to enable ecosystem effects. The startups can show agile management, customer discovery, or cutting-edge technology to the most sclerotic corporate teams or researchers. They can help overcome skepticism or correct misinformation about innovative technology or new trends. Or, simply, startups could provide juice for the press. Four strategies are in use today:

1. **Enlarged audience.** You can open events, seminars, workshops, video content, or inspirational talks (all of which would in any case be scheduled for participants) to the public or to a selected audience, e.g., corporate

managers. These activities have a relative scalability in audience numbers, so it is convenient to make them more inclusive. Example: Techstars Startup Weekend's Sunday night pitches often become a pivotal meetup for the local startup community.

2. **Mixed teams.** You can invite the intended targets of ecosystem effects to temporarily join the entrepreneurs for a task, challenge, toy project, or codevelopment project. Example: Stora Enso Accelerator.
3. **Role models.** The founders are tasked as speakers, event organizers, or seminar lecturers at local ecosystem hubs. Example: return-value activities in Start-Up Chile for students, universities, or local businesses.
4. **Mixed panels.** The intended targets are invited on discussion panels with mentors or entrepreneurs, or on juries for startup pitches. Example: again, Techstars Startup Weekend pitch nights.

KEY TAKEAWAYS

- **Mentor management is a crucial task.** Mentors are generally volunteers—think of them as another kind of customer for whom you need to craft a captivating user experience. Mentor management and matching require seniority and credibility. Even a pull system, whereby mentors get picked by startups, needs refereeing—a task that can be done by the program team or delegated to a paid "coach" who accompanies the same startup throughout the entire program. Research suggests that concentrating mentor sessions at the beginning accelerates learning and avoids premature satisficing.
- **Training serves the runners-up.** Educational formats are essential to fill knowledge gaps, but it's challenging to keep the content relevant for an entire batch of startups. Training seems to have only short-term effects and to impact the runners-up more than the champions. In this respect, force participation only to top priority workshops, leaving the others as opt in or custom.

- **Peer collaboration must be proactive.** Highly successful cohort-based programs pride themselves on their peer and alumni community and follow-on interactions. Proactively fostering a culture of transparency and cross-help turns out to be a decisive factor in creating value from peers—simply sitting in the same office seems insufficient.
- **Access to networks is a top reason for participation.** Brokerage and networking are at the core of most startup programs, and one of the main reasons why startups participate. Although often criticized for not being the innovation panacea they are held to be, demo days still have good reasons to exist. They exercise a focusing function (imposing tension in the program), create artificial scarcity for busy partners such as senior leaders or investors, and provide hype and marketing for the program.
- **Use staged funding.** The way in which capital funds are delivered (e.g., debt, equity) and when—at the start, in a substage, or at graduation—matters at least as much as the sheer quantity of money. Avoid overloading a startup with red tape and distractions. Staged financing, the practice of investing or distributing funds to startups in tranches, has been scientifically proven to be efficient.
- **Plan activities for ecosystem effects.** To artificially force ecosystem effects, you can: open the program's events to a local audience (for instance, when you invite an inspirational speaker); create temporary mixed teams to solve specific challenges or toy problems; ask participants to speak at universities or other local ecosystem hubs; or invite senior leaders or politicians to public panels with startups.

PART THREE

COMPLETING THE PUZZLE

16

SYSTEMS OF PROGRAMS

The Startup Community Way[1] by Brad Feld and Ian Hathaway shows how startup communities are complex, adaptable systems. A system is any group of interacting, interrelated, or interdependent components that form a unified whole. Any stimulus on a complex, adaptable system produces unpredictable effects because its parts move and react to the stimulus in ways that are beyond our current modeling ability.

The book *The Rainforest*[2] by Victor W. Huang and Greg Horowitt has a similar thesis: entrepreneurial ecosystems are highly interconnected and complex systems, where the equilibrium between different actors and actions can be hard to describe and control. Furthermore, a large organization is a complex system itself. Its internal stability is based on relationships and politics between hundreds or thousands of human beings, each one with their own agendas, projects, desires, needs, and fears.

Startup programs lie at the intersection of these complex systems—the startup community on the external side, and a large organization on the internal side. As we argued in Chapter 2, startup programs are not just the intersection but the purposive connectors of those complex systems, by design and mission. Any kind of stimulus from the entrepreneurial or organizational ecosystem will influence the program, and likewise any action the program takes, for good or ill, will produce a stimulus on one or both of those systems. The effects of a startup program originate from injecting new opportunities, skill sets, and funding into an ecosystem during the program activities. Every component of the offering, such as funding, free credits, and mentors, will create unpredictable changes, not only for the startups applying and those in the program, but also for other programs, corporate managers, politicians, and organizations. Later, every graduated startup will contribute to the external ecosystem with new jobs, inventions, and connections. At the very least, each graduate will become an ambassador or a detractor for future editions, altering the program's reputation and therefore the sourcing of new startups. As we have argued, such ecosystem effects are inevitable—and that's simply because a startup program's existential mission is precisely to create those interactions, changes, and opportunities. It is exactly these interdependencies that make startup program design so crucial.

In this chapter we will look one step further, to an additional complication to this complexity: there is rarely just one startup program. Startup programs are very often surrounded by other startup programs—either internally or externally, or more often in both ecosystems. Startup programs inside the same organization are obviously interconnected—they tap the same resources and support the same business. But startup programs run by different organizations in the same entrepreneurial ecosystem are also interconnected because they all serve the same startup community. Such interdependencies between startup programs are as inevitable as the ecosystem effects we discussed before.

Multiple interconnected startup programs create what we call a *system of programs*, an ensemble of initiatives that provide opportunities not just for individual startup–organization partners, but also across the system as a whole. Programs in the same system can compete or cooperate, like any other business. For instance, they can subtract startups from one another or, on the flip side, amicably redirect startups to a program that is a better fit. Two programs that work with startups of different maturities can cooperate by sending the best graduates of the earlier-stage program to the later-stage program, and so on.

In some situations, planning a system of programs may make more sense than designing an individual startup program—this is more applicable perhaps inside an organization, where senior leadership can act as strategists, but it is sometimes also applicable when policymakers intervene to foster the growth of a system of programs within a region or across different organizations. And as with single startup programs, rigorous, intentional design is also key for systems of programs. Good design, in the case of systems of programs, would correspond to abundant and well-defined synergies between programs and a virtuous, constructive competition. On the other hand, bad design would be, for instance, when planning ignored one of the macro-areas of fertilization, exploration, and exploitation (see Chapter 9), or when too many competing programs deplete the reservoir (see Chapter 10).

Discussing the design of a system of programs would likely require an entire new book, so we will not attempt to be exhaustive in just one chapter. However, this book would not be complete without at least an introduction to this topic. The first part of this chapter will look at systems of programs built inside the same organization, while the second part will briefly discuss systems of programs across different organizations in the same entrepreneurial ecosystem.

The System Inside the Organization

This chapter focuses on how programs work with and feed off each other. A system of programs within the same organization is essentially a set of solutions to a set of different or overlapping objectives (Circle 2). In other words, your "portfolio of programs" builds over time around a "portfolio of problems" that startups "get hired" to solve for your organization. The most common scenarios for internal systems are:

1. All of your startup programs are under one roof. They grow organically, and it is easy to rearrange them yearly (*planned portfolio*). Anyone at your organization who wants to engage with startups goes through your unit and is directed to one of your portfolio programs.
2. Startup programs are under multiple roofs but all on the same campus (GV and Google for Startups, for example).

These situations are a bit more complex (*emergent portfolio*). Various actors within the same organization talk to startups, but these groups don't always talk to each other. The "startup guys" in a large organization sometimes are so busy searching and supporting startups that they do not talk with the rest. They create their own paradise island and live there, solving the startups' problems, but maybe losing contact with the organization's current problems. Sometimes the same startup is approached by competing at worst, ignorant at best internal functions. Worse still, other times not only do external startups get an inconsistent message from the organization, but the programs compete for internal resources like funding, or internal allies or clients, such as business units or problem owners.

3. You are starting "Program One" with the intent of creating a portfolio of programs.

A practical example of emergent portfolio is what happened historically with corporate venture capital. Originally CVC was the only way to engage with startups. Then, primarily because organizations were using CVC for multiple "jobs," from identifying a promising opportunity to investing in backup technology,[3] the other startup program templates that were living inside of CVC sprang out. Programs became more specialized at one job, such as challenges for sourcing specific solutions, accelerators for investing in very early-stage startups, hackathons for community engagement.

Now that there are so many different models, you have the possibility to either start mega and reduce gradually by spinning out lesser programs and optimizing them, or starting small and building up one edition after the other.

You should think about whether your organization will be more tolerant of spinning out programs from one initial mega-program if each solves a specific problem, or it would prefer to focus programs on subproblems at first and then merge them if needed. It is a question of strategy and budget.

Either way, you will most likely end up having a system of interconnected programs, immersed in the general entrepreneurial and innovation ecosystem surrounding them.

The KJ Matrix

To help sort out internal program portfolio strategy we use what we call the KJ Matrix, a map showing the organization's objectives discussed in Chapter 2 against the control proximity the organization exerts (tight or loose) and whether it acts internally or externally (Table 16.1). We named it "KJ" after Kelly Johnson, the founder of the legendary Skunk Works,[4] Lockheed Martin's Advanced Development Programs—a unit with a high degree of autonomy and unhampered by bureaucracy tasked with working on advanced or secret projects—essentially, an archetype of corporate exploration and, potentially, entrepreneurship.

Internal and external can be both literal and figurative. Skunk Works was external in two senses: it worked with external contractors to build the plane (as opposed to in-house), and it sat in a tent outside the office to add autonomy.

The KJ Matrix is a diagnostic tool plotting innovation actions against various internal and external actors. The organization's objectives (or problems) are in the left column. Along with the other columns, there are the four possible combinations of control and distance: internal and tight, internal and loose, external and tight, external and loose. Startup programs are in the two rightmost columns (external). Examples of internal solutions are R&D (internal and tight) and intrapreneurship programs (internal and loose).

The KJ Matrix addresses an internal organizational issue. It visualizes the actions undertaken for each objective, and highlights overlaps, redundancies, and shortcomings. This analysis can help detect any blind spots and decide what program should cover each gap.

Before starting a new program, you should identify the problem or objective it is trying to solve (Circle 2). Once you identify the problem, stay on the same row of the KJ Matrix and see what else is happening, internally or not, around that problem. Maybe the R&D department is already working on an internal solution, or maybe a spin-off is getting ready to take off. The KJ Matrix suggests what other activities might be underway and points to where to look for them. As you will see, in many cases, it shows more than one startup program model in the same cell. That is natural, because the model depends not just on the objective (i.e., the Circle 2 indicated on the row), but also on what you can do or offer, and the available startups (Circles 1 and 3).

TABLE 16.1 An example of KJ Matrix

Organizational Objectives / Solution	Internal and Tight	Internal and Loose	External and Tight	External and Loose
Financial investing	Buy back your own stocks	Invest on market (stocks, etc.)	Financial CVC&A	Financial CVC&A
Strategic investing	Internal R&D on strategic projects	Invest in internal startups Leverage unutilized technology	Strategic CVC&A	Strategic CVC&A
Innovation procurement	Internal R&D	Innovation Lab (e.g., Skunkworks) Internal venture building Leverage unutilized technology	External venture building M&A	Matchmaking programs + commercial partnerships Challenge
Innovation ecosystem building	[Implicitly external]	[Implicitly external]	Technology platform (e.g., App Store)	Business platform (e.g., partnering marketplace)
Startup ecosystem building	[Implicitly external]	[Implicitly external]	Incubator	Competition Hackathon Accelerator Business platform (e.g., fair: SXSW, Techcrunch Disrupt, Web Summit)
Mindset shift and organizational culture	HR programs Innovation training / workshops	Innovation Lab (e.g., Skunk Works) Intrapreneurship programs	Reciprocal education (mixed teams; e.g., Google.org Fellows, Stora Enso Accelerator)	Accelerator (e.g., Techstars) Hackathon

(continued)

TABLE 16.1 An example of KJ Matrix (continued)

Organizational Objectives / Solution	Internal and Tight	Internal and Loose	External and Tight	External and Loose
Mission-driven education and venture creation	[Implicitly external]	[Implicitly external]	Incubator	Competition, Challenge, Hackathon, Accelerator, Student program
Ideation	Internal ideation platforms Design sprints (Oregon energy trust?)	Innovation Lab (e.g., Skunk Works) Intrapreneurship programs	Open innovation platform	Hackathon Challenge Student program (e.g., Hacking for Defense) Open innovation platform
Validation	Design sprints	Innovation Lab (e.g., Skunkworks) Intrapreneurship programs	Codevelopment program Venture client	Accelerator Challenge
Trend discovery and market intelligence	Internal market research Internal technology scouting	Innovation outposts	Hire BDO, McKinsey, etc.	Accelerator cohort (e.g., Techstars)
Talent hiring	Job fairs, advertise on linked	Headhunters (hired)	M&A (acqui-hiring)	Hackathon (for HR selection) Open source community
R&D capital	Internal R&D budget	Public funding on internal R&D projects	Venture client (if with venture backed startups with own funding)	Public funding with research consortia
Press and media coverage	Internal PR & MarCom	PR agencies (hired)	Press releases on startup programs or startup success stories	Independent press (e.g., press releases from supported startups)
Reputation and brand	Internal PR & MarCom	PR agencies (hired) Successful innovations from internal startups	Own partner network (with investors, other programs)	Hired innovation firms' network

Consider building or updating your own organization's KJ Matrix before starting any new program. After this analysis, ask if you still want to solve the problem with startups. If yes, then follow the tips of Part Two, finding synergies with whatever other initiative is out there.

The Planned Portfolio

The planned portfolio approach answers the question of which startups to engage with and for what purpose, starting from a blank page. It is rarely seen in the real world because it is unlikely that you can plan the KJ Matrix top-down once and for all, without iterations and adjustments. The process is usually chaotic at first, while you figure out what parts of your organization need startups the most and what units are willing to accept the hardship of working with them. However, the planned approach is potentially valuable for brainstorming, like a Renaissance "ideal city" utopia.

One by one, you should engage with internal allies, business units, and corporate units until you find the first enthusiasts who know they have a problem and actively want it solved by startups. After that, following an innovation diffusion curve,[5] you can identify the early adopters and later the majority of internal adopters. Each time, you add a startup program solving the units' problems or supporting their objectives.

Solution sourcing is a straightforward example, but there are other cases where internal stakeholders may have a culture problem or ecosystem problem and they want to work with you, external vendors, or startups. In time, you will build a "portfolio of problems" and an associated "portfolio of programs" organically under the same roof as more and more issues are added. This type of planned portfolio approach often wins support from the C-suite and is awarded a multiyear budget.

Entropy Happens: The Emergent Portfolio

Unlike the planned portfolio but more common so far in the real world is the emergent portfolio. Startup programs can represent "islands of freedom" within an organization, sometimes entire archipelagos of freedom, but they also tend to pop up in parallel, and when multiple programs within the same organization start to compete for funding or branding, things can get complicated.

Sometimes these programs spend too much time figuring out their role inside the organization, scouting allies, and looking for problem owners willing to admit they need startups, and too little time catering to startups in the reservoir. Other times, instead, they spend too little time internally and cannot integrate with the rest of the organization.

This chaotic situation of multiple programs popping up in different parts of the same organization is natural, like entropy. Adam's eighth-grade science teacher had a great way of teaching about the second law of thermodynamics, which says that entropy always increases with time. He explained that your bedroom never gets automatically cleaner over time, but it does seem to get automatically messy. The same is true with startup programs, and even organizations well versed in startup engagement practices face this issue:

- Google has Google for Startups and Google Ventures (now called GV, and independent). They are two different initiatives that emerged in a decentralized (organic) way as a result of different instantiations of the Startup Program Strategy Canvas.
- To make it even more confusing Google for Startups contains a "portfolio" of six or seven startup programs, and so we could say that Google has a "system of systems" of programs.
- Salesforce has four or five different fund types, and each of those types has subsidiary funds.
- Allianz experienced an evolution of sequential programs, parallel programs, and then merging all the programs into one[6] (not to be confused with keeping separate programs under the same consolidated business unit).

Several other corporations and government organizations in our research have multiple programs. If such disorder should happen, it is possible to audit startup programs and merge them—just like you might do an org-chart change every few years. For example, you can take programs that pursue the same Circle 2 objective and merge them. Or you can uniformize your internal signaling and create a single point-of-contact for internal business units willing to engage with startups.

Having a balanced portfolio approach is essential with startup programs. You may start with internal early adopters and champions who get it, but eventually, you have to balance the problems and the business units from the KJ matrix. This balance generally comes from top management or a general approach to innovation governance and is outside of each program team's control zone.

Sometimes, however, programs emerge to solve problems that the company still wants solved, but an earlier program has failed to make much headway. This is likely a red flag. Internal competition might be good because it stimulates people to do better, but one should always keep in mind that, in the context of startup programs, it's the startups that are the ones bringing the solution, and programs (whether they are competing or not) are just a framework. In this case the underperforming program should be redesigned, not ambushed.

The System Outside the Organization

Save for underdeveloped ecosystems, almost any entrepreneurial ecosystem hosts mutliple programs: private accelerators, university incubators, community hackathons, corporate programs, and so on. In such ecosystems, entropy can be even stronger than within organizations because in external systems independent and uncoordinated initiatives are the norm. This variety undoubtedly enriches the entrepreneurial ecosystem, so at a macro level it is positive. From the perspective of a single program, however, that means more competition. But it can also mean more synergic opportunities, depending on your strategy.

Competing with External Programs

Suppose you operate in a local ecosystem of 500,000 to 1 million people. It's neither a small town nor a metropolis. Reasonably, not more than 1 percent of those people participate in the local entrepreneurial ecosystem, i.e., 5,000 to 10,000 at maximum, likely many less. There is only space for a certain number of startup events, accelerators, and incubators, and it's not high. More than 5 or 10 hackathons in parallel during the same weekend might struggle to fill the room. And 5 or 10 accelerators would have to scout nationally or at least regionally, or they might exhaust the promising opportunities in the local backlog.

Sometimes, competition is intentional. One incumbent program is underperforming, and an alternative can stimulate more excellence. It happens externally, but also internally. However, when your program competes with others in the same ecosystem, you could deplete the shared geographical reservoir faster. This happens, for instance, when two accelerators in town tap on the same vertical, such as digital health startups (Figure 16.1). For this reason the reservoir's status should be analyzed and monitored. Is there enough "repletion" for two programs? Are local universities, startup community meetups, business angels, and investors producing enough quality deal flow to sustain two accelerators? Design should answer these questions, as market aspects are part of startup program design.

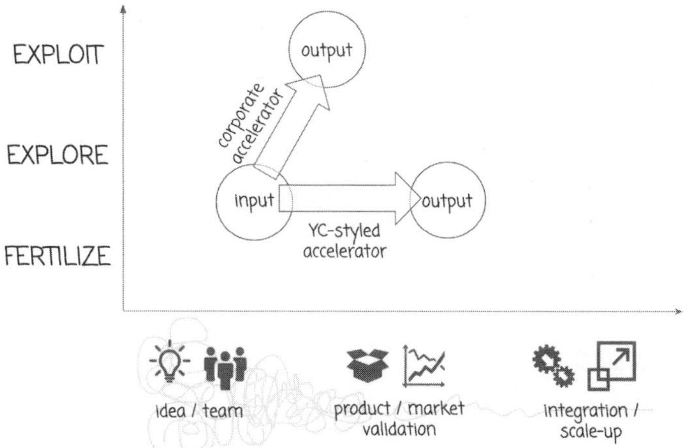

FIGURE 16.1 Programs can be represented as arrows stretching from input to output states of participants. Horizontal axis: the startup journey. Vertical axis: a metaphorical sequence of fertilize, explore, and exploit. Here, two programs serve the same input segment but propose two different directions.

Competition means that your offer should be more effective for your ecosystem, to have a "good enough" deal flow. At the same time, differentiation and specialization become even more influential. Figure 16.1 also shows how two programs, both called "accelerators," actually accelerate in different directions. The YC-style accelerator keeps the startup in exploration mode. In contrast, the corporate accelerator might not move a startup forward as fast (the image exaggerates to make the point), but it can provide a customer.

Finding Synergies with External or Internal Programs

Programs in the same system give their best when they cooperate. Innovation and entrepreneurship are not zero-sum games and working together can potentially make everyone a winner.

To create synergies, you can compose a system with programs that fuel each other—the outputs of earlier programs feed the later programs (Figure 16.2). You can also plug into other innovation initiatives that are not "startup programs," according to our definition, but that are highly synergic with creating similar opportunities, such as intrapreneurship programs, innovation outposts, business schools, or coders meetups.

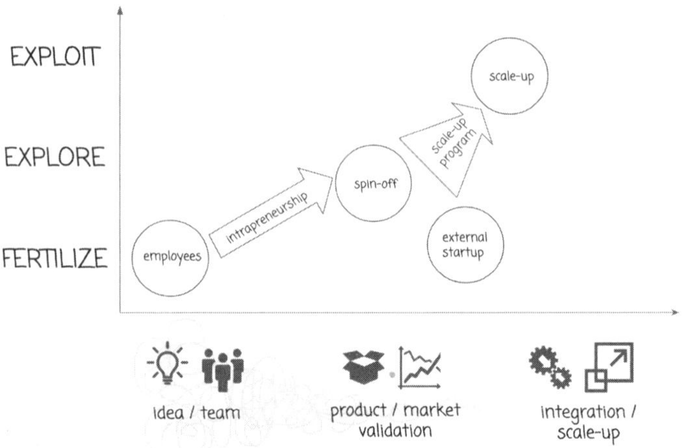

FIGURE 16.2 Two programs are combined in sequence. The first, fully internal, creates teams of entrepreneurial employees (intrapreneurship). The second scales up ventures into the corporation's exploitation space. Input teams can be internal or external.

In an interoperating system, startups can move from program to program following a growth path. Synergies between internal and external programs are frequent. Startups originating from internal innovation activities (e.g., an intrapreneurship program) can later join an external accelerator.

Programs can also redistribute their deal flow, redirecting promising startups to other partner programs that are a better fit (e.g., for maturity level or vertical). You can do vertical redistribution among programs covering different industries or sectors. For instance, two vertical accelerators inside the same ecosystem, one in energy and one in manufacturing, can create a synergy by redirecting startups to each other according to the strategic fit of a startup with each program. Another kind of redistribution happens when using different programs for different maturity levels. For example, TechPeaks partnered as a pre-accelerator with world-class accelerators or incubators (such as Founders Institute among others) to get access to the applicants those accelerators discarded because they were too early-stage for them.

Suppose you are confident enough in your own program and are able to see the big picture. In that case, you can intentionally allow YC to accelerate companies or even select them, and you can let other investors invest in them. When those startups become a match for one of your programs, you enter the game.

How to Differentiate

For independent startup program founders, this should be the first section of this book to read. If you are not designing a program for any organization, but you intend to build a new organization around the program, then start by studying the competitive landscape before deciding how you will position in it.

Analyzing other programs in your ecosystem is also essential for choosing to compete or cooperate. There is no need for a detailed mapping (you want to avoid "analysis paralysis"); startup programs constantly pivot and adjust their strategy in any case. However, a general idea can guide design decisions connected to Circle 3 and the target segment: Is it overserved? Is there a sufficient quantity and quality of startups? What are the sources of new startups, which replenish the deal flow?

After the analysis, you need to decide your value proposition—an exercise that should involve the steps discussed in Chapter 12. Your program could exploit one or more of the following strategies:

- **Underserved input.** An underserved target segment creates a tremendous opportunity for innovation (and positioning). TechPeaks followed this strategy for the first edition, positioning as a program for aspirant entrepreneurs without a team. In 2013 that was a far underserved segment in the global startup scene, and the program acquired immediate visibility.
- **Underserved output.** Thinking in systems helps create a new program that benefits the whole corporate or regional system and helps build alliances with upstream or downstream programs. For instance, if the entrepreneurial ecosystem has many venture funds but they all struggle with deal flow, there is an opportunity for an incubator or accelerator that outputs startups ready to raise a VC round.
- **Underserved vertical.** An underserved industry or technology specialization sets the program apart from the rest of the competitors inside the same ecosystem, because a vertical demarks a reservoir. Take the Ocean Solutions Accelerator: its narrow and application-oriented focus drives applications worldwide.
- **Better-quality support.** Of course, you can beat the competition by providing better support, including wider networks, more experienced mentors, access to better labs, and so on. It is a direct and potentially costly competitive strategy but it also helps keep the ecosystem performing.
- **More incentives.** Adding captivating features to the offer can also be expensive. The most intuitive incentives are to provide more funding or require less equity. It is the equivalent of a price war, where the highest bidder sets the threshold for everybody else, but as a price war, it may be self-destructive. Another incentive can be a certification, a cheap perk for university-driven programs. Falmouth Launchpad run by Falmouth University in England, for example, incentivizes aspirant entrepreneurs to join its venture builder with the opportunity to gain an MSc in Entrepreneurship.

KEY TAKEAWAYS

- **Ecosystem whiplash.** Startup communities are complex, adaptable systems. Startup programs always operate inside an entrepreneurial and an organizational ecosystems; they cannot be expected to be unaffected by the surrounding ecosystems. Any offering, partner, or graduated startup will create feedback loops that you should anticipate rather than being at their mercy.
- **Portfolio of problems, portfolio of programs.** A system of programs internal to the same organization is essentially a set of solutions to a group of different or overlapping objectives. In other words, your "portfolio of programs" builds over time around a "portfolio of problems" that startups "get hired" to solve for your organization. One by one, you should engage with internal allies, business units, and corporate units, until you find the first enthusiasts who know they have a problem and actively want it solved by startups, and then gradually move to the majority of the organization.
- **Synergic and parallel programs.** Programs in the same system give their best when they cooperate. Innovation and entrepreneurship are not zero-sum games, and working together can potentially make everyone a winner. To create synergies, you can compose a system with programs that fuel each other—the outputs of earlier programs feed the later programs. You can also run parallel programs that cope with different innovation paths. Finally, you can plug into other innovation initiatives such as intrapreneurship programs, innovation outposts, business schools, or coders meetups.

OUTSOURCING THE PROGRAM

When you sit with the CEO, everything is all right, and you feel the permission to partner with startups. But when later you walk on the work floor of the business lines, you don't feel surrounded by so many believers.

—Anonymous interviewee

It can be challenging to introduce a startup program in a large organization. The world of startups defies the logic of many corporate and government hierarchies.

You don't need to do everything alone. There are plenty of innovation firms that are eager to help. They maintain proprietary databases and access to deal flow, are adept in design thinking and lean validation methodologies, and have invested in startups or partnered with them. They can accompany you through the whole journey.

You should seriously consider outsourcing a part or all of your startup program. This chapter will investigate what you could delegate to external suppliers, and in which situations you should do it. Also, you should consider using tested models, even though we warned multiple times throughout this book against that choice if it is blind. In summary, this chapter addresses:

1. External providers: when to hire them and for what
2. Applying a model "as is": success cases and failures

When to Hire an External Provider

For large organizations, building a startup collaboration strategy on their own can be challenging. Hundreds of private innovation firms have mastered the art of engaging with startups and offering their services to corporations and governments. They have built a reputation in the startup community through various means.

Some, such as Techstars or Startupbootcamp, began their journeys as startup accelerators and investors and later moved into supporting corporations, governments, or regions around startup collaborations and ecosystem building.

Mass Challenge and other not-for-profit organizations entered the sector as a startup program of a different type, usually a competition or a coworking space. Later, some of these organizations moved to structure an offer more targeted on corporate and government partners, sponsors, or clients.

Many others started from consultancy, directly supporting corporate clients and later developing or acquiring competencies in startups—from the Big Four down to boutique consultancies. A few innovators built on firsthand expertise in corporate innovation and became independent consultants to distribute that knowledge to more organizations. A few more players came directly from the entrepreneurial ranks—former digital entrepreneurs who lived the scene as founders and then turned from product to consultants.

The Startup Program Strategy Canvas can guide the internal situation analysis and understand what kind of service is most needed (Figure 17.1).

Hire for Circle 1: When You Need to Build Capacity

Large organizations have it all: a recognized brand, access to a vast partner network, and maybe an institutional role. Smaller or less visible organizations, such as a farming company in the Midwest or a brewing company in New England, although

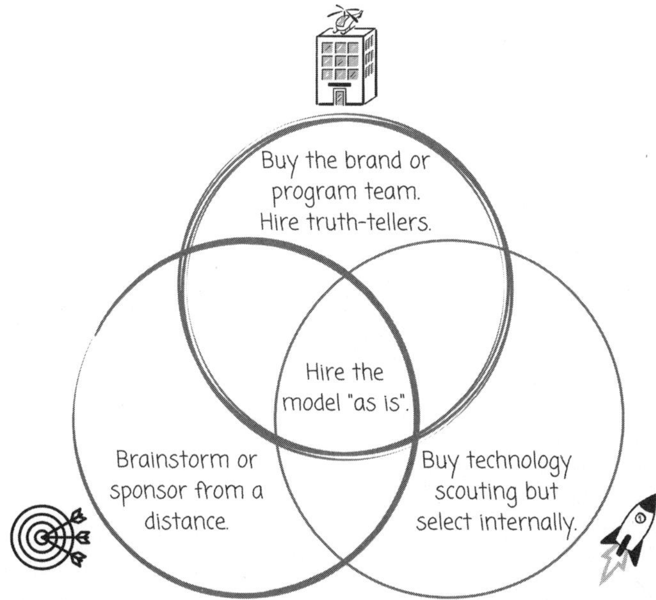

FIGURE 17.1 Different reasons to hire external providers depending on which Circle is problematic.

successful in their own right, might be powerless when mobilizing startups. They are not known for innovations—or maybe they even have a negative reputation about not being innovative, such as for some government agencies.

If one of your internal factors is not ready for startup collaboration, you may want to hire an external provider to provide what is needed. For example, you may need help with branding, the program team, internal culture, or other issues:

Branding. Cobranding with an established player in the startup community can solve a visibility issue. The partner will vet the program with its brand and track record instead of you. It will also mobilize its partner network to get referrals to the most exciting startups for your case. However, be aware that some whales of the global entrepreneurial ecosystem may let you have only a minimal part in the selection process—and sometimes for good reasons, as we will argue shortly.

Program team. When you have an operational problem or a lack of direct experience, you can resort to an external provider to supply a ready-to-go program team. Almost any innovation firm has refined its version of a program—from hackathons to accelerators. If you need help in operations, mentor management, and leadership, go with a firm's own format because it will already have optimized the nuts and bolts and developed processes to cope with outliers or emergencies. Verify if the team has experience with the startups' maturity stage you are targeting:

- For idea-team startups, choose a provider with proven community management skills.
- For late-stage startups, hire someone with an industry network and, possibly, previous experience in your vertical.
- Early-stage startups are somewhere in the middle.

If you aim for solution sourcing or ecosystem building, form a shadow team in your organization to support the external operations and help external providers navigate your organization and your entrepreneurial ecosystem.

Culture and internal buy-in. "Sometimes what a company needs are truth-tellers that run interviews, talk to the board of directors, and understand who is onboard," Lesa Mitchell of Techstars said. External providers can derive authority from neutrality to internal politics and be instrumental in implementing faster change. To this aim, "buy from IBM": choose providers with enough authority to command trust in the executive ranks.

Other issues. If your problems in Circle 1 lie in a lack of readiness in assets or in capturing value, external providers cannot help as much—not on those issues directly, at least. You will need to fertilize internally through seminars, workshops, and gradual programs, building momentum until you can fly independently. External providers can help you create a long-term vision of how your programs will evolve from fertilizing to exploring or exploiting (Chapter 7).

Being ready to capture a program's value cannot be delegated: external innovation firms cannot replace your organization in that. However, management consultants can help articulate the proposition to other internal business units and organize the process.

Hire for Circle 2: When You Have Unclear Objectives

Having clear goals might be more challenging than it appears. The imperative might be working with startups, no matter how—or why. This thrust may come from fear of disruption or an executive's momentary passion for a specific technology, or the coolness of startups. Or just from inexperience or a lot of confusion.

That's OK. The decision to harness startups' opportunities with a portfolio of equity investments or to integrate startups' products can be delayed after testing the water. The only mistake would be to rest on the beach instead of diving deep after the initial one or two runs.

If the long-term objective is still unclear, why not stay at the window for some time and watch the experts play their game? Here you have at least two options: sponsoring or cocreation with a provider:

Sponsor. You can build knowledge with a light-touch sponsorship, gaining a front seat in an existing program. Your organization can prolong a one-off approach to startup collaborations in parallel with this tactic until you decide. The number of organizations that started in this way is uncountable.

The challenge of this approach is how to involve senior leadership and key decision makers. Just sponsoring may not contribute to clarifying their mind on how to proceed—unless they get into that front seat. Do not take a distant position when you sponsor; try to stay as close as possible to the front line.

Cocreation. An external innovation firm can help you clarify your needs. It is actually in their own interest to do it. It is not rare that innovation firms get hired to execute a model that was preselected by the organization, but which later turns out to be the wrong program for the goals in the mind of who selected it. For instance, they can be asked to run a hackathon because "the CEO said so" and then later be blamed for the lack of results, even when they executed the hackathon to perfection—and grow a bad reputation or lose the client. Perhaps, the organization didn't need a hackathon, but an incubator (or a challenge, or any other model), but the provider had no say in it.

Many innovation firms provide more than one model, so if you let them brainstorm your priorities with you at the beginning, they will be able to guide you in choosing the model without preconceptions. The brainstorming usually takes one of two forms, or a combination of both: (a) a set of interviews to major internal stakeholders, to map your needs and opinions about them, and/or (b) a one- or two-day innovation workshop to cocreate the program. Because such clarifications are also in the provider's interest, you might even get some of these services at a discount or for free.

Hire for Circle 3: When You are Weak at Sourcing

One of the main assets of external providers is their sourcing capability and proprietary reservoir. An organization cannot build a partner network in universities, investors, and accelerators overnight. Innovation firms might have access to professional software to source leads from the web, and trained personnel for technology and startup scouting that would cost you time and money to build or hire on your own.

Startup sourcing and scouting can be conveniently outsourced, provided that your organization can, alone or with its suppliers, accomplish the following:

1. **Delineate the target profile.** One of the toughest challenges for your outsourcer will not be finding startups, but rather understanding which startups matter for you. Even when your organization specifies a technology or industry, your engineers can always push back on a brilliant startup because it conflicts with their internal project ("not invented here" syndrome). External providers can easily scout 5,000 to 10,000 potential candidates in a few weeks, and they will shortlist from 50 to 300 for you. It is in your interest that the preselection does not accidentally leave out any possible match, so work with them to define the startup description and problem brief in an actionable way.
2. **Build an internal selection process.** External scouts can supply a shortlist, but it is up to your organization to

identify startups with a strong match. The last stage of a recruitment process can only be internal, whether your goal is solution sourcing, financial investment, or ecosystem building. Your people know so much more of the organizational strategy than any external provider ever could learn, so unless you are just testing the waters (see the previous section), they must sit in the judge's chair. You could always let your provider pick a few wild cards—outliers that you would not consider but that are surprising given your provider's knowledge of market and technology trends.

There might be circumstances when it is more reasonable to stay out of selection and let the experts do the job for you. For example, if the organization's goal is a financial investment and your selectors have little experience of startups as an asset class, let the experts pick for you. It is easy to be swayed by momentary fashions or a charismatic founder with spectacular pitching skills.

"Hiring" a Model "As Is"

One option can also be to outsource the whole program to an innovation firm and its model or to reimplement someone else's model "as is." For instance, Puerto Rico's Parallel18 is a local instantiation of Start-Up Chile's model, with minor modifications. Similarly, many investor-driven accelerators simply execute a copycat of Y Combinator's or Techstars' models.

Earlier in this book, we warned against this practice. The peculiar characteristics and context of each organization too often impose model adaptations. When you "hire" a model, you are assuming that your organization and the startup community you are serving are equivalent to those of the original model. Sometimes this is true, but every time it needs to be questioned.

There are two notable cases for which a copycat can work. The first is for more straightforward programs, such as hackathons or challenges. And the second is when your context is very similar and you make the proper adjustments to cope with the few differences from the original situation.

Take Parallel18 and its replica of Start-Up Chile: both countries, although with their own characteristics, were after global digital talents (same Circle 3) to reposition their country as an operational base on the international map of digital entrepreneurship while also educating the locals (same Circle 2). Whereas Chile offers a base in Latin America and connections with the local extractive industry, Puerto Rico leverages its position, both geographical and political, as a bridge between the United States and Latin America. Still, it mobilized a similar kind of internal commitment from the government that made the original program possible in Chile (similar Circle 1, with adaptations).

Provider as an External Sandbox

External providers have one additional function: they inherently create a sandbox outside the organization to protect startups from distractions while still opening a gateway for your organization into the startup world.

For financial goals, completely external programs bring the advantage of cultivating startups while not hindering their growth with corporate or government chains. The startups' business development and value must be the priority objective for programs with financial goals. Only the startup's growth can create a win for both the startup and its financiers, in this case (Chapter 3). Any interference due to one of the financiers' strategic reasons would hurt everyone else. If financial gain is the primary objective, the startup's focus on creating more value should prevail over one shareholder's particular interests.

Players such as Techstars, Startupbootcamp, or others, for the most part, reproduce the same blueprint independently of who sponsors them. They apply minor adaptations according to industry, geography, and other specific characteristics of the ecosystem in which a new program operates, but the structure stays almost the same.

The reason for this relative inflexibility is to put founders first. Founders create value for all investors, and also for their corporate or government sponsors. Their success is the sponsors' success—that is, if the startup's rapid growth is what creates value for the organizational sponsor.

Chapters 4 and 5 discussed solution sourcing and ecosystem building, two cases in which rapid growth is not a prerequisite for the organizational sponsor's gain. Growth is still positive for both cases. A more developed startup can scale better, invest in R&D, update its product, and conveniently serve a corporation that partnered as a launching customer (or "venture client"). And in ecosystems, the more business a startup does on the platform, the higher the orchestrator's metrics. However, rapid growth is *not* a guaranteed advantage. A solid business means more stable jobs, a more reliable supplier, and a local partner. Instead, rapidly moving toward an exit might mean the supplier is busy making its valuation target, or it might migrate to an international hub far from home, or it might become more expensive to acquire.

For these reasons, external providers could be the only way for your organization to access high-growth startups. That is because, when an established organization runs a startup program internally without an expert provider, the parent's strategy gravitational force of its core business could decelerate a startup instead of providing a shortcut forward (Figure 17.2)—and startups know it.

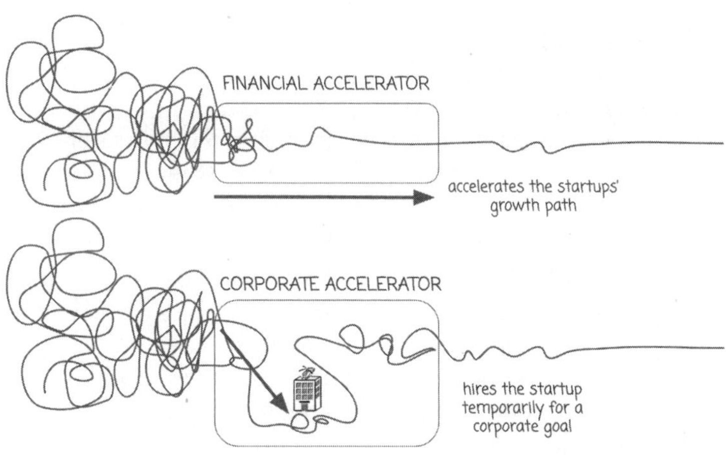

FIGURE 17.2 A corporate accelerator might hire a startup for a different task, potentially decelerating its growth path temporarily.

The consequence is that high-growth startups may stay away, while instead the pipeline gets filled with short-termist BS or PS startups that take the perks and disappear (remember the incentives dry-up problem). The misalignment of objectives and incentives keeps the startup's growth out of focus for these corporate programs and may condemn them to mediocrity before launching their first call.

In this respect, when specialized operators don't alter the program they designed for growth, they are doing a favor rather than an injustice to their client. By keeping the model "as is," they are not just using their expertise to the maximum level: they also create the conditions to engage with high-growth founders who may not respond to the other, decelerating type of value proposition.

KEY TAKEAWAYS

- **Use the Canvas to assess when to hire a provider.** The Startup Program Strategy Canvas can help decide what to outsource to an external provider. For Circle 1 (lack of readiness), consider outsourcing if your brand is underdeveloped in the startup community; if your program team is incomplete or inexperienced; or if you need an external authority to win internal resistance. For Circle 2 (unclear objectives), consider sponsoring other programs and get a sneak peek at results, or buying an innovation workshop to clarify the goals. For Circle 3 (weak at sourcing), you can easily outsource the scouting, but you must assist your provider in delineating the right targets and selecting them.
- **External sandbox.** External providers have one additional function: they inherently create a sandbox outside the organization to protect startups from distractions while still opening a gateway for your organization into the startup world. For financial goals, completely external programs bring the advantage of cultivating startups while not hindering their growth with corporate or government chains.

THE FUTURE OF STARTUP PROGRAMS

Throughout this book, we have discussed the many obstacles along the path of successful startup engagement and support programs. For some organizations, the future will continue to be business as usual—the same old constellation of internal turf wars, "not invented here" syndrome, misalignment of objectives, vanity metrics, irrelevant benchmarks, or unaware or lazy program designers copying and pasting a template blindly out of its context.

But we hope that the future will be different for our readers—a confident step toward a more contextual approach to startup program design based on the elements represented in the three Circles of our Startup Program Strategy Canvas.

How Startup Program Design Can Change the Future

This book brings about a more conscious approach to adapting to your context the startup program templates and models that have proven effective in other contexts.

Part One showed how a difference in one of the external Circles starts a domino effect that affects the Intersection and may even bring a dysfunctionality by breaking the balance with the other Circles.

Part Two laid out the path to rebuild that balance from the ground up, supposing that no one template works in your circumstances and that you have to imagine an entirely new program model.

FIGURE 18.1 Difficulties that startup program design can help solve, mapped on the Startup Program Strategy Canvas.

Armed with a new consciousness and new building blocks, you can address all the critical issues that have affected the choice, planning, and implementation of startup programs so far. The problems startup program design can solve for large organizations can be summarized as follows, directly on the Canvas (Figure 18.1):

- **Circle 1: Organization's uniqueness and readiness.** It is hard to create a compelling case for corporate venturing with senior leaders and middle management at the same time: the former may focus on the longer term, and the latter at daily operations. You need to minimize opposition and counter detractors as much as possible. The first step is assessing the organization's strengths and weaknesses and what it can offer to startups in a given moment, without misrepresentation. Then, you build up more capabilities and momentum step by step, until you can really harvest the power of unique collaborations in future programs.

- **Circle 2: Program objectives.** It can be challenging to pinpoint goals that are understood and shared by all the parties involved in the program, including—if that is the case—internal business units or external partners. The program team may have its own goals and agenda, and the overlap with the general strategy can be real or not, communicated or not. Identify success scenarios and outcome metrics, as well as metrics describing the positive ecosystem feedback loop. Create usable outputs enabling the organization's value capture.
- **Circle 3: Target startups.** Look beyond the stereotypes of the "best startups" (future unicorns) and clarify what "best" signifies in the context at hand. Understand the needs and motivations of the startup community that can contribute to the program's objectives.
- **Intersection: Program.** Focus on crafting a fair exchange of value between organizations and startups, striking a balance of offer and ask. Align both sides' motivations for the duration needed to produce results out of the collaboration: with a fair quid pro quo when a short-term partnership is sufficient; with the right conditions for growth, integration, retention, or commitment when you need long-term collaborations to harvest the results you are pursuing.

Iterations

A rational, waterfall approach to design would be to analyze the three Circles first, derive all the requirements, and then, based on the free design dimensions, identify the parameters for the Intersection that best respect the conditions.

But this is not what happens in most real cases: the specs are not as straightforward to obtain, the way to produce and capture value is unclear, and only testing can tell what works in your ecosystem and what does not. Iterative design is inevitable.

To gain a reference point to start the iterative process, program designers use a tested template. This practice will not change. However, we hope that design mistakes will be spotted sooner, saving millions of dollars for organizations and precious time for startups.

Generations

In startups, there are many examples of family trees and generational fights. One of Silicon Valley's best known generational rivalries is that between Oracle and Salesforce.[1] Marc Benioff left a senior vice president position in Larry Ellison's Oracle in 1999 to found Salesforce, of which he serves as the CEO. Ellison invested $2 million in Salesforce and became its inaugural board member. The two men and their companies became competitors in the rise of enterprise software as a service, with harsh words exchanged at times. In 2020, Salesforce surpassed Oracle in market cap for the first time. Meanwhile, Salesforce Ventures participated in a Series E funding round in Twilio, a rising star in the sector, topping a market cap of $60 billion at the end of 2020. In a metaphorical sense, Twilio could be considered Oracle's grandchild.

Startup programs have also gone through generations and waves as a global industry—which often mirrors the journey of individual startup programs as they evolve in their approach to collaborations. Corporate venture capital is arguably in its fourth[2] or fifth wave, given the current shift back toward financial goals. The startup program industry, in general, is likely undergoing its third wave (Figure 18.2):

- The first wave of programs included startup competitions, hackathons, and incubators, centered on community building and connecting a broader network of entrepreneurs, investors, and ecosystem actors.
- The second wave expanded to advanced incubators, accelerators, matchmaking events, and internal mindset

programs all seeking to collect and validate new ideas and scale the best.

- A return to a focus on financial impact is leading the third wave. After the reality check of self-referential actions and "innovation theater," organizations align startup programs with the performance indicators typical of the core business.

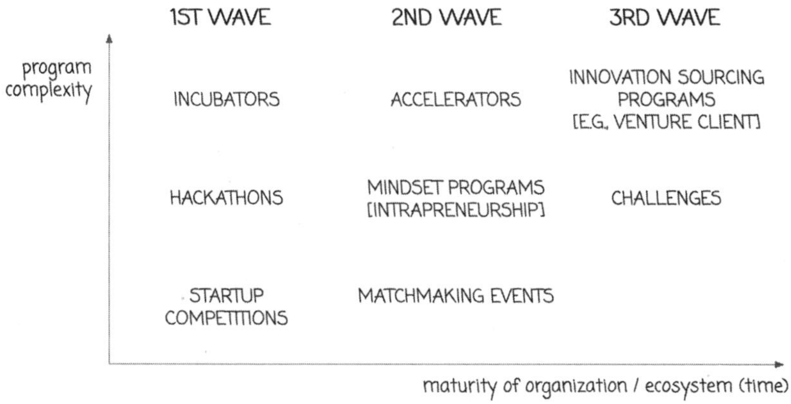

program complexity	1ST WAVE	2ND WAVE	3RD WAVE
	INCUBATORS	ACCELERATORS	INNOVATION SOURCING PROGRAMS [E.G. VENTURE CLIENT]
	HACKATHONS	MINDSET PROGRAMS [INTRAPRENEURSHIP]	CHALLENGES
	STARTUP COMPETITIONS	MATCHMAKING EVENTS	

maturity of organization / ecosystem (time)

FIGURE 18.2 Typically, an organization goes through three waves of startup programs. The same waves were observed at macro level globally starting from 2005.

For the future, we envision a fourth wave of startup programs emerging, both at the level of the individual organization and the industry level, as a more mature mix of the previous waves. Based on our research and interviews, we foresee four dominating trends:

1. **More self-sustainable programs** or more attention to obtaining measurable results to present a compelling case to stakeholders and sponsors.
2. **More involvement of the organization's internal ranks**—not just in the operational phase, but also earlier, during program design and setup.
3. **More attention to the post-graduation phase**, either by extending the activities into the follow-on stage or creating more interoperable systems of programs.

4. **More hybridization and polymorphism of models**, following a more self-aware interpretation of the context in which a startup program operates.

Trend #1: Sustainability and Measurable Results

Like any other unit of a large organization, startup programs are called on sooner or later to become economically sustainable—or, alternatively, to demonstrate some measurable impact (e.g., in social or environmental terms) that provides ground for sponsors to confirm their support. After an initial *bona fide* period in which temporary vanity metrics can cope with public relations, press, hype, or participation, all startup programs must expose some sort of data endorsing their usefulness.

We project that vanity metrics will disappear for programs at all stages, even during the initial grace period. Senior leaders will invoke more thorough planning of when significant metrics will emerge, with a step-by-step road map on reaching that state. While accelerators, incubators, and similar programs have survived on PR metrics for a long time, senior leaders now have an increased awareness of how these instruments work (and, maybe, disillusionment after some failed experiments). It will not be long before they put healthy pressure downward on program managers to become more concrete in driving results from day one.

But the pressure to account for data and metrics will also come from the outside, not just from the inside. The global startup community is wary of "innovation theater" acts and practices and demands more commitment, clarity of objectives, and transparency of results. Startup entrepreneurs and their institutional backers have been repeatedly disappointed by corporate and government programs' defiance, to the point that trust now has to be rebuilt from the foundations, starting below the ground floor. Data and demonstrated success stories are one inalienable tool to that end.

To the defense of program managers, impact measurement was not a priority for many years. With most startup communities worldwide not seeing their first modern accelerator until 2010 or even 2015, program managers were busy instilling the fundamental blocks of internal and external innovation culture, reformulating failure as learning, or accepting risk-takers in the ranks of sane people. While those aspects still require additional work, startup programs cannot live out of that anymore. Culture alone does not pay the bills.

Program managers need to change their attitude toward reporting and communicating their results. Some entered the industry out of a vocational calling, a true passion for startups and entrepreneurs, and a desire to help innovate. Until recently, this group could not care less for metrics. Like prophets of a new religion, they felt that open innovation and entrepreneurial support programs were the *right things to do* and believed that one day everyone would join in the enlightenment too—only to see their budget cut at the third or fourth year.

Others became program managers moving internally from other functions, such as marketing and communication, engineering, R&D, corporate development, or M&A. For those that did not do it for passion, it was for career development. The latter frequently acted as bureaucrats to maximize any metric they were assigned—and if it was PR, then it was PR. Others still thought they knew what they were doing, but they didn't—innovation practices are not something that books can easily teach. However, now these managers are learning and, among other issues, they are correcting the metrics, too.

All this said, the world still lacks metric models acknowledged as a general benchmark for cases that are *not* related to startup growth (i.e., anything beyond valuation, revenues, funds raised, exits). This absence poses managerial problems because the impact of startup programs on the P&L and ROI is a lagging indicator and cannot inform decisions on what to correct when the action is still live, and whether to stay bullish or pull the plug. Every program needs its tailored metrics.

Metrics are needed to *communicate* what the program is achieving (or striving to achieve), *align* the rest of the organization on its significance, and *win* the internal support necessary to make an impact. So, more and more, we will see internal discussions about metrics, with program teams setting up key performance indicators from the start (or as soon as possible after the early tests). In other words, we believe that OKRs, V2MOMs, and their cousins are coming to startup programs sooner rather than later.

How This Book Helped

In Part One, we illustrated the startup program's interdependence on the circumstances (the three Circles). There is no holy grail in program templates. The context, and especially Circle 2, defines success for the program and its metrics. A program can legitimately be compared only to others implementing the same objectives and operating in similar contexts.

Specifically, Chapter 2 showed how templates, when copied without adaptation, impose implicit assumptions on the contextual Circles—metrics being one of them. Suppose an organization implements a CVC or accelerator. In that case, the benchmark metrics of CVC will inevitably influence the expectations (internally, from stakeholders, or externally, from the entrepreneurial ecosystem), even if an intelligent analysis would suggest otherwise.

These reasons can be helpful to convince your colleagues and stakeholders to sit down together and agree on what metrics matter to you and your organization and build a compelling case for the program.

We have also distinguished program outputs from ecosystem effects or externalities, such as press or culture, that close a feedback loop onto the external and internal ecosystems. Consequently, outcomes and ecosystem benefits should each have their own distinctive set of metrics. Press coverage and cultural metrics should be read as a by-product of a startup program and be functional to improving the outputs in the subsequent editions—and never as the primary output (Chapters 1 and 9).

Trend #2: Preparing the Internal Ground

Consistently throughout our research, we have collected anecdotal evidence that the perceived reasons for startup program failure are primarily internal. Alberto Onetti of Mind the Bridge emphasized this aspect when he reported his research on the success factors of corporate venturing: "They are four: (1) Top-level buy-in; (2) Expect opposition; (3) Get some quick wins to increase the internal reputation and stimulate internal competition; (4) Focus more on building your internal ecosystem rather than the external one." About the last point, he insisted, "The program team should spend more time walking the corridors than talking to startups."

Many program managers have already realized that their Achilles heel is inside, in an inadequate preparation of the internal ground with senior leaders, detractors, partners, and the lack of connection with the internal innovation pipeline—when that pipeline exists (Circle 1). Shell Ventures, a CVC, has activated four paid "implementation managers," essentially internal business developers that steadily bridge and connect startups and business units. Robert Bosch Venture Capital, another CVC, complemented its investment activities with a venture client unit, Open Bosch, dedicated to the same task.

We project that this trend will continue and amplify, with programs of all sorts directing more focus and resources to plow the internal ecosystem of R&D, business units, and corporate development. More organizations will follow leaders such as Enel Innovability or Open Bosch, who have created networks of internal ambassadors, innovation managers, or "spiders in the web," acting as point-of-contact with the startup program team.

The program team, on its end, will increasingly be an orchestrator of this cross-functional and cross-unit body of "innovation connectors." At the top level, senior leaders' buy-in (e.g., a CIO or similar, if not the CEO herself) will continue to be the key to opening gates, taming detractors, and removing internal roadblocks.

The same considerations apply equally to internal government departments or local ecosystem partners. The program should devise an appropriate activation strategy for these subjects to maximize value capture. Start-Up Chile pivoted along these lines already in 2015 when it insisted on the local business involvement.

The principles from *The Rainforest* (mentioned in Chapter 16) apply to any innovation or entrepreneurial ecosystem, internal or external. In any ecosystem, there are tribes, and if transaction costs between tribe A are B are socially high, it is harder to innovate. We project that it will increasingly become part of the program team's mission (and likely of its performance indicators) to connect external and internal partners, and eventually also internal and internal.

How This Book Helped

Circle 1 of our Canvas regards the uniqueness and readiness of the internal ecosystem. By singling it out and placing it on the top of the Canvas, we have intentionally highlighted its importance to encourage a more realistic consideration of its critical function. It is there—you cannot hide from it (Chapter 2).

The readiness profile presented in Chapter 8 will help you discuss with your colleagues which features to activate in the next edition, and which to delay to future editions when your organization is readier to deliver.

Finally, in Chapter 7, we argued how starting small and progressively scaling programs up can incrementally build internal buy-in and internal innovation culture. Alternatively, systems of programs can achieve a similar objective (Chapter 16). In essence, you can use startup programs to fertilize better startup programs. Simpler programs, such as hackathons or competition, can set the stage for more ambitious programs such as incubators, accelerators, and venture funds.

Trend #3: More Follow-on and Additional Systems

We project that startup programs in the future will plan more activities and alumni involvement in the follow-on stage, post-graduation. Also, we believe that interoperating program systems will become more widespread, creating a value chain from initial engagement to outcomes. Both evolutions will have the same roots:

1. Acquire more control on long-term partnerships' results
2. Diversify and deepen the foothold in the startup community when addressing multiple objectives at once with startup programs

The intensification of activities and services for startups in the follow-on stage is already a best practice of top-tier accelerators of the caliber of Techstars and YC. Their alumni services include: exclusive networking and investing opportunities, job boards and talent scouting, cross-collaborations, and online communities (e.g., YC's Bookface alumni platform). Other programs will follow—to create more opportunities, extend their brand, and collect success metrics.

In addition to the normal alumni services, several organizations will create more sophisticated follow-on programs. According to GAN (Global Accelerator Network), accelerators have already started, with many raising follow-on funds. The average size of follow-on funds of accelerators ballooned to more than double from 2017 to 2018, with 27 percent of accelerators having one.[3]

Systems of programs are already in place in major corporations, including Google, SAP, Amazon, Salesforce, Robert Bosch, SAP, Novartis, and Bayer. Some build on one another's programs' outputs, whereas others diversify the targets.

As noted in Chapters 1 and 16, until the dot-com bubble, CVCs were doing everything. Then startup programs began to diversify. They were initiated and run by different units, sometimes in uncommunicative silos, or they grew inside an umbrella unit that grouped them all. Over time, organizations alternated between two extreme situations—from a single "startup unit" to many, and back to one again.

There will be more self-awareness and a better organization of the pipeline and the interaction of programs in the future. The pressure to deliver (see Trend #1) is growing, and managers are learning. More and more interoperating program systems will be planned, not produced randomly "as you go."

Thanks to planning, we project that the "startup guys" will be more integrated with their parent organization, not isolated like corporate oddities. Improved integration, in turn, will benefit startup selection and program design.

The net advantages will spill over, not just on the organizations, but also on startups, because they will experience more relevant programs for their stage of maturity, technology, and current needs.

How This Book Helped

Chapter 1 showed how each program is a process, with inputs, outputs, and outcomes. Chapter 2 argued how post-graduation objectives require a thorough planning of alliances and value capturing mechanisms in the follow-on stage.

Chapters 3 to 6 illustrated the preconditions of long-term alignment and how, without them, even if you apply a template by the school, partnerships will break up.

Chapter 9 discussed fertilization, exploration, and exploitation, posing a strategic design decision on what objectives should be prioritized, given the state of your organization. Chapters 12 to 15 shed light on how to craft and adjust the value proposition, structure, selection, and activities to pursue the specific objectives that your system requires. Finally, Chapter 16 discussed the very concept of program systems.

Trend #4: The Accelerator is Dead, Long Live the Accelerator

Around 2015 the proliferation of accelerators was such that some experts predicted a Darwinian selection of the fittest, something like a lemming's suicide run because of the unproven business model (many small equity tickets) and a winner-take-all market. Instead, programs that dubbed themselves "startup accelerators" in 2020 had likely more than doubled in five years.[4]

However, the vast majority of those "startup accelerators" have far less in common with the original model introduced by YC than the name would suggest. Many focus on community building instead of financial goals; others specialize in an industry or a niche technology. Most do not take equity. Some last five weeks, others nine months. In summary, while "startup accelerators" multiply in numbers, it's not the original "Accelerator" anymore. The big-A model has been polymorphed and hybridized in all sorts of ways.

Hybridization is pervasive today in the startup program industry, and we predict that it will continue to expand. Polymorphism will become the new norm, and the boundaries between models will become even fuzzier.

This trend is inevitable because of context's overwhelming influence over models (shown in the Startup Program Strategy Canvas). As corporations and governments grow more aware of the role startups play in their strategy, they will customize more. And since each organization has its peculiarities, objectives, uniqueness, and readiness level for startup collaborations, every new entrant will morph, adapt, and hybridize existing templates even more.

Even if new entrants should stop (unlikely anytime soon), startups will continue to play a role in innovation and economic development; and startup programs will keep changing following the way startups change.

How This Book Helped

This book has pursued nothing else than a paradigm shift. We purposely did not ever say, "Here are the models—accelerator, venture fund, hackathon, and so on—each with these characteristics; we'll guide you to choose the right one." There is no right or wrong model because models are not monolithic, unmodifiable entities. While models are undoubtedly distinctive, they are all just different forms of startup programs, with shared characteristics that can be hybridized and mixed (Chapter 1).

Chapter 2 highlighted the strategic aspects of model selection and adaptation, epitomized by the Startup Program Strategy Canvas. It has shown how the three Circles determine the central Intersection and how, by changing one Circle, the Intersection also changes. These are tools for more informed and aware customization and hybridization at a strategic level.

In Part Two, we have illustrated several design challenges and proposed solutions for each of them. Once again, we purposely did not suggest a rigid methodology. Instead, our problem-solution duos can be used as *design patterns* to address specific problems.

Final Remarks

Every organization is different. Simply copying a startup program from another organization does not work. We hope our book convinces you to strive for a deep understanding of your organization's readiness to collaborate with startups and then to design a program that adapts from successful approaches used by comparable organizations—but all the while staying faithful to your unique context. Finally, as you measure and evaluate results, allow your program to evolve in concert with your changing context, as well as the changes in the startup environment both locally and globally.

We're confident that if you follow the processes we've outlined, you'll be on a path to creating a successful and sustainable startup program that fosters innovation and growth, and helps solve your organization's problems.

Acknowledgments

The following people were interviewed and/or mentioned in the book. We deeply appreciate their knowledge and specialization in their respective fields, and their openness to share as part of our research. We gratefully thank them for their cooperation and dedication to developing startup communities and startup programs.

Lingy Au, Lightning Accelerator

Bill Barber, Banca Intesa San Paolo Innovation EcoSystems Executive Advisor

Francesco Baruffi, former Head of Open Innovation Projects at Emil Banca

Jeremy Basset, CEO at CO:CUBED, former Head of Unilever Foundry

Klaus Beetz

Naomi Berlin, Strategy Sales Director at Cambridge Innovation Center

Lisa Besserman, former Head of Program, Global Incubator at Indeed.com

Chalermyuth Boonma, former Head of Bootcamp at dtac Accelerate

Paolo Borella, Cofounder and former Board Member of Vertical Accelerator

Katarina Brud, Director of MobilityXlab

Joanna Buczkowska-McCumber, Executive Director of League of Innovators

Luis Caldas de Oliveira, Deputy Director of iStartLab at Instituto Superior Técnico Lisboa

Arturo Calle, Startup Peru, Founder & CEO of Suruna

Oslene Carrington, Founder of the Guyana Economic Development Trust (GEDT)

Lisa Cashmore, Vice President, Start and Scale at Communitech

Matteo Cevese, Innovation Manager Startup Acceleration at Hub Innovazione Trentino

Kim Cheolhoon, CEO and Founder of StarthubKorea

Cynthia Cheung, Youth Social Entrepreneurship and Innovation Consultant at The United Nations Development Programme, Youth Co:lab

Bernabé Chumpitazi, former Innovation Manager at Initiative France

Augusto Coppola, CEO Cloud Accelerator

Ed Cullinan, former Lead, Transformation Program at ATCO Group

Gabby Czertok, Founder and CEO of The Builders

Tatjana De Kerros, Head of Venturing at RicoLab

Franck Debane, CEO at Tango

Stefano De Panfilis, Chief Operations Officer at FIWARE Foundation

Federica Destro, Program & Community Specialist at Zambon Open Accelerator

Gianluca Dettori, General Partner Barcamper Ventures and Kauffman Fellow

Jose Deustua, Managing Director at UTEC Ventures, Peru

Sebastián Díaz Mesa, former CEO of Start-Up Chile, Startup Heatmap

Alberto Di Minin, Full Professor of Innovation Management & Policy at Scuola Superiore Sant'Anna

Wojciech Drewczynski, CEO at Space3ac

Dan D'Souza, Internal Innovation and Venture Building Team at L Marks

Craig Elias, Entrepreneur-in-Residence at Bow Valley College in Calgary

Sergio Escobar, CEO at BCF Ventures

Melanie Ewan, Cofounder and Managing Partner at Volition Advisors

Alex Farcet, Cofounder of Startupbootcamp and Rainmaking

Brad Feld, Managing Director at Foundry Group

Sofia Fernandes, Head of Business Development at Building Global Innovators

Tamasha Fernando, Project Manager—Entrepreneurship Education & Women Empowerment, government of Sri Lanka

Otto Freijser, Founding Partner and Lean Innovation Lead at Perpetulon

Miguel Fontes, Executive Director at Startup Lisboa

Gregor Gimmy, Managing Director at 27pilots and founder of BMW Startup Garage

Michele Giordani, Managing Partner & Cofounder at Gellify

Guido Giordano, Director of Venture Programs at Invest Ottawa

Vlad Gliga, Cofounder and CEO of Rubik Hub

Google For Startups

Johannes Grabowski, Open Bosch Cofounder, Robert Bosch Venture Capital GmbH

Charles Graham-Brown, Chief Investment Officer & Partner at Seedstars

Elisa Grasso, former Program Director at Startupbootcamp

Tobias Gutmann, Professor of Product Innovation at EBS Universität für Wirtschaft und Recht

Eric Harr, Cofounder & CEO, The Laudato sì Challenge

Holly Harrington, former Content & Strategy Head, Startup Launchpad

Pär Hedberg, CEO and Founder of Sting Startup Ecosystem

Marco Hernàiz, Founder & CEO at OPI Digital Group

Chris Heuer, Entrepreneur in Residence & Founder at Mentor Bureau

Imre Hild, Manging Partner at Global Traction

Jordan Jocius, Director at The Founder Institute, Waterloo-Toronto Corridor

Jane Kearns, Vice President Growth Services, MaRS Discovery District

Diana Kander

Riam Kanso, Founder & CEO at Conception X

Chris Kay, CEO and Cofounder at Multiplicity

Colin Keogh, Cofounder at The Rapid Foundation

Tristan Kromer, Innovation Coach & Founder at Kromatic

Paul Lancaster, Founder and Director at Plan Digital Limited

Andrea Landini, Head of Community at Gellify

Miryam Lazarte, CEO and Cofounder at LatAm Startups

Dawn LeBlanc, Managing Director at Hartford InsurTech Hub

Jon Letts, Program Operations Manager at Sustainable Ocean Alliance

Christian Lindener, Global Head of Disruptive Ventures at Airbus

Vanessa Liu, VP at SAP.iO Foundries, North America

Maria Ljungberg, CEO Propel Capital and Director Investor Relations at Sting

Sunny Madra, Vice President at Ford X, Ford Motor Company

Bettina Maestre

Bostjan Makarovic, Chair of the Board of Trustees at Chaitech Santa Lucia

Filippo Mansani, Head of Innovation and High-Technology Capital Goods at ITA, Italian Trade Agency

Dimitri Maroulis, former Venture Partner and Global Program Director at Antler

Ash Maurya, Founder and CEO at Leanstack

Gordon McCarthy, former EIR at Propel ICT, currently Director, Global Sales at Novonix

Christopher McLachlan, Head of Company Builder at EnBW Energie Baden-Württemberg AG

Lesa Mitchell, Managing Director at Techstars

Gabriele Molari, former Innovation Manager at Tetra Pak

Piera Morlacchi, Associate Professor of Entrepreneurship and Organization Studies, University of Sussex Business School

Agustín Moro, Global Director Partnerships at Telefónica

Gene Murphy, Cofounder at Startup Boost

Norman Musengimana, Founder & CEO at BizSkills Academy Inc.

Rick Myllenbeck Evan Nisselson, General Partner at LDV Capital

Zafrul Noordin, Founder at Andalus Ventures

Michele Novelli, Board Member and Senior Advisor at Digital Magics Fintech

Pierre-Simon Ntiruhungwa, Cofounder and Head of Founders of the Future

Monica Obogeanu, Startup Programs Manager at Orange Fab

Paul Orlando, Founder at Startups Unplugged

Martina Palmese, former Brand, Innovation and CSR Specialist at QVC

Fabián Pérez, former Ecosystem Coordinator at Cowo Centre for Innovation and Entrepreneurship

Stefan Perkmann Berger, Managing Director and Cofounder of WhatAVenture

Tina Peterson, Founder and Manager, T-Mobile Accelerator at T-Mobile

Reijo Pold, MD at Innovation Heads

Paolo Privitera, Mentor at 500 Startups, Google Launchpad, Chinaccelerator/Mox

John Ramey, former DARPA startup program designer

Alex Reynolds, Data and Intelligence Lead at L Marks

Terry Rock, President & CEO at Platform Calgary

Inês Santos Silva, Managing Partner at Aliados Consulting and formerly Startup Pirates

Nicolas Sassoli, former Head of Startup Unit at Almacube

Jeff Schumacher, Founder & CEO of NAX Group

Christoph Selig, Start-up manager at Kilometer1

Jay Shah, former Director of Velocity entrepreneurship program

Mahdi Shariff, Senior Advisor and Interim CIO at Slush China

Tetiana Siianko, former Head of Acceleration Programs at Foodtech Sweden

Giulia Silenzi, Director of Innovation and Head of Food Tech Accelerator at Deloitte

Abdullah Snobar, Executive Director of The DMZ Ryerson

Marius Starcke, former Partner at WhatAVenture GmbH

Peter Stern, Venture Partner at LDV Capital

Lukas Strniste, CEO and Founder at EnterpriseUp

Paul Sturrock, Cofounder at FastForward London

Manuel Tanger, Cofounder and Head of Open Innovation at Beta-i

Fabio Tentori, CEO of Enel Innovation Hubs

Mirko Trasciatti, Chief Operating Officer at Startupbootcamp ItalianTech London

Daniel Twal, Head of Corporate Innovation at ISDI Accelerator

Marius Ursache, CEO and Cofounder at Metabeta

Alex von Mühlenen, Founder and Chief Executive Officer at Resilient

Kristin Welch, Strategy & Operations at Ford X

Bianca Welds, formerly PitchIT Caribbean

Andrea Welling, Regional Director, BC at Futurpreneur Canada

Colin Weston, Cofounder and Community Leader at Startup Vancouver

Jelte Wingender, Corporate Innovation, Senior Manager at Innoway

Felix Wong, Head of Growth at AngelHub

Jon Worren, former Venture & Corporate Programs at MaRS Discovery District

Ray Wu, former cofounder, Operations and Growth at Magicbus

David Yiptong, Director, Programs at Platform Calgary

Paolo Zanzi, Head of Quality, Organization and Innovation at Bayer

Na'im Zerbes, Program Manager at SecondMuse

We would also like to express our gratitude to the editorial team from McGraw Hill and associated partners, whose exceptional professionalism and patience have played a vital role in bringing this book to fruition: Donya Dickerson, Stephen Isaacs, Noah Schwartzberg, Cheryl Segura, Kevin Commins, Steve Straus, and Richard Camp. First books can be particularly rough-going, and this one was probably rougher than most—it was very much a team effort.

Notes

INTRODUCTION

1. The first attempt to draw a distinction, in our records, is in: Cohen, Susan L., 2013, "What Do Accelerators Do? Insights from Incubators and Angels," *Innovations: Technology, Governance, Globalization* 8 (3–4): 19–25.
2. Steve Blank, a serial entrepreneur, corporate innovator, and active blogger, is considered one of the initiators of the lean startup movement with his book: Steven Gary Blank, 2007, *The Four Steps to the Epiphany* (Wiley). The quoted definition of startup appeared on his blog in 2010: https://steveblank.com/2010/01/25/whats-a-startup-first-principles/.
3. For alternative definitions, see (1) Weiblen, T., and H. W. Chesbrough, 2015, "Engaging with Startups to Enhance Corporate Innovation," *California Management Review* 57, no. 2; (2) Selig, C. J., and G. H. Baltes, 2020, "Strengthening Organizational Ambidexterity Through Corporate Entrepreneurship Activities," IEEE International Conference on Engineering, Technology and Innovation (ICE/ITMC).

CHAPTER 1

1. Docherty, M., 2015, *Collective Disruption* (Polarity Press). Other approaches are separation, switching, self-organization.
2. O'Reilly, C.A., and M. L. Tushman, 2013, "Organizational Ambidexterity: Past, Present, and Future," *Academy of Management Perspectives* 27, no. 4: 324–338; O'Reilly,

C.A., and M. L. Tushman, 2004, "The Ambidextrous Organization," *Harvard Business Review.*

3. Agafitei, I. G., and S. Avasilcai, 2015, "A Case Study on Open Innovation on Procter & Gamble. Part II: Co-creation and digital involvement," *IOP Conference Series Materials Science and Engineering* 95(1):012150, DOI: 10.1088/1757-899X/95/1/012150.
4. Steiber, Annika, and Sverker Alänge, 2021, "Corporate-Startup Collaboration: Effects on Large Firms' Business Transformation," *European Journal of Innovation Management* 24.2 (0001): 235–257.
5. World Food Programme, 2021, "Imara Tech: Ending Manual Labour on Small Farms," https://innovation.wfp.org/project/imara-tech.
6. Arch Grants, 2020, "Accelerating Economic Development," https://archgrants.org/our-impact/our-impact-1/.
7. CB Insights, 2017, "The History of CVC: From Exxon and DuPont to Xerox and Microsoft, How Corporates Began Chasing the Future," https://www.cbinsights.com/research/report/corporate-venture-capital-history/.
8. Eckblad, J., T. Gutmann, and C. Lindener, 2019, *2019 Corporate Venturing Report.* Tilburg: Corporate Venturing Research Group, TiSEM, Tilburg University.
9. Stanford, K., and V. Le, "CVC's Sea Change: Tracking the Strategy's Shift," *PitchBook Data Inc*, December 2020. The 2020 data is from the first three quarters.
10. "Corporate VCs Are Moving the Goalposts," 2016, *Harvard Business Review*, https://hbr.org/2016/11/corporate-vcs-are-moving-the-goalposts.
11. Interview of authors with Prof. Alberto Onetti, Chairman Mind the Bridge, 2020.
12. Clarisse, B., M. Wright, J. Van Hove, 2015, "A Look Inside Accelerators," Nesta.
13. Cohen, Susan L., 2013, op. cit.
14. Kariv, D., 2019, *Educating Entrepreneurs: Innovative Models and New Perspectives* (Routledge).

15. Grimaldi, R., A. Grandi, 2005, "Business Incubation and New Venture Creation: An Assessment of Incubating Models," *Technovation* 25, 111–121.
16. Ibid.
17. Waters-Lynch, J., J. Potts, T. Butcher, J. Dodson, and J. Hurley, 2016, "Coworking: A Transdisciplinary Overview," http://dx.doi.org/10.2139/ssrn.2712217.
18. Wikipedia, 2021, s.v. "Hackathon," https://en.wikipedia.org/wiki/Hackathon#Etymology.
19. Feld, B., 2012, *Startup Communities* (Wiley).
20. Nasa Space App Challenge, 2021, https://www.spaceappschallenge.org/.
21. Written interview to Agustín Moro and Pablo Ramos Martinez, 2020.
22. Start-Up Chile website, https://www.startupchile.org/about-us/; interviews with Sebastián Díaz Mesa, former CEO of Start-Up Chile, 2018–2020.
23. Data obtained from the official website, https://www.startupchile.org/impact/.
24. Skunk Works is an official pseudonym for Lockheed Martin's Advanced Development Programs (ADP). The designation "skunkworks" describes a group within an organization given a high degree of autonomy, with the task of working on advanced or secret projects. Wikipedia, s.v. "Skunk Works," https://en.wikipedia.org/wiki/Skunk_Works.
25. Onetti, A., 2021, "Turning Open Innovation into Practice: Trends in EUROPEAN Corporates," *Journal of Business Strategy* 42, no. 1, 51–58. https://doi.org/10.1108/JBS-07-2019-0138.
26. Daniels, M., 2018, "Why Your Corporate Accelerator Is Failing—and How to Fix It," *The Globe and Mail*, https://www.theglobeandmail.com/business/small-business/growth/article-why-your-corporate-accelerator-is-failing-and-how-to-fix-it/.
27. Steiber, Annika, and Sverker Alänge, 2021, "Corporate-Startup Collaboration: Effects on Large Firms' Business

Transformation," *European Journal of Innovation Management*, 24.2 (0001), 235–257.

28. Schwartz, B., 2004, *The Paradox of Choice: Why Less Is More* (Harper Perennial).
29. Capria Ventures LLC, *2015 Global Best Practices Report on Incubation and Acceleration*, https://unitus.vc/wp-content/uploads/2015/10/Unitus-Seed-Fund-2015-Global-Best-Practices-Survey-of-Incubators-and-Accelerators-1.pdf.
30. Carman, D., 2013, "The Excubator: A New Kind of Incubator," *Blackline Review*, http://blacklinereview.com/the-excubator-a-new-kind-of-incubator/.
31. The word "ideathon" is widely documented in the United States in universities (e.g., University of Washington, https://c21.washington.edu/our-programs/ideathon) or corporate activities (e.g., Cisco, https://www.cisco.com/c/m/en_in/customer-experience-academy.html#~about).
32. Interview with the authors, 2020.
33. Fehder, Daniel C., and Yael V. Hochberg, 2014, "Accelerators and the Regional Supply of Venture Capital Investment," SSRN: https://ssrn.com/abstract=2518668 or http://dx.doi.org/10.2139/ssrn.2518668; and Bone, J., J. Gonzalez-Uribe, C. Haley, and H. Lahr, 2019, "The Impact of Business Accelerators and Incubators in the UK," *BEIS Research Paper Number 2019/009*. Both studies found a correlation between the onset of activities of the first accelerator in a region and the amount of venture capital invested in technology companies, whereas that of non-tech companies remains unaffected (control group). In the British study, the increase of available venture capital five years after the inception of an accelerator was found to be over 240 percent higher.
34. Bazen, J., 2018. "Analysis of the Effects of Creative Hackathons on Participants, Challenge Providers and the Entrepreneurial Ecosystem," *Saxion, Enschede*. On a survey of 157 students who participated in a series of hackathons, 55 percent of those not already involved in a startup project (54 percent of total respondents) indicated that participation

in the hackathon had "some" or "quite a lot" of influence on their intention to start a business.

35. Pompa, C., 2013, "Literature Review on the Impact of Business Incubation, Mentoring, Investment and Training on Start-up Companies," Overseas Development Institute.
36. Stam, E., and B. Spigel, 2016, "Entrepreneurial Ecosystems," *Utrecht School of Economics*, Discussion Papers Series 16-13, https://www.uu.nl/sites/default/files/rebo_use_dp_2016_1613.pdf.
37. Feld, B., and I. Hathaway, 2020, *The Startup Community Way: Evolving an Entrepreneurial Ecosystem* (Wiley).
38. Stangler, D. and Bell-Masterson, J., 2015, "Measuring an entrepreneurial ecosystem," *Kauffman Foundation*, https://www.kauffman.org/entrepreneurship/reports/measuring-an-entrepreneurial-ecosystem/.

CHAPTER 2

1. Palmer, M., 2020, "This Is Why Corporate Accelerators Fail—Your Answers," *Sifted*, https://sifted.eu/articles/why-corporate-accelerators-fail/.
2. Feld, B., and I. Hathaway, 2020, op. cit.
3. Ackoff, Russell L., 1999, *Ackoff's Best: His Classic Writings on Management* (Wiley). A famous quote from Prof. Ackoff is: "A system is never the sum of its parts; it's the product of their interaction." See also https://www.youtube.com/watch?v=a0ooqJ-pOH4.
4. Drucker, Peter F., 2000, *The Essential Drucker*, (Routledge).
5. Wikipedia, s.v. "Ikigai," https://en.wikipedia.org/wiki/Ikigai.
6. A unicorn is a privately held company that received a valuation of one billion dollars or more. Wikipedia, s.v. "Unicorn (finance)," https://en.wikipedia.org/wiki/Unicorn_(finance).
7. Wikipedia, s.v. "Know thyself," https://en.wikipedia.org/wiki/Know_thyself.
8. Objectives and Key Results (OKR), see Doerr, J., 2018, *Measure What Matters* (Penguin).
9. Vision Values Methods Obstacles Measures (V2MOM), see Benioff, M., 2020, "Create strategic Company Alignment

with a V2MOM," the 360 blog, https://www.salesforce.com/blog/how-to-create-alignment-within-your-company/.

10. This focus on using startup programs to reposition a brand from a traditional industry in the digital era is reported by several studies. For instance, see Mocker, V., S. Bielli, C. Haley, 2015, "Winning Together: A Guide to Successful Corporate-Startup Collaborations," Nesta, https://ec.europa.eu/futurium/en/system/files/ged/43-nesta-winning-together-guidestartupcollab.pdf. The authors list four macro-objectives for corporate-startup collaboration programs: (1) rejuvenating corporate culture, (2) innovating big brands, (3) solving business problems, (4) expanding into future markets. Motivation (2) is described as follows: "Working with startups . . . modifies the external perception of corporate brands among their customers, partners and future employees." Examples for that motivation are found in the programs by Telefónica, Accenture, and Microsoft.
11. In scientific and business literature, the association of corporate venturing with the creation of real options has been widely explored. One of the foundational papers is: Vanhaverbeke, W., V. Van de Vrande, H. W. Chesbrough, 2008, "Understanding the Advantages of Open Innovation Practices in Corporate Venturing in Terms of Real Options," *Creativity and Innovation Management* 17(4): 251–258, DOI: 10.1111/j.1467-8691.2008.00499.x. A real option is the right, but not the obligation, to take an action in the future, and typically consists of two distinct actions: option creation and option exercise. Corporate venturing (and startup programs within it) implement the option creation action. To exercise the option, firms may create equity alliances, joint ventures, exclusivity agreements, spin-ins, or outright acquisitions.
12. Chesbrough, H., 2002, "Making Sense of Corporate Venture Capital," *Harvard Business Review* 80(3): 90+. In the article, Chesbrough highlights six significant reasons for strategic investing that can advance a corporation's own growth, notably: (1) "Promoting a standard"—when

investment involves startups directly or indirectly promoting a technology standard that is favorable to the corporation's own growth; (2) "Stimulating demand"—when investment is in startups producing complementary products; (3) "Leveraging underutilized technology"—this regards startups that spun out of the corporation, and in this respect it does not pertain this book; (4) "Experimenting with new capabilities"—when investments are in startups disrupting the corporation's own business, in a form of defensive self-disruption and to acquire insider information from such companies; (5) "Developing a backup technology"—also related to defensive self-disruption; (6) "Exploring strategic whitespace"—when investing in companies serving markets currently outside of the corporation's range, to both gather market intelligence and hedge against disruption.

13. Real example from a challenge on open innovation platform HeroX in January 2021, https://www.herox.com/magnet.
14. Granstrand, O., and M. Holgersson, 2020, "Innovation Ecosystems: A Conceptual Review and a new Definition," *Technovation* 90–91, ISSN 0166-4972, https://doi.org/10.1016/j.technovation.2019.102098. The authors define: "An innovation ecosystem is the evolving set of actors, activities, and artifacts, and the institutions and relations, including complementary and substitute relations, that are important for the innovative performance of an actor or a population of actors," and "An innovation ecosystem could in other words include an actor system with collaborative (complementary) and competitive (substitute) relations with or without a focal firm, and an artifact system with complementary and substitute relations." Although in the more general sense an innovation ecosystem can exist without a focal firm, in this book we use the term with reference to the presence of a focal firm.
15. Stam and Spiegel, op. cit. The authors define: "Entrepreneurial ecosystems are defined as a set of interdependent actors and factors coordinated in such a way that they enable productive entrepreneurship within a particular territory." Among startup entrepreneurs and investors, the term *startup*

ecosystem is common as well. For example, see Wikipedia: "A startup ecosystem is formed by people, startups in their various stages and various types of organizations in a location (physical or virtual), interacting as a system to create and scale new startup companies. These organizations can be further divided into categories such as universities, funding organizations, support organizations (like incubators, accelerators, coworking spaces etc.), research organizations, service provider organizations (like legal, financial services etc.) and large corporations." Wikipedia, s.v. "Startup ecosystem," https://en.wikipedia.org/wiki/Startup_ecosystem. The concept of entrepreneurial ecosystem is highly related to that of startup community, and it contains it.

16. Baghai, M., S. Coley, D. White, 1999, "The Alchemy of Growth—Practical Insights for Building the Enduring Enterprise," 1999 © McKinsey, *Orion Business.*
17. Nagji, B., and G. Tuff, 2012, "Managing Your Innovation Portfolio," *Harvard Business Review*, 90(5), 66–74. Igor Ansoff, a mathematician, first published his matrix in 1957, showing four marketing strategies based on product and target market considerations.
18. Lazarow, A., 2020, "Startups, It's Time to Think Like Camels—Not Unicorns," *Harvard Business Review*, https://hbr.org/2020/10/startups-its-time-to-think-like-camels-not-unicornsarticle.
19. Blank, Steve, 2013, "Why the Lean Start-up Changes Everything," *Harvard Business Review*, https://hbr.org/2013/05/why-the-lean-start-up-changes-everything.
20. Founder-market fit conventionally describes a situation when the founder team of a startup has the right skills and possibly an unfair advantage to profitably launch a new high-growth business in a given market. This fit may come from a deep experience or knowledge of a particular industry or technology, or a strong motivation. Wilson, T., 2020, "Investing at Founder-Market Fit," Medium, https://medium.com/@taw/investing-at-founder-market-fit-9fa49ec97079; Canning, J., 2020, "The Importance of Founder-Market Fit & How to

Highlight It While Fundraising," *Forbes*, https://www.forbes.com/sites/jilliancanning/2020/01/15/the-importance-of-founder-market-fit--how-to-highlight-it-while-fundraising/.

21. The Lean Startup literature is full of references about problem-solution fit and product-market fit. See for example: Maurya, Ash, 2012, *Running Lean*, 2nd ed. (O'Reilly).
22. Product-market fit is a condition used in product management to indicate a sufficient maturity level of a product to be able to satisfactorily serve its reference market and start scaling-up of production and customer acquisition. See for instance: Blank, Steve, 2005, *The Four Step to the Epiphany* (K & S Ranch).
23. Interview of the authors with Jay Shah, 2019.
24. In fact, Entrepreneur First had just run its initial batch or two when TechPeaks was conceived, and Antler was far from existing yet.

CHAPTER 3

1. Frommer, D., and R. Molla, 2017, "It's Been 10 Years Since Microsoft Invested in Facebook—Now Facebook Is Worth Almost as Much as Microsoft," Vox Recode, https://www.vox.com/2017/10/23/16412108/facebook-microsoft-2007-investment-market-cap-chart.
2. *NVCA 2020 Yearbook*, National Venture Capital Association and PitchBook Data Inc., 2020.
3. Bertoni, F., M. G. Colombo, and A. Quas, 2017, "The Role of Governmental Venture Capital in the Venture Capital Ecosystem: An Organizational Ecology Perspective," *Entrepreneurship: Theory and Practice* 43(4), DOI: https://doi.org/10.1177/1042258717735303.
4. *NVCA 2020 Yearbook*, op. cit.
5. The internal rate of return (IRR) measures the profitability of investments and is used when comparing different asset classes. It expresses the annual rate of return that an investment is expected to generate.
6. *US Venture Capital*, Cambridge Associates, March 2020, https://www.cambridgeassociates.com/wp-content/uploads/2020/07/WEB-2020-Q1-USVC-Benchmark-Book.pdf. See

also: Wright, M., and R. Chopra, 2010, "Returns to Venture Capital," in D. J. Cumming, *Venture Capital: Investment Strategies, Structures and Policies* (John Wiley & Sons), Chapter 19, DOI: https://doi.org/10.1002/9781118266908.ch19.

7. *Private Investments*, Cambridge Associates, September 2020, https://www.sec.gov/files/cambridge-associates-private-investments.pdf.
8. Kaplan, S., and A. Schoar, 2005, "Private Equity Performance: Returns, Persistence and Capital Flows," *The Journal of Finance* LX, no. 4, DOI: https://doi.org/10.1111/j.1540-6261.2005.00780.x.
9. Deal flow is a term used by venture capitalists to describe the rate at which business proposals and investment pitches are being received. Rather than a rigid quantitative measure, the rate of deal flow is somewhat qualitative and is meant to indicate whether business is good or bad. https://www.investopedia.com/terms/d/dealflow.asp.
10. Gompers, Paul A., W. Gornall, S. N. Kaplan, and I. A. Strebulaev, 2016, "How Do Venture Capitalists Make Decisions?," Stanford University Graduate School of Business Research Paper No. 16-33, European Corporate Governance Institute (ECGI)—Finance Working Paper No. 477/2016, DOI: http://dx.doi.org/10.2139/ssrn.2801385.
11. Thiel, Peter, with B. Masters, 2014, *Zero to One* (Virgin Books), ISBN: 978-0804139298.
12. Wikipedia, s.v. "Patient capital," https://en.wikipedia.org/wiki/Patient_capital.
13. Criticism against corporate venture capital (and corporate accelerators) is widespread in the industry and the global startup community. See, for instance: Lagourgue, S., 2018, "The Pitfalls of Corporate Venture Capital—and How to Avoid Them," MaRS, https://www.marsdd.com/news/the-pitfalls-of-corporate-venture-capital-and-how-to-avoid-them/. The author reports the proceedings of a panel hosted by MaRS in Toronto, Canada, during which six pitfalls of CVC emerged (the brackets indicate how they relates to our Circles): (1) The corporation takes a hands-off approach (lack

of business unit commitment in Circle 1); (2) The corporation lacks a clearly defined venture group (lack of Intersection); (3) The corporation lacks a mandate to become a customer (conflicting expectations in Circle 3 and 1); (4) It's not a long-term relationship (lack of alignment in Circle 2 and 3); (5) The corporation does not understand the niche (not the right people or networks in Circle 1); (6) Only one corporate investor sits at the table (because it may prevent the start-ups from working with competitors—conflicting objectives in Circle 2).

14. For a history of corporate venture capital from its origins to 2017 with data of growth trends in the decade after the Great Recession, see this report by CB Insights, 2017, "The History of CVC: From Exxon and DuPont to Xerox and Microsoft, How Corporates Began Chasing 'the Future,'" https://www.cbinsights.com/research/report/corporate-venture-capital-history/. Also, we reviewed over 50 corporate accelerators in search of a case in which the corporation declared to act as a purely financial investor, but could not find any. The research was carried out through the inspection of online websites. In some rare cases it was complemented by interviews with the respective program managers.
15. Ibid.
16. Prats, J., and J. Siota, "How Corporations Can Better Work With Startups," *Harvard Business Review*, June 2019, https://hbr.org/2019/06/how-corporations-can-better-work-with-startups.
17. Rolfes, M., and A. Pentland, 2016, "Working Paper on Organizational Dynamics in Corporate Venture Capital Firms," https://ui.adsabs.harvard.edu/abs/2016arXiv161100970R/abstract.
18. "Corporate VCs are Moving the Goalposts," *Harvard Business Review*, November 2016, 24–25, https://hbr.org/2016/11/corporate-vcs-are-moving-the-goalposts.
19. The Cambridge Dictionary gives the following definition of strategic investment: "investment by a company that is intended to make it more successful over time." s.v. "strategic

investment," https://dictionary.cambridge.org/dictionary/english/strategic-investment. In general, other definitions also stress that financial gain is not the sole reason for investing.

20. There have been several attempts at identifying one-size-fits-all measures for strategic objectives in CVC&A; however, to our knowledge none has reached the status of a standard. For example, in a workshop in 2018, veteran CVC manager David Horowitz guided a group of fellows to list five categories of relevant strategic KPIs for CVC: (1) Access to new technology, (2) Trend spotting and market intelligence, (3) Commercial relationships, (4) M&A pipeline, (5) Launching businesses in new markets. David Horowitz, 2018, "Measuring Success in Corporate Venture Capital: How to Identify KPIs for Strategic Investment Programs," Medium, https://medium.com/touchdownvc/measuring-success-in-corporate-venture-capital-43ee88337988. However, hardly any CVC pursues all of those goals at the same time, making comparisons on so many different measurable dimensions even harder.
21. Chesbrough, H., 2002, op. cit.
22. Romans, A., 2016, *Masters of Corporate Venture Capital: Collective Wisdom from 50 VCs Best Practices for Corporate Venturing* (CreateSpace).
23. Mind the Bridge social media.
24. Chesbrough, H., 2002, op. cit.
25. https://www.salesforce.com/company/ventures/funds/.
26. Written interview of the authors with the Wayra team, 2020. After the relaunch in 2018, Wayra focuses now on later-stage startups ($1–5 million valuation) with a proven fit with Telefónica's strategic projects.

CHAPTER 4

1. The Goldilocks principle consists in choosing a solution that has "just the right" mix of the desirable features. In the children's story of Goldilocks and the three bears, the protagonist Goldilocks is a young girl who chooses a soup that is neither too hot nor too cold—"just right."

2. Talk on CorporateInnovators.eu, 2020.
3. Case study accessed through LH Startup MAQER's website, https://lhstartupmaqer.com/leena-ai/.
4. Story from the interview of the authors with Gabby Czertok, 2020.
5. Interviewed informally during the research for this book, requested anonymity.
6. Mattes, Frank, and Dr. Ralph-Christian Ohr, 2018, *Scaling-up Corporate Startups: Turn Innovation Concepts into Business Impact.*
7. Birkinshaw, J., and S. Meghani, 2016, "Innovation at Unilever: The Foundry. Unilever Foundry Case Study," London Business School.
8. Econic, 2016, "Why BMW's Startup Garage Invented the Venture Client Model," https://blog.markgrowth.com/why-bmws-startup-garage-invented-the-venture-client-model-a6e5c4da2559.
9. Garcia B., J. M., and F. Monteiro, 2019, "Enel's Innovability: Global Open Innovation and Sustainability," INSEAD.
10. Talk on CorporateInnovators.eu, 2020.

CHAPTER 5

1. Jacobides, M. G., 2013, "Blackberry Forgot to Manage the Ecosystem," *Harvard Business Review*, https://hbr.org/2013/08/blackberry-forgot-to-manage-the.
2. Adner, R., 2012, "Amazon vs. Apple: Competing Ecosystem Strategies," *Harvard Business Review*, https://hbr.org/2012/03/amazon-vs-apple-competing-ecos.
3. Jacobides, M. G., 2019, "In the Ecosystem Economy, What's Your Strategy?," *Harvard Business Review*, https://hbr.org/2019/09/in-the-ecosystem-economy-whats-your-strategy.
4. Jacobides, M. G. 2019. "Amazon's Ecosystem Grows Bigger and Stronger by the Day. Should We Be Worried?," *Forbes*, https://www.forbes.com/sites/lbsbusinessstrategyreview/2019/05/09/amazons-ecosystem-grows-bigger-and-stronger-by-the-day-should-we-be-worried/.

5. An alternative definition of entrepreneurial ecosystem can be found in: Novotny, A., E. Rasmussen, T. H. Clausen, and J. Wiklund, eds., 2020, *Research Handbook on Start-Up Incubation Ecosystems* (Cheltenham, UK: Edward Elgar Publishing), doi: https://doi.org/10.4337/9781788973533.
6. In general, innovation ecosystem is connected to the concept of business ecosystem, at least for what concerns this book. Lingens, B., M. Böger, S. Gackstatter, and A. Lemaire, 2019, "Business Ecosystems: Partnership of Equals for Corporates, SMEs and Startups." Also: Altman, E. J., and M. L. Tushman, 2017, "Platforms, Open/User Innovation, and Ecosystems: A Strategic Leadership Perspective," in Furman, J., A. Gawer, B. Silverman, S. Stern, *Advances in Strategic Management, Entrepreneurship, Innovation, and Platforms*, 37 (Bingley, UK: Emerald Group Publishing, Ltd.).
7. Maurya, Ash, 2016, *Scaling Lean: Mastering the Key Metrics for Startup Growth* (Portfolio Penguin).
8. Jacobides, M. G., A. Sundararajan, and M. Van Alstyne, 2019, "Platforms and Ecosystems: Enabling the Digital Economy," World Economic Forum, http://www3.weforum.org/docs/WEF_Digital_Platforms_and_Ecosystems_2019.pdf.
9. Niccolai, J., 2008, "Microsoft Offers Free Software to Web Startups," *PC World*, https://www.pcworld.com/article/153333/free_microsoft_apps.html.
10. The educational program was delivered in so-called AppCademy events, where a selection of the funded teams are flown to Aalto University in Helsinki to undertake a two- to four-week intensive coaching session. These events included extensive coaching and training in branding and positioning, design and user experience excellence, development, monetization, marketing, communications, and much more.
11. Llewellyn, D. W. T., D. Sharapov, and E. Autio, 2016, "Linking Entrepreneurial and Innovation Ecosystems: The Case of AppCampus," in *Entrepreneurial Ecosystems and the Diffusion of Startups* (Edward Elgar). See also https://arcticstartup.com/lets-say-farewell-to-appcampus/.

12. Lardinois, F., 2017, "Microsoft Is Giving ISVs New Incentives to Deploy on Azure," Techcrunch, https://techcrunch.com/2017/05/10/microsoft-is-giving-isvs-new-incentives-to-deploy-on-azure/.
13. Tilley, A., 2020, "Microsoft Seeks Startup Partnerships in Battle with Amazon Over Cloud," *Wall Street Journal*, https://www.wsj.com/articles/microsoft-seeks-startup-partnerships-in-battle-with-amazon-over-cloud-11600077601.
14. The APN Global Startup Program is an invite-only go-to-market program built to support mid-to-late-stage startups that have raised institutional funding, achieved product-market fit, and are ready to scale. https://aws.amazon.com/partners/global-startup/.
15. Jones, G., 2020, "FIWARE Accelerator: More Open Source Ecosystem than Accelerator," CompassList, July 16, 2020, https://www.compasslist.com/insights/fiware-accelerator-more-open-source-ecosystem-than-accelerator.
16. B. Clarisse, M. Wright, and J. Van Hove, 2015, "A Look Inside Accelerators," Nesta. The authors distinguish startup accelerators into three archetypes: investor-led accelerators, matchmaker accelerators, and ecosystem accelerators. The latter type "typically have government agencies as a main stakeholder. The government agencies are interested in stimulating startup activity, either within a specific region or within a specific technological domain."
17. https://en.wikipedia.org/wiki/Digital_nomad.
18. https://www.helsinkibusinesshub.fi/90-day-finn-program-invites-u-s-tech-professionals-to-experience-finlands-unique-work-life-balance/.
19. Applied Analysis, 2017, *The Economic Impact of Downtown Project*, http://dtplv.com/wp-content/uploads/2017/03/DTP-economic-impact.pdf.
20. https://www.kauffman.org/.

CHAPTER 6

1. The Sustainable Development Goals (SDGs) were adopted by all United Nations Member States in 2015 as a universal call

to action to end poverty, protect the planet, and ensure that all people enjoy peace and prosperity by 2030. Accessible at: https://sdgs.un.org/goals.

2. Haltiwanger, J., R. S. Jarmin, and J. Miranda, 2013, "Who Creates Jobs? Small Versus Large Versus Young," *Review of Economics and Statistics* 95, no. 2, 347–361. The study refers to comprehensive data tracking all firms and establishments in the US nonfarm business sector for the period 1976 to 2005 from the Census Bureau's Longitudinal Business Database (LBD).
3. "Show Me Jobs: The Impact of First-Time Employers on Job Creation in Missouri," MOsourcelink, 2019.
4. Morris, R., and L. Török, 2018, "Fostering Productive Entrepreneurship Communities: Key Lessons on Generating Jobs, Economic Growth and Innovation," Endeavor Insight.
5. Ayyagari, M., A. Demirguc-Kunt, and V. Maksimovic, 2014, "Who Creates Jobs in Developing Countries?," *Small Bus Econ* 43:75–99.
6. Motoyama, Y., and J. Wiens, 2015, "Guidelines for Local and State Governments to Promote Entrepreneurship," Ewing Marion Kauffman Foundation. The authors suggest that the inexperience of public officers in selecting and supporting early-stage ventures makes venture capital investing an inefficient use of public funds. Likewise, they contend that the focus of traditional incubators on providing office space and cutting overhead is hardly effective or conductive to a surge of champion startups. In face of these shortcomings, the authors suggest a number of actions to redesign existing venture funds and incubators: for example, involve local entrepreneurs in award selection and mentorship and integrate the recipient companies in the local ecosystem (for the complete list see the article).
7. Isenberg, D., and R. Brown, 2014, "For a Booming Economy, Bet on High Growth Firms, Not Small Businesses," *Harvard Business Review*.
8. Bhatia, A. K., and N. Levina, 2020, "Can Entrepreneurship Be Taught in a Classroom?," *Harvard Business Review*,

https://hbr.org/2020/08/can-entrepreneurship-be-taught-in-a-classroom.

9. Motoyama, Y., and J. Wiens, op. cit.
10. Email interview of the authors with Jane Kearns.
11. https://tiphub.vc/.
12. Baird, R., 2019, "Why Entrepreneurs Are Better Judges of New Ideas than Expert Investors," Village Capital blog, https://unreasonablegroup.com/articles/entrepreneurs-actually-best-judges-of-new-ideas/.
13. https://blog.google/outreach-initiatives/google-org/googleorg-fellowship/.
14. https://www.atlas.vet/fellowship.

CHAPTER 7

1. Ries, Eric, 2017, *The Startup Way: How Entrepreneurial Management Transforms Culture and Drives Growth* (Portfolio Penguin).
2. A minimum viable product is a product with the smallest possible feature set able to capture the attention and satisfy the needs of your early adopters.
3. Innovation theater is an innovation practice that doesn't produce a measurable and accountable result. Blank, S., 2019, "Why Companies Do 'Innovation Theater' Instead of Actual Innovation," *Harvard Business Review*, https://hbr.org/2019/10/why-companies-do-innovation-theater-instead-of-actual-innovation.

CHAPTER 8

1. Net Promoter, Net Promoter System, Net Promoter Score, NPS, and the NPS-related emoticons are registered trademarks of Bain & Company, Inc., Fred Reichheld and Satmetrix Systems, Inc.
2. Mattes, F., and R.-C. Ohr, 2018, op. cit. The authors describe how most large corporations concentrate on the initial stages of innovation (namely, ideation and validation) or on the last (growth of a standardized business model) and fail to put in place an operational model to scale up those initial tests to

when they enter a standardized execution stage. They also demonstrate how this applies across all three innovation playfields of McKinsey's three-horizon model: Horizon 1, or "Optimize the Core"—exploiting the core business; Horizon 2 or "Reshape the Core"—adapting tested technologies from other contexts; and Horizon 3, or "Create the New"—exploring globally new business models and technologies.

3. Zimmerman, T., S. Gardiner, J. Wallis, 2015, "A Guide to Self-Disruption: Driving Growth Through Enterprise Innovation Strategies in the Digital Age," Accenture.
4. Startup programs that test new technologies or new business models operate in Horizons 2 or 3 of McKinsey's model, and thus they incur into similar challenges as internal innovation projects in those horizons do.
5. In the late 2010's Bayer ran an innovation coaching program for employees, driven by an Innovation Ambassador in each country and based on volunteer participation. Source: interview of the authors with Paolo Zanzi, innovation ambassador Bayer Italy, 2019.
6. Garcia B., J. M., and F. Monteiro, 2019, op. cit. The system of Enel's innovation managers and communities of practice was also illustrated to one of the authors, Paolo Lombardi, in an interview and a public presentation by Fabio Tentori, head of Enel Innovation Hubs, in 2019.
7. Javier Suàrez, Seguros Bolívar S.A., interviewed by Marco Marinucci of Mind the Bridge, 2021, https://www.youtube.com/watch?v=WmMZ8m2JRVQ.
8. Research by Mind the Bridge, reported by prof. Alberto Onetti in his interview with the authors.
9. Golden, J., A. Sridharan, R. A. Burgelman, 2019, "An Overview of Corporate Venture Capital," Stanford Graduate School of Business.
10. In "The State of Art of Open Innovation—Report 2020" by Mind the Bridge with the support of the International Chamber of Commerce, https://mindthebridge.com/the-state-of-art-of-open-innovation-2020-report/, out of 50 corporations classified as "corporate startup stars" and "open

innovation challengers" by an expert committee (on a total sample of hundreds), 80 percent include innovation outcomes in their incentive programs. In a similar report dating 2019 and referring only to European companies accessed here, 36 percent of "corporate startup stars" were reported to extend innovation-commanded incentives to all employees, not only those directly working in innovation.

11. Plenty of blogs speak enthusiastically of digital nomadism and remote work even before the end of 2019. The general concept is that the availability of jobs that require only a laptop and an internet connection increased dramatically during the decade 2010–2020. Remote jobs included software programming, writing, computer-aided design, customer service, and digital marketing, among the most popular.
12. Plenty of research points in this direction. KPMG's Benchmarking Innovation Impact 2020 Report is a recent source. The report revealed that, among the full respondent set of 215 innovation leaders in Fortune 1000 companies, 52 percent cited politics, turf wars, or lack of alignment as the biggest obstacle to success of innovation actions. "One key to longevity and impact for innovation teams in any industry is that they find ways to collaborate with other parts of the organization," says Scott Kirsner, CEO and cofounder of Innovation Leader, quoted in the same report. "Creating allies and supporters is key, because there are always internal conflicts and resource debates you'll need to work through."
13. This point originated out of conversations with Augusto Coppola, former managing director of LUISS Enlabs Accelerator, and with Paolo Borella, cofounder and ex-CEO of Vertical.vc. It is also supported by the insider observation of one of the authors, Adam Berk, of the foundation and evolution of Google Launchpad under the direction of Roy Geva Glasberg.
14. These considerations stem from a number of sources, including also our direct experience and the interview with Charles Graham-Brown of Seedstars. In 2019, he said: "We consider the program manager to be more operational, whereas the

Entrepreneur in Residence, which is the other figure that we have, absolutely needs to be an entrepreneur. The program manager for me is detail-oriented, it has good communication and community building skills because they need to be the ones reaching out to mentors, to investors to come to demo day, working with the partners, connecting the startups together. They are kind of the glue that holds it all together and drives it forward."

15. That operators of different kinds of startup programs need different skills is a shared feeling in the industry, although we could not find any specific data. Ingo Ramesohl, managing director at Robert Bosch Venture Capital, for instance, in his interview with Alberto Onetti on Mind the Chat, 2020, https://www.youtube.com/watch?v=DPz8yKSzP68, said that early-stage investments at the accelerator stage were a different job. Vice versa, accelerator leaders rarely possess the financial or entrepreneurial background that venture fund teams require.
16. An Entrepreneur in Residence (EiR) is typically a serial entrepreneur or an experienced industry leader who is in a break between companies and looking for the next opportunity. EiRs are hired to coach startups and to stand by in case one of the startups needs to complete its management team.
17. From the press release of the National University of Singapore (NUS), dated November 2019: "The bespoke six-month part-time programme will combine the best of both organisations including platforms, funding and ecosystems. . . . This unique programme allows talents to keep their current jobs, while they explore finding the right partners and launching their new ventures. With Antler's methodology, founders with software or deep tech skills will be matched to those with a business background, to create a strong founding team." Further details about the design of this program were disclosed by Dimitri Maroulis of Antler during a series of interviews with the authors in 2019, from which emerged the target of large corporations' senior managers.

18. CB Insights, 2018, "A Guide to Corporate Innovation: 19 Strategies to Drive Innovation Now," https://www.cbinsights.com/research/corporate-innovation-strategy-guide/.

CHAPTER 9

1. For balanced scorecards (BSC), see Kaplan, R.S., and D.P. Norton, 1992, "The Balanced Scorecard: Measures That Drive Performance," *Harvard Business Review* (January–February 1992): 71–79. For Result-Based Management (RBM), see https://en.wikipedia.org/wiki/Results-based_management. For Management by Objectives (MBO), see Drucker, P., 1954, *The Practice of Management* (New York: Harper & Row). For Objectives and Key Results (OKR), see Doerr, J., 2018, *Measure What Matters* (Penguin). For Vision Values Methods Obstacles Measures (V2MOM), see Benioff, M., 2020, "Create Strategic Company Alignment with a V2MOM," the 360 blog, https://www.salesforce.com/blog/how-to-create-alignment-within-your-company/.
2. Compared to OKR, the objective there is the same as here. The outcomes are related to key results in OKR, but where key results associate a numerical metric straight away, outcomes can or not have an associated metric.
3. Osterwalder, A., Y. Pigneur, A. Smith, F. Etiemble, 2020, *The Invincible Company: How to Constantly Reinvent Your Organization with Inspiration from the World's Best Business Models* (Wiley).
4. Blank, S., 2019, "McKinsey's Three Horizons Model Defined Innovation for Years. Here's Why It No Longer Applies," *Harvard Business Review*, https://hbr.org/2019/02/mckinseys-three-horizons-model-defined-innovation-for-years-heres-why-it-no-longer-applies.
5. Several studies and literature point to this recommendation, which, beyond being intuitive, is repeated by operators in interviews and case studies. For instance, Unilever's whitepaper "The State of Innovation: A Deep Dive into Corporate-Startup Partnerships from The Unilever Foundry," 2017, revealed that the "four key elements that make

collaboration a success in the long-term are: senior buy-in, transparency and streamlined processes, clear objectives and processes for scaling up, education and learnings." The quantitative research was conducted with 204 Unilever Brand Managers and 114 startups.https://www.theunileverfoundry.com/highlights/future-of-corporate-and-startup-innovation.html.

6. As of 2020, The Unilever Foundry made three investments in startups, according to Crunchbase. The objective has never been complete ownership, though. In the cited London Business School case study, Jeremy Basset, former Unilever Foundry and one of the initiators, is reported to have said: "The idea wasn't for Unilever to buy out these startups, because experience told us that would kill their entrepreneurial spark; rather it was about creating a commercial opportunity that worked for both sides."
7. Attributed to Marc Mathieu, former global senior vice president of marketing and leader of the initiation of The Unilever Foundry, London Business School case study, op. cit.
8. Sebastián Díaz Mesa, interview with the authors, 2020.
9. Interview of the authors with Maria Ljungberg, 2020.
10. This emerged in the interview of the authors with Kristine Welch, FordX, in 2019.
11. This and the previous remarks emerged in informal conversations and research. One of such conversations happened during an online talk by Lars Roessler, founder of BSH Startup Kitchen, in 2020 on CorporateInnovators.eu. In reply to our question on how they compute the value of a startup collaboration project in BSH, he made a distinction in the type of business impact: product development or process improvement, each having different mechanics. For the earlier it is about the opportunity cost of internal development; for the latter it is about cost savings.
12. Emerged in the interview of the authors with Dawn LeBlanc, InsurTech Hub Hartford, 2019.
13. This output was suggested by Craig Elias, the founder of 150 Startups, a nonprofit entrepreneurial course for students

delivered in Calgary, Canada. In his interview with the authors in 2020, Elias said, "We try to measure whether or not we turn someone into a 'role model.' Role models are those who, at any point when they are done, find a way to inspire others to follow in their footsteps by sharing their story with other students in some sort of public or private format on campus, for instance, when someone on a student entrepreneurship panel shares their story." Elias's definition is inspired by the work on role models of Daniel Isenberg, founding executive director of the Babson Entrepreneurship Ecosystem Platform and adjunct professor at Columbia Business School.

14. Interview with the authors, 2019, and interview on CorporateInnovators.eu, 2020.
15. Garcia B., J.M., F. Monteiro, op. cit.
16. Talk given on CorporateInnovators.eu, 2020, by Christopher McLachlan, head of Company Builder at EnBW Energie Baden-Württemberg AG.
17. The accelerator requested anonymity. Research conducted by one of the authors, Paolo, and his team in 2019.

CHAPTER 10

1. https://www.crunchbase.com/, https://pitchbook.com/, https://dealroom.co/. Other popular ones are https://www.cbinsights.com/ or https://mattermark.com/.

CHAPTER 11

1. Cohen, S. L., C. B. Bingham, and B. L. Hallen, 2018, "The Role of Accelerator Designs in Mitigating Bounded Rationality in New Ventures," *Administrative Science Quarterly*, 1–45, 0001839218782131.
2. The research was conducted in 2019 over a sample of 32 Italian corporations running corporate acceleration or incubation programs for external startups. In all cases but two the programs were internal. The key performance indicators varied, but the most frequent were performance indicators—metrics that the program team could be held accountable for.

3. Available on the book website, https://startupprogramdesign.com/.
4. Osterwalder, Alexander, and Yves Pigneur, 2010, *Business Model Generation* (Wiley).
5. Kaplan, S., and A. Schoar, 2005, op. cit.
6. Cumming, D., and N. Dai, 2011, "Fund Size, Limited Attention and Valuation of Venture Capital Backed Firms," *Journal of Empirical Finance* 18, no. 1, pp. 2–15.
7. Computed on 302 exits on 1,801 investments, for a total of $6,195 million as of 2018. Data from Seed-DB, https://www.seed-db.com/accelerators.
8. Ibid.
9. Abdullah, S., 2018, "How Long Does It Take a Startup to Exit?," Crunchbase Blog, https://about.crunchbase.com/blog/startup-exit/.

CHAPTER 12

1. For example, both Oasis500 and Zinc Catalyst coach the applicants with validation bootcamps and pitch training to elevate the quality of applications. Activities similar to those of the activation stage (e.g., mentorship, speakers, networking events) may populate the follow-on stage, too, just less frequently or intensively—such as alumni community reunions and exchanges.
2. Video of interview, https://www.youtube.com/watch?v=AaFRh-X9vvI.
3. Company builders have been given diverse names: startup studio, venture builder, startup factory, startup foundry, and startup generator, among others. Since we didn't find any clear and consistent semantic difference, this book adopts "company builder" for uniformity and treats the others as synonyms. As we write, company builders are enjoying a golden age as internal innovation programs for corporations. In this book we explicitly look at programs that build companies with external entrepreneurs, as opposed to employees who are turned into entrepreneurs. See Gutmann, T., 2018, "Harmonizing Corporate Venturing Modes: An Integrative

Review and Research Agenda," *Management Review Quarterly*, for the function of venture builders in a corporate innovation program strategy.

4. See note 2 in this chapter.
5. The story was collected by the authors in a series of interviews in 2020 with Paolo Borella, former CEO and chairman of Vertical.vc, the innovation firm supporting Stora Enso in the program together with Aalto University.
6. Data published by the program, https://archgrants.org/our-impact/.
7. Zukin, S., and M. Papadantonakis, 2018, "Hackathons as Co-optation Ritual: Socializing Workers and Institutionalizing Innovation in the 'New' Economy," *Research in the Sociology of Work* 31, "Precarious Work."
8. This is a real startup challenge that was active at the time of writing, run by an American publicly traded corporation—purposely anonymized.
9. Cohen, S. L., C. B. Bingham, and B. L. Hallen, 2018, op. cit.
10. This is a real case, kept anonymous for respect.

CHAPTER 13

1. Adapted from presentations found online and internal confirmation from a Techstars employee, accessed at https://www2.slideshare.net/BertierLuyt/techstars-paris-accelerator-74513537.
2. Everyone in Techstars (including also the founders who participated in an accelerator) refers to weeks two to four as "mentor madness." Jag Singh, managing director at Techstars Berlin, created an extensive wiki of what happens in the Berlin programs he runs, accessed at https://jag.eu/help/mentor-madness/: "During the Techstars program, each company meets up to ten mentors every day over a period of three weeks, meeting with around a hundred mentors in total. It's all incredibly intense." Also, startup Eversend (2019 batch) wrote: "Here at the Berlin program, there's a whopping 78 mentors with in-depth experience of their respective industries. In the past two weeks, we met with every. single.

one. of the 78, for 25 minutes each. That's over 32 hours of exposure to an incredibly diverse range of expertise, external questioning, and intense introspection of our business," accessed at https://medium.com/eversendapp/our-startup-life-at-techstars-berlin-mentor-madness-43e08400761f.

3. Cohen, S. L., C. B. Bingham, and B. L. Hallen, 2018, op. cit. The authors suggest that concentrating consultation (mentorship) in the early phases of an accelerator is more effective than distributing it over the course of the program. See also Chapter 15.
4. Anonymized, interviewed during an online talk on CorporateInnovators.eu, 2020.
5. From the Seedstars blog, https://www.seedstars.com/content-hub/learning-resources/what-have-we-learned-running-our-acceleration-program-fully-online-past-5-years/.
6. Interview with the authors, 2020. See also Devin Coldewey, 2019, "In the Accelerator over the Sea: Aboard the Sustainable Ocean Alliance's Floating Startup Program," *TechCrunch*, https://techcrunch.com/2019/10/16/in-the-accelerator-over-the-sea/.
7. Cassidy, Mike, 2008, "Speed as THE Primary Business Strategy," Slideshare.net, https://www.slideshare.net/dmc500hats/best-strategy-is-speed-startup2startup-may-2008.
8. Gross, Bill, 2015, "What Factors Matter Most for Company Success?," TED Talk, Vancouver, Canada, https://www.youtube.com/watch?v=mGY_9sFg2qM.
9. A service blueprint is a map of a service delivery process, showing both what the client experiences and what happens behind the stage.
10. Techstars Startup Weekend, https://startupweekend.org/organizers.

CHAPTER 14

1. González-Uribe, J., and S. Reyes, 2018, "Selection Issues," Chapter 5 in *Accelerators: Successful Venture Creation and Growth* (Edward Elgar).

2. Online video interview to Michael Seibel, CEO at Y Combinator, November 2020, op. cit., https://www.youtube.com/watch?v=CkZizhfSErk.
3. Roberts, P. W., and S. A. Lall, 2019, *Observing Accelerators* (Palgrave Macmillan).
4. González-Uribe, J., and S. Reyes, 2021, "Identifying and Boosting 'Gazelles': Evidence from Business Accelerators," *Journal of Financial Economics* 139, no. 1, pp. 260–287, ISSN 0304-405X, https://doi.org/10.1016/j.jfineco.2020.7.12.
5. F6S: https://www.f6s.com/. YouNoodle: https://younoodle.com/.
6. Thiel, P., with B. Masters, 2014, op. cit.
7. Freytag, R., 2019, "On a Growth Track with Startups: How Established Companies Can Pursue Innovation," *Strategy & Leadership* 47, no. 4, pp. 26–33, https://doi.org/10.1108/SL-05-2019-0070.
8. Baghai, M., S. Coley, and D. White, 1999, op. cit.
9. Baird, R., 2019, op. cit.
10. Wrobel, B., and M. Massey, 2020, "Deciding Together: Flipping the Power Dynamics in Impact Investing," Beeck Center, https://beeckcenter.medium.com/deciding-together-flipping-the-power-dynamics-in-impact-investing-b4c3d086f818.
11. González-Uribe, J., and S. Reyes, 2021, op. cit.: the authors measure the effect of what they call "generosity" in a three-year study of an accelerator in Colombia. They conclude that about 34 percent of all selected startups were admitted because of luck in the judge's draft.
12. See, for instance: Balachandra, L., T. Briggs, K. Eddleston, and C. Brush, 2019, "Don't Pitch Like a Girl! How Gender Stereotypes Influence Investor Decisions," *Entrepreneurship Theory and Practice* 43, no. 1, pp. 116–137; or Thébaud, S., 2015, "Accounting for Gender Biases in Entrepreneurship and Innovation," *Social Forces* 94, no. 1, pp. 61–86.
13. González-Uribe, J., and S. Reyes, 2021, op. cit.

14. Perkmann Berger, S., and A. Matjacic, 2018, *The Startup Factory*, WhatAVenture white paper, https://www.whataventure.com/whitepaper/startup-factory.
15. The study specifically refers to the influence of arrangements in the selection process on the financial performance of the selected startups. For other performance that is not purely financial we could not find any scientific study. The study is illustrated in Roberts, P. W., and S. A. Lall, op. cit.
16. "Analysis of Accelerators' Good Practices," *Annex 8.5 to Deliverable 2.4, FI-IMPACT*, June 2016. The study analyzed the 16 FIWARE Accelerators initiated by as many private-public partnerships in 2014 and targeting digital startups in verticals from agrifood to smart cities, and from mobile apps to energy. Save for five of them, the partners in the other accelerators did not have any previous experience with startup programs. Startups were requested to fill in up to 50 long questions per application. As a survey established, such forms were ex post unanimously considered "too bureaucratic" by all program managers. And yet, 16 accelerators adopted them.

CHAPTER 15

1. GAN is an association of accelerators that follow the Techstars model. Global Accelerator Network Infographic 2019, https://www.gan.co/data/2019-infographic/.
2. Cusolito, A. P., E. Dautovic, and D. McKenzie, 2019, "Can Government Intervention Make Firms More Investment-Ready? A Randomized Experiment in the Western Balkans," *The Review of Economics and Statistics*, doi : https://doi.org/10.1162/rest_a_00882.
3. Cohen, S. L., C. B. Bingham, and B. L. Hallen, 2018, op. cit.
4. These reasons come from informal research done by the authors in hundreds of startup events and programs.
5. Cusolito, A.P., E. Dautovic, and D. McKenzie, op. cit.
6. The startups belonged to six distinct cohorts, from 2013 to 2018, and were interviewed in 2019, after all had graduated. The accelerator requested anonymity because the research

was conducted as part of an internal evaluation project and has not been made publicly available.

7. Chafkin, M., 2015, "The Y Combinator Chronicles—Giddiness, Terror, Cornbread: Here's What a Y Combinator Dinner Is Really Like," *Fast Company*, https://www.fastcompany.com/3040961/giddiness-terror-cornbread-heres-what-a-y-combinator-dinner-is-r.
8. Cohen, S.L., C. B. Bingham, and B. L. Hallen, op. cit.
9. Susan L. Cohen, 2013, op. cit.
10. Kushner, R., 2018, *Accelerate This!* (CreateSpace Independent Publishing Platform). The sentence is part of a longer paragraph where Kat Mañalac attributes the need of a demo day to the need to create tension and increase the stakes, which in turn improve the founders' productivity in the three-month duration of the program.
11. Y Combinator, 2021, "Demo Day FAQ," https://www.ycombinator.com/demoday/faq/#q6c.
12. The founder referred to a rule that required each startup to ask for three bids for every single item bought with the public funds provided by a government accelerator. In government programs, specifically, reducing bureaucracy might be hard or out of the program's control.
13. Dahiya, S., and K. Ray, 2012, "Staged Investments in Entrepreneurial Funding," *Journal of Corporate Finance* 18, no. 5, pp. 1193–1216.
14. Global Accelerator Network, op. cit. Out of 105 accelerators in the GAN Community, 27 percent had a follow-on fund in 2018 of an average size of $29.2 million per accelerator, up from $14 million in 2017.

CHAPTER 16

1. Feld, B., and I. Hathaway, 2020, op. cit.
2. Huang, V. W., and G. Horowitt, 2012, *The Rainforest: The Secret for Building the Next Silicon Valley* (Regenwald).
3. Chesbrough, H., 2002, op. cit.
4. Wikipedia, s.v. "Skunk Works," https://en.wikipedia.org/wiki/Skunk_Works.

5. Rogers, Everett, 2003, *Diffusion of Innovations*, 5th ed. (Simon and Schuster), ISBN 978-0-7432-5823-4.
6. Gutmann, T., D. Kanbach, and S. Seltman, 2019, "Exploring the Benefits of Corporate Accelerators: Investigating the SAP Industry 4.0 Startup Program," *Problems and Perspectives in Management* 17, no.3, pp. 218–232.

CHAPTER 18

1. Novet, J., 2020, "Marc Benioff's Salesforce Has Eclipsed Larry Ellison's Oracle in Market Cap," CNBC, https://www.cnbc.com/2020/07/10/salesforce-eclipses-oracle-in-market-cap.html.
2. CB Insights, 2017, "The History of CVC: From Exxon and DuPont to Xerox and Microsoft, How Corporates Began Chasing 'The Future,' " op. cit.
3. Global Accelerator Network, 2019, "2019 Data Report," https://www.gan.co/data/2019-infographic/.
4. We found two data points for 2016: The Gust Global Accelerator Report 2016 accounted for 579 accelerators worldwide, while F6S reportedly had more than 700. Sources, respectively: https://gust-marketing-production.herokuapp.com/accelerator_reports/2016/global and https://www.linkedin.com/pulse/what-future-accelerators-tzahi-zack-weisfeld/. In February 2021, based on online research by the authors, F6S reported 1,143 accelerators and Crunchbase reported 3,141.

Index

About the Authors

Back in 2008, in the midst of the global economic crisis, many organizations and individuals turned to entrepreneurship as it became increasingly viable to set up a startup. There was a palpable expansion in the new startup scene with the rise of incubators, communities, events, and meetups, allowing cross-fertilization of ideas and the creation of networks. At this time, authors Paolo and Adam were both getting their first tastes of this young and agile world of startups.

Your authors have been through everything you are going through and offer, in addition to theory, the practical advice and actionable tips derived from studying about 500 cases globally.

Paolo Lombardi cofounded two startups of his own before creating the startup accelerator Techpeaks in the Italian Alps, together with an international team including investors (LDV Capital, Earlybird Venture Capital) and research stakeholders (University of Trento, FBK – Bruno Kessler Foundation). The accelerator was the first international and public program of its kind in Europe, and the program's design was closely inspired by Y Combinator, Start-Up Chile, and Startup Weekend. This experience promoted a steep learning curve, after which Paolo moved laterally to design and manage over two dozen other programs with corporations and public institutions, including projects with the World Bank, the European Commission, and Italy's main telco operator, TIM. Paolo was a Fulbright Fellow at Santa Clara University, California, a visiting researcher at the University of Glasgow, United Kingdom, and holds a double PhD in Computer Vision and Artificial Intelligence from the Universities of Pavia,

Italy, and Paris Sud, France. He has been a Business Accelerator manager at the European Institute of Technology – EIT Digital, and a Scientific Officer at the European Commission. He is an external lecturer of Innovation and Entrepreneurship at Polytechnic University of Milan, Bocconi Business School, and the University of Trento, Italy. Paolo has coached and supported the business development and fund-raising of hundreds of startups in the incubators, accelerators, and hackathons he has created or directed in digital, robotics, social impact, and creative industries.

Adam Berk is an out-of-the-box thinker, a lean entrepreneur, lean teacher, and serial entrepreneur who helps large organizations implement innovation at scale. He is one of the lucky ones who has found his *one* thing—that intersection between what one is good at, what one loves (and can be paid for), and what the world needs. His work in that intersection includes mentoring startups in startup programs like Google's AI for Social Good Accelerator, the World Food Programme Innovation Accelerator, and digitalundivided. He helps grantees and traditional startups with hypothesis testing, customer discovery and design sprints, assumptions mapping and prioritization, strategy, expansion into the US market, adoption of OKRs as they scale, and hiring. He advises the programs themselves, formally or informally, as to their design.

Adam's journey to this place follows the Startup Program Strategy Canvas quite remarkably. After graduating with a degree in Economics from Emory University in 2000, he started in Circle 3—a startup guy. He started neighborrow.com, one of the very first sharing economy companies in the world, with Dave Tomback, learning many important lessons along the way, the most important of which was to understand deeply "What problem are you solving?" Now in Circle 2, if you'll indulge the metaphor, Adam spent time teaching, mentoring, coaching, and empathizing with product teams, embracing a lean startup and design thinker's mentality. This led naturally to Circle 1, the org. Adam broke into corporate innovation consulting when Sonja Kresojevic was putting together a team to work on the Pearson Lean Product Lifecycle. There, he took what he knew about lean and agile and gained applicable experience into corporate politics, governance, and how budgets work in the real word. From there more corporate and government work naturally led to "the Intersection" working on some of the great startup programs of the world. Already brought into a large org, to understand and solve problems using lean startup and design thinking and agility, and with startup experience—it was only natural to help theese orgs not only to think like startups but also to engage with startups directly.

He is dedicated to helping organizations that are raising the standards (both economic and otherwise) for all people around the world.